EXPLORING PHILOSOPHY

EXPLORING PHILOSOPHY

An Introductory Anthology

EDITED BY

Steven M. Cahn

New York   Oxford

OXFORD UNIVERSITY PRESS

2000

Oxford University Press

Oxford   New York
Athens   Auckland   Bangkok   Bagotá   Buenos Aires   Calcutta
Cape Town   Chennai   Dar es Salaam   Delhi   Florence   Hong Kong
Istanbul
Karachi   Kuala Lumpur   Madrid   Melbourne   Mexico City   Mumbai
Nairobi   Paris   São Paulo   Singapore   Taipei   Tokyo   Toronto
Warsaw

and associated companies in

Berlin   Ibadan

Published by Oxford University Press, Inc.,
198 Madison Avenue, New York, New York, 10016
http://www.oup-usa.org

Library of Congress Cataloging-in-Publication Data

Exploring philosophy : an introductory anthology / [edited by]
Steven M. Cahn.
    p. cm.
  ISBN 0-19-513619-5
  ISBN 0-19-513352-8 (pbk.)
  1. Philosophy Introductions. I. Cahn. Steven M.
  BD21 .E96 1999
  100—dc21
                                                    99-29797
                                                       CIP

Printing (last digit): 10 9 8 7 6 5 4

Printed in the United States of America
on acid-free paper

To my mother,
Evelyn Baum Cahn

Contents

Preface

Those who begin the study of philosophy may easily become discouraged. Many classic texts are daunting in their complexity, and much contemporary writing is intended primarily for a professional audience.

A few prominent philosophers of our day write in a style understandable by all, but nonspecialists are often left unaware of this work. They may never realize that serious discussion of central problems of philosophy can proceed without arcane terminology, unexplained references, or convoluted arguments.

The guiding principle of this book is that reading clear, recent essays by noted philosophers, along with the most accessible and influential historical sources, offers an inviting avenue to the subject. Here many of these materials have been shortened to sharpen their focus and make them easier to understand. Nevertheless, four *Dialogues* of Plato and the first two *Meditations* of Descartes are presented unabridged.

The issues I have chosen to include are drawn from numerous fields of philosophy, but the emphasis is not on covering all areas or viewpoints. Rather, I have sought selections that offer fair accounts of differing opinions. The authors, however, defend their own positions, and readers may disagree. In these matters no one has the last word; discussion will continue. But at least what these writers have to say is comprehensible, and I hope their straightforwardness will encourage an understanding of philosophical inquiry and an appreciation of its importance and fascination. The historical sources, which are grouped together, present more difficulty than the other selections and can be omitted entirely without having any effect on the continuity of the contemporary readings.

Finally, note that some of these selections were written when the custom was to use the noun "man" and the pronoun "he" to refer to all persons, regardless of sex. With this proviso, let us now embark on exploring philosophy.

Acknowledgments

I am deeply grateful to my editor, Robert Miller, for his dependable advice and unfailing encouragement. I also wish to thank the staff of Oxford University Press for its generous assistance and Ian Gardiner for his skilled proofreading. I benefited from the wise counsel of David Rosenthal, the insight and support of Tziporah Kasachkoff, and specific suggestions regarding the contents of the volume offered by Eric Lindermayer, Allyson Robichaud, Andrea Tschemplik, and several anonymous reviewers. I appreciate especially that Professor Tschemplik, who teaches at George Washington University, provided explanatory notes for Plato's *Meno* and *Phaedo*.

Maureen Eckert, my research assistant at The Graduate School of The City University of New York, deserves special recognition. I drew on her judgments regarding the appropriateness of selections considered for inclusion. She also provided valuable help in preparing the manuscript for publication.

My commentary reflects, as usual, stylistic suggestions offered by my brother, Victor L. Cahn, playwright, actor, and Professor of English at Skidmore College. The title of the book was proposed by my wife, Marilyn, to whom I owe so much more.

PART 1

INTRODUCTION

What Is Philosophy?

Monroe C. Beardsley and
Elizabeth Lane Beardsley

The study of philosophy is unlike the study of any other subject. No
dates, formulas, or rules need be memorized. No field work is necessary, and no technical equipment required. The only prerequisite
is an inquiring mind.

About what do philosophers inquire? The word *philosophy* is of
Greek origin and literally means "the love of wisdom." But what
sort of wisdom do philosophers love?

The answer is provided in our first selection. Its authors are Eliz-
abeth Lane Beardsley (1914–1990), a philosopher who taught at
Lincoln University and then at Temple University, and her husband,
Monroe C. Beardsley (1915–1985), a President of the American
Philosophical Association, who taught at Swarthmore College and
then at Temple University.

While the best way to understand the nature of philosophical
inquiry is to consider some specific philosophical issues, an
overview of the subject is helpful, and that is what the Beardsleys
provide.

Philosophical questions grow out of a kind of thinking that is familiar to all
of us: the thinking that we do when we ask ourselves whether something
that we believe is reasonable to believe. "Reasonable" has a broad, but definite, meaning here: a reasonable belief is simply a belief for which a good
reason can be given. Reasonable beliefs are logically justifiable. It would
seem that a belief that is reasonable stands a better chance of being true than
one that is not, so anyone who is interested in the truth of his beliefs should
be concerned about their reasonableness.

All of us have known, long before we approached the systematic study
of philosophy, what it is like to want to make a belief reasonable, and also
what it is like not to care whether a belief is reasonable or not. We have all
had the experience of accepting beliefs without worrying about their logical
justification, for we have all been children. We absorbed the beliefs of our
parents, or the opinions current in our society or culture, without thinking

Excerpted from *Philosophical Thinking: An Introduction*, by Monroe C. Beardsley and
Elizabeth L. Beardsley, copyright © 1965 by Harcourt, Inc., reprinted by permission
of the publisher.

about them very much or looking at them with a critical eye. We may not even have been fully aware that we had them; we may have acted on them without ever having put them into words. As long as our own experience did not seem to conflict with those early beliefs, or those beliefs did not seem to clash with one another, it did not occur to us to question them or to inquire into the reasons that could be given for them.

But a growing individual cannot grow for very long without sometimes wondering whether his most cherished beliefs have any foundation. This experience, too, dates back to childhood. When, for example, a child notices that the Santa Claus on the street corner is about as tall as his father, while the one in the department store is a good deal taller, and is moved to ask questions about Santa's location and stature, he is looking critically at a belief and inquiring into its reasons.

As we emerge from childhood, we continue to have experiences of this kind and to acquire further beliefs. Some beliefs we go on accepting without checking up on their reasonableness; other beliefs we do question, some of them very seriously. But two things happen to many of us. First, the questioned beliefs increase in proportion to the unquestioned beliefs. And second, the questioning process, once begun, is carried on for longer and longer times before it is allowed to end. The child who is told that the department store Santa is "really" Santa Claus, while those in the street are merely trusted helpers, may be satisfied for a time, but at some later stage he will probably ask himself what reason there is for believing *this* to be true, especially if he compares notes with his cousin from another city, who has been provided with a different candidate for the "real Santa Claus." The junior high school student who has been told he should accept what his science teacher says because the latter knows his subject may wonder why the teacher is judged to be a qualified authority in this field. If provided with satisfactory assurances, he will call a halt to his questioning process at that stage; but later on, perhaps in college, he may be moved to ask why we should ever accept anything told us by "authorities," no matter how well qualified. Should we not rely entirely on our own firsthand experience? Is anything else really *knowledge?*

The search for good reasons for our beliefs, and for good reasons for the reasons, can be carried as far as we wish. If it is carried far enough, the searcher finds himself confronted by questions of a peculiar kind: the questions of philosophy. Among these questions you will find some that you have already thought about, as well as others that will be unfamiliar to you. Many of them, however, originally came to be asked because someone undertook a critical examination of his ordinary beliefs.

Philosophical Questions

As our first example, let us trace the origin of a few philosophical questions that arise out of the moral aspects of life. People sometimes say, "He ought to be put in jail for that." Sometimes this is only an exclamation of anger at some instance of meanness or brutality; sometimes it leads to action, however, for juries do put people in jail because (if the jurors are conscientious) they believe that this punishment is just. Suppose you hear a friend remark, about the recent conviction of someone who has violated the law—a holdup man, a venal judge, an industrialist who has conspired to fix prices, a civil rights demonstrator who has blocked a construction site—that the jail sentence is deserved. After you hear all the relevant details, you may agree with him. But even so, you might still wonder whether you are right, and—not because you plan to do anything about the case, but merely because you would like to be sure you *are* right—you may begin to ask further, more searching, questions.

Why does the man deserve to be sent to jail? Because he committed a crime, of course. Yes, but why should he be sent to jail for committing a crime? Because to disobey the laws of the state is wrong. But *why?* Just because certain people you don't even know, perhaps people who died years before you were born, passed a law against, let us say, spitting in the subway or disorderly conduct, how does that obligate you to obey the law? This line of questioning, as we can foresee, will, if carried far, lead into some perplexing questions about the moral basis of the law, the tests of right and wrong, the purposes of government and society. For example, we may discover that in approving the jail sentence we are assuming that the existence of a government is so important to maintain that governments have the right, under certain conditions, to deprive any citizen of his liberties. This assumption is a philosophical belief. And when we ask whether or not it is true, we are asking a philosophical question.

But consider how the questioning might turn into a different channel. Granted that the act was illegal, there still remains the question whether the man should be punished. Sometimes people do wrong things because they are feeble-minded or mentally ill, and we do not regard them as punishable. Well, in this case, it might be said, the man is responsible for his action. Why responsible? Because he was free when he committed it—free to commit the act or to refrain from committing it. He had, some would say, free will. Indeed, all men have free will—though they do not always exercise it. Then what reason is there to believe that this, in turn, is true? How do we know there is such a thing as free will? Again, we seem to have uncovered an underlying belief that lies deeper than the lawyer's or the juror's immediate problems, something they do not themselves discuss, but (according to one theory) take for granted. We have reached another belief that can be called philosophical, and exposed another philosophical question: do human beings have free will?

Let us see what it is about these questions that makes them philosophical. One of the first things that might be noticed about them is that they are highly *general.* One question is more general than another if it is about a broader class of things: about brown cows rather than about Farmer Jones's

brown cow . . . , or about cows rather than about brown cows, or about animals rather than about cows. A question about everything there is would be
the most general of all—we shall be trying in due course to answer such
questions. Most philosophical questions are highly general: Are all right actions those that promote human happiness? Is all knowledge based on sense
experience? Or—to recall those that turned up in our example—do all human beings have free will? Do all citizens owe certain obligations to their
governments? Those who specialize in subjects other than philosophy may
be interested in particular things or events, such as individual crimes or
criminals. Or they may be interested in things or events of certain limited
kinds, such as the psychological or sociological causes of crime. The philosopher goes into action when questions are raised about much larger classes,
such as the class of human beings or of knowledge. Those who limit their in-
vestigations are entirely justified in doing so, for human knowledge could
scarcely develop otherwise. Courts would never get their work done if every
judge felt called upon to solve wide-ranging questions about guilt and responsibility before he could get down to the business of trying a particular
case. But somebody, sometime, must ask those broad questions and try to
answer them. That is the job of the philosopher.

Some questions count as philosophical because of a second, and even
more important, quality: they are highly *fundamental*. The beliefs that a particular person has at a particular time constitute a more or less orderly system, depending on the extent to which they are logically interconnected,
some being reasons for others, some of the others being in turn reasons for
still others, etc. When you are pressed for your reason for predicting rain, if
you reply that you observe dark clouds, then in your thinking at that time
the second belief is more fundamental than the first. Of course a belief that is
very fundamental in one person's thinking may not be at all fundamental in
another's; that is one reason why each person comes at philosophy a little
differently from everyone else. But there are some beliefs that are pretty sure
to be fundamental in the thinking of anyone who holds them at all, and it is
these that we have in mind when we speak of fundamental beliefs and fundamental questions without mentioning any particular believer.

When one belief supports another, but is not itself supported by it, it is
logically more fundamental; there is more to it, so to speak, and therefore, in
principle at least, it is capable of supporting a wider range of other beliefs.
Thus, of two beliefs, the more fundamental one is probably the one that underlies and supports more of your other beliefs. If you should discover that
you were mistaken about a particular fact, you would probably not have to
revise many of your other beliefs to accommodate this change. But, for example, a belief in the immortality of the soul may be tied up with many other beliefs about morality, religion, education, and science. A highly fundamental question is a question about the truth of a highly fundamental belief.
And such questions are philosophical ones. The more general a question is,
the more fundamental it is likely to be, because it will range over a larger

area. But this is not necessarily true. For example, the question, "Are all men selfish?" and the question, "Do all men wear shoes?" are equally general, since they are about all men; but they are not equally fundamental, since the former has important consequences for our beliefs about the nature of moral obligation (which includes a host of beliefs about particular obligations), while little seems to depend upon the latter. On the other hand, the philosophical question, "Does God exist?" does not seem to be general at all, for it is about a single being. Nevertheless, this question is fundamental for many people, since many other beliefs about human beings and the physical universe may depend upon the answer to it—and some of these beliefs are themselves highly general.

We do not know how to set up any rules telling exactly how general or how fundamental a question must be in order for it to be considered a philosophical one. Philosophers themselves might not all agree on the proper classification of every question you can think of. But if the demand for good reasons is pressed, beginning with any belief, it will gradually pass beyond the scope of various special fields of knowledge and investigation, and at some point it will bring to light a question that many philosophers would be interested in, and would recognize—perhaps with joy, and perhaps, if it is a very tough one, with uneasiness—as their very own.

Philosophical Examination

Any thinking that concerns the truth of a philosophical belief is *philosophical thinking*. It may take the form of accepting a belief as true and investigating its logical connections with other beliefs; this may be called *exploring* the belief. Or it may take the form of questioning the belief and attempting to determine whether it is based on good reasons; this may be called *examining* the belief. Professional philosophers are those who have made philosophical thinking their vocation; but they have no monopoly on that activity. It is pursued by specialists in other fields—by scientists, historians, literary critics—whenever they inquire into the fundamental questions about their own disciplines. And it is pursued by all intelligent human beings who want to understand themselves and their world. Professional philosophers who genuinely respect their subject do not erect "No Trespassing" signs around philosophical questions.

In order to illustrate a little more fully what is involved in the process of examining a belief philosophically, let us take an example from history—let us begin with the belief that such-and-such a culture flourished hundreds of years before the Christian era in Central Africa or Nigeria. When the historian tells us this, we believe him. But if we have some intellectual curiosity, we might wonder how he knows it. Since the culture had no written language, he cannot rely on documents. And since their thatched houses and all the organic materials they once used in their daily life (wood, hide, cloth) would long ago have disintegrated in the tropical climate, the African historian has less to go on than his colleagues in other areas.[1] The usual methods developed by archaeologists are seldom available to him. It is hard to find organic materials on which to use the carbon-14 dating method (based on the constant rate of decay of this isotope in living organisms), though some artifacts have been dated in this way. Because of the rapid decay of dead wood and the eccentricities of seasonal growth, he cannot make much use of dendrochronology (dating by tree rings). But suppose the historian answers our challenge by using another method, thermoluminescence. In pottery there are uranium impurities that radiate naturally, but this radiation is trapped until the pottery is heated to a very high temperature. When the radiation rate for a particular substance is known, it is possible to determine how long ago the pottery was baked by measuring the amount of radiation built up in it.

Now we began with a question asked by the historian, "When did this culture flourish?" and the historian gave his answer. But when we ask him for his reasons he appeals to principles of physics: for example, that the radiation rate of this kind of pottery is always such-and-such. If we ask him, "How do you know this?" he will, of course, conduct us to the physicist and advise us to direct our question to him—he is the expert on radiation. Suppose we do so. Presumably the physicist's answer will be something of this sort: "We have tested various samples in our laboratory under controlled conditions, and found that the radiation rate is constant." Now, "constant" here means that it holds not only for last week's laboratory samples, but for the same substance a thousand years ago and a thousand years hence.

Our historical curiosity is satisfied, and we would ordinarily be content to accept the physicist's conclusion, too. But, however irritating it may be, let us continue to press our question ruthlessly. "Why do you say," we ask the physicist, "that just because the radiation rate was constant all last week, it must have been the same thousands of years ago?" At first he may not quite know what we are after. "Well," he might say, hoping to appease us, "my experiments have shown that the radiation rate is independent of various environmental conditions, such as moisture, and I have reason to believe that the *relevant* conditions were the same in the past as they are now." If we are astute as well as doggedly persistent, we can point out something to him in return: "But you seem to be assuming a general proposition that whenever the same conditions exist, the same effects will occur—'Like causes, like effects,' or something of the sort."

Granted that if this general principle holds true, the physicist's particular law about the constancy of radiation rate can be justified—but again we can ask, "How do we know that like causes produce like effects? How do we know that an event always has certain relevant causal conditions, and that whenever these conditions recur, the effect must recur, too?" Now we have left the physicist behind, too, and crossed over into the mysterious territory of philosophy. For we have asked a highly general question—since it is about all events, without exception, including everything that has happened or ever will happen. And it seems to be a highly fundamental question, since the assumption that every event has a cause, if it is true, must underlie an enormous number of other beliefs, not only in history and physics but in the common affairs of ordinary life.

Indeed, at this point we seem to have left everyone behind but the philosopher. And that is one of the peculiarities of this subject. When Harry Truman was President, he had a sign over his desk that said, "The buck stops here." The philosopher does his intellectual work under a similar sign, for there is no one to whom he can pass on a question with the plea that it is too general or too fundamental for him to deal with. The philosopher—and with him anyone else who is doing philosophical thinking—stands at the end of the line.

Here are two more samples of thinking that begin with a nonphilosophical belief but lead gradually but directly into philosophy. We present them in the form of brief dialogues.

Dialogue I

A: You ought to have written to your parents last Sunday.

B: Why?

A: Because you promised you would write every Sunday.

B: I know I did, but I've been awfully busy. Why was it so important to keep my promise?

A: Not just *that* promise—*any* promise. It's wrong ever to break a promise.

B: Well, I used to think that, but now I'm not sure. What makes you think it's always wrong to break promises?

A: My reason is simply that most people in our society disapprove of it. You know perfectly well that they do.

B: Of course I know that most people in our society disapprove of breaking promises, but does that prove it really is always wrong to do it? The majority opinion in our society could be mistaken, couldn't it? I don't see why it should be taken for granted that what most Americans *think* is wrong and what really *is* wrong should always coincide. What's the connection between the two?

Dialogue II

A: In my paper for political science I had to define "democracy." "Democracy" means "government by the people collectively."

B: What made you choose that definition?

A: I looked up the word in the dictionary, of course.

B: How do you know your dictionary is right? My dictionary doesn't always give the same definitions as yours.

A: Oh, but mine is larger and more recent, so it's bound to be more reliable.

B: Yes, but language is constantly changing, and words like "democracy" are used in lots of different ways. I think one shouldn't feel bound by any dictionary definition. Every writer should feel free to define any word as he wishes.

A: But that would be chaotic. Besides, you wouldn't really have definitions at all, in that case.

B: Why wouldn't you have definitions? There's no such thing as *the* "one true meaning" of a word, is there? Words mean whatever people make them mean, so why shouldn't I select my own meanings and put them in definitions of my own?

Very different topics are discussed in these brief conversations; but they follow a similar pattern. In each case, speaker A makes an opening remark of a fairly specific sort, speaker B asks A to give a good reason for his opening statement, and A does provide what, on the level of ordinary common-sense thinking, would be regarded as a satisfactory reason. Many conversations would end at this stage; but B is disposed to probe more deeply, to uncover the assumptions underlying A's reasons, and to ask whether these more basic assumptions, in turn, are reasonable. Notice how the beliefs being questioned become more general and more fundamental as the questioning goes on. In each of the little dialogues, B pushes A over the brink into philosophy. At the end of each, he raises a question concerning the truth of a philosophical belief—and there the matter is left, for the time being.

But you may not be content to leave it at that. If you feel some frustration or impatience with the way A and B are arguing, you are on the verge of doing some philosophical thinking yourself. Wouldn't you like to ask B some searching questions—for example, about the way in which he is using some of his key words? This would all be a lot clearer, you may have said to yourself while you were reading Dialogue I, if we were sure just what the word "wrong" means here. Maybe it means simply "disapproved by a majority of people in one's own society." In that case, what happens to B's final question? Isn't he confused? But *does* "wrong" mean only this? And take the term "free will," which was used in one of the other examples of philosophical thinking discussed above. How can we decide whether it is reasonable to believe that human beings have this mysterious thing without saying precisely what it is?

If you have been thinking for yourself along these lines, or (even if you haven't) if you can now see the sense in raising these questions about the meaning of key words, you will be able to sympathize with a good deal of what contemporary philosophers have been doing. Philosophers at all periods have been concerned to analyze the meaning of basic philosophical terms, but this task has received more attention from twentieth-century philosophers—or from many of them, at least—than ever before. By "key words" in philosophy we mean simply those words that are used in statements of beliefs that are highly general and fundamental, and in questions about these beliefs. A question about the meaning of such a word, such as the question, "What does 'cause' mean?" is itself highly fundamental, since the notion of causality plays a pervasive part in our thinking, and much might depend upon being clear about it. And we can see how it is that questions about the meaning of particular terms have led philosophers very naturally to still more fundamental questions about meaning itself, along with other basic characteristics of language. This further stage of interest in language is displayed in Dialogue II, in which speaker B is not content to accept A's remarks about the definition of the word "democracy" without questioning his assumptions about the very process of definition itself. Here B reveals a conviction (which we all can share) that we ought to be as clear as possible about the words in which we express our beliefs.

Increased clearness in your own beliefs is, then, one of the three chief benefits you can derive from a study of philosophy—if, as we hope, you are not content merely to learn about the theories and arguments of the great philosophers (interesting and valuable as that is), but will make this study an active exercise in philosophical thinking.

The second benefit, partly dependent on the first, is increased assurance that your beliefs are reasonable. A belief whose reasons have been examined deeply enough to reach the level of philosophical questioning rests on a firmer foundation than one that has been examined less thoroughly. This does not mean that everyone should become a professional philosopher (though we cannot help hoping that some readers of this book will ultimately make that choice). Admittedly, the philosopher's desire to base his beliefs on good reasons is unusually persistent and intense: the philosopher would not only rather be right than President—he would rather be right than anything. But all of us who want assurance that our beliefs are well grounded should do some philosophical thinking about some of them, at least, in order to secure the firmest possible grounds.

The third benefit which the study of philosophy can confer upon our beliefs is increased consistency. For philosophical thinking forces each of us to see whether his fundamental beliefs in different areas of experience form a logically coherent whole. We have already encountered . . . a pair of philosophical beliefs that seem in danger of clashing head-on in a contradiction. You will recall how we found that the philosophical examination of a belief about an African culture seemed to uncover an underlying assumption that every event happens under such conditions that when they are repeated, the same sort of event must happen again—in other words, that every event happens in accordance with a law of nature. And when we examined the assumptions underlying punishment we found that these seem to include the assumption that human beings have free will. To have free will is to be able to act in two different ways under precisely the same conditions. But if it is ever true that a man could have acted differently under the same conditions—i.e., that the conditions did not completely determine his action— then here is *one event* (namely the action) that did *not* happen in accordance with any law of nature. Perhaps further examination would clear things up;

but it looks as if we have here a contradiction in beliefs. Philosophical thinking has diagnosed it, and further philosophical thinking is the only thing that will provide a cure.

The three values we have cited—clarity, reasonableness, and consistency—are basic intellectual values. But perhaps you are saying to yourself something like this: "I can see that studying philosophy may help me improve my beliefs, but, after all, there is more to life than thinking and believing. What I most want from my education is to improve my *actions*. How can philosophical thinking help me to *live* better?"

Part of our answer here is that we must beware of drawing too sharp a line between beliefs and actions. Our beliefs—including philosophical beliefs—have a considerable influence on our actions. This influence can be seen most directly in one area of philosophy, where we are concerned with questions of value, but answers to some other basic philosophical questions may also possess some power to affect, however indirectly, the way we live. Although knowledge may be valuable for its own sake, as well as for its practical consequences, it is not wrong to expect philosophy to have its effects. It would be wrong, however, to ask every philosophical belief to show a direct and simple connection with human action. Perhaps the growing appreciation of the importance of basic research in science may foster an appreciation of the quest for answers to other highly fundamental questions, without insistence on immediate practical results.

In saying that beliefs influence actions, we do not mean to lose sight of the effect of emotions on human conduct. Temporary emotions, as well as more enduring emotional attitudes, are often powerful enough to make us behave in ways counter to what we believe intellectually. Philosophical thinking can do a great deal to clarify and harmonize our beliefs at all levels, and to strengthen their foundations. But the philosopher is no substitute for the psychiatrist, or for the parents and teachers of our early years who help create our emotional make-up. Yet many philosophers have claimed that the experience of thinking about philosophical questions can affect our emotional attitudes as well as our beliefs.

When we detach our minds from immediate practical matters and from the limited boundaries of particular fields of specialization, we experience a kind of release from petty and provincial concerns. The experience of thinking as human beings who are trying to understand themselves and their universe may produce a serenity and breadth of mind that can in time become enduring attitudes.

NOTE

1. For this example, and the details concerning it, we are indebted to Harrison M. Wright, "Tropical Africa: The Historian's Dilemma," *Swarthmore Alumni Magazine* (October, 1963).

Defence of Socrates

⧫⧫

PLATO

Philosophers build on the work of their predecessors, and the intellectual links that form the chain of the history of philosophy extend back to ancient Greece, more than five centuries before the Christian era. While only tantalizing fragments remain from the writings of the earliest philosophers, three men made such enormous contributions to the development of the subject that all philosophers acknowledge their overwhelming impact: Socrates (c. 470–399 B.C.E.), Plato (c. 429–347 B.C.E.), and Aristotle (384–322 B.C.E.).

Their relationship is unusual. Socrates wrote nothing but in conversation was able to befuddle the most powerful minds of his day. Plato, his devoted student, responded to Socratic teaching not, as one might suppose, by being intimidated but by becoming the greatest of philosophical writers, whose *Dialogues,* mostly featuring the character Socrates, form the foundation of all subsequent Western philosophy. Such a towering figure as Plato could have been expected to produce mere disciples, but, after studying with Plato for more than two decades, Aristotle developed his own comprehensive philosophical system, opposed in many respects to that of Plato, and so powerful in its own right that throughout history its impact has rivalled that of Plato. Surely Socrates and Plato were remarkable teachers as well as philosophers.

The *Defence of Socrates* (or *Apology* as it is sometimes titled) is an account of the trial of Socrates, who, after having been found guilty of impiety, was put to death by the Athenian democracy. Socrates' speech to the jury, as related by Plato, has come down through the ages as an eloquent defense of Socrates' life and of philosophy itself.

Are the words actually those Socrates spoke? Scholars disagree, but a plausible answer is provided by David Gallop, Professor

Emeritus of Philosophy at Trent University in Ontario, Canada, the author of the translation from the Greek that we are using:

> [I]t is inconceivable that any speaker could have improvised before a real court such an artfully structured, nuanced, and polished composition as Plato's *Defence of Socrates.* That is not to say that the work falsifies any biographical facts about Socrates, still less that its content is wholly invented. For we all know to the contrary, it may even in some places faithfully reproduce what Socrates said in court. But whatever blend of fact and fiction it contains, the speech as a whole is a philosophical memoir, intended to convey a sense of Socrates' mission and the supreme injustice of his conviction. It remains, above all, an exhortation to the practice of philosophy. No less than Plato's dramatic dialogues, it is designed to draw its readers into philosophical reflection, so that they may recover for themselves the truths to which the master had borne witness.
>
> If that is the chief aim of the *Defence,* its fidelity to fact becomes a secondary issue.

To assist you in reading the *Defence,* Notes and an Index of Names prepared by the translator are provided at the end.

I don't know[1] how you, fellow Athenians, have been affected by my accusers, but for my part I felt myself almost transported by them, so persuasively did they speak. And yet hardly a word they have said is true. Among their many falsehoods, one especially astonished me: their warning that you must be careful not to be taken in by me, because I am a clever speaker. It seemed to me the height of impudence on their part not to be embarrassed at being refuted straight away by the facts, once it became apparent that I was not a clever speaker at all—unless indeed they call a "clever" speaker one who speaks the truth. If that is what they mean, then I would admit to being an orator, although not on a par with them.

As I said, then, my accusers have said little or nothing true; whereas from me you shall hear the whole truth, though not, I assure you, fellow Athenians, in language adorned with fine words and phrases or dressed up, as theirs was: you shall hear my points made spontaneously in whatever words occur to me—persuaded as I am that my case is just. None of you should expect anything to be put differently, because it would not, of course, be at all fitting at my age, gentlemen, to come before you with artificial speeches, such as might be composed by a young lad.

One thing, moreover, I would earnestly beg of you, fellow Athenians. If you hear me defending myself with the same arguments I normally use at the bankers' tables in the market-place (where many of you have heard me) and elsewhere, please do not be surprised or protest on that account. You see, here is the reason: this is the first time I have ever appeared before a court of law, although I am over 70; so I am literally a stranger to the diction of this place. And if I really were a foreigner, you would naturally excuse me, were I to speak in the dialect and style in which I had been brought up; so in the present case as well I ask you, in all fairness as I think, to disregard my manner of speaking—it may not be as good, or it may be better—but to consider and attend simply to the question whether or not my case is just; because that is the duty of a judge, as it is an orator's duty to speak the truth.

To begin with, fellow Athenians, it is fair that I should defend myself against the first set of charges falsely brought against me by my first accusers, and then turn to the later charges and the more recent ones. You see, I have been accused before you by many people for a long time now, for many years in fact, by people who spoke not a word of truth. It is those people I fear more than Anytus and his crowd, though they too are dangerous. But those others are more so, gentlemen: they have taken hold of most of you since childhood, and made persuasive accusations against me, yet without an ounce more truth in them. They say that there is one Socrates, a "wise man," who ponders what is above the earth and investigates everything beneath it, and turns the weaker argument into the stronger.[2]

Those accusers who have spread such rumour about me, fellow Athenians, are the dangerous ones, because their audience believes that people who inquire into those matters also fail to acknowledge the gods. Moreover, those accusers are numerous, and have been denouncing me for a long time now, and they also spoke to you at an age at which you would be most likely to believe them, when some of you were children or young lads; and their accusations simply went by default for lack of any defence. But the most absurd thing of all is that one cannot even get to know their names or say who they were—except perhaps one who happens to be a comic playwright.[3] The ones who have persuaded you by malicious slander, and also some who persuade others because they have been persuaded themselves, are all very hard to deal with: one cannot put any of them on the stand here in court, or cross-examine anybody, but one must literally engage in a sort of shadow-boxing to defend oneself, and cross-examine without anyone to answer. You too, then, should allow, as I just said, that I have two sets of accusers: one set who have accused me recently, and the other of long standing to whom I was just referring. And please grant that I need to defend myself against the latter first, since you too heard them accusing me earlier, and you heard far more from them than from these recent critics here.

Very well, then. I must defend myself, fellow Athenians, and in so short a time[4] must try to dispel the slander which you have had so long to absorb. That is the outcome I would wish for, should it be of any benefit to you and to me, and I should like to succeed in my defence—though I believe the task to be a difficult one, and am well aware of its nature. But let that turn out as God wills: I have to obey the law and present my defence.

Let us examine, from the beginning, the charge that has given rise to the slander against me—which was just what Meletus relied upon when he drew up this indictment. Very well then, what were my slanderers actually saying when they slandered me? Let me read out their deposition, as if they were my legal accusers:

"Socrates is guilty of being a busybody, in that he inquires into what is beneath the earth and in the sky, turns the weaker argument into the stronger, and teaches others to do the same."

The charges would run something like that. Indeed, you can see them for yourselves, enacted in Aristophanes' comedy: in that play, a character called "Socrates" swings around, claims to be walking on air,[5] and talks a lot of other nonsense on subjects of which I have no understanding, great or small.

Not that I mean to belittle knowledge of that sort, if anyone really is learned in such matters—no matter how many of Meletus' lawsuits I might have to defend myself against—but the fact is, fellow Athenians, those subjects are not my concern at all. I call most of you to witness yourselves, and I ask you to make that quite clear to one another, if you have ever heard me in discussion (as many of you have). Tell one another, then, whether any of you has ever heard me discussing such subjects, either briefly or at length; and as a result you will realize that the other things said about me by the public are equally baseless.

In any event, there is no truth in those charges. Moreover, if you have heard from anyone that I undertake to educate people and charge fees, there is no truth in that either—though for that matter I do think it also a fine thing if anyone *is* able to educate people, as Gorgias of Leontini, Prodicus of Ceos, and Hippias of Elis profess to. Each of them can visit any city, gentlemen, and persuade its young people, who may associate free of charge with any of their own citizens they wish, to leave those associations, and to join with them instead, paying fees and being grateful into the bargain.

On that topic, there is at present another expert here, a gentleman from Paros; I heard of his visit, because I happened to run into a man who has spent more money on sophists[6] than everyone else put together—Callias, the son of Hipponicus. So I questioned him, since he has two sons himself.

"Callias," I said, "if your two sons had been born as colts or calves, we could find and engage a tutor who could make them both excel superbly in the required qualities—and he'd be some sort of expert in horse-rearing or agriculture. But seeing that they are actually human, whom do you intend to engage as their tutor? Who has knowledge of the required human and civic qualities? I ask, because I assume you've given thought to the matter, having sons yourself. Is there such a person," I asked, "or not?"

"Certainly," he replied.

"Who is he?" I said; "Where does he come from, and what does he charge for tuition?"

"His name is Evenus, Socrates," he replied; "He comes from Paros, and he charges 5 minas."[7]

I thought Evenus was to be congratulated, if he really did possess that skill and imparted it for such a modest charge. I, at any rate, would certainly be giving myself fine airs and graces if I possessed that knowledge. But the fact is, fellow Athenians, I do not.

Now perhaps one of you will interject: "Well then, Socrates, what is the difficulty in your case? What is the source of these slanders against you? If you are not engaged in something out of the ordinary, why ever has so much rumour and talk arisen about you? It would surely never have arisen, unless you were up to something different from most people. Tell us what it is, then, so that we don't jump to conclusions about you."

That speaker makes a fair point, I think; and so I will try to show you just what it is that has earned me my reputation and notoriety. Please hear me out. Some of you will perhaps think I am joking, but I assure you that I shall be telling you the whole truth.

You see, fellow Athenians, I have gained this reputation on account of nothing but a certain sort of wisdom. And what sort of wisdom is that? It is a human kind of wisdom, perhaps, since it might just be true that I have wisdom of that sort. Maybe the people I just mentioned possess wisdom of a superhuman kind; otherwise I cannot explain it. For my part, I certainly do not possess that knowledge; and whoever says I do is lying and speaking with a view to slandering me—

Now please do not protest, fellow Athenians, even if I should sound to you rather boastful. I am not myself the source of the story I am about to tell you, but I shall refer you to a trustworthy authority. As evidence of my wisdom, if such it actually be, and of its nature, I shall call to witness before you the god at Delphi.[8]

You remember Chaerephon, of course. He was a friend of mine from youth, and also a comrade in your party, who shared your recent exile and restoration.[9] You recall too what sort of man Chaerephon was, how impetuous he was in any undertaking. Well, on one occasion he actually went to the Delphic oracle, and had the audacity to put the following question to it—as I said, please do not make a disturbance, gentlemen—he went and asked if there was anyone wiser than myself; to which the Pythia responded that there was no one. His brother here will testify to the court about that story, since Chaerephon himself is deceased.

Now keep in mind why I have been telling you this: it is because I am going to explain to you the origin of the slander against me. When I heard the story, I thought to myself: "What ever is the god saying? What can his riddle mean? Since I am all too conscious of not being wise in any matter, great or small, what ever can be mean by pronouncing me to be the wisest? Surely he cannot be lying: for him that would be out of the question."

So for a long time I was perplexed about what he could possibly mean. But then, with great reluctance, I proceeded to investigate the matter somewhat as follows. I went to one of the people who had a reputation for wisdom, thinking there, if anywhere, to disprove the oracle's utterance and declare to it: "Here is someone wiser than I am, and yet you said that I was the wisest."

So I interviewed this person—I need not mention his name, but he was someone in public life; and when I examined him, my experience went something like this, fellow Athenians: in conversing with him, I formed the opinion that, although the man was thought to be wise by many other people, and especially by himself, yet in reality he was not. So I then tried to show him that he thought himself wise without being so. I thereby earned his dislike, and that of many people present; but still, as I went away, I thought to myself: "I am wiser than that fellow, anyhow. Because neither of us, I dare say, knows anything of great value; but he thinks he knows a thing when he doesn't; whereas I neither know it in fact, nor think that I do. At any rate, it appears that I am wiser than he in just this one small respect: if I do not know something, I do not think that I do."

Next, I went to someone else, among people thought to be even wiser than the previous man, and I came to the same conclusion again; and so I was disliked by that man too, as well as by many others.

Well, after that I went on to visit one person after another. I realized, with dismay and alarm, that I was making enemies; but even so, I thought it my duty to attach the highest importance to the god's business; and therefore, in seeking the oracle's meaning, I had to go on to examine all those with any reputation for knowledge. And upon my word,[10] fellow Athenians—because I am obliged to speak the truth before the court—I truly did experience something like this: as I pursued the god's inquiry, I found those held in the highest esteem were practically the most defective, whereas men who were supposed to be their inferiors were much better off in respect of understanding.

Let me, then, outline my wanderings for you, the various "labours" I kept undertaking,[11] only to find that the oracle proved completely irrefutable. After I had done with the politicians, I turned to the poets—including tragedians, dithyrambic poets,[12] and the rest—thinking that in their company I would be shown up as more ignorant than they were. So I picked up the poems over which I thought they had taken the most trouble, and questioned them about their meaning, so that I might also learn something from them in the process.

Now I'm embarrassed to tell you the truth, gentlemen, but it has to be said. Practically everyone else present could speak better than the poets themselves about their very own compositions. And so, once more, I soon realized this truth about them too: it was not from wisdom that they composed their works, but from a certain natural aptitude and inspiration, like that of seers and sooth-sayers—because those people too utter many fine words, yet know nothing of the matters on which they pronounce. It was obvious to me that the poets were in much the same situation; yet at the same time I realized that because of their compositions they thought themselves the wisest people in other matters as well, when they were not. So I left, believing that I was ahead of them in the same way as I was ahead of the politicians.

Then, finally, I went to the craftsmen, because I was conscious of knowing almost nothing myself, but felt sure that amongst them, at least, I would find much valuable knowledge. And in that expectation I was not disappointed: they did have knowledge in fields where I had none, and in that respect they were wiser than I. And yet, fellow Athenians, those able craftsmen seemed to me to suffer from the same failing as the poets: because of their excellence at their own trade, each claimed to be a great expert also on matters of the utmost importance; and this arrogance of theirs seemed to eclipse their wisdom. So I began to ask myself, on the oracle's behalf, whether I should prefer to be as I am, neither wise as they are wise, nor ignorant as they are ignorant, or to possess both their attributes; and in reply, I told myself and the oracle that I was better off as I was.

The effect of this questioning, fellow Athenians, was to earn me much hostility of a very vexing and trying sort, which has given rise to numerous slanders, including this reputation I have for being "wise"—because those present on each occasion imagine me to be wise regarding the matters on which I examine others. But in fact, gentlemen, it would appear that it is only the god who is truly wise; and that he is saying to us, through this oracle, that human wisdom is worth little or nothing. It seems that when he says "Socrates," he makes use of my name, merely taking me as an example—as if to say, "The wisest amongst you, human beings, is anyone like Socrates who has recognized that with respect to wisdom he is truly worthless."

That is why, even to this day, I still go about seeking out and searching into anyone I believe to be wise, citizen or foreigner, in obedience to the god. Then, as soon as I find that someone is not wise, I assist the god by proving that he is not. Because of this occupation, I have had no time at all for any activity to speak of, either in public affairs or in my family life; indeed, because of my service to the god, I live in extreme poverty.

In addition, the young people who follow me around of their own accord, the ones who have plenty of leisure because their parents are wealthiest, enjoy listening to people being cross-examined. Often, too, they copy my example themselves, and so attempt to cross-examine others. And I imagine that they find a great abundance of people who suppose themselves to possess some knowledge, but really know little or nothing. Consequently, the people they question are angry with me, though not with themselves, and say that there is a nasty pestilence abroad called "Socrates," who is corrupting the young.

Then, when asked just what he is doing or teaching, they have nothing to say, because they have no idea what he does; yet, rather than seem at a loss, they resort to the stock charges against all who pursue intellectual inquiry, trotting out "things in the sky and beneath the earth," "failing to acknowledge the gods," and "turning the weaker argument into the stronger."

They would, I imagine, be loath to admit the truth, which is that their pretensions to knowledge have been exposed, and they are totally ignorant. So because these people have reputations to protect, I suppose, and are also both passionate and numerous, and have been speaking about me in a vigorous and persuasive style, they have long been filling your ears with vicious slander. It is on the strength of all this that Meletus, along with Anytus and Lycon, has proceeded against me: Meletus is aggrieved for the poets, Anytus for the craftsmen and politicians, and Lycon for the orators. And so, as I began by saying, I should be surprised if I could rid your minds of this slander in so short a time, when so much of it has accumulated.

There is the truth for you, fellow Athenians. I have spoken it without concealing anything from you, major or minor, and without glossing over anything. And yet I am virtually certain that it is my very candour that makes enemies for me—which goes to show that I am right: the slander against me is to that effect, and such is its explanation. And whether you look for one now or later, that is what you will find.

So much for my defence before you against the charges brought by my first group of accusers. Next, I shall try to defend myself against Meletus, good patriot that he claims to be, and against my more recent critics. So once again, as if they were a fresh set of accusers, let me in turn review their deposition. It runs something like this:

"Socrates is guilty of corrupting the young, and of failing to acknowledge the gods acknowledged by the city, but introducing new spiritual beings instead."

Such is the charge: let us examine each item within it.

Meletus says, then, that I am guilty of corrupting the young. Well I reply, fellow Athenians, that Meletus is guilty of trifling in a serious matter, in that he brings people to trial on frivolous grounds, and professes grave concern about matters for which he has never cared at all. I shall now try to prove to you too that that is so.

Step forward, Meletus, and answer me. It is your chief concern, is it not, that our younger people shall be as good as possible?

—It is.

Very well, will you please tell the judges who influences them for the better—because you must obviously know, seeing that you care? Having discovered me, as you allege, to be the one who is corrupting them, you bring me before the judges here and accuse me. So speak up, and tell the court who has an improving influence.

You see, Meletus, you remain silent, and have no answer. Yet doesn't that strike you as shameful, and as proof in itself of exactly what I say—that you have never cared about these matters at all? Come then, good fellow, tell us who influences them for the better.

—The laws.

Yes, but that is not what I'm asking, excellent fellow. I mean, which *person*, who already knows the laws to begin with?

—These gentlemen, the judges, Socrates.

What are you saying, Meletus? Can these people educate the young, and do they have an improving influence?

—Most certainly.

All of them, or some but not others?

—All of them.

My goodness, what welcome news, and what a generous supply of benefactors you speak of! And how about the audience here in court? Do they too have an improving influence, or not?

—Yes, they do too.

And how about members of the Council?[13]

—Yes, the Councillors too.

But in that case, how about people in the Assembly, its individual members, Meletus? They won't be corrupting their youngers, will they? Won't they all be good influences as well?

—Yes, they will too.

So every person in Athens, it would appear, has an excellent influence on them except for me, whereas I alone am corrupting them. Is that what you're saying?

—That is emphatically what I'm saying.

Then I find myself, if we are to believe you, in a most awkward predicament. Now answer me this. Do you think the same is true of horses? Is it everybody who improves them, while a single person spoils them? Or isn't the opposite true: a single person, or at least very few people, namely the horse-trainers, can improve them; while lay people spoil them, don't they, if they have to do with horses and make use of them? Isn't that true of horses as of all other animals, Meletus? Of course it is, whether you and Anytus deny it or not. In fact, I dare say our young people are extremely lucky if only one person is corrupting them, while everyone else is doing them good.

All right, Meletus. Enough has been said to prove that you never were concerned about the young. You betray your irresponsibility plainly, because you have not cared at all about the charges on which you bring me before this court.

Furthermore, Meletus, tell us, in God's name, whether it is better to live among good fellow citizens or bad ones. Come sir, answer: I am not asking a hard question. Bad people have a harmful impact upon their closest companions at any given time, don't they, whereas good people have a good one?

—Yes.

Well, is there anyone who wants to be harmed by his companions rather than benefited?—Be a good fellow and keep on answering, as the law requires you to. Is there anyone who wants to be harmed?

—Of course not.

Now tell me this. In bringing me here, do you claim that I am corrupting and depraving the young intentionally or unintentionally?

—Intentionally, so I maintain.

Really, Meletus? Are you so much smarter at your age than I at mine as to realize that the bad have a harmful impact upon their closest companions at any given time, whereas the good have a beneficial effect? Am I, by contrast, so far gone in my stupidity as not to realize that if I make one of my companions vicious, I risk incurring harm at his hands? And am I, therefore, as you allege, doing so much damage intentionally?

That I cannot accept from you, Meletus, and neither could anyone else, I imagine. Either I am not corrupting them—or if I am, I am doing so unintentionally[14]; so either way your charge is false. But if I am corrupting them unintentionally, the law does not require me to be brought to court for such mistakes, but rather to be taken aside for private instruction and admonition—since I shall obviously stop doing unintentional damage, if I learn better. But you avoided association with me and were unwilling to instruct me. Instead you bring me to court, where the law requires you to bring people who need punishment rather than enlightenment.

Very well, fellow Athenians. That part of my case is now proven: Meletus never cared about these matters, either a lot or a little. Nevertheless, Meletus, please tell us in what way you claim that I am corrupting our younger people. That is quite obvious, isn't it, from the indictment you drew up? It is by teaching them not to acknowledge the gods acknowledged by the city, but to accept new spiritual beings instead? You mean, don't you, that I am corrupting them by teaching them that?

—I most emphatically do.

Then, Meletus, in the name of those very gods we are now discussing, please clarify the matter further for me, and for the jury here. You see, I cannot make out what you mean. Is it that I am teaching people to acknowledge that some gods exist—in which case it follows that I do acknowledge their existence myself as well, and am not a complete atheist, hence am not guilty on that count—and yet that those gods are not the ones acknowledged by the city, but different ones? Is that your charge against me—namely, that they are different? Or are you saying that I acknowledge no gods at all myself, and teach the same to others?

—I am saying the latter: you acknowledge no gods at all.

What ever makes you say that, Meletus, you strange fellow? Do I not even acknowledge, then, with the rest of mankind, that the sun and the moon are gods?[15]

—By God, he does not, members of the jury, since he claims that the sun is made of rock, and the moon of earth!

My dear Meletus, do you imagine that it is Anaxagoras you are accusing?[16] Do you have such contempt for the jury, and imagine them so illiterate as not to know that books by Anaxagoras of Clazomenae are crammed with such assertions? What's more, are the young learning those things from me when they can acquire them at the bookstalls, now and then, for a drachma at most, and so ridicule Socrates if he claims those ideas for his own, especially when they are so bizarre? In God's name, do you really think me as crazy as that? Do I acknowledge the existence of no god at all?

—By God no, none whatever.

I can't believe you, Meletus—nor, I think, can you believe yourself. To my mind, fellow Athenians, this fellow is an impudent scoundrel who has framed this indictment out of sheer wanton impudence and insolence. He seems to have devised a sort of riddle in order to try me out: "Will Socrates the Wise tumble to my nice self-contradiction?[17] Or shall I fool him along with my other listeners?" You see, he seems to me to be contradicting himself in the indictment. It's as if he were saying: "Socrates is guilty of not acknowledging gods, but of acknowledging gods"; and yet that is sheer tomfoolery.

I ask you to examine with me, gentlemen, just how that appears to be his meaning. Answer for us, Meletus; and the rest of you, please remember my initial request not to protest if I conduct the argument in my usual manner.

Is there anyone in the world, Meletus, who acknowledges that human phenomena exist, yet does not acknowledge human beings?—Require him to answer, gentlemen, and not to raise all kinds of confused objections. Is there anyone who does not acknowledge horses, yet does acknowledge equestrian phenomena? Or who does not acknowledge that musicians exist, yet does acknowledge musical phenomena?

There is no one, excellent fellow: if you don't wish to answer, I must answer for you, and for the jurors here. But at least answer my next question yourself. Is there anyone who acknowledges that spiritual phenomena exist, yet does not acknowledge spirits?

—No.

How good of you to answer—albeit reluctantly and under compulsion from the jury. Well now, you say that I acknowledge spiritual beings and teach others to do so. Whether they actually be new or old is no matter: I do at any rate, by your account, acknowledge spiritual beings, which you have also mentioned in your sworn deposition. But if I acknowledge spiritual beings, then surely it follows quite inevitably that I must acknowledge spirits. Is that not so?—Yes, it is so: I assume your agreement, since you don't answer. But we regard spirits, don't we, as either gods or children of gods? Yes or no?

—Yes.

Then given that I do believe in spirits, as you say, if spirits are gods of some sort, this is precisely what I claim when I say that you are presenting us with a riddle and making fun of us: you are saying that I do not believe in gods, and yet again that I do believe in gods, seeing that I believe in spirits.

On the other hand, if spirits are children of gods,[18] some sort of bastard offspring from nymphs—or from whomever they are traditionally said, in each case, to be born—then who in the world could ever believe that there were children of gods, yet no gods? That would be just as absurd as accepting the existence of children of horses and asses—namely, mules—yet rejecting the existence of horses or asses!

In short, Meletus, you can only have drafted this either by way of trying us out, or because you were at a loss how to charge me with a genuine offense. How could you possibly persuade anyone with even the slightest intelligence that someone who accepts spiritual beings does not also accept divine ones, and again that the same person also accepts neither spirits nor gods nor heroes? There is no conceivable way.

But enough, fellow Athenians. It needs no long defence, I think, to show that I am not guilty of the charges in Meletus' indictment; the foregoing will suffice. You may be sure, though, that what I was saying earlier is true: I have earned great hostility among many people. And that is what will convict me, if I am convicted: not Meletus or Anytus, but the slander and malice of the crowd. They have certainly convicted many other good men as well, and I imagine they will do so again; there is no risk of their stopping with me.

Now someone may perhaps say: "Well then, are you not ashamed, Socrates, to have pursued a way of life which has now put you at risk of death?"

But it may be fair for me to answer him as follows: "You are sadly mistaken, fellow, if you suppose that a man with even a grain of self-respect should reckon up the risks of living or dying, rather than simply consider, whenever he does something, whether his actions are just or unjust, the deeds of a good man or a bad one." By your principles, presumably, all those demigods who died in the plain of Troy[19] were inferior creatures—yes, even the son of Thetis,[20] who showed so much scorn for danger, when the alternative was to endure dishonour. Thus, when he was eager to slay Hector, his mother, goddess that she was, spoke to him—something like this, I fancy:

My child, if thou dost avenge the murder of thy friend, Patroclus,
And dost slay Hector, then straightway [so runs the poem]
Shalt thou die thyself, since doom is prepared for thee
Next after Hector's

But though he heard that, he made light of death and danger, since he feared far more to live as a base man, and to fail to avenge his dear ones. The poem goes on:

Then straightway let me die, once I have given the wrongdoer
His deserts, lest I remain here by the beak-prowed ships,
An object of derision, and a burden upon the earth.

Can you suppose that he gave any thought to death or danger?

You see, here is the truth of the matter, fellow Athenians. Wherever a man has taken up a position because he considers it best, or has been posted there by his commander, that is where I believe he should remain, steadfast in danger, taking no account at all of death or of anything else rather than dishonour. I would therefore have been acting absurdly, fellow Athenians, if when assigned to a post at Potidaea, Amphipolis, or Delium[21] by the superiors you had elected to command me, I remained where I was posted on those occasions at the risk of death, if ever any man did; whereas now that the god assigns me, as I became completely convinced, to the duty of leading the philosophical life by examining myself and others, I desert that post from fear of death or anything else. Yes, that would be unthinkable; and then I truly should deserve to be brought to court for failing to acknowledge the gods' existence, in that I was disobedient to the oracle, was afraid of death, and thought I was wise when I was not.

After all, gentlemen, the fear of death amounts simply to thinking one is wise when one is not: it is thinking one knows something one does not know. No one knows, you see, whether death may not in fact prove the greatest of all blessings for mankind; but people fear it as if they knew it for certain to be the greatest of evils. And yet to think that one knows what one does not know must surely be the kind of folly which is reprehensible.

On this matter especially, gentlemen, that may be the nature of my own advantage over most people. If I really were to claim to be wiser than anyone in any respect, it would consist simply in this: just as I do not possess adequate knowledge of life in Hades, so I also realize that I do not possess it; whereas acting unjustly in disobedience to one's betters, whether god or human being, is something I *know* to be evil and shameful. Hence I shall never fear or flee from something which may indeed be a good for all I know, rather than from things I know to be evils.

Suppose, therefore, that you pay no heed to Anytus, but are prepared to let me go. He said I need never have been brought to court in the first place; but that once I had been, your only option was to put me to death. He declared before you that, if I got away from you this time, your sons would all be utterly corrupted by practising Socrates' teachings. Suppose, in the face of that, you were to say to me:

"Socrates, we will not listen to Anytus this time. We are prepared to let you go—but only on this condition: you are to pursue that quest of yours and practise philosophy no longer; and if you are caught doing it any more, you shall be put to death."

Well, as I just said, if you were prepared to let me go on those terms, I should reply to you as follows:

"I have the greatest fondness and affection for you, fellow Athenians, but I will obey my god rather than you; and so long as I draw breath and am able, I shall never give up practising philosophy, or exhorting and showing the way to any of you whom I ever encounter, by giving my usual sort of message. 'Excellent friend,' I shall say; 'You are an Athenian. Your city is the most important and renowned for its wisdom and power; so are you not ashamed that, while you take care to acquire as much wealth as possible, with honour and glory as well, yet you take no care or thought for understanding or truth, or for the best possible state of your soul?'

"And should any of you dispute that, and claim that he does take such care, I will not let him go straight away nor leave him, but I will question and examine and put him to the test; and if I do not think he has acquired goodness, though he says he has, I shall say, 'Shame on you, for setting the lowest value upon the most precious things, and for rating inferior ones more highly!' That I shall do for anyone I encounter, young or old, alien or fellow citizen; but all the more for the latter, since your kinship with me is closer."

Those are my orders from my god, I do assure you. Indeed, I believe that no greater good has ever befallen you in our city than my service to my god; because all I do is to go about persuading you, young and old alike, not to care for your bodies or for your wealth so intensely as for the greatest possible well-being of your souls. "It is not wealth," I tell you, "that produces goodness; rather, it is from goodness that wealth, and all other benefits for human beings, accrue to them in their private and public life."

If, in fact, I am corrupting the young by those assertions, you may call them harmful. But if anyone claims that I say anything different, he is talking nonsense. In the face of that I should like to say: "Fellow Athenians, you may listen to Anytus or not, as you please; and you may let me go or not, as you please, because there is no chance of my acting otherwise, even if I have to die many times over—"

Stop protesting, fellow Athenians! Please abide by my request that you not protest against what I say, but hear me out; in fact, it will be in your interest, so I believe, to do so. You see, I am going to say some further things to you which may make you shout out—although I beg you not to.

You may be assured that if you put to death the sort of man I just said I was, you will not harm me more than you harm yourselves. Meletus or Anytus would not harm me at all; nor, in fact, could they do so, since I believe it is out of the question for a better man to be harmed by his inferior. The latter may, of course, inflict death or banishment or disenfranchisement; and my accuser here, along with others no doubt, believes those to be great evils. But I do not. Rather, I believe it a far greater evil to try to kill a man unjustly, as he does now.

At this point, therefore, fellow Athenians, so far from pleading on my own behalf, as might be supposed, I am pleading on yours, in case by condemning me you should mistreat the gift which God has bestowed upon you—because if you put me to death, you will not easily find another like me. The fact is, if I may put the point in a somewhat comical way, that I have been literally attached by God to our city, as if to a horse—a large thoroughbred, which is a bit sluggish because of its size, and needs to be aroused by some sort of gadfly. Yes, in me, I believe, God has attached to our city just such a creature—the kind which is constantly alighting everywhere on you, all day long, arousing, cajoling, or reproaching each and every one of you. You will not easily acquire another such gadfly, gentlemen; rather, if you take my advice, you will spare my life. I dare say, though, that you will get angry, like people who are awakened from their doze. Perhaps you will heed Anytus, and give me a swat: you could happily finish me off, and then spend the rest of your life asleep—unless God, in his compassion for you, were to send you someone else.

That I am, in fact, just the sort of gift that God would send to our city, you may recognize from this: it would not seem to be in human nature for me to have neglected all my own affairs, and put up with the neglect of my family for all these years, but constantly minded your interests, by visiting each of you in private like a father or an elder brother, urging you to be concerned about goodness. Of course, if I were gaining anything from that, or were being paid to urge that course upon you, my actions could be explained. But in fact you can see for yourselves that my accusers, who so shamelessly level all those other charges against me, could not muster the impudence to call evidence that I ever once obtained payment, or asked for any. It is I who can call evidence sufficient, I think, to show that I am speaking the truth—namely, my poverty.

Now it may perhaps seem peculiar that, as some say, I give this counsel by going around and dealing with others' concerns in private, yet do not venture to appear before the Assembly, and counsel the city about your business in public. But the reason for that is one you have frequently heard me give in many places: it is a certain divine or spiritual sign[22] which comes to me, the very thing to which Meletus made mocking allusion in his indictment. It has been happening to me ever since childhood: a voice of some sort which comes, and which always—whenever it does come—restrains me from what I am about to do, yet never gives positive direction. That is what opposes my engaging in politics—and its opposition is an excellent thing, to my mind; because you may be quite sure, fellow Athenians, that if I had tried to engage in politics, I should have perished long since, and should have been of no use either to you or to myself.

And please do not get angry if I tell you the truth. The fact is that there is no person on earth whose life will be spared by you or by any other majority, if he is genuinely opposed to many injustices and unlawful acts, and tries to prevent their occurrence in our city. Rather, anyone who truly fights for what is just, if he is going to survive for even a short time, must act in a private capacity rather than a public one.

I will offer you conclusive evidence of that—not just words, but the sort of evidence that you respect, namely, actions. Just hear me tell my experiences, so that you may know that I would not submit to a single person for fear of death, contrary to what is just; nor would I do so, even if I were to lose my life on the spot. I shall mention things to you which are vulgar commonplaces of the courts; yet they are true.

Although I have never held any other public office in our city, fellow

Athenians, I have served on its Council. My own tribe, Antiochis, happened
to be the presiding commission[23] on the occasion when you wanted a collective trial for the ten generals who had failed to rescue the survivors from the
naval battle.[24] That was illegal, as you all later recognized. At the time I was
the only commissioner opposed to your acting illegally, and I voted against
the motion. And though its advocates were prepared to lay information
against me and have me arrested, while you were urging them on by shout-
ing, I believed that I should face danger in siding with law and justice, rather
than take your side for fear of imprisonment or death, when your proposals
were contrary to justice.

    Those events took place while our city was still under democratic rule.
But on a subsequent occasion, after the oligarchy had come to power, the
Thirty summoned me and four others to the round chamber,[25] with orders to
arrest Leon the Salaminian, and fetch him from Salamis[26] for execution; they
were constantly issuing such orders, of course, to many others, in their wish
to implicate as many as possible in their crimes. On that occasion, however, I
showed, once again not just by words, but by my actions, that I couldn't care
less about death—if that would not be putting it rather crudely—but that my
one and only care was to avoid doing anything sinful or unjust. Thus, powerful as it was, that regime did not frighten me into unjust action: when we
emerged from the round chamber, the other four went off to Salamis and arrested Leon, whereas I left them and went off home. For that I might easily
have been put to death, had the regime not collapsed shortly afterwards.
There are many witnesses who will testify before you about those events.

    Do you imagine, then, that I would have survived all these years if I had
been regularly active in public life, and had championed what was right in a
manner worthy of a brave man, and valued that above all else, as was my
duty? Far from it, fellow Athenians: I would not, and nor would any other
man. But in any public undertaking, that is the sort of person that I, for my
part, shall prove to have been throughout my life; and likewise in my private
life, because I have never been guilty of unjust association with anyone, including those whom my slanderers allege to have been my students.[27]

    I never, in fact, was anyone's instructor[28] at any time. But if a person
wanted to hear me talking, while I was engaging in my own business, I never grudged that to anyone, young or old; nor do I hold conversation only
when I receive payment, and not otherwise. Rather, I offer myself for questioning to wealthy and poor alike, and to anyone who may wish to answer in
response to questions from me. Whether any of those people acquires a good
character or not, I cannot fairly be held responsible, when I never at any time
promised any of them that they would learn anything from me, nor gave
them instruction. And if anyone claims that he ever learnt anything from me,
or has heard privately something that everyone else did not hear as well,
you may be sure that what he says is untrue.

    Why then, you may ask, do some people enjoy spending so much time
in my company? You have already heard, fellow Athenians: I have told you

the whole truth—which is that my listeners enjoy the examination of those who think themselves wise but are not, since the process is not unamusing. But for me, I must tell you, it is a mission which I have been bidden to undertake by the god, through oracles and dreams,[29] and through every means whereby a divine injunction to perform any task has ever been laid upon a human being.

That is not only true, fellow Athenians, but is easily verified—because if I do corrupt any of our young people, or have corrupted others in the past, then presumably, when they grew older, should any of them have realized that I had at any time given them bad advice in their youth, they ought now to have appeared here themselves to accuse me and obtain redress. Or else, if they were unwilling to come in person, members of their families—fathers, brothers, or other relations—had their relatives suffered any harm at my hands, ought now to put it on record and obtain redress.

In any case, many of those people are present, whom I can see: first there is Crito, my contemporary and fellow demesman, father of Critobulus here; then Lysanias of Sphettus, father of Aeschines here; next, Epigenes' father, Antiphon from Cephisia, is present; then again, there are others here whose brothers have spent time with me in these studies: Nicostratus, son of Theozotides, brother of Theodotus—Theodotus himself, incidentally, is deceased, so Nicostratus could not have come at his brother's urging; and Paralius here, son of Demodocus, whose brother was Theages; also present is Ariston's son, Adimantus, whose brother is Plato here; and Aeantodorus, whose brother is Apollodorus here.

There are many others I could mention to you, from whom Meletus should surely have called some testimony during his own speech. However, if he forgot to do so then, let him call it now—I yield the floor to him—and if he has any such evidence, let him produce it. But quite the opposite is true, gentlemen: you will find that they are all prepared to support me, their corruptor, the one who is, according to Meletus and Anytus, doing their relatives mischief. Support for me from the actual victims of corruption might perhaps be explained; but what of the uncorrupted—older men by now, and relatives of my victims? What reason would they have to support me, apart from the right and proper one, which is that they know very well that Meletus is lying, whereas I am telling the truth?

There it is, then, gentlemen. That, and perhaps more of the same, is about all I have to say in my defence. But perhaps, among your number, there may be someone who will harbour resentment when he recalls a case of his own: he may have faced a less serious trial than this one, yet begged and implored the jury, weeping copiously, and producing his children here, along with many other relatives and loved ones, to gain as much sympathy as possible. By contrast, I shall do none of those things, even though I am running what might be considered the ultimate risk. Perhaps someone with those thoughts will harden his heart against me; and enraged by those same thoughts, he may cast his vote against me in anger. Well, if any of you are so inclined—not that I expect it of you, but if anyone *should* be—I think it fair to answer him as follows:

"I naturally do have relatives, my excellent friend, because—in Homer's own words—I too was 'not born of oak nor of rock,' but of human parents; and so I do have relatives—including my sons,[30] fellow Athenians. There are three of them: one is now a youth, while two are still children. Nevertheless, I shall not produce any of them here, and then entreat you to vote for my acquittal."

And why, you may ask, will I do no such thing? Not out of contempt or disrespect for you, fellow Athenians—whether or not I am facing death boldly is a different issue. The point is that with our reputations in mind—yours and our whole city's, as well as my own—I believe that any such behaviour would be ignominious, at my age and with the reputation I possess; that reputation may or may not, in fact, be deserved, but at least it is believed that Socrates stands out in some way from the run of human beings. Well, if those of you who are believed to be pre-eminent in wisdom, courage, or any other form of goodness, are going to behave like that, it would be demeaning.

I have frequently seen such men when they face judgment: they have significant reputations, yet they put on astonishing performances, apparently in the belief that by dying they will suffer something unheard of—as if they would be immune from death, so long as you did not kill them! They seem to me to put our city to shame: they could give any foreigner the impression that men preeminent among Athenians in goodness, whom they select from their own number to govern and hold other positions, are no better than women.[31] I say this, fellow Athenians, because none of us who has even the slightest reputation should behave like that; nor should you put up with us if we try to do so. Rather, you should make one thing clear: you will be far more inclined to convict one who stages those pathetic charades and makes our city an object of derision, than one who keeps his composure.

But leaving reputation aside, gentlemen, I do not think it right to entreat the jury, nor to win acquittal in that way, instead of by informing and persuading them. A juror does not sit to dispense justice as a favour, but to determine where it lies. And he has sworn, not that he will favour whomever he pleases, but that he will try the case according to law. We should not, then, accustom you to transgress your oath, nor should you become accustomed to doing so: neither of us would be showing respect towards the gods. And therefore, fellow Athenians, do not require behaviour from me towards you which I consider neither proper nor right nor pious—more especially now, for God's sake, when I stand charged by Meletus here with impiety: because if I tried to persuade and coerce you with entreaties in spite of your oath, I clearly *would* be teaching you not to believe in gods; and I would stand literally self-convicted, by my defence, of failing to acknowledge them. But that is far from the truth: I do acknowledge them, fellow Athenians, as none of my accusers do; and I trust to you, and to God, to judge my case as shall be best for me and for yourselves.

For many reasons, fellow Athenians, I am not dismayed by this outcome[32]—your convicting me, I mean—and especially because the outcome has come as no surprise to me. I wonder far more at the number of votes cast on each side, because I did not think the margin would be so narrow. Yet it seems, in fact, that if a mere thirty votes had gone the other way, I should have been acquitted.[33] Or rather, even as things stand, I consider that I have been cleared of Meletus' charges. Not only that, but one thing is obvious to everyone: if Anytus had not come forward with Lycon to accuse me, Meletus would have forfeited 1,000 drachmas, since he would not have gained one-fifth of the votes cast.

But anyhow, this gentleman demands the death penalty for me. Very well, then: what alternative penalty[34] shall I suggest to you, fellow Athenians? Clearly, it must be one I deserve. So what do I deserve to incur or to pay, for having taken it into my head not to lead an inactive life? Instead, I have neglected the things that concern most people—making money, managing an estate, gaining military or civic honours, or other positions of power, or joining political clubs and parties which have formed in our city. I thought myself, in truth, too honest to survive if I engaged in those things. I did not pursue a course, therefore, in which I would be of no use to you or to myself. Instead, by going to each individual privately, I tried to render a service for you which is—so I maintain—the highest service of all. Therefore that was the course I followed: I tried to persuade each of you not to care for any of his possessions rather than care for himself, striving for the utmost excellence and understanding; and not to care for our city's possessions rather than for the city itself; and to care about other things in the same way.

So what treatment do I deserve for being such a benefactor? If I am to make a proposal truly in keeping with my deserts, fellow Athenians, it should be some benefit; and moreover, the sort of benefit that would be fitting for me. Well then, what *is* fitting for a poor man who is a benefactor, and who needs time free for exhorting you? Nothing could be more fitting, fellow Athenians, than to give such a man regular free meals in the Prytaneum;[35] indeed, that is far more fitting for him than for any of you who may have won an Olympic race with a pair or a team of horses: that victor brings you only the appearance of success, whereas I bring you the reality; besides, he is not in want of sustenance, whereas I am. So if, as justice demands, I am to make a proposal in keeping with my deserts, that is what I suggest: free meals in the Prytaneum.

Now, in proposing this, I may seem to you, as when I talked about appeals for sympathy, to be speaking from sheer effrontery. But actually I have no such motive, fellow Athenians. My point is rather this: I am convinced that I do not treat any human being unjustly, at least intentionally—but I cannot make you share that conviction, because we have conversed together so briefly. I say this, because if it were the law here, as in other jurisdictions, that a capital case must not be tried in a single day, but over several,[36] I think you could have been convinced; but as things stand, it is not easy to clear oneself of such grave allegations in a short time.

Since, therefore, I am persuaded, for my part, that I have treated no one unjustly, I have no intention whatever of so treating myself, nor of denouncing myself as deserving ill, or proposing any such treatment for myself. Why should I do that? For fear of the penalty Meletus demands for me, when I say that I don't know if that is a good thing or a bad one? In preference to that, am I then to choose one of the things I know very well to be bad, and demand that instead? Imprisonment, for instance? Why should I live in prison, in servitude to the annually appointed prison commissioners? Well then, a fine, with imprisonment until I pay? That would amount to what I just mentioned, since I haven't the means to pay it.

Well then, should I propose banishment? Perhaps that is what you would propose for me. Yet I must surely be obsessed with survival, fellow Athenians, if I am so illogical as that. You, my fellow citizens, were unable to put up with my discourses and arguments, but they were so irksome and odious to you that you now seek to be rid of them. Could I not draw the inference, in that case, that others will hardly take kindly to them? Far from it, fellow Athenians. A fine life it would be for a person of my age to go into exile, and spend his days continually exchanging one city for another, and being repeatedly expelled—because I know very well that wherever I go, the young will come to hear me speaking, as they do here. And if I repel them, they will expel me themselves, by persuading their elders; while if I do not repel them, their fathers and relatives will expel me on their account.

Now, perhaps someone may say: "Socrates, could you not be so kind as to keep quiet and remain inactive, while living in exile?" This is the hardest point of all of which to convince some of you. Why? Because, if I tell you that that would mean disobeying my god, and that is why I cannot remain inactive, you will disbelieve me and think that I am practising a sly evasion. Again, if I said that it really is the greatest benefit for a person to converse every day about goodness, and about the other subjects you have heard me discussing when examining myself and others—and that an unexamined life is no life for a human being to live—then you would believe me still less when I made those assertions. But the facts, gentlemen, are just as I claim them to be, though it is not easy to convince you of them. At the same time, I am not accustomed to think of myself as deserving anything bad. If I had money, I would have proposed a fine of as much as I could afford: that would have done me no harm at all. But the fact is that I have none—unless you wish to fix the penalty at a sum I could pay. I could afford to pay you 1 mina, I suppose, so I suggest a fine of that amount—

One moment, fellow Athenians. Plato here, along with Crito, Critobulus, and Apollodorus, is urging me to propose 30 minas,[37] and they are saying they will stand surety for that sum. So I propose a fine of that amount, and these people shall be your sufficient guarantors of its payment.

For the sake of a slight gain in time, fellow Athenians, you will incur infamy and blame from those who would denigrate our city, for putting Socrates to death[38]—a "wise man"—because those who wish to malign you will say I am wise, even if I am not; in any case, had you waited only a short time, you would have obtained that outcome automatically. You can see, of course, that I am now well advanced in life, and death is not far off. I address that not to all of you, but to those who condemned me to death; and to those same people I would add something further.

Perhaps you imagine, gentlemen, that I have been convicted for lack of arguments of the sort I could have used to convince you, had I believed that I should do or say anything to gain acquittal. But that is far from true. I have been convicted, not for lack of arguments, but for lack of brazen impudence and willingness to address you in such terms as you would most like to be addressed in—that is to say, by weeping and wailing, and doing and saying much else that I claim to be unworthy of me—the sorts of thing that you are so used to hearing from others. But just as I did not think during my defence that I should do anything unworthy of a free man because I was in danger, so now I have no regrets about defending myself as I did; I should far rather present such a defence and die, than live by defending myself in that other fashion.

In court, as in warfare, neither I nor anyone else should contrive to escape death at any cost. On the battlefield too, it often becomes obvious that one could avoid death by throwing down one's arms and flinging oneself upon the mercy of one's pursuers. And in every sort of danger there are many other means of escaping death, if one is shameless enough to do or to say anything. I suggest that it is not death that is hard to avoid, gentlemen, but wickedness is far harder, since it is fleeter of foot than death. Thus, slow and elderly as I am, I have now been overtaken by the slower runner; while my accusers, adroit and quick-witted as they are, have been overtaken by the faster, which is wickedness. And so I take my leave, condemned to death by your judgment, whereas they stand for ever condemned to depravity and injustice as judged by Truth. And just as I accept my penalty, so must they. Things were bound to turn out this way, I suppose, and I imagine it is for the best.

In the next place, to those of you who voted against me, I wish to utter a prophecy. Indeed, I have now reached a point at which people are most given to prophesying—that is, when they are on the point of death. I warn you, my executioners, that as soon as I am dead retribution will come upon you—far more severe, I swear, than the sentence you have passed upon me. You have tried to kill me for now, in the belief that you will be relieved from giving an account of your lives. But in fact, I can tell you, you will face just the opposite outcome. There will be more critics to call you to account, people whom I have restrained for the time being though you were unaware of my doing so. They will be all the harder on you since they are younger, and you will rue it all the more—because if you imagine that by putting people to death you will prevent anyone from reviling you for not living rightly, you are badly mistaken. That way of escape is neither feasible nor honourable. Rather, the most honourable and easiest way is not the silencing of others, but striving to make oneself as good a person as possible. So with that prophecy to those of you who voted against me, I take my leave.

As for those who voted for my acquittal, I should like to discuss the outcome of this case while the officials are occupied, and I am not yet on the way to the place where I must die. Please bear with me, gentlemen, just for this short time: there is no reason why we should not have a word with one another while that is still permitted.

Since I regard you as my friends, I am willing to show you the significance of what has just befallen me. You see, gentlemen of the jury—and in applying that term to you, I probably use it correctly—something wonderful has just happened to me. Hitherto, the usual prophetic voice from my spiritual sign was continually active, and frequently opposed me even on trivial matters, if I was about to do anything amiss. But now something has befallen me, as you can see for yourselves, which one certainly might consider—and is generally held—to be the very worst of evils. Yet the sign from God did not oppose me, either when I left home this morning, or when I appeared here in court, or at any point when I was about to say anything during my speech; and yet in other discussions it has very often stopped me in mid-sentence. This time, though, it has not opposed me at any moment in anything I said or did in this whole business.

Now, what do I take to be the explanation for that? I will tell you: I suspect that what has befallen me is a blessing, and that those of us who suppose death to be an evil cannot be making a correct assumption. I have gained every ground for that suspicion, because my usual sign could not have failed to oppose me, unless I were going to incur some good result.

And let us also reflect upon how good a reason there is to hope that death is a good thing. It is, you see, one or other of two things: either to be dead is to be nonexistent, as it were, and a dead person has no awareness whatever of anything at all; or else, as we are told, the soul undergoes some sort of transformation, or exchanging of this present world for another. Now if there is, in fact, no awareness in death, but it is like sleep—the kind in which the sleeper does not even dream at all—then death would be a marvellous gain. Why, imagine that someone had to pick the night in which he slept so soundly that he did not even dream, and to compare all the other nights and days of his life with that one; suppose he had to say, upon consideration, how many days or nights in his life he had spent better and more agreeably than that night; in that case, I think he would find them easy to count compared with his other days and nights—even if he were the Great

King of Persia,[39] let alone an ordinary person. Well, if death is like that, then for my part I call it a gain; because on that assumption the whole of time would seem no longer than a single night.

On the other hand, if death is like taking a trip from here to another place, and if it is true, as we are told, that all of the dead do indeed exist in that other place, why then, gentlemen of the jury, what could be a greater blessing than that? If upon arriving in Hades, and being rid of these people who profess to be "jurors," one is going to find those who are truly judges, and who are also said to sit in judgment there[40]—Minos, Rhadamanthys, Aeacus, Triptolemus, and all other demigods who were righteous in their own lives—would that be a disappointing journey?

Or again, what would any of you not give to share the company of Orpheus and Musaeus, of Hesiod and Homer? I say "you," since I personally would be willing to die many times over, if those tales are true. Why? Because my own sojourn there would be wonderful, if I could meet Palamedes, or Ajax, son of Telamon, or anyone else of old who met their death through an unjust verdict. Whenever I met them, I could compare my own experiences with theirs—which would be not unamusing, I fancy—and best of all, I could spend time questioning and probing people there, just as I do here, to find out who among them is truly wise, and who thinks he is without being so.

What would one not give, gentlemen of the jury, to be able to question the leader of the great expedition against Troy,[41] or Odysseus, or Sisyphus, or countless other men and women one could mention? Would it not be unspeakable good fortune to converse with them there, to mingle with them and question them? At least that isn't a reason, presumably, for people in that world to put you to death—because amongst other ways in which people there are more fortunate than those in our world, they have become immune from death for the rest of time, if what we are told is actually true.

Moreover, you too, gentlemen of the jury, should be of good hope in the face of death, and fix your minds upon this single truth: nothing can harm a good man, either in life or in death; nor are his fortunes neglected by the gods. In fact, what has befallen me has come about by no mere accident; rather, it is clear to me that it was better I should die now and be rid of my troubles. That is also the reason why the divine sign at no point turned me back; and for my part, I bear those who condemned me, and my accusers, no ill will at all—though, to be sure, it was not with that intent that they were condemning and accusing me, but with intent to harm me—and they are culpable for that. Still, this much I ask of them. When my sons come of age, gentlemen, punish them: give them the same sort of trouble that I used to give you, if you think they care for money or anything else more than for goodness, and if they think highly of themselves when they are of no value. Reprove them, as I reproved you, for failing to care for the things they should, and for thinking highly of themselves when they are worthless. If you will do that, then I shall have received my own just deserts from you, as will my sons.

But enough. It is now time to leave—for me to die, and for you to live—though which of us has the better destiny is unclear to everyone, save only to God.

NOTES

1. It is striking that the *Defence of Socrates* begins, as it ends, with a disavowal of knowledge.
2. Socrates' reputation for skill in argument enabled Aristophanes to caricature him as an instructor in logical trickery. Cf. *Clouds* (112–15).
3. The reference is to Aristophanes.
4. Speeches in Athenian lawcourts were timed.
5. This describes Socrates' first appearance in the *Clouds* (223–5), where he is swung around in a basket in the air, and says he is walking on air and thinking about the sun.
6. Professional educators who offered instruction in many subjects.
7. A mina equalled 100 silver drachmas. At the end of the fifth century a drachma was roughly equivalent to one day's pay for a man employed in public works. Evenus' fees were therefore not as "modest" as Socrates pretends.
8. The god Apollo, though nowhere named in the *Defence*, is the deity whose servant Socrates claim to be. In what follows, however, when he speaks of "the god," it is not always clear whether he means Apollo, or a personal God distinct from any deity of traditional Greek religion.
9. Politicians of the democratic party had fled from Athens during the regime of the Thirty Tyrants. They returned under an amnesty in 403 B.C. when the Thirty were overthrown.
10. Literally, "by the dog," a favourite Socratic oath, which may have originated as a euphemism.
11. Socrates alludes to the labours of Heracles, twelve tasks of prodigious difficulty imposed upon a hero of legendary strength and courage.
12. The dithyramb was an emotionally powerful lyric poem, performed by a chorus of singers and dancers.
13. The Athenian Council was a body of 500, with fifty members from each of the ten tribes, elected annually by lot from citizens over the age of 30. In conjunction with the magistrates it carried on state business, and prepared an agenda for the Assembly.
14. Socrates' denial that he corrupts the young intentionally relies upon the principle that human beings never intentionally follow a course of action which they know or believe to be harmful to themselves. Since, in Socrates' view, all wrongdoing is harmful to the agent, it follows that all wrongdoing is unintentional, and curable by the removal of ignorance. This doctrine, one of the so-called Socratic Paradoxes, is often summarized in the slogan "Virtue is Knowledge." It is elaborated in the *Meno*.
15. The sun and moon, even though not the objects of an official cult at Athens, were widely believed to be divine.
16. According to one tradition, Anaxagoras had been prosecuted for heresies regarding the composition of the sun and moon.

17. The "riddle" which Socrates attributes to Meletus consists in the self-contradictory statement "Socrates acknowledges gods and does not acknowledge gods." Greek riddles often take the form of paradoxes generated by apparent self-contradiction.
18. Spirits were sometimes begotten by gods through union with nymphs or mortals.
19. Site of the legendary war between the Greeks and Trojans, which is the context of Homer's *Iliad.*
20. Achilles, heroic Greek warrior in the Trojan War. As the offspring of a goddess mother by a mortal father, he is referred to as a "demigod."
21. Potidawa, in Thrace, was the scene of a campaign in 432 B.C.
22. Socrates here confirms that his well-known mysterious "sign" had been used to substantiate the charge of "introducing new spiritual realities."
23. Fifty representatives from each of the ten tribes who made up the Council took turns during the year to provide an executive for the entire body.
24. In 406 B.C., after a sea-battle off the Ionian coast at Arginusae, several Athenian commanders were charged for their failure to rescue the shipwrecked survivors and recover the dead. A motion to try them collectively was endorsed by the Council and referred to the Assembly. Although a collective trial was unconstitutional, the motion was passed by the Assembly after a stormy debate, and six surviving commanders were convicted and executed.
25. A building also called the "sun-shade" from its shape. It was commandeered as a seat of government by the Thirty.
26. An island separated by a narrow channel from the coast of Africa.
27. Socrates is probably alluding, especially, to two of his former associates who had become notorious enemies of the Athenian democracy, Alcibiades and Critias. The former was a brilliant but wayward politician, who had turned against Athens and helped her enemies. The latter was an unscrupulous oligarch, who had become a leading member of the Thirty Tyrants.
28. Socrates here, in effect, contrasts himself with the sophists, in that he did not set himself up as a professional teacher.
29. For example, the Delphic oracle, whose answer had led Socrates to undertake his mission. Dreams had long been believed to be a source of divine communication with human beings, and are often so treated by Plato.
30. At the time of the trial Socrates had two little boys, Sophroniscus and Menexenus, and an older son, Lamprocles.
31. This is one of many disparaging remarks in Plato about women. Open displays of emotion, especially grief, are regarded as distinctively female, an indulgence of the "female side" of our nature.
32. The verdict was "Guilty." Socrates here begins his second speech, proposing an alternative to the death penalty demanded by the prosecution.
33. With a jury of 500, this implies that the vote was 280–220, since at the time of Socrates' trial an evenly split vote (250–250) would have secured his acquittal.
34. The court had to decide between the penalty demanded by the prosecution and a counter-penalty proposed by the defence, with no option of substituting a different one.
35. The Prytaneum was the building on the north-east slope of the Acropolis, in which hospitality was given to honoured guests of the state, and to Olympic victors and other sports-heroes.

36. This was the law at Sparta, because of the irrevocability of capital punishment.
37. This seems to have been a normal amount for a fine, and was a considerable sum.
38. The jury has now voted for the death penalty, and Socrates begins his final speech.
39. This monarch embodied the popular ideal of happiness.
40. It is not clear whether Socrates envisages them merely as judging disputes among the dead, or as passing judgment upon the earthly life of those who enter Hades.
41. Agamemnon, chief of the Greek forces in the Trojan War.

INDEX OF NAMES

Adimantus: older brother of Plato.

Aeacus: one of the three judges in Hades. He also appears as a judge and lawgiver of the island Aegina, and an arbiter of disputes among the gods.

Aeantodorus: brother of APOLLODORUS, but otherwise unknown.

Aeschines: devotee of Socrates, who wrote speeches for the lawcourts, taught oratory, and was admired as an author of Socratic dialogues. A few fragments of his writings are extant.

Ajax: Greek hero of the Trojan War, mentioned as a victim of an "unjust verdict." This refers to the award of Achilles' armour to ODYSSEUS in a contest with Ajax. The latter's resulting madness and suicide are the subject of *Ajax,* one of the extant tragedies by Sophocles.

Anaxagoras: Presocratic philosopher, originally from Clazomenae in Ionia. Important fragments of his work are extant. He spent many years in Athens and was prominent in Athenian intellectual life.

Antiphon: from Cephisia, father of EPIGENES and supporter of Socrates at his trial, but not otherwise known.

Anytus: leading Athenian democratic politician and accuser of Socrates, and the main instigator of the prosecution.

Apollodorus: ardent devotee of Socrates, notorious for his emotional volatility.

Ariston: Athenian of distinguished lineage, and father of Plato.

Aristophanes: *c.* 450–385. The most famous playwright of Athenian Old Comedy. Eleven of his plays and many fragments are extant.

Callias: wealthy Athenian patron of sophistic culture.

Cebes: citizen of Thebes in Boeotia, who had studied there with the Pythagorean philosopher Philolaus. A disciple of Socrates.

Chaerephon: long-time faithful follower of Socrates. Expelled from Athens in 404 during the regime of the Thirty Tyrants, he returned when the democracy was restored in the following year. The comic poets nicknamed him "the bat" from his squeaky voice.

Crito: Socrates' contemporary, fellow demesman, and one of his closest friends.

Critobulus: son of CRITO and member of the Socratic circle, who was present at Socrates' trial and death.

Cronus: mythical son of URANUS (Heaven) and Gaea (Earth), father of ZEUS, and his predecessor as chief among the gods. He mutilated his father, married his sister Rhea, and devoured his children, except for Zeus, who overthrew him.

Daedalus: legendary artist, craftsman, and inventor. His many marvellous works included the labyrinth for the Minotaur in the palace of King Minos of Crete, and wings for himself and his son, Icarus. He was also believed to have made statues that could open their eyes, walk, and move their arms.

Demodocus: father of THEAGES.

Epigenes: an associate of Socrates. He was present at Socrates' death.

Euthyphro: self-proclaimed expert on religious law. Since Plato portrays him as somewhat eccentric, it is a nice irony that his name should mean "Straight-Thinker" or "Right-Mind."

Evenus: a professional teacher of human excellence, or "sophist."

Gorgias: c. 480–376, from Leontini in Sicily; commonly but perhaps wrongly classified as a "sophist." He cultivated an artificial but influential prose style, and gave lessons in rhetoric, or effective public speaking.

Hades: the underworld inhabited by the dead. The name belongs, properly, to the mythical king of that realm, who was the brother of ZEUS and Poseidon.

Hector: son of Priam, and leading Trojan hero in the war between Greece and Troy. In HOMER's Iliad he kills PATROCLUS, squire of Achilles, who in turn avenges his friend's death by slaying Hector.

Hephaestus: lame god of fire and of the forge, and associated with volcanoes in Greek mythology. He was cast out of heaven by his mother HERA because he was deformed. In revenge he sent her a golden throne to which she was chained with invisible bonds when she sat upon it.

Hera: daughter of CRONUS, wife and sister of ZEUS, and mother of HEPHAESTUS.

Hesiod: one of the earliest extant Greek poets. His Theogony contains an account of the origin of the traditional gods. His Works and Days is a didactic poem giving moral and practical precepts about rural life.

Hippias: itinerant teacher or "sophist," probably a close contemporary of Socrates, who claimed expertise in many subjects.

Hipponicus: member of wealthy Athenian family, and father of CALLIAS.

Homer: greatest epic poet of Greece, and composer of the Iliad and the Odyssey. The Iliad contains episodes from the legendary Trojan War, while the Odyssey recounts the travels and adventures of the hero ODYSSEUS during his journey home after the war.

Leon: resident of Salamis, unjustly arrested and murdered by the Thirty Tyrants in 404.

Lycon: Athenian politician and co-accuser of Socrates with MELETUS and ANYTUS.

Lysanias: of Sphettus, father of AESCHINES, but otherwise unknown.

Meletus: youthful co-accuser of Socrates with ANYTUS and LYCON. He drew up the indictment against Socrates, but was evidently a mere tool of Anytus.

Minos: legendary king of Crete, and traditional judge in the underworld.

Musaeus: mythical bard or singer, closely connected with ORPHEUS.

Nicostratus: supporter of Socrates, present at his trial, but otherwise unknown.

Odysseus: legendary hero in HOMER's Iliad, and central figure in the Odyssey, which recounts his wanderings after the Trojan War.

Orpheus: legendary bard and founder of the archaic mystical or religious movement known as "Orphism."

Palamedes: Greek hero of the Trojan War, credited with invention of the alphabet.

Paralius: supporter of Socrates who was present at his trial, but is not otherwise known.

Patroclus: squire and close friend of Achilles in HOMER's Iliad, slain by HECTOR and avenged by Achilles.

Prodicus: itinerant teacher from Ceos, and one of the sophists.

Proteus: mythical "old man of the sea," who eluded all attempts at capture by constantly changing his form.

Rhadamanthys: with AEACUS and MINOS one of the three traditional judges in the underworld.

Simmias: citizen of Thebes and follower of Socrates, who was prepared to finance his escape.

Sisyphus: mythical wrongdoer, famous for his endless punishment in the underworld. His task was to push a boulder up to the top of a hill, from which it always rolled down again.

Tantalus: mythical king of Phrygia, possessing proverbial wealth. In one tradition he tried to make himself immortal by stealing the food of the gods. For this he was punished by being made to stand in water which receded as soon as he stooped to drink, and to stretch out for fruit which the wind always blew away from his grasp.

Telamon: legendary king of Salamis and father of AJAX.

Theages: disciple of Socrates, whose brother PARALIUS was present at the trial, though Theages himself was already dead.

Theodotus: associate of Socrates who died before his trial, but is not otherwise known.

Theozotides: father of NICOSTRATUS and THEODOTUS. Though deceased by the time of Socrates' trial, he is known to have introduced two important democratic measures after the fall of the Thirty Tyrants. Plato may therefore have mentioned him to counter suspicion that Socrates had antidemocratic leanings.

Thetis: sea-nymph or goddess, given in marriage to the mortal Peleus. Achilles was her only child.

Triptolemus: mythical agricultural hero from Eleusis, and a central figure in its mystery cults.

Uranus: heaven or the sky, conceived in mythology as child and husband of Gaea (earth). Chief deity before his son CRONUS.

Zeus: son of CRONUS, and chief among the Olympian gods.

PART 2

REASONING

The Scope of Logic

✧✧✧

WESLEY C. SALMON

To assert a belief is simple; defending it is far more difficult. Yet if a belief is not defended adequately, why accept it?

Saying something is true does not make it true. Suppose Smith says that Charles Darwin, who developed the theory of evolution, and Abraham Lincoln were both born on February 12, 1809. Jones denies this claim. If saying something is true proves it true, then what Smith says is true and what Jones says is also true—which is impossible, since one of them denies exactly what the other affirms. Their statements are contradictory, and asserting them both amounts to saying nothing at all. (Incidentally, Smith is correct.)

To reason effectively, we need to avoid contradiction and accept beliefs that are adequately defended. But what are the appropriate standards by which we can determine if our beliefs are consistent with each other and well-confirmed by the available evidence? Logic is the subject that offers answers to these questions, and the scope of logic is explained in the following essay by Wesley C. Salmon, Professor of Philosophy at the University of Pittsburgh, who served as President of the American Philosophical Association.

The remainder of my remarks should be read after Salmon's article. So please proceed now to the selection, and return to this point after finishing it.

In his last paragraph Salmon refers to deductive correctness as "validity." If you have followed his account to that point, you will realize that a valid argument may have false premises and a false conclusion, false premises and a true conclusion, or true premises and a true conclusion. What is not possible is for a valid argument to have true premises and a false conclusion, for a valid argument is one in which if the premises are true, then so is the conclusion.

For purposes of review, consider the following arguments:

1. The capital of Massachusetts is Springfield. No banks are located in the capital of Massachusetts. Therefore, Springfield has no banks.
2. The capital of Massachusetts is Springfield. Springfield is the

Logic, 2d edition, by Salmon, © 1983. Reprinted by permission of Prentice-Hall, Inc., Upper Saddle River, NJ.

home of the Boston Red Sox. Therefore, the capital of Massachusetts is the home of the Boston Red Sox.
3. The capital of Massachusetts is Boston. Boston is the home of the
   Boston Red Sox. Therefore, the capital of Massachusetts is the
   home of the Boston Red Sox.

Example (1) illustrates a valid argument with false premises and
a false conclusion. Example (2) illustrates a valid argument with
false premises and a true conclusion. Example (3) illustrates a valid
argument with true premises and a true conclusion.

A valid argument with true premises is referred to by philosophers as a "sound" argument. Since a sound argument has true
premises and its conclusion follows from its premises, the conclusion of a sound argument is sure to be true. No wonder philosophers prize sound arguments.

In one of his celebrated adventures, Sherlock Holmes comes into possession
of an old felt hat. Although Holmes is not acquainted with the owner of the
hat, he tells Dr. Watson many things about the man—among them, that he is
highly intellectual. This assertion, as it stands, is unsupported. Holmes may
have evidence for his statement, but so far he has not given it.

Dr. Watson, as usual, fails to see any basis for Holmes's statement, so he
asks for substantiation. "For answer Holmes clapped the hat upon his head.
It came right over the forehead and settled upon the bridge of his nose. 'It is
a question of cubic capacity,' said he; 'a man with so large a brain must have
something in it.'"[1] Now, the statement that the owner of the hat is highly intellectual is no longer an unsupported assertion. Holmes has given the evidence, so his statement is supported. It is the conclusion of an argument. . . .

An argument consists of one statement which is the conclusion and one
or more statements of supporting evidence. The statements of evidence are
called "premises." There is no set number of premises which every argument
must have, but there must be at least one.

When Watson requested a justification for the statement about the owner of the hat, Holmes gave an indication of an argument. Although he did
not spell out his argument in complete detail, he did say enough to show
what it would be. We can reconstruct it as follows:

a]   1. This is a large hat.

     2. Someone is the owner of this hat.

     3. The owners of large hats are people with large heads.

     4. People with large heads have large brains.

     5. People with large brains are highly intellectual.

     6. The owner of this hat is highly intellectual.

This is an argument; it consists of six statements. The first five statements are the premises; the sixth statement is the conclusion.

The premises of an argument are supposed to present evidence for the conclusion. Presenting evidence in premises involves two aspects. First, the premises are statements of fact. Second, these facts are offered as *evidence for* the conclusion. There are, consequently, two ways in which the premises may fail to present evidence for the conclusion. First, one or more of the premises may be false. In this case, the *alleged* facts are not facts at all; the *alleged* evidence does not exist. Under these circumstances, we can hardly be said to have good grounds for accepting the conclusion. Second, even if the premises are all true—that is, even if the premises do accurately state the facts—they may not have an appropriate relation to the conclusion. In this case, the facts are as stated in the premises, but these facts are not *evidence for* the conclusion. In order for facts to be evidence for a conclusion they must be properly relevant to that conclusion. Obviously, it will not do merely to give any true statements to support a conclusion. The statements must have some bearing upon that conclusion.

If an argument is offered as a justification of its conclusion, two questions arise. First, are the premises true? Second, are the premises properly related to the conclusion? If either question has a negative answer, the justification is unsatisfactory. It is absolutely essential, however, to avoid confusing these two questions. In logic we are concerned with the second question only. When an argument is subjected to logical analysis, the question of relevance is at issue. *Logic deals with the relation between premises and conclusion, not with the truth of the premises.*

One of our basic purposes is to provide methods of distinguishing between logically correct and incorrect arguments. *The logical correctness or incorrectness of an argument depends solely upon the relation between premises and conclusion.* In a logically correct argument, the premises have the following relation to the conclusion: *If the premises were true, this fact would constitute good grounds for accepting the conclusion as true.* If the facts alleged by the premises of a logically correct argument are, indeed, facts, then they do constitute good evidence for the conclusion. That is what we shall mean by saying that the premises of a logically correct argument *support* the conclusion. The premises of an argument support the conclusion if the truth of the premises would constitute good reason for asserting that the conclusion is true. When we say that the premises of an argument support the conclusion, we are *not* saying that the premises are true; we are saying that there would be good evidence for the conclusion *if* the premises were true.

The premises of a logically incorrect argument may *seem* to support the conclusion, but actually they do not. Logically incorrect arguments are called "fallacious." Even if the premises of a logically incorrect argument were true, this would not constitute good grounds for accepting the conclusion. The premises of a logically incorrect argument do not have the proper relevance to the conclusion.

Since the logical correctness or incorrectness of an argument depends solely upon the relation between premises and conclusion, *logical correctness or incorrectness is completely independent of the truth of the premises.* In particular, it is wrong to call an argument "fallacious" just because it has one or more false premises. Consider the argument concerning the hat in example *a.* You may already have recognized that there is something wrong with the argument from the size of the hat to the intellectuality of the owner; you might have been inclined to reject it on grounds of faulty logic. It would have been a mistake to do so. The argument is logically correct—it is not fallacious—but it does have at least one false premise. As a matter of fact, not everyone who has a large brain is highly intellectual. However, you should be able to see that the conclusion of this argument would have to be true if all of the premises were true. It is not the business of logic to find out whether people with large brains are intellectual; this matter can be decided only by scientific investigation. Logic *can* determine whether these premises support their conclusion.

As we have just seen, a logically correct argument may have one or more false premises. A logically incorrect or fallacious argument may have true premises; indeed, it may have a true conclusion as well.

b]   *Premises:*   All mammals are mortal.

All dogs are mortal.

Conclusion: All dogs are mammals.

This argument is obviously fallacious. The fact that the premises and the conclusion are all true statements does not mean that the premises support the conclusion. They do not. . . . It happens that the conclusion, "All dogs are mammals," is true, but there is nothing in the premises which provides any basis for it.

Since the logical correctness or incorrectness of an argument depends solely upon the relation between the premises and the conclusion and is completely independent of the truth of the premises, we can analyze arguments without knowing whether the premises are true—indeed, we can do so even when they are known to be false. This is a desirable feature of the situation. It is often useful to know what conclusions can be drawn from false or doubtful premises. For example, intelligent deliberation involves the consideration of the consequences of various alternatives. We may construct arguments with various premises in order to see what the consequences are. In so doing, we do not pretend that the premises are true; rather, we can examine the arguments without even raising the question of the truth of the premises. Up to this point we have proceeded as if the only function of arguments is to provide justifications for conclusions. We see now that this is only one among several uses for arguments. In general, arguments serve to show the conclusions that can be drawn from given premises, whether these premises are known to be true, known to be false, or are merely doubtful.

For purposes of logical analysis it is convenient to present arguments in standard form. We shall adopt the practice of writing the premises first and identifying the conclusion by a triplet of dots.

c]   Everyone who served on the jury was a registered voter.

            Jones served on the jury.

            ∴ Jones was a registered voter.

This argument is logically correct. Outside of logic books, we should not expect to find arguments expressed in this neat form. We must learn to recognize arguments when they occur in ordinary prose, for they are not usually set off in the middle of the page and labeled. Furthermore, we have to identify the premises and the conclusion, for they are not usually explicitly labeled. It is not necessary for the premises to precede the conclusion. Sometimes the conclusion comes last, sometimes first, and sometimes in the middle of the argument. For stylistic reasons arguments may be given in a variety of ways; for example, any of the following variations of *c* would be quite proper:

d]   Everyone who served on the jury was a registered voter and
            Jones served on the jury; *therefore,* Jones was a registered voter.

e]   Jones was a registered voter *because* Jones served on the jury, and
            everyone who served on the jury was a registered voter.

f]   *Since* everyone who served on the jury was a registered voter,
            Jones *must have been* a registered voter, *for* Jones served on the
            jury.

The fact that an argument is being given is usually conveyed by certain words or phrases which indicate that a statement is functioning as a premise or as a conclusion. Terms like "therefore," "hence," "consequently," "so," and "it follows that" indicate that what comes immediately after is a conclusion. The premises from which it follows should be stated nearby. Also, certain verb forms which suggest necessity, such as "must have been," indicate that the statement in which they occur is a conclusion. They indicate that this statement follows necessarily (i.e., deductively) from stated premises. Other terms indicate that a statement is a premise: "since," "for," and "because" are examples. The statement which follows such a word is a premise. The conclusions based upon this premise should be found nearby. Terms which indicate parts of arguments should be used if, and only if, arguments are being presented. If no argument occurs, it is misleading to use these terms. For instance, if a statement is prefaced by the word "therefore," the reader has every right to expect that it follows from something which has already been said. When arguments are given, it is important to indicate that fact, and to indicate exactly which statements are intended as premises and which as conclusions. It is up to the reader to be sure he understands which statements are premises and which are conclusions before he proceeds to subject arguments to analysis.

There is another respect in which arguments encountered in most contexts fail to have the standard logical form. When we subject arguments to logical analysis, all of the premises must be given explicitly. Many arguments, however, involve premises which are so obvious that it would be sheer pedantry to state them in ordinary speech and writing. We have already seen an example of an argument with missing premises. Holmes's argument about the hat was incomplete; we attempted to complete it in example *a*. Outside a logic book, example *c* might appear in either of the following forms, depending on which premise is considered more obvious:

g]   Jones must have been a registered voter, for he served on the jury.

h]   Jones was a registered voter, because everyone who served on the jury was a registered voter.

In neither case would there be any difficulty in finding the missing premise.

It would be unreasonable to insist that arguments always be presented in complete form without missing premises. Nevertheless, the missing premise can be a great pitfall. Although a missing premise is often a statement too obvious to bother making, sometimes a missing premise can represent a crucial hidden assumption. When we attempt to complete the arguments we encounter, we bring to light the assumptions which would be required to make them logically correct. This step is often the most illuminating aspect of logical analysis. It sometimes turns out that the required premises are extremely dubious or obviously false.

Logical analysis of discourse involves three preliminary steps which we have discussed.

1. Arguments must be recognized; in particular, unsupported statements must be distinguished from conclusions of arguments.
2. When an argument has been found, the premises and conclusions must be identified.
3. If the argument is incomplete, the missing premises must be supplied.

When an argument has been set out in complete and explicit form, logical standards can be applied to determine whether it is logically correct or fallacious. . . .

What we have said so far applies to all types of arguments. The time has come to distinguish two major types: *deductive* and *inductive*. There are logically correct and incorrect forms of each. Here are correct examples.

a]   *Deductive:* Every mammal has a heart.

           All horses are mammals.

           ∴ Every horse has a heart.

b]   *Inductive:* Every horse that has ever been observed has had a heart.

           ∴ Every horse has a heart.

There are certain fundamental characteristics which distinguish between correct deductive and correct inductive arguments. We will mention two primary ones.

	DEDUCTIVE		INDUCTIVE
I.	If all of the premises are true, the conclusion *must be true.*	I.	If all of the premises are true, the conclusion is probably true but not necessarily true.
II.	All of the information or factual content in the conclusion was already contained, at least implicitly, in the premises.	II.	The conclusion contains information not present, even implicitly, in the premises.

It is not difficult to see that the two examples satisfy these conditions.

Characteristic I. The only way in which the conclusion of *a* could be false—that is, the only possible circumstance under which it could fail to be true that every horse has a heart—is that either not all horses are mammals or not all mammals have hearts. In other words, for the conclusion of *a* to be false, one or both of the premises must be false. If both premises are true, the conclusion must be true. On the other hand, in *b,* it is quite possible for the premise to be true and the conclusion false. This would happen if at some future time, a horse is observed which does not have a heart. The fact that no horse without a heart has yet been observed is some evidence that none ever will be. In this argument, the premise does not necessitate the conclusion, but it does lend some weight to it.

Characteristic II. When the conclusion of *a* says that all horses have hearts, it says something which has already been said, in effect, by the premises. The first premise says that all mammals have hearts, and that includes all horses according to the second premise. In this argument, as in all other correct deductive arguments, the conclusion states explicitly or reformulates information already given in the premises. It is for this reason that deductive arguments also have characteristic I. The conclusion must be true if the premises are true, because the conclusion says nothing which was not already stated by the premises. On the other hand, the premise of our inductive argument *b* refers only to horses that have been observed up to the present, while the conclusion refers to horses that have not yet been observed. Thus, the conclusion makes a statement which goes beyond the information given in the premise. It is because the conclusion says something not given in the premise that the conclusion might be false even though the premise is true. The additional content of the conclusion might be false, rendering the conclusion as a whole false. Deductive and inductive arguments fulfill different functions. The deductive argument is designed to make explicit the content of the premises; the inductive argument is designed to extend the range of our knowledge.

We may summarize by saying that the inductive argument expands the content of premises by sacrificing necessity, whereas the deductive argument achieves necessity by sacrificing any expansion of content.

It follows immediately from these characteristics that deductive correctness (known as *validity* . . .) is an all or nothing affair. An argument either qualifies fully as a correct deduction or it fails completely; there are no degrees of deductive validity. The premises either completely necessitate the conclusion or they fail entirely to do so. Correct inductive arguments, in contrast, admit of degrees of strength, depending upon the amount of support the premises furnish for the conclusion. There are degrees of probability which the premises of an inductive argument can supply to a conclusion, but the logical necessity which relates premises to conclusion in a deductive argument is never a matter of degree.

NOTE

1. A. Conan Doyle, "The Adventure of the Blue Carbuncle," *Adventures of Sherlock Holmes* (New York and London: Harper & Row, n.d.), p. 157. Direct quotation and use of literary material from this story by permission of the Estate of Sir Arthur Conan Doyle.

Improving Your Thinking

✧✧

STEPHEN F. BARKER

Effective reasoning calls for avoiding fallacious arguments and clarifying ambiguous terms. Our next selection, by Stephen F. Barker, Professor of Philosophy at Johns Hopkins University, addresses both these issues.

You can strengthen your own thinking by being alert to some commonly used words that are so notoriously vague that their appearance in any argument signals trouble. Here are some examples:

subjective, natural, relative, pragmatic, diverse. Next time you hear someong use one of these terms, ask what it means. Everyone will benefit from the clarification.

1. Fallacies

If we want to become more skillful at playing chess, or football, or any other game, it is a good idea to study not only the shrewd moves that experts make, but also the poor moves that less experienced players make—we can learn from their mistakes. Similarly, as we try to improve our ability to reason logically, we should not confine our attention to specimens of good reasoning; we should also consider plenty of tempting examples of bad reasoning. By becoming more aware of how these bad arguments are bad, we strengthen our ability to distinguish between good and bad reasoning.

In ordinary talk the term "fallacy" is often loosely applied to any sort of mistaken belief or untrue sentence. "It's a fallacy to believe that handling a toad causes warts," people say. Here the thing being called a fallacy is just a belief, not a piece of reasoning. But in logic the term "fallacy" is restricted to mistakes in reasoning: a *fallacy* is a logical mistake in reasoning, especially one that it is tempting to make. There is a logical fallacy only when there are premises and a conclusion which is erroneously thought to be proved by them.

Many types of fallacies have been given special names, especially those types that are rather tempting and likely to deceive people. . . .

An argument is called a *petitio principii* (or begging of the question) if the argument fails to prove anything because it somehow takes for granted what it is supposed to prove. Suppose a man says "Jones is insane, you know," and we reply "Really? Are you sure?" and he responds, "Certainly, I can prove it. Jones is demented; therefore he is insane." This is a valid argument in the sense that if the premise is true, the conclusion must be true too; but the argument is unsatisfactory, for it does not really prove anything. The premise is merely another statement of the conclusion, so that practically anyone who doubts the truth of the conclusion ought to be equally doubtful about the truth of the premise, and the argument is useless for the purpose of convincing us of the truth of the conclusion. Thus the argument takes for granted just what it is supposed to prove; it begs the question.

Consider a longer chain of reasoning:

"We must not drink liquor."

"Why do you say that?"

"Drinking is against the will of Allah."

"How do you know?"

"The Koran says so."

"But how do you know that the Koran is right?"

"Everything said in the Koran is right."

"How do you know that?"

"Why, it's all divinely inspired."

"But how do you know that?"

"Why, the Koran itself declares that it is divinely inspired."

"But why believe that?"

"You've got to believe the Koran, because everything in the Koran is right."

This chain of reasoning is a more extended case of begging the question; the speaker is reasoning in a large circle, taking for granted one of the things that is supposed to be proved.

One specific form of *petitio principii,* or begging of the question, has a special name of its own: the fallacy of *complex question.* This is the fallacy of framing a question so as to take for granted something controversial that ought to be proved.

Suppose Mr. White is trying to prove that Mr. Green has a bad character, and White asks Green the famous question "Have you stopped beating your wife yet?" If Green answers "Yes" to this question, White will argue that Green is admitting to having been a wife-beater; if he answers "No," then White will argue that Green is admitting to still being a wife-beater. The questioner has framed his question in such a way as to take for granted that Green has a wife whom he has been beating. The fallacy is that this is a controversial proposition that is at least as doubtful as is the conclusion (that Green has a bad character) supposedly being established. It is not proper in this debate to take for granted this controversial proposition; it needs to be proved if White is to make use of it at all. . . .

One important type of fallacy . . . is the *ad hominem* fallacy. An argument is *ad hominem* (Latin: "to the man") if it is directed at an opponent in a controversy rather than being directly relevant to proving the conclusion under discussion. Such arguments are often, but not always, fallacious. For example, suppose someone argues: "Of course Karl Marx must have been mistaken in maintaining that capitalism is an evil form of economic and social organization. Why, he was a miserable failure of a man who couldn't even earn enough money to support his family." This is an *ad hominem* argument, for it attacks Marx the man instead of offering direct reasons why his views are incorrect. . . .

Another quite different fallacy of irrelevance is the appeal to unsuitable authority. . . . We commit this fallacy when we appeal to some admired or famous person as if that person were an authority on the matter being discussed—but when we have no good reason for thinking that the person is a genuine authority on it. Of course it is not always fallacious to appeal to authorities, but we are not entitled to appeal to persons as authorities unless there are good reasons for believing them to be authorities, and we should not trust an authority outside his or her special proven field of competence. A famous guitarist may be an expert on one type of music, but this does not make her an authority on philosophy of life. A movie star may be an authority on how to look attractive to the opposite sex, but is not likely to be an authority on which pain reliever is most healthful or which toothpaste tastes best. . . .

We conclude with . . . the fallacy of *black-and-white* thinking. A wife may say to her husband "So you think the soup is too cold, do you? Well, I suppose you would like to have had it scalding hot then, instead." The second remark is presented as if it followed logically from the first, and yet there is no logical connection whatever. But people find it very easy to fall into this sort of thinking in extremes, especially in the heat of controversy.

2.   Definitions

When we encounter words that cause confusion because their meanings are ambiguous, it is often helpful to define them. . . .

Definitions that are useful in preventing ambiguity may be subdivided into two types. Some of them serve the purpose of describing the meaning that a word already has in language. We might call these *analytical* definitions. In giving this kind of definition of a word, the speaker does not aim to change its meaning; he aims only to characterize the meaning it already has. Dictionary definitions are of this type. When a definition has this purpose, we can properly ask whether the definition is correct or incorrect.

In order to be correct in its description of the meaning of a word, an analytical definition must not be *too broad*; that is, it must not embrace things that do not really belong. (To define "pneumonia" as "disease of the lungs" would be too broad, for there are many lung diseases besides pneumonia.) Also, in order to be correct in its description of the meaning of a word, an analytical definition must not be *too narrow*; that is, it must not exclude things that really belong. (To define "psychosis" as "schizophrenia" would be too narrow, for there are other kinds of psychoses. . . .)

Finally, a definition cannot serve much useful purpose if it is circular. . . . For example, to define "straight line" as "the line along which a ray of light travels when it goes straight" is circular and uninformative. . . .

A second type of definition useful in preventing ambiguity is the *stipulative* definition, whose purpose is to declare how a speaker intends that a certain word, phrase, or symbol shall be understood ("Let 'S' mean 'Samoans'"; "Let 'heavy truck' mean 'truck that can carry a load of 5 tons or more'"; etc.). Perhaps the expression being defined is one that previously had no meaning, or perhaps it had a different or a vaguer meaning. At any rate, the point of the stipulative definition is that the expression now is deliberately endowed with a particular meaning. Obviously, a stipulative definition cannot be of much use if it is unclear or circular. However, we do not have to worry about whether it is too broad or too narrow, for that sort of correctness cannot pertain to stipulative definitions. A stipulative definition is arbitrary, in that it expresses only the speaker's intention to use the word in the stipulated manner, and the speaker is, after all, entitled to use it in any desired way, so long as it does not cause confusion.

In order to avoid causing confusion, however, a stipulative definition should not assign to a word that already has an established meaning some new meaning that is likely to be confused with it. Consider the following dialogue:

SMITH: General Green is insane, you know. He ought to be dismissed.

JONES: He is? I agree that we should not have insane persons serving in the Army. But how do you know he's insane?

SMITH: It's obvious. He says he believes in extrasensory perception, and according to my definition—surely I'm entitled to use words as I please—anyone who does that is insane.

Here the stipulative definition is used to promote ambiguity rather than to prevent it. In the ordinary sense of the term "insane," Jones agrees with Smith that insane persons ought not to be generals. But Smith offers no evidence that General Green is insane in this sense. All that Smith shows is that the general is "insane" in a special, idiosyncratic sense of the word. From that, nothing follows about whether he ought to be dismissed. Smith is causing confusion by failing to keep distinct these two very different senses of the word; this happens because he fails to recognize the difference here between a stipulative and an analytical definition. . . .

The two kinds of definitions mentioned so far both aim to inform us about verbal usage. . . . It would be a mistake, however, to suppose that everything called a definition belongs to one of these two kinds. In fact, the profoundest and most valuable definitions usually do not fit tidily into either kind. When Newton defined force as the product of mass times acceleration, when Einstein defined simultaneity of distant events in terms of the transmission of light rays . . . [w]hat these definitions did was to propose new verbal usages growing out of the previously established usages. It was felt that these new usages perfected tendencies of thought implicit in the old usages and offered more insight into the subject matter being treated.

We might give the name *revelatory* definitions to definitions like these, which do not fit into either of the two categories of stipulative and analytical. Revelatory definitions constitute a third category. Further examples of revelatory definitions can be found in other, diverse fields. For example, when a nineteenth-century writer defined architecture as frozen music, he was not trying to describe how the word "architecture" is used in our language. (He took it for granted that his readers would know what kinds of constructions are considered architecture.) Nor was he proposing some arbitrary new usage. We should not censure his definition on the ground that it is unhelpful for the purpose of preventing ambiguity; that is not the purpose of this kind of definition. This definition is a metaphor, and it suggests a new way of looking at architecture, comparing the structural organization of the parts of a building with the structural organization of the parts of a musical composition. In trying to decide whether the definition is a good one or not, we must reflect about the extent and validity of this comparison between music and buildings; the definition is a good one if and only if the comparison is revealing. . . .

How frequently are definitions needed? People sometimes think that one always should define one's terms at the beginning of any discussion. But this idea becomes absurd if carried too far. Suppose that we as speakers did undertake to define all our terms in noncircular ways. However far we proceeded, we would always still have . . . undefined terms; therefore this task is an impossible one to complete. Moreover, we do have a fairly adequate understanding of the meanings of many words that we have never bothered to define and also of many words that we would not know how to define satisfactorily even if we tried. Thus, it would be foolish to try indiscriminately to define all or even most of our terms before proceeding with our thinking. What we should do at the beginning of a discussion is seek definitions of those particular words which are especially likely to make trouble in the discussion because they are harmfully ambiguous, obscure, or vague.

This is especially true with regard to discussions in which confusion is caused by failure to notice the different meanings of a term. A *verbal dispute* is a dispute arising solely from the fact that some word is being used with different meanings; this kind of dispute can be settled merely by giving the definitions that clarify the situation (though to say this is not to say that such disputes always are *easy* to settle).

The American philosopher William James gives a classic example of such a verbal dispute. . . . Suppose there is a squirrel on the trunk of a tree, and a man walks around the tree. The squirrel moves around the tree trunk so as to stay out of sight, always facing the man but keeping the tree between them. Has the man gone around the squirrel or not? Some of James's friends disputed hotly for a long time about this question. Here is a purely verbal dispute; it can be settled by pointing out that in one sense the man has gone "around" the squirrel, for he has moved from the north to the west and then to the south and east of the squirrel's location, but in another sense the man has not gone "around" the squirrel, for the squirrel has always been facing him. Once we have pointed out these two different senses of the word, we have done all that can reasonably be done; there is nothing more worth discussing (though this does not ensure that discussion will cease). With a verbal dispute like this, giving definitions is the way to resolve the dispute. But it would be utterly wrong to assume that all disputes are verbal in this way.

There are many serious problems for the settling of which definitions are not needed, and there are many other problems where if definitions help, they mark only the beginning of the thinking needed to resolve the issue.

Fixing Belief

✧✧

MORRIS R. COHEN AND ERNEST NAGEL

Sound reasoning requires that our beliefs be well-founded. But what method should we employ for deciding what to believe?

This question is addressed in the next essay, written by two of the most eminent American philosophers of the twentieth century: Morris R. Cohen (1880–1947), Professor of Philosophy at The City College of New York, and his student Ernest Nagel (1901–1985), who became Professor of Philosophy at Columbia University. Both men served as President of the American Philosophical Association, and both were legendary teachers, although Cohen's pedagogical style was intimidating, while Nagel's was supportive.

Both greatly admired the work of Charles Sanders Peirce (1839–1914), a seminal figure in the development of American philosophy, and his classic essay "The Fixation of Belief" contains the central ideas that Cohen and Nagel present here in highly accessible form.

Most of our beliefs . . . rest on the tacit acceptance of current attitudes or on our own unreflective assumptions. Thus we come to believe that the sun revolves around the earth daily because we see it rise in the east and sink in the west; or we send a testimonial to the makers of a certain toothpaste to the effect that it is an excellent preserver of teeth because we have had no dental trouble since we have used that preparation; or we offer alms to some beggar because we perceive his poverty by his rags and emaciated appearance. But too often and sometimes, alas! too late, we learn that not all "seeing" is "believing." Beliefs so formed do not stand up against a more varied experience. There is too little agreement in opinions so formed and too little security in

From *An Introduction to Logic and Scientific Method*. Reprinted by permission of Hackett Publishing Co., Inc. All rights reserved.

acting upon them. Most of us then find ourselves challenged to support or change our opinions. And we do so by diverse methods.

The Method of Tenacity

Habit or inertia makes it easier for us to continue to believe a proposition simply because we have always believed it. Hence, we may avoid doubting it by closing our mind to all contradictory evidence. That frequent verbal reiteration may strengthen beliefs which have been challenged is a truth acted upon by all organized sects or parties. If anyone questions the superior virtues of ourselves, our dear ones, our country, race, language, or religion, our first impulse and the one generally followed is to repeat our belief as an act of loyalty and to regard the questioning attitude as ignorant, disloyal, and unworthy of attention. We thus insulate ourselves from opinions or beliefs contrary to those which we have always held. As a defense of this attitude the believer often alleges that he would be unhappy if he were to believe otherwise than he in fact does. But while a change in opinion may require painful effort, the new beliefs may become habitual, and perhaps more satisfying than the old ones.

This method of tenacity cannot always secure the stability of one's beliefs. Not all men believe alike, in part because the climate of opinion varies with historical antecedents, and in part because the personal and social interests which men wish to guard are unlike. The pressure of opinions other than one's own cannot always be so disregarded. The man who tenaciously holds on to his own way occasionally admits that not all those who differ from him are fools. When once the incidence of other views is felt, the method of tenacity is incapable of deciding between conflicting opinions. And since a lack of uniformity in beliefs is itself a powerful source of doubt concerning them, some method other than the method of tenacity is required for achieving stable views.

The Method of Authority

Such a method is sometimes found in the appeal to authority. Instead of simply holding on doggedly to one's beliefs, appeal is made to some highly respected source to substantiate the views held. Most propositions of religion and conduct claim support from some sacred text, tradition, or tribunal whose decision on such questions is vested with finality. Political, economic, and social questions are frequently determined in similar fashion. What one should wear at a funeral, what rule of syntax one should follow in writing, what rights one has in the product of his labor, how one should behave in some social crisis like war—these are problems repeatedly resolved by the authoritative method.

We may distinguish two forms of the appeal to authority. One form is inevitable and reasonable. It is employed whenever we are unable for lack of time or training to settle some problem, such as, What diet or exercise will relieve certain distressing symptoms? or, What was the system of weights which the Egyptians used? We then leave the resolution of the problem to experts, whose authority is acknowledged. But their authority is only relatively final, and we reserve the right to others (also competent to judge), or to ourselves (finding the time to acquire competence), to modify the findings of our expert. The second form of the appeal to authority invests some sources with infallibility and finality and invokes some external force to give sanction to their decisions. On questions of politics, economics, and social conduct, as well as on religious opinions, the method of authority has been used to root out, as heretical or disloyal, divergent opinions. Men have been frightened and punished into conformity in order to prevent alternative views from unsettling our habitual beliefs.

The aim of this method, unanimity and stability of belief, cannot be achieved so long as authorities differ. Buddhists do not accept the authorities of the Christians, just as the latter reject the authority of Mahomet and the Koran. In temporal matters experts frequently disagree and are often found in error. Moreover, authoritative regulation of all beliefs is not feasible practically, and much must be left to be decided in some other way. The method of authority has thus to be supplemented, if not replaced, by some other method for resolving doubt and uncertainty.

The Method of Intuition

A method repeatedly tried in order to guarantee stable beliefs is the appeal to "self-evident" propositions—propositions so "obviously true" that the understanding of their *meaning* will carry with it an indubitable conviction of their *truth*. Very few men in the history of philosophy and that of the sciences have been able to resist at all times the lure of intuitively revealed truths. . . .

Unfortunately, it is difficult to find a proposition for which at some time or other "self-evidence" has not been claimed. Propositions regarded as indubitable by many, for example, that the earth is flat, have been shown to be false. It is well known that "self-evidence" is often a function of current fashions and of early training. The fact, therefore, that we feel absolutely certain, or that a given proposition has not before been questioned, is no guarantee against its being proved false. Our intuitions must, then, be tested.

The Method of Science or Reflective Inquiry

None of the methods for settling doubts we have examined so far is free from human caprice and willfulness. As a consequence, the propositions which are held on the basis of those methods are uncertain in the range of their application and in their accuracy. If we wish clarity and accuracy, order and consistency, security and cogency, in our actions and intellectual allegiances we shall have to resort to some method of fixing beliefs whose efficacy in resolving problems is independent of our desires and wills. Such a method, which takes advantage of the objective connections in the world around us, should be found reasonable not because of its appeal to the idiosyncrasies of a selected few individuals, but because it can be tested repeatedly and by all men.

The other methods discussed are all inflexible, that is, none of them can admit that it will lead us into error. Hence none of them can make provision for correcting its own results. What is called *scientific method* differs radically from these by encouraging and developing the utmost possible doubt, so that what is left after such doubt is always supported by the best available evidence. As new evidence or new doubts arise it is the essence of scientific method to incorporate them—to make them an integral part of the body of knowledge so far attained. Its method, then, makes science progressive because it is never too certain about its results. . . . It appeals to no special revelation or authority whose deliverances are indubitable and final. It claims no infallibility, but relies upon the methods of developing and testing hypotheses for assured conclusions. . . . The method makes possible the noting and correction of errors by continued application of itself. . . .

It is this self-corrective nature of the method which allows us to challenge any proposition, but which also assures us that the theories which science accepts are more probable than any alternative theories. By not claiming more certainty than the evidence warrants, scientific method succeeds in obtaining more logical certainty than any other method yet devised.

Testing Hypotheses

✿✿✿

STEVEN M. CAHN, PATRICIA KITCHER, AND GEORGE SHER

The scientific method of explanation involves formulating a hypothesis and testing it, then accepting, rejecting, or modifying it in light of the experimental results. But how do we test a hypothesis? That is the subject of the following selection I wrote with Patricia Kitcher,

Professor of Philosophy at Columbia University, and George Sher, Professor of Philosophy at Rice University. At one time we were colleagues in the Department of Philosophy at the University of Vermont.

As you read about hypothesis testing, you may wonder about the source of hypotheses. How are they developed? No mechanical procedures are available; the answer lies in creative imagination. But while scientific method gives free rein to ingenuity, it requires that our intuitions be accepted only if they pass the rigors of careful testing.

It is a commonplace that people—most notably scientists and detectives—test hypotheses and accept those hypotheses that pass the tests they have devised. For example, imagine that a problem has developed in a small rural town. Residents are falling sick, complaining of severe nausea, abdominal pains, and other symptoms. The local doctor hypothesizes that the trouble has been caused by the opening of a new chemical plant that is emptying waste within a mile of one of the lakes that yield the town's supply of drinking water. The hypothesis can be tested in a number of different ways. The residents might check the consequences of only drinking water from lakes that are not close to the chemical plant. Or they might examine the effects on laboratory animals of drinking water obtained shortly after large amounts of waste had been ejected from the plant. It is relatively easy to see how the doctor's hypothesis might fail such tests. The residents might find that using water from different lakes achieved nothing, and that the sickness continued to spread. Equally, it is evident how the hypothesis could pass the tests. One might discover, for example, that the health of laboratory animals was dramatically affected by providing them with water obtained shortly after an episode of waste disposal.

The case just described indicates the general way in which a hypothesis might be tested. Frequently we advance a claim—a hypothesis—whose truth or falsity we are unable to ascertain by relatively direct observation. We cannot just look and see what causes the sickness in the rural town; we cannot just look and see if the earth moves, or if the continents were once part of a single land mass, or if the butler committed the crime. In evaluating such hypotheses, we consider what things we would expect to observe if the hypothesis were true. Then we investigate to see if these expectations are borne out. If they are, then the hypothesis passes the test, and its success counts in its favor. If they are not, then the failure counts against the hypothesis.

We can make our description of the process of hypothesis testing more precise as follows. For any hypothesis H, an *observational consequence* of H is a statement that meets two conditions: First, it must be possible to ascertain the truth or falsity of the statement by using observation; second, the statement must follow deductively from H. Then we can represent cases of success and failure with tests as follows. Suppose that O is an observational consequence of H. Then, as a matter of deductive logic, it is true that

$$\text{If H then O}$$

If we are fortunate to observe the truth of O, then we give the following argument:

$$F_1 \quad \frac{\text{If H then O}}{\text{H}}$$

If experience is unkind to H, and we observe that O is false, we give the different argument:

$$F_2 \quad \frac{\begin{array}{l}\text{If H then O}\\ \text{Not O}\end{array}}{\text{Not H}}$$

There is an important asymmetry between F_1 and F_2. The latter is conclusive in a way that the former is not. Notice that F_2 is a deductively valid form of argument. Hence, if we know that the premises are true, we have a guarantee that the conclusion is true. However, F_1 is not deductively valid: it is possible that the premises should be true and the conclusion false. However, we become ever more justified in accepting a hypothesis as we find that a numerous and varied collection of its observational consequences prove true. Although we may balk at accepting an argument of the form F_1, we find it hard to resist more elaborate arguments, taking such forms as:

$$F_3 \quad \begin{array}{l}\text{If H then } O_1\\ \text{If H then } O_2\\ \cdot\\ \cdot\\ \cdot\\ \text{If H then } O_n\\ O_1\\ O_2\\ \cdot\\ \cdot\\ \cdot\\ \underline{O_n}\\ \text{H}\end{array}$$

where n is a large number and the O statements $O_1, \ldots, O_n$ form a varied collection of claims about what might be observed. For example, if Sherlock Holmes infers from the hypothesis that Moriarty was the culprit, observational consequences to the effect that the grandfather clock should have stopped at midnight, that a single goblet should be missing from the curio cabinet, that the rug in the hallway should show traces of clay on its underside . . . , and if we discover that all of these effects are to be found, then we may justifiably conclude that the hypothesis is correct. Here again, arguments of form F_3, like those of form F_1, are deductively invalid.

When a hypothesis passes tests, the results do not guarantee that the hypothesis is true, but the larger the number of cases and the more varied they are, the higher is our rational confidence in the hypothesis. Moreover, a single failure spells doom. One observational consequence that is not borne out shows us that the hypothesis is wrong. However strikingly successful Holmes's hypothesis about Moriarty may have been, we must abandon it if it implies an effect we find to be absent. Suppose that it follows from the hypothesis that there should be a size 12A footprint in the flowerbed beneath the kitchen window. Then, for all the success with the grandfather clock, the missing goblet, and the hallway rug, the absence of that footprint defeats Holmes's hypothesis.

At this stage we ought to acknowledge that observational consequences of a single hypothesis are hard to come by. Indeed, our discussion of Holmes's hypothesis about Moriarty is extremely fanciful. By itself, that hypothesis does not imply any such results about observation as those that we have ascribed to it. To make predictions about clocks, clay, and curios we have to appeal to all sorts of other premises, unspoken *auxiliary assumptions.* When our predictions go awry, we can always lay the blame on one of these auxiliary assumptions. Saving the central hypothesis, we choose to reject some other statement that is used in deriving from it the observational result that has proved faulty.

What this means is that the simple argument form F_2, while deductively valid, does not often provide us with a realistic account of what goes on in abortive tests. The following form of argument is much more widely applicable:

$$F_4 \quad \text{If H and } (A_1 \text{ and } A_2 \text{ and } \ldots \text{ and } A_n) \text{ then O}$$
$$\underline{\text{Not O}}$$
$$\text{Not H or not } (A_1 \text{ and } A_2 \text{ and } \ldots \text{ and } A_n)$$

F_4, like F_2, is deductively valid. However, it lacks the bite of F_2, for it leaves open the possibility that, given uncomfortable observational findings, we may lay the blame on some auxiliary assumption (i.e., A_1 or A_2 or . . . or A_n).

In the abstract, it may be hard to understand how this could ever work, or how the rejection of auxiliary assumptions could ever be justified. So we shall conclude our discussion of hypothesis testing by describing a classic case. In 1543, Nicolaus Copernicus published an astronomical treatise, claiming that the earth revolves annually about the sun. Orthodox astronomers pointed out that, if Copernicus were right, then, at different times of the year, we should observe the fixed stars from different angles. (Compare: As you run around a running track, the objects you see are seen at different angles from different points of the track.) Yet we do not observe any change in the angle at which we see the fixed stars. So Copernicus is instantly refuted! However, the alleged refutation is too quick. As Galileo (and other Copernicans) pointed out, the prediction that the fixed stars should be seen at different angles at different times of the year does not follow from the claim that the earth revolves annually about the sun. One must also assume that the stars are relatively close, for if they are very distant, the shifts in angle will not be big enough for us to detect. Thus Galileo rejected an auxiliary assumption, and maintained that the universe is much bigger than his predecessors had supposed. He was vindicated in the nineteenth century, when minute differences in the angles at which the fixed stars appear were finally detected.

Science and Common Sense

❖❖

ERNEST NAGEL

> The use of scientific method may strike you as little more than reliance on common sense. And scientific method is indeed a refinement and systemization of common sense. But what more can be said to help clarify their relationship? That is the theme of the next essay, written by Ernest Nagel, the noted philosopher of science who was coauthor of one of our previous selections (pp. 56–59).
>
> With this article we come to the end of this section devoted to reasoning. Now we are ready to use our powers of reason in exploring the problems of philosophy.

From *The Structure of Science.* Reprinted by permission of Hackett Publishing Co., Inc. All rights reserved.

Long before the beginnings of modern civilization, men acquired vast funds of information about their environment. They learned to recognize substances which nourished their bodies. They discovered the uses of fire and developed skills for transforming raw materials into shelters, clothing, and utensils. They invented arts of tilling the soil, communicating, and governing themselves. Some of them discovered that objects are moved more easily when placed on carts with wheels, that the sizes of fields are more reliably compared when standard schemes of measurement are employed, and that the seasons of the year as well as many phenomena of the heavens succeed each other with a certain regularity. . . . The acquisition of reliable knowledge concerning many aspects of the world certainly did not wait upon the advent of modern science and the self-conscious use of its methods. Indeed, in this respect, many men in every generation repeat in their own lives the history of the race: they manage to secure for themselves skills and competent information, without benefit of training in the sciences and without the calculated adoption of scientific modes of procedure.

If so much in the way of knowledge can be achieved by the shrewd exercise of native gifts and "common-sense" methods, what special excellence do the sciences possess, and what do their elaborate intellectual and physical tools contribute to the acquisition of knowledge? The question requires a careful answer if a definite meaning is to be associated with the word "science." . . .

No one seriously disputes that many of the existing special sciences have grown out of the practical concerns of daily living: geometry out of problems of measuring and surveying fields, mechanics out of problems raised by the architectural and military arts, biology out of problems of human health and animal husbandry, chemistry out of problems raised by metallurgical and dyeing industries, economics out of problems of household and political management, and so on. To be sure, there have been other stimuli to the development of the sciences than those provided by problems of the practical arts; nevertheless, these latter have had, and still continue to have, important roles in the history of scientific inquiry. In any case, commentators on the nature of science who have been impressed by the historical continuity of common-sense convictions and scientific conclusions have sometimes proposed to differentiate between them by the formula that the sciences are simply "organized" or "classified" common sense.

It is undoubtedly the case that the sciences are organized bodies of knowledge and that in all of them a classification of their materials into significant types or kinds (as in biology, the classification of living things into species) is an indispensable task. It is clear, nonetheless, that the proposed formula does not adequately express the characteristic differences between science and common sense. A lecturer's notes on his travels in Africa may be very well organized for the purposes of communicating information interestingly and efficiently, without thereby converting that information into what has historically been called a science. A librarian's card catalogue represents an invaluable classification of books, but no one with a sense for the historical association of the word would say that the catalogue is a science. The obvious difficulty is that the proposed formula does not specify what *kind* of organization or classification is characteristic of the sciences.

Let us therefore turn to this question. A marked feature of much information acquired in the course of ordinary experience is that, although this information may be accurate enough within certain limits, it is seldom accompanied by any explanation of why the facts are as alleged. Thus societies which have discovered the uses of the wheel usually know nothing of frictional forces, nor of any reasons why goods loaded on vehicles with wheels are easier to move than goods dragged on the ground. Many peoples have learned the advisability of manuring their agricultural fields, but only a few have concerned themselves with the reasons for so acting. The medicinal properties of herbs like the foxglove have been recognized for centuries, though usually no account was given of the grounds for their beneficent virtues. Moreover, when "common sense" does attempt to give explanations for its facts—as when the value of the foxglove as a cardiac stimulant is explained in terms of the similarity in shape of the flower and the human heart—the explanations are frequently without critical tests of their relevance to the facts. Common sense is often eligible to receive the well-known advice Lord Mansfield gave to a newly appointed governor of a colony who was unversed in the law: "There is no difficulty in deciding a case—only hear both sides patiently, then consider what you think justice requires, and decide accordingly; but never give your reasons, for your judgment will probably be right, but your reasons will certainly be wrong."

It is the desire for explanations which are at once systematic and controllable by factual evidence that generates science; and it is the organization and classification of knowledge on the basis of explanatory principles that is the distinctive goal of the sciences. More specifically, the sciences seek to discover and to formulate in general terms the conditions under which events of various sorts occur, the statements of such determining conditions being the explanations of the corresponding happenings. This goal can be achieved only by distinguishing or isolating certain properties in the subject matter studied and by ascertaining the repeatable patterns of dependence in which these properties stand to one another. In consequence, when the inquiry is successful, propositions that hitherto appeared to be quite unrelated are exhibited as linked to each other in determinate ways by virtue of their place in a system of explanations. In some cases, indeed, the inquiry can be carried to remarkable lengths. Patterns of relations may be discovered that are pervasive in vast ranges of fact, so that with the help of a small number of explanatory principles an indefinitely large number of propositions about these facts can be shown to constitute a logically unified body of knowledge. The unification sometimes takes the form of a deductive system, as in the case of demonstrative geometry or the science of mechanics. Thus a few principles, such as those formulated by Newton, suffice to show that propositions concerning the moon's motion, the behavior of the tides, the paths of projectiles, and the rise of liquids in thin tubes are intimately related, and that all these propositions can be rigorously deduced from those principles conjoined with various special assumptions of fact. In this way a systematic explanation is achieved for the diverse phenomena which the logically derived propositions report.

Not all the existing sciences present the highly integrated form of systematic explanation which the science of mechanics exhibits, though for many of the sciences—in domains of social inquiry as well as in the various divisions of natural science—the idea of such a rigorous logical systematization continues to function as an ideal. But even in those branches of departmentalized inquiry in which this ideal is not generally pursued, as in much historical research, the goal of finding explanations for facts is usually always present. Men seek to know why the thirteen American colonies rebelled from England while Canada did not, why the ancient Greeks were able to repel the Persians but succumbed to the Roman armies, or why urban and commercial activity developed in medieval Europe in the tenth century and not before. To explain, to establish some relation of dependence between propositions superficially unrelated, to exhibit systematically connections between apparently miscellaneous items of information are distinctive marks of scientific inquiry.

A number of further differences between common sense and scientific knowledge are almost direct consequences of the systematic character of the latter. A well-recognized feature of common sense is that, though the knowledge it claims may be accurate, it seldom is aware of the limits within which its beliefs are valid or its practices successful. A community, acting on the rule that spreading manure preserves the fertility of the soil, may in many cases continue its mode of agriculture successfully. However, it may continue to follow the rule blindly, in spite of the manifest deterioration of the soil, and it may therefore be helpless in the face of a critical problem of food supply. On the other hand, when the reasons for the efficacy of manure as a fertilizer are understood, so that the rule is connected with principles of biology and soil chemistry, the rule comes to be recognized as only of restricted validity, since the efficiency of manure is seen to depend on the persistence of conditions of which common sense is usually unaware. Few who know them are capable of withholding admiration for the sturdy independence of those farmers who, without much formal education, are equipped with an almost endless variety of skills and sound information in matters affecting their immediate environment. Nevertheless, the traditional resourcefulness of the farmer is narrowly circumscribed: he often becomes ineffective when some break occurs in the continuity of his daily round of living, for his skills are usually products of tradition and routine habit and are not informed by an understanding of the reasons for their successful operation. More generally, common-sense knowledge is most adequate in situations in which a certain number of factors remain practically unchanged. But since it is normally not recognized that this adequacy does depend on the constancy of such factors—indeed, the very existence of the pertinent factors may not be recognized—common-sense knowledge suffers from a serious incompleteness. It is the aim of systematic science to remove this incompleteness, even if it is an aim which frequently is only partially realized.

The sciences thus introduce refinements into ordinary conceptions by the very process of exhibiting the systematic connections of propositions about matters of common knowledge. Not only are familiar practices thereby shown to be explicable in terms of principles formulating relations between items in wide areas of fact; those principles also provide clues for altering and correcting habitual modes of behavior, so as to make them more effective in familiar contexts and more adaptable to novel ones. This is not to say, however, that common beliefs are necessarily mistaken, or even that they are inherently more subject to change under the pressure of experience than are the propositions of science. Indeed, the age-long and warranted stability of common-sense convictions, such as that oaks do not develop overnight from acorns or that water solidifies on sufficient cooling, compares favorably with the relatively short life span of many theories of science. The essential point to be observed is that, since common sense shows little interest in systematically explaining the facts it notes, the range of valid application of its beliefs, though in fact narrowly circumscribed, is not of serious concern to it. . . .

Implicit in the contrasts between modern science and common sense already noted is the important difference that derives from the deliberate policy of science to expose its cognitive claims to the repeated challenge of critically probative observational data, procured under carefully controlled conditions. As we had occasion to mention previously, however, this does not mean that common-sense beliefs are invariably erroneous or that they have no foundations in empirically verifiable fact. It does mean that common-sense beliefs are not subjected, as a matter of established principle, to systematic scrutiny in the light of data secured for the sake of determining the accuracy of those beliefs and the range of their validity. It also means that evidence admitted as competent in science must be obtained by procedures instituted with a view to eliminating known sources of error; and it means, furthermore, that the weight of the available evidence for any hypothesis proposed as an answer to the problem under inquiry is assessed with the help of canons of evaluation whose authority is itself based on the performance of those canons in an extensive class of inquiries. Accordingly, the quest for explanation in science is not simply a search for any *prima facie* plausible "first principles" that might account in a vague way for the familiar "facts" of conventional experience. On the contrary, it is a quest for explanatory hypotheses that are genuinely testable, because they are required to have logical consequences precise enough not to be compatible with almost every conceivable state of affairs. The hypotheses sought must therefore be subject to the possibility of rejection, which will depend on the outcome of critical procedures, integral to the scientific quest, for determining what the actual facts are.

The difference just described can be expressed by the dictum that the conclusions of science, unlike common-sense beliefs, are the products of scientific method. However, this brief formula should not be misconstrued. It must not be understood to assert, for example, that the practice of scientific method consists in following prescribed rules for making experimental discoveries or for finding satisfactory explanations for matters of established fact. There are no rules of discovery and invention in science, any more than there are such rules in the arts. Nor must the formula be construed as maintaining that the practice of scientific method consists in the use in all inquiries of some special set of techniques (such as the techniques of measurement employed in physical science), irrespective of the subject matter or the problem under investigation. Such an interpretation of the dictum is a caricature of its intent; and in any event the dictum on that interpretation is preposterous. Nor, finally, should the formula be read as claiming that the practice of scientific method effectively eliminates every form of personal bias or source of error which might otherwise impair the outcome of the inquiry, and more generally that it assures the truth of every conclusion reached by inquiries employing the method. . . . But despite this fact the historical record of what has been achieved by this policy in the way of dependable and systematically ordered knowledge leaves little room for serious doubt concerning the superiority of the policy over alternatives to it.

PART 3

KNOWLEDGE
AND SELF

Appearance and Reality

BERTRAND RUSSELL

An ancient philosophical question is whether we can trust the evidence of our senses. We seem to see water on the highway ahead, but, when we reach the place that had appeared wet, the area is dry. We think we hear a person cry, but it is only the blowing of the wind. Since our senses sometimes lead us astray, when, if ever, should we rely on them? This issue is central to one of the fundamental fields of philosophical inquiry: the theory of knowledge, or, as philosophers often refer to it, "epistemology," from the Greek word *epistēmē*, meaning "knowledge."

The relation between what seems to be the case and what is the case, between appearance and reality, is the theme of our next selection. Its author is Bertrand Russell (1872–1970), the English philosopher, mathematician, writer, and social activist, winner of the 1950 Nobel Prize for Literature and one of the most prominent figures of the twentieth century.

Is there any knowledge in the world which is so certain that no reasonable man could doubt it? This question, which at first sight might not seem difficult, is really one of the most difficult that can be asked. When we have realized the obstacles in the way of a straightforward and confident answer, we shall be well launched on the study of philosophy—for philosophy is merely the attempt to answer such ultimate questions, not carelessly and dogmatically, as we do in ordinary life and even in the sciences, but critically, after exploring all that makes such questions puzzling, and after realizing all the vagueness and confusion that underlie our ordinary ideas.

In daily life, we assume as certain many things which, on a closer scrutiny, are found to be so full of apparent contradictions that only a great amount of thought enables us to know what it is that we really may believe. In the search for certainty, it is natural to begin with our present experiences, and in some sense, no doubt, knowledge is to be derived from them. But any statement as to what it is that our immediate experiences make us know is very likely to be wrong. It seems to me that I am now sitting in a chair, at a table of a certain shape, on which I see sheets of paper with writing or print.

By turning my head I see out of the window buildings and clouds and the sun. I believe that the sun is about ninety-three million miles from the earth; that it is a hot globe many times bigger than the earth; that, owing to the earth's rotation, it rises every morning, and will continue to do so for an indefinite time in the future. I believe that, if any other normal person comes into my room, he will see the same chairs and tables and books and papers as I see, and that the table which I see is the same as the table which I feel pressing against my arm. All this seems to be so evident as to be hardly worth stating, except in answer to a man who doubts whether I know anything. Yet all this may be reasonably doubted, and all of it requires much careful discussion before we can be sure that we have stated it in a form that is wholly true.

To make our difficulties plain, let us concentrate attention on the table. To the eye it is oblong, brown and shiny, to the touch it is smooth and cool and hard; when I tap it, it gives out a wooden sound. Any one else who sees and feels and hears the table will agree with this description, so that it might seem as if no difficulty would arise; but as soon as we try to be more precise our troubles begin. Although I believe that the table is "really" of the same colour all over, the parts that reflect the light look much brighter than the other parts, and some parts look white because of reflected light. I know that, if I move, the parts that reflect the light will be different, so that the apparent distribution of colours on the table will change. It follows that if several people are looking at the table at the same moment, no two of them will see exactly the same distribution of colours, because no two can see it from exactly the same point of view, and any change in the point of view makes some change in the way the light is reflected.

For most practical purposes these differences are unimportant, but to the painter they are all-important: the painter has to unlearn the habit of thinking that things seem to have the colour which common sense says they "really" have, and to learn the habit of seeing things as they appear. Here we have already the beginning of one of the distinctions that cause most trouble in philosophy—the distinction between "appearance" and "reality," between what things seem to be and what they are. The painter wants to know what things seem to be, the practical man and the philosopher want to know what they are; but the philosopher's wish to know this is stronger than the practical man's, and is more troubled by knowledge as to the difficulties of answering the question.

To return to the table. It is evident from what we have found, that there is no colour which preeminently appears to be *the* colour of the table, or even of any one particular part of the table—it appears to be of different colours from different points of view, and there is no reason for regarding some of these as more really its colour than others. And we know that even from a given point of view the colour will seem different by artificial light, or to a colour-blind man, or to a man wearing blue spectacles, while in the dark there will be no colour at all, though to touch and hearing the table will be unchanged. This colour is not something which is inherent in the table, but something depending upon the table and the spectator and the way the light falls on the table. When, in ordinary life, we speak of *the* colour of the table, we only mean the sort of colour which it will seem to have to a normal spectator from an ordinary point of view under usual conditions of light. But the other colours which appear under other conditions have just as good a right to be considered real; and therefore, to avoid favouritism, we are compelled to deny that, in itself, the table has any one particular colour.

The same thing applies to the texture. With the naked eye one can see the grain, but otherwise the table looks smooth and even. If we looked at it through a microscope, we should see roughnesses and hills and valleys, and all sorts of differences that are imperceptible to the naked eye. Which of these is the "real" table? We are naturally tempted to say that what we see through the microscope is more real, but that in turn would be changed by a still more powerful microscope. If, then, we cannot trust what we see with the naked eye, why should we trust what we see through a microscope? Thus, again, the confidence in our senses with which we began deserts us.

The *shape* of the table is no better. We are all in the habit of judging as to the "real" shapes of things, and we do this so unreflectingly that we come to think we actually see the real shapes. But, in fact, as we all have to learn if we try to draw, a given thing looks different in shape from every different point of view. If our table is "really" rectangular, it will look, from almost all points of view, as if it had two acute angles and two obtuse angles. If opposite sides are parallel, they will look as if they converged to a point away from the spectator; if they are of equal length, they will look as if the nearer side were longer. All these things are not commonly noticed in looking at a table, because experience has taught us to construct the "real" shape from the apparent shape, and the "real" shape is what interests us as practical men. But the "real" shape is not what we see; it is something inferred from what we see. And what we see is constantly changing in shape as we move about the room; so that here again the senses seem not to give us the truth about the table itself, but only about the appearance of the table.

Similar difficulties arise when we consider the sense of touch. It is true that the table always gives us a sensation of hardness, and we feel that it resists pressure. But the sensation we obtain depends upon how hard we press the table and also upon what part of the body we press with; thus the various sensations due to various pressures or various parts of the body cannot be supposed to reveal *directly* any definite property of the table, but at most to be *signs* of some property which perhaps *causes* all the sensations, but is not actually apparent in any of them. And the same applies still more obviously to the sounds which can be elicited by rapping the table.

Thus it becomes evident that the real table, if there is one, is not the same as what we immediately experience by sight or touch or hearing. The real table, if there is one, is not *immediately* known to us at all, but must be an inference from what is immediately known. Hence, two very difficult questions at once arise; namely, (1) Is there a real table at all? (2) If so, what sort of object can it be?

It will help us in considering these questions to have a few simple terms of which the meaning is definite and clear. Let us give the name of "sense-data" to the things that are immediately known in sensation: such things as colours, sounds, smells, hardnesses, roughnesses, and so on. We shall give the name "sensation" to the experience of being immediately aware of these things. Thus, whenever we see a colour, we have a sensation *of* the colour, but the colour itself is a sense-datum, not a sensation. The colour is that *of* which we are immediately aware, and the awareness itself is the sensation. It is plain that if we are to know anything about the table, it must be by means of the sense-data—brown colour, oblong shape, smoothness, etc.—which we associate with the table; but, for the reasons which have been given, we cannot say that the table *is* the sense-data, or even that the sense-data are directly properties of the table. Thus a problem arises as to the relation of the sense-data to the real table, supposing there is such a thing. . . .

In fact, almost all philosophers seem to be agreed that there is a real table: they almost all agree that, however much our sense-data—colour, shape, smoothness, etc.—may depend upon us, yet their occurrence is a sign of something existing independently of us, something differing, perhaps, completely from our sense-data, and yet to be regarded as causing those sense-data whenever we are in a suitable relation to the real table. . . .

[I]t will be well to consider for a moment what it is that we have discovered so far. It has appeared that, if we take any common object of the sort that is supposed to be known by the senses, what the senses *immediately* tell us is not the truth about the object as it is apart from us, but only the truth about certain sense-data which, so far as we can see, depend upon the relations between us and the object. Thus what we directly see and feel is merely "appearance," which we believe to be a sign of some "reality" behind. But if the reality is not what appears, have we any means of knowing whether there is any reality at all? And if so, have we any means of finding out what it is like?

Such questions are bewildering, and it is difficult to know that even the strangest hypotheses may not be true. Thus our familiar table, which has roused but the slightest thoughts in us hitherto, has become a problem full of surprising possibilities. The one thing we know about it is that it is not what it seems.

What Can I Know?

D. Z. PHILLIPS

> Philosophers often test fundamental beliefs by raising doubts about them, then considering possible ways of resolving the doubts. The previous selection by Bertrand Russell raised doubts about the evidence of our senses and concluded that a familiar table is not what it seems. Our next article, by D. Z. Phillips, Professor of Philosophy at the University of Wales, Swansea, maintains that Russell's doubts can be answered and that we do know the table as it is.
>
> Here is a typical instance of philosophers disagreeing. Which, if either, is correct? Just as each member of a jury at a trial needs to make a decision and defend a view after considering all the relevant evidence, so each philosophical inquirer needs to make a decision and defend a view after considering all the relevant arguments. The challenge and excitement of philosophy is that, after taking account of the work others have done, the responsibility for reaching conclusions is your own.

What is philosophy about? Before I went to university, but knowing that philosophy was going to be one of the subjects I was to study there, I read a well-known introduction to philosophy in the hope of answering that question. My first impression was that the philosopher is an ultra-cautious person. Philosophers do not rush into saying that we know this or that, as most people do. They step back and think about things. Although we say we know all sorts of things, strictly speaking—philosophers conclude—we do not.

Given this view of philosophy, it seemed to me that the usefulness of philosophy was evident. Philosophy is a way of sharpening our thinking. It teaches us to be cautious, and not to be over-hasty in reaching our conclusions. By imposing its strict demands, philosophy tightens up our standards of knowledge. Our day-to-day assumptions are shot through with contradictions and inconsistencies. A great deal of reflection is necessary before we can arrive at what we really know. Philosophy is an indispensable guide in this reflection. This view of the usefulness of philosophy was reflected in the views of many educationalists, and this is still the case. They favour introductory classes in philosophy even for those whose primary intentions are to

From *Introducing Philosophy*. Copyright © 1996 by Blackwell Publishers. Reprinted by permission of the publisher.

study other subjects. The pencil needs to be sharpened before it can write with sufficient care about other topics.

This straightforward view of philosophy was given a severe jolt, however, when I read further and discovered the kinds of things that many philosophers were prepared to doubt.[1] They doubt things that we ordinarily would not doubt. The list that I read in the introduction to philosophy was surprising, to say the least. The philosopher told me that it seemed to him, at a certain moment, that he was sitting in a chair at a table which had a certain shape, on which he saw sheets of paper with writing or print on them. By turning his head he could see buildings, clouds, and the sun through the window. He believed that the sun is about ninety-three million miles away from the Earth and that, owing to the Earth's rotation, it rises every morning and will continue to do so for an indefinite time in the future. He believed that if any other normal person came into the room, that person would see the same chairs, tables, books, and papers as he saw. Further, he believed that the table he saw was the same table as he felt pressing against his arm.

What puzzled me was this: on the one hand, the philosopher wrote that all these things seemed so evident as to be hardly worth stating; but on the other hand, he said that all these facts could be reasonably doubted and that much reflection is needed before we can arrive at a description of the situation which would be wholly true. Of course, he was quite prepared to admit that most people would not bother to question these facts. They would see no point in doing so. My initial reaction was to think that the majority were correct on this issue. Suddenly, in view of what the philosopher was prepared to doubt, philosophy, so far from appearing to be a useful subject, now appeared to be a complete waste of time. The philosophical doubt seemed to be, not a tightening up of standards, but a trivial game; the kind of game which irritates parents when, on the first visit home after commencing the subject, budding philosophers confront them with the question, "So you think there's a table here, do you?" Recently, some philosophers have reacted in the same way to philosophers' doubts. They have asked why philosophers should give young people doubts that they would never have had in the first place if the philosophers had not opened their mouths. On this view, philosophy does not clarify our confusions—it creates them.

My new reaction, however, simply led to a new puzzle. Why should we doubt what seems so evident as to not need stating? Surely, it is not enough simply to accuse philosophers of indulging in trivial pursuits. They take their doubts seriously. I felt there was something wrong about these doubts, but did not know why. Whether we like it or not, people have always been puzzled about the doubts that philosophers discuss. I felt it was insufficient to say to someone who has doubts about whether we *know* something, "Well, we *do,* so that's that." Even if we feel that there is something odd about the philosophical doubts, that response will not help the doubter. The doubter is not going to accept the answer on authority. If the doubt is misplaced, we have to show the route by which it is reached. Unless we show the road to confusion, there is no road back from it. . . .

How do I come to know anything? Before I know anything my mind must have been like an empty receptacle, waiting to receive knowledge. Where is this knowledge to come from? Surely, from something outside myself, something which will furnish my mind with knowledge. How else am I to become acquainted with "yellow," "red," "hardness," "softness," "hot," "cold," "sweetness," "bitterness," and so on? These are experiences that I receive as a result of my interaction with the external world. I call the experiences that I have "ideas," "impressions," or "sensations." These are the furnishings of my mind, the data on which any knowledge I have relies.

But, now, a sceptical worry surfaces. If the sensory experiences of my mind are my necessary starting-point in my search for knowledge, how do I ever get beyond them? I say that these experiences come from an external world, but how do I know this? If my mind is acquainted only with its own ideas, how do I know—how can I know—whether these ideas refer to anything? How can I know that they refer to an external world? The very *possibility* of knowledge of an external world seems thrown into question.

Consider "seeing" as an example; seeing a table, let us say. I want to say that this experience came about as a result of something external to itself, namely, the table. But how can I ever know that? How do I get from my experience, my idea of the table, to the real table? If I have an experience called "seeing a table," I have an obvious interest in knowing whether it refers to a table. My experience may have been caused by some other object, or by no object at all. Light conditions may create the illusion that I am seeing a table. But how can I find out whether my experience does refer to a table, or to some other object, or whether it is illusory? If I want to know what causes the bulge in my sock, I can take out the object causing the bulge, a golf ball, let us say, and find out by doing so. In this example I have an independent access to the cause of the bulge in my sock. But when I want to know the cause of the ideas in my mind, I can have no independent access to their cause. But in that case, how do I know that they are caused by anything or refer to anything? I seem to be locked in the circle of my own ideas.

Let us suppose that my mental experience takes the form of an image of an apple. How can I know whether I am seeing an apple or imagining an apple? If I am imagining an apple, my experience makes no contact with a real apple. But, once again, I can only check this if I have independent access to the apple, the very access which seems to be denied to me. How on Earth am I going to get out of this predicament? . . .

Perhaps we ought to question the initial starting-point of the challenge, the assumption that all I am acquainted with are the ideas of my own mind. What is it that makes this assumption attractive? Think of examples such as hearing a car in the distance. It may be said that to say I hear a car is to say more than I know, strictly speaking. I am going beyond the immediate datum of my experience. That immediate datum is a sound. That is what I can be said to know. In saying that it is the sound of a car, I am interpreting the sound, perhaps by association with other occasions, and so on.

For examples such as these, the illegitimate assumption is made that *all* our experiences are based on minimal, immediate data. Thus, although there is nothing wrong in saying that I see a book, I am told that this is a very complex claim. What I experience immediately, it is said, is not a book, but a certain diversity of light and colour. These immediate data are self-authenticating. We cannot be mistaken about them. They are called *sense-data*. When we say that we see tables and chairs we are clearly going beyond our immediate experience of sense-data. The sceptical challenge can now be reformulated in these terms: What is the relation between our experience of sense-data and our claim to experience an external world? How can we ever get from sense-data to knowledge of the external world? Claims about the external world always stand in need of evidence. Sense-data, on the other hand, provide the evidence. But the problem is that sense-data can never provide sufficient justification for saying that we are in contact with an external world. Let us see why.

What qualifies as an example of an indubitable immediate experience? "I hear a car" clearly does not qualify, since that is a claim that I could be mistaken about. But "I hear a purring engine-like noise" will not qualify either, since I could be mistaken about that too. I may have forgotten that I have cotton-wool in my ears, and the noise may, in fact, be quite a loud one. Will "I hear a noise" qualify as a minimal, immediate experience? No, because I may be mistaken about that too. What I am hearing is simply noises in my head. And so we arrive at a minimal sense-datum: "It seems to me now as if I were hearing a noise."

The outcome of our quest for an example of a minimal sense-experience is not encouraging. We must not forget that the purpose of locating such data was to provide evidence for claims concerning the external world. We were supposed to be enabled to *advance* from such data to statements concerning the external world. But the location of such data constitutes, not an advance to, but a retreat from any claims about the external world. In terms of our example, the retreat takes the following form: "I hear a car"—"I seem to hear a car"—"It seems to *me* I hear a car"—"It seems to me *now* that I hear a purring-noise"—"It seems to me now as though I were hearing a purring-noise."

Why did we go in search of minimal sense-data in the first place? We did so because we felt that any statement about an external world can always be doubted, and thus stands in need of evidence. What we know immediately are minimal sense-data. But is this true? . . . [W]e doubt in circumstances that we call unfavourable. But what of favourable circumstances? Can I doubt that I hear a car in these? The car may be coming directly towards me. I may be sitting in the car or driving it. There may be no room for doubt at all. It would be absurd to suggest that there is always room for doubt because I may have forgotten that I had cotton-wool in my ears. It would be odd to say that any kind of judgement or verdict on the basis of sense-data is necessary when, in favourable circumstances, we hear a car. Verdicts are needed, for the most part, when we are not in a position to hear or see things clearly. But if I am sitting at a table, leaning on it, and so on, I am not giving a verdict on anything. My sitting at a table is not a claim which stands in need of evidence. It is not a claim at all. When I see a book, select it, pick it up, turn its pages, and read it, I am not verifying anything. I am simply seeing, selecting, picking up, turning the pages, and reading a book.

Whether a statement stands in need of evidence depends on the circumstances in which it is made. Once this is admitted, we can see that there is no absolute distinction between two kinds of statement—one kind of statement which always stands in need of evidence, and another kind of statement which always provides evidence. So we cannot say that any statement about the external world stands in need of evidence and that it is the function of statements about sense-data to provide such evidence. But once this absolute distinction is rejected, we reject the terms of the sceptical challenge at the same time. It can no longer be said that we *must* show how knowledge of an external world can be arrived at on the basis of the immediate data of our experience. Indeed, when circumstances are favourable, the onus is not on us to say when we can stop doubting and be able to assert "I see a book." The onus is on the sceptic to tell us why we should have started to doubt in the first place. . . .

[W]e are sometimes mistaken about what we think we perceive. I see a stick partly immersed in water and think it is bent. Later I find out that I was mistaken. The stick was not bent. But what I saw was bent. What, then, did I see? It is tempting to reply, "Not the stick, but the appearance of the stick." What "appears," the sense-datum, does not guarantee any reference to what is really the case. By such an argument, experiences become a "something" between me and objects in the external world. In the case of illusions the "something" that I experience does not refer to anything, whereas in the case of perceptions it does.

But this conception of a sense-datum, the necessary object of my experience, is a confused one. If I think I see a bent stick which later turns out to be straight, I do not need to postulate anything other than the stick to account for my mistake. I do not see "the appearance" of the stick. It is the stick that looks bent. It is the *same* thing, namely, the stick, which—in certain conditions—appears to be bent when it is not. The phenomenon of deception does not necessitate the postulation of two realms, one of sense-data and the other of physical objects. That being so, we are not faced with the task of showing how we move from the first realm to the second. . . .

The unintelligibility involved in the notions of two realms, one of sense-data, and the other of external objects, is a far-reaching one. It may seem as if, irrespective of what we say of the latter, sense can be made of the notion of the mind and its sensory-experiences. After all, according to the sceptic, this is our necessary starting-point in our search for knowledge. But, logically, this is not the case. If we sever the connection between the notion of experience and our normal surroundings, the notion of the mind and its experiences will itself become unintelligible.

Consider the simple instruction, "Think of a harbour." I cannot obey it unless I know something about harbours. I must be able to recognize a harbour. Unless I can do this, someone will retort when I describe what I am thinking, "No, that's not a harbour. You're thinking of something else." My thinking, my mental image of a harbour, is not self-authenticating. It is by reference to harbours and our dealings with them that the correctness of my thinking will be assessed. I can obey the instructions, "Think of a triangle," or "Think of the colour 'red,'" only because I have a wider acquaintance with triangles and colours. But the sceptic thinks that we can strip away these wider surroundings and still speak intelligibly of the mind and its ideas. To him, the mind, so conceived, is unproblematic. What is problematic, it is claimed, is how we can ever know that we are in contact with the external world. The reverse is true. If we forget our external surroundings, the notion of the mind and its ideas becomes a meaningless concatenation of sensory data. The intelligibility of private experiences depends on external surroundings that we share.

NOTE

1. [S]ee Russell, *The Problems of Philosophy,* one of the most famous introductions to philosophy.

The Problem of Induction

BERTRAND RUSSELL

We now return to the writings of Bertrand Russell and consider a different problem about knowledge. This one is raised by reflecting on our common practice of assuming that the laws of nature that have held in the past will continue to hold in the future.

We have learned that bread nourishes us; stones do not. But do
we have good reason to believe that the laws of nature will remain
constant? Starting tomorrow, might stones nourish us and bread be
inedible? That is the question Russell challenges us to answer.

In this case he is not urging that we change our basic beliefs but
that we seek to understand their justification. In other words, he
asks that we engage in philosophical inquiry.

It is obvious that if we are asked why we believe that the sun will rise tomorrow, we shall naturally answer, "Because it always has risen every day."
We have a firm belief that it will rise in the future, because it has risen in the
past. If we are challenged as to why we believe that it will continue to rise as
heretofore, we may appeal to the laws of motion: the earth, we shall say, is a
freely rotating body, and such bodies do not cease to rotate unless something
interferes from outside, and there is nothing outside to interfere with the
earth between now and tomorrow. Of course it might be doubted whether
we are quite certain that there is nothing outside to interfere, but this is not
the interesting doubt. The interesting doubt is as to whether the laws of motion will remain in operation until tomorrow. If this doubt is raised, we find
ourselves in the same position as when the doubt about the sunrise was first
raised.

The *only* reason for believing that the laws of motion will remain in operation is that they have operated hitherto, so far as our knowledge of the
past enables us to judge. It is true that we have a greater body of evidence
from the past in favour of the laws of motion than we have in favour of the
sunrise, because the sunrise is merely a particular case of fulfilment of the
laws of motion, and there are countless other particular cases. But the real
question is: Do *any* number of cases of a law being fulfilled in the past afford
evidence that it will be fulfilled in the future? If not, it becomes plain that we
have no ground whatever for expecting the sun to rise tomorrow, or for expecting the bread we shall eat at our next meal not to poison us, or for any of
the other scarcely conscious expectations that control our daily lives. It is to
be observed that all such expectations are only *probable*; thus we have not to
seek for a proof that they *must* be fulfilled, but only for some reason in
favour of the view that they are *likely* to be fulfilled.

Now in dealing with this question we must, to begin with, make an important distinction, without which we should soon become involved in
hopeless confusions. Experience has shown us that, hitherto, the frequent
repetition of some uniform succession or coexistence has been a *cause* of our
expecting the same succession or coexistence on the next occasion. Food that
has a certain appearance generally has a certain taste, and it is a severe
shock to our expectations when the familiar appearance is found to be associated with an unusual taste. Things which we see become associated, by

habit, with certain tactile sensations which we expect if we touch them; one of the horrors of a ghost (in many ghost stories) is that it fails to give us any sensations of touch. Uneducated people who go abroad for the first time are so surprised as to be incredulous when they find their native language not understood.

And this kind of association is not confined to men; in animals also it is very strong. A horse which has been often driven along a certain road resists the attempt to drive him in a different direction. Domestic animals expect food when they see the person who usually feeds them. We know that all these rather crude expectations of uniformity are liable to be misleading. The man who has fed the chicken every day throughout its life at last wrings its neck instead, showing that more refined views as to the uniformity of nature would have been useful to the chicken.

But in spite of the misleadingness of such expectations, they nevertheless exist. The mere fact that something has happened a certain number of times causes animals and men to expect that it will happen again. Thus our instincts certainly cause us to believe that the sun will rise tomorrow, but we may be in no better a position than the chicken which unexpectedly has its neck wrung. We have therefore to distinguish the fact that past uniformities *cause* expectations as to the future, from the question whether there is any reasonable ground for giving weight to such expectations after the question of their validity has been raised.

The problem we have to discuss is whether there is any reason for believing in what is called "the uniformity of nature." The belief in the uniformity of nature is the belief that everything that has happened or will happen is an instance of some general law to which there are *no* exceptions. The crude expectations which we have been considering are all subject to exceptions, and therefore liable to disappoint those who entertain them. But science habitually assumes, at least as a working hypothesis, that general rules which have exceptions can be replaced by general rules which have no exceptions. "Unsupported bodies in air fall" is a general rule to which balloons and airplanes are exceptions. But the laws of motion and the law of gravitation, which account for the fact that most bodies fall, also account for the fact that balloons and airplanes can rise; thus the laws of motion and the law of gravitation are not subject to these exceptions.

The belief that the sun will rise tomorrow might be falsified if the earth came suddenly into contact with a large body which destroyed its rotation; but the laws of motion and the law of gravitation would not be infringed by such an event. The business of science is to find uniformities, such as the laws of motion and the law of gravitation, to which, so far as our experience extends, there are no exceptions. In this search science has been remarkably successful, and it may be conceded that such uniformities have held hitherto. This brings us back to the question: Have we any reason, assuming that they have always held in the past, to suppose that they will hold in the future?

It has been argued that we have reason to know that the future will resemble the past, because what was the future has constantly become the past, and has always been found to resemble the past, so that we really have experience of the future, namely of times which were formerly future, which we may call past futures. But such an argument really begs the very question at issue. We have experience of past futures, but not of future futures, and the question is: Will future futures resemble past futures? This question is not to be answered by an argument which starts from past futures alone. We have therefore still to seek for some principle which shall enable us to know that the future will follow the same laws as the past.

Will the Future Be Like the Past?

FREDERICK L. WILL

> Frederick L. Will (1909–1998) was Professor of Philosophy at the University of Illinois at Urbana-Champaign and served as President of the American Philosophical Association. His son is George F. Will, the writer and political commentator.
>   Frederick Will devoted much of his research to issues related to inductive reasoning, and one of his best-known articles is a reply to Russell's doubts about the justification of induction. After reading Will's answer to Russell, consider whose position you find more compelling.

Suppose that there was somewhere in the world an enclosure beyond which it was impossible for anyone ever to go or to make any observations. Nothing could be seen, heard, or in any other way perceived beyond the border. The territory beyond the enclosure, for ever barred from human perception, is the land of Future. The territory within the enclosure is the land of Present and Past, but since it is overwhelmingly the latter, it all goes under the name of Past. Now suppose that someone within the enclosure is interested in some proposition about the way things behave beyond the enclosure, say, a simple and homely proposition about chickens, to the effect that beyond the enclosure roosters fight more than hens. And he wonders what evidence, if any, there is for this proposition. Of course he cannot observe this to be true. He must base it upon his observation in the land of Past; and if he does base it upon the observed fact that roosters in the land of Past fight more than hens, he must assume that in this respect chickens beyond the enclosure behave like chickens within it, so that, knowing that in the latter area roosters are the more pugnacious, he may employ this knowledge as evidence that things are this way also in the former area. This is an assumption which no empirical evidence, confined as it must be to evidence in Past, can be employed to support. Any attempt to support it with such evidence must itself assume that in respect to the phenomena involved differences between Past and Future are negligible; and since that is exactly what the reasoning is attempting to establish, the process is patently circular.

This is the kind of metaphor which makes friends, and influences people, in this case, to draw the wrong conclusions. There are several faults in the analogy. The chief one is that, as represented, the border between Past and Future is stationary, while in the temporal situation it is not. To duplicate the temporal situation in this respect the analogy should represent the border as constantly moving, revealing as it does constantly, in territory which has hitherto been Future, hens and roosters similar as regards difference in disposition to those already observed in Past. The matter of evidence for the proposition about hens and roosters is then also different. If this proposition is in a position analogous to the beliefs about uniformity which are represented in modern scientific laws, the situation is something like this. Previously inhabitants in Past had drawn more sweeping conclusions concerning the difference between the disposition to fight of male and female chickens. They have discovered recently that in respect to young chicks and pullets this generalization did not hold. They have therefore revised the proposition to exclude all the known negative instances and speak only and more surely of the behaviour of hens and roosters, meaning by these latter terms just fully grown and developed female and male chickens.

So far as there is any record, chickens in Past have verified this rule; so far as there is any record, every chicken revealed by the ever-receding border has likewise verified it; so far as there is any record there has not been one negative instance. Is it not the case that the inhabitants of Past do have evidence for the proposition that all chickens obey this rule, those already in Past, which they call "Past-chickens" and those also which are not yet in Past but which will be subsequently revealed by the moving border, and which they call not unnaturally "Future-chickens"? They have a vast number of positive instances of the rule, and no negative instances, except those in respect to which the rule has already been revised. In view of the present evidence that in all cases, year after year and century after century, the progressively revealed chickens have verified and do verify this rule, must one not conclude that the inhabitants of Past do have evidence for this proposition, and that anyone is wrong who says that they have actually no evidence one way or other?

The sceptic, however, is still prepared to argue his case, and his argument, in terms of the present analogy, has a now familiar ring. That the inhabitants of Past have no evidence whatsoever about the behaviour of Future-chickens, he will insist; and as grounds he will point out that although the border does progressively recede and reveal chickens like those previously observed in Past, these are really not Future-chickens. By the very fact that they have been revealed they are no longer Future-chickens, but are now Past-chickens. Observation of them is not observation of Future-chickens, and any attempt to reason from such observation to conclusions about Future-chickens must therefore assume that Future-chickens are like Past-chickens. For the inhabitants of Past, in these efforts to know the land beyond the border, this is both an inescapable and unknowable presumption.

What should one say of an argument of this kind? Only through some logical slip, one feels strongly, would it be possible to arrive at such a conclusion. One would have thought that the receding border was a matter upon which the inhabitants of Past may legitimately congratulate themselves in the light of their interest in learning what Future-chickens, when they become Past, are going to be like. If the border had not yet begun to recede they would indeed be in an unfortunate position for securing such knowledge. But happily this is not the case. The border is constantly receding. And granting that it will constantly recede, revealing always more of the land of Future, and even granting also that this means that there is an inexhaustible area to be revealed, the inhabitants of Past are in the fortunate position that with the progressive recession they may learn more and more about chickens, Past and Future. They may derive hypotheses from their experience of what has already been revealed and proceed further to test these by the progressive revelations of Future, in the light of which they may be confirmed, refuted, or revised. The sceptic's argument amounts to the assertion that all this apparent good fortune is really illusory and that the sorry Pastians are actually in no better position with respect to knowing about Future-chickens and Future-things generally than they would be if the border never moved at all. For the movement of the border does not reveal Future-chickens, since Future is by definition the land beyond the border. No matter how much or how little is revealed, by the very fact that it is revealed and on this side of the border it is not Future but Past, and therefore, since the land of Future always is beyond observation, no empirical method can produce any evidence that what is in that land is in any way similar to what is not. That this rendering of the sceptic's position, though in the language of the above metaphor, is undistorted and fair may be seen by consulting the words of an illustrious modern sceptic and follower of Hume, Bertrand Russell. In his chapter, "On Induction," in *The Problems of Philosophy*, Russell expressed the matter in this fashion:

> It has been argued that we have reason to know that the future will resemble the past, because what was the future has constantly become the past, and has always been found to resemble the past, so that we really have ex-

perience of the future, namely of times which were formerly future, which we may call past futures. But such an argument really begs the very question at issue. We have experience of past futures, but not of future futures, and the question is: Will future futures resemble past futures? This question is not to be answered by an argument which starts from past futures alone. We have therefore still to seek for some principle which shall enable us to know that the future will follow the same laws as the past.

This is the central difficulty urged by Hume, Russell, and others in arguing that there can never be any empirical evidence that the future will be like the past. Empirically, in Russell's language, it is possible to have evidence only that this has been true of past and possibly present futures, not that it will be true of future futures. It is the situation in the land of Past all over again. There are generalizations which are constantly being confirmed by experience. But every time a confirming instance occurs it is nullified as evidence by the argument that it is not really a confirming instance at all. For by the fact that it has occurred it is an instance of a past future, and therefore it tells nothing whatever about future futures. In treating of the land of Past it was suggested that there is involved in arguing in this manner a logical slip or error. It remains to investigate how this is the case.

Suppose that in 1936, to take but a short span of time, a man says that in the above-defined sense the future will be like the past. In 1936, if he could somehow have shown that 1937 would be like 1936, this would have been evidence for his statement, as even a sceptic would admit. But in 1937, when he does establish that 1937 is like 1936, it has somehow ceased to be evidence. So long as he did not have it, it was evidence; as soon as he gets it it ceases to be. The constant neutralization of the evidence which is effected in this argument is effected by the same kind of verbal trick which children play upon one another in fun. Child A asks child B what he is going to do tomorrow. B replies that he is going to play ball, go swimming, or what not. Thereupon A says, "You can't do that."

B: Why not?
A: Because tomorrow never comes. When tomorrow comes it won't be tomorrow; it will be today. You can never play tomorrow; you can only play today.

Again, if a prophet announces that next year will bring a utopia, and if each succeeding year, when the predicted utopia does not come, he defends himself by pointing out that he said "next year" and that obviously this is not next year, no reasonable person would pay much attention to him. Such a person would realize, on a moment's reflection, that the prophet is being deceptive with the word "next." In 1936, "next year" means "1937"; in 1937 it means "1938." Since every year "next year" means a different year, a year yet to come, what the prophet says can never be verified or disproved. If in

1936 he meant by this phrase 1937, as he sensibly should, then this state-ment can be verified or refuted in 1937. But if, when 1937 comes, he insists that he did not mean 1937, but "next year," and if in 1938 he again insists that he did not mean that year, and so on, then what he seems to be mean-ing by "next year" is the $n + 1$th year where n is the ever progressing num-ber of the present year. No one should alter his present activities or his plans for the future on the basis of such a prediction, for, of course, it really is not a prediction. While in the form of a statement about the future it does not say anything about the future, anything which could possibly be true or false in the infinity of time, if infinity it is, which yet remains to transpire. For what the prophet is saying is that utopia will come next year, and by his own interpretation of the words "next year" he is affirming that next year will never come. In other words, at the time which never comes, and hence when nothing occurs, a utopia will occur. This is not even sensible speech; it is a contradiction.

In a similar though less simple way those who employ the sceptical ar-gument about uniformity to show that there is no evidence whatever for any statement about the future are being themselves deceived and are deceiving others by their use of expressions like "next," "future," "future future," and "past future." The man who said in 1936 that the future would be like the past, that mere differences in temporal position make no difference in the be-haviour of nature which is described in scientific laws, meant, as he sensibly should, that this was true of the years 1937, 1938, and so on. He said some-thing of the form "all A's are B's" and it has been possible since 1936 to ex-amine the A's of 1937 to 1952 and to see whether what he said is confirmed or disproved by the available evidence. If, however, now that it is 1952, and all this evidence is in, he should remark that since it is 1952 the years 1937–52 are no longer future and therefore have ceased to be evidence for the propo-sition, then he is guilty of using, or rather abusing, the word "future" in the way in which the prophet in the previous example was abusing the word "next." For the only basis for his contention that the observed A's are not confirming evidence, or what is the same thing, that they are confirming in-stances only if one assumes quite circularly that the future is like the past, is in his illusive use of the word "future." Time does pass, and, because it does, the present is a constantly changing one; and the point of reference for the use of words like "future" and "past" is accordingly different. The correct conclusion to be drawn from the fact that time passes is that the future is constantly being revealed and that, in consequence, we have had and shall have the opportunity to learn more and more accurately what the laws of na-ture's behaviour are and how therefore the future will be like the past.

Free Will or Determinism?

STEVEN M. CAHN

Philosophers sometimes consider questions about the fundamental nature of the world. Does every event have a cause? Do human beings possess free will? Does each person consist of a soul connected to a body? Is life after death possible? Such issues belong to the field of philosophy known as "metaphysics," a Greek term meaning "after physics," so-called because when Aristotle's works were first catalogued more than two millenia ago, the treatise in which he discussed such matters was placed after his treatise on physics.

In the next essay I consider the metaphysical claim that free will is an illusion, and that, therefore, we should not hold people morally responsible for their actions. The discussion begins with an account of one of the twentieth century's most famous criminal trials. How did it involve an issue in metaphysics? Let us see.

In 1924 the American people were horrified by a senseless crime of extraordinary brutality. The defendants were eighteen-year-old Nathan Leopold and seventeen-year-old Richard Loeb. They were the sons of Chicago millionaires, brilliant students who had led seemingly idyllic lives. Leopold was the youngest graduate in the history of the University of Chicago, and Loeb the youngest graduate in the history of the University of Michigan. Suddenly they were accused of the kidnapping and vicious murder of fourteen-year-old Bobby Franks, a cousin of Loeb's. Before the trial even began, Leopold and Loeb both confessed, and from across the country came an outcry for their execution.

The lawyer who agreed to defend them was Clarence Darrow, the outstanding defense attorney of his time. Since Leopold and Loeb had already admitted their crime, Darrow's only chance was to explain their behavior in such a way that his clients could escape the death penalty. He was forced to argue that Leopold and Loeb were not morally responsible for what they had done; that they were not to be blamed for their actions. But how could he possibly maintain that position?

Darrow's defense was a landmark in the history of criminal law. He argued that the actions of his clients were a direct and necessary result of hereditary and environmental forces beyond their control.[1] Leopold suffered from a glandular disease that left him depressed and moody. Originally shy with girls, he had been sent to an all-girls school to cure his shyness but had sustained deep psychic scars from which he never recovered. In addition, his parents instilled in him the belief that his wealth absolved him of any responsibility toward others. Pathologically inferior because of his diminutive size, and pathologically superior because of his wealth, he became an acute schizophrenic.

Loeb suffered from a nervous disorder that caused fainting spells. During his unhappy childhood he had often thought of committing suicide. He was under the control of a domineering governess and was forced to lie and cheat to deceive her. His wealth led him to believe he was superior to all those around him, and he developed a fascination for crime, an activity in which he could demonstrate his superiority. By the time he reached college he was severely psychotic.

In his final plea Darrow recounted these facts. His central theme was that Leopold and Loeb were in the grip of powers beyond their control. They themselves were victims.

> I do not know what it was that made these boys do this mad act, but I do know there is a reason for it. I know they did not beget themselves. I know that any one of an infinite number of causes reaching back to the beginning might be working out in these boys' minds, whom you are asked to hang in malice and in hatred and in injustice, because someone in the past has sinned against them. . . . What had this boy to do with it? He was not his own father; he was not his own mother; he was not his own grandparents. All of this was handed to him. He did not surround himself with governesses and wealth. He did not make himself. And yet he is to be compelled to pay.[2]

Darrow's plea was successful, for Leopold and Loeb escaped execution and were sentenced to life imprisonment. Although they had committed crimes and were legally responsible for their actions, the judge believed they were not morally responsible, for they had not acted freely.

If the line of argument that Darrow utilized in the Leopold–Loeb case is sound, then not only were Leopold and Loeb not to blame for what they had done, but no person is ever to blame for any actions. As Darrow himself put it, "We are all helpless."[3] But is Darrow's argument sound? Does the conclusion follow from the premises, and are the premises true?

We can formalize his argument as follows:

Premise 1:   No action is free if it must occur.

Premise 2:   In the case of every event that occurs, antecedent conditions, known or unknown, ensure the event's occurrence.

Conclusion: Therefore, no action is free.

Premise (1) assumes that an action is free only if it is within the agent's power to perform it and within the agent's power not to perform it. In other words, whether a free action will occur is up to the agent. If circumstances require the agent to perform a certain action or require the agent not to perform that action, then the action is not free.

Premise (2) is the thesis known as "determinism." Put graphically, it is the claim that if there were at any time a being who knew the position of every particle in the universe and all the forces acting on each particle, then that being could predict with certainty every future event. Determinism does not presume such a being exists; the being is only imagined in order to illustrate what the world would be like if determinism were true.

Darrow's conclusion, which is supposed to follow from premises (1) and (2), is that no person has free will. Note that to have free will does not imply being free with regard to all actions, for only the mythical Superman is free to leap tall buildings at a single bound. But so long as at least some of an agent's actions are free, the agent is said to have free will. What Darrow's argument purports to prove is that not a single human action that has ever been performed has been performed freely.

Does the conclusion of Darrow's argument follow from the premises? If premise (2) is true, then every event that occurs must occur, for its occurrence is ensured by antecedent conditions. Since every action is an event, it follows from premise (2) that every action that occurs must occur. But according to premise (1), no action is free if it must occur. Thus, if premises (1) and (2) are true, it follows that no action is free—the conclusion of Darrow's argument.

Even granting that Darrow's reasoning is unassailable, we need not accept the conclusion of his argument unless we grant the truth of his premises. Should we do so?

Hard determinism is the view that both premises of Darrow's argument are correct. In other words, a hard determinist believes that determinism is true and that, as a consequence, no person has free will.[4] Determinists note that whenever an event occurs, we all assume that a causal explanation can account for the occurrence of the event. Suppose, for example, you feel a pain in your arm and are prompted to visit a physician. After examining you, the doctor announces that the pain had no cause, either physical or psychological. In other words, you were supposed to be suffering from an uncaused pain. On hearing this diagnosis you would surely switch doctors. After all, no one may be able to discover the cause of your pain, but surely something is causing it. If nothing were causing it, you wouldn't be in pain. This same line of reasoning applies whether the event to be explained is a loud noise, a change in the weather, or an individual's action. If the event were uncaused, it wouldn't have occurred.

However, we may agree that the principle of determinism holds in the vast majority of cases, yet doubt its applicability in the realm of human action. While causal explanations may be found for rocks falling and birds flying, people are far more complex than rocks or birds.

The determinist responds to this objection by asking us to consider any specific action: for instance, your decision to read this book. You may suppose your decision was uncaused, but did you not wish to acquire information about philosophy? The determinist argues that your desire for such information, together with your belief that the information is found in this book, caused you to read. Just as physical forces cause rocks and birds to do things, so human actions are caused by desires and beliefs.

If you doubt this claim, the determinist can call attention to our success in predicting people's behavior. For example, a store owner who reduces prices can depend on increasing visits by shoppers; an athlete who wins a major championship can rely on greater attention from the press. Furthermore, when we read novels or see plays, we expect to understand why the characters act as they do, and an author who fails to provide such explanations is charged with poor writing. The similarity of people's reactions to the human condition also accounts for the popularity of the incisive psychological insights of a writer such as La Rochefoucauld, the French aphorist. We read one of his maxims, for instance, "When our integrity declines, our taste does also,"[5] and nod our heads with approval, but are we not agreeing to a plausible generalization about the workings of the human psyche?

Granted, people's behavior cannot be predicted with certainty, but the hard determinist reminds us that each individual is influenced by a unique combination of hereditary and environmental factors. Just as each rock is slightly different from every other rock and each bird is somewhat different from every other bird, so human beings differ from each other. But just as rocks and birds are part of an unbroken chain of causes and effects, so human beings, too, are part of that chain. Just as a rock falls because it breaks off from a cliff, so people act because of their desires and beliefs. And just as a rock has no control over the wind that causes it to break off, so people have no control over the desires and beliefs that cause them to act. In short, we are said to have no more control over our desires and beliefs than Leopold and Loeb had over theirs. If you can control your desire for food and your friend cannot, the explanation is that your will is of a sort that can control your desire and your friend's will is of a sort that cannot. That your will is of one sort and your friend's will of another is not within the control of either of you. As one hard determinist has written, "If we can overcome the effects of early environment, the ability to do so is itself a product of the early environment. We did not give ourselves this ability; and if we lack it we cannot be blamed for not having it."[6]

At this point in the argument an antideterminist is apt to call attention to recent developments in physics that have been interpreted by some thinkers as a refutation of determinism. They claim that work in quantum mechanics demonstrates that certain subatomic events are uncaused and inherently unpredictable. Yet some physicists and philosophers of science argue that determinism has not been refuted, since the experimental results can be understood in causal terms.[7] The outcome of this dispute, however, seems irrelevant to the issue of human freedom, since the events we are discussing are not subatomic, and indeterminism on that level is compatible with the universal causation of events on the much larger level of human action.

Here, then, is a summary of hard determinism: According to this view, determinism is true and no person has free will. Every event that occurs is caused to occur, for otherwise why would it occur? Your present actions are events caused by your previous desires and beliefs, which themselves are accounted for by hereditary and environmental factors. These are part of a causal chain extending back far before your birth, and each link of the chain determines the succeeding link. Since you obviously have no control over events that occurred before your birth, and since these earlier events determined the later ones, it follows that you have no control over your present actions. In short, you do not have free will.

The hard determinist's argument may appear plausible, yet few of us are inclined to accept its shocking conclusion. We opt, therefore, to deny one of its two premises. *Soft determinism* is the view that the conclusion is false because premise (1) is false. In other words, a soft determinist believes both that determinism is true and that human beings have free will. The implication of the position is that an action may be free even if it is part of a causal chain extending back to events outside the agent's control. While this view may at first appear implausible, it has been defended throughout the centuries by many eminent philosophers, including David Hume and John Stuart Mill.

An approach employed explicitly or implicitly by many soft determinists has come to be known as "the paradigm-case argument." Consider it first in another setting, where its use is a classic of philosophical argumentation.

In studying physics we learn that ordinary objects like tables and chairs are composed of sparsely scattered, minute particles. This fact may lead us to suppose that such objects are not solid. As Sir Arthur Eddington, the noted physicist, put it, a "plank has no solidity of substance. To step on it is like stepping on a swarm of flies."[8]

Eddington's view that a plank is not solid was forcefully attacked by the British philosopher L. Susan Stebbing. She pointed out that the word "solid" derives its meaning from examples such as planks.

> For "solid" just is the word we use to describe a certain respect in which a plank of wood resembles a block of marble, a piece of paper, and a cricket ball, and in which each of these differs from a sponge, from the interior of a soap-bubble, and from the holes in a net. . . . The point is that the common usage of language enables us to attribute a meaning to the phrase "a solid plank"; but there is no common usage of language that provides a meaning for the word "solid" that would make sense to say that the plank on which I stand is not solid.[9]

In other words, a plank is a paradigm case of solidity. Anyone who claims that a plank is not solid does not know how the word "solid" is used in the English language. Note that Stebbing is not criticizing Eddington's scientific views; but only the manner in which he interpreted them.

The paradigm-case argument is useful to soft determinists; for in the face of the hard determinist's claim that no human action is free, soft determinists respond by pointing to a paradigm case of a free action, for instance, a person walking down the street. They stipulate that the individual is not under the influence of drugs, is not attached to ropes, is not sleepwalking, and so on; in other words, they refer to a normal, everyday instance of a person walking down the street. Soft determinists claim that the behavior described is a paradigm case of a free action, clearly distinguishable from instances in which a person is, in fact, under the influence of drugs, attached to ropes, or sleepwalking. These latter cases are not examples of free actions, or are at best problematic examples, while the case the soft determinists cite is clear and seemingly indisputable. Indeed, according to soft determinists, anyone who claims the act of walking down the street is not free does not know how the word "free" is used in English. Thus people certainly have free will, for we can cite obvious cases in which they act freely.

How do soft determinists define a "free action"? According to them, actions are free if the persons who perform them wish to do so and could, if they wished, not perform them. If your arm is forcibly raised, you did not act freely, for you did not wish to raise your arm. If you were locked in a room, you would also not be free, even if you wished to be there, for if you wished to leave, you couldn't.

Soft determinists emphasize that once we define "freedom" correctly, any apparent incompatibility between freedom and determinism will disappear. Consider some particular action I perform that is free in the sense explicated by soft determinists. Granting that the action is one link in a causal chain extending far back beyond my birth, nevertheless, I am free with regard to that action, for I wish to perform it, and if I did not wish to, I would not do so. This description of the situation is consistent with supposing that my wish is a result of hereditary and environmental factors over which I have no control. The presence of such factors is, according to the soft determinist, irrelevant to the question of whether my action is free. I may be walking down a particular street because of my desire to buy a coat and my belief that I am heading toward a clothing store, and this desire and belief may themselves be caused by any number of other factors. But, since I desire to walk down the street and could walk down some other street if I so desired, it follows that I am freely walking down the street. By this line of reasoning soft determinists affirm both free will and determinism, finding no incompatibility between them.

Soft determinism is an inviting doctrine, for it allows us to maintain a belief in free will without having to relinquish the belief that every event has a cause. Soft determinism, however, is open to objections that have led some philosophers to abandon the position.

   The fundamental problem for soft determinists is that their definition of "freedom" does not seem in accordance with the ordinary way in which we use the term. Note that soft determinists and hard determinists offer two different definitions of "freedom." According to the hard determinist, an action is free if it is within my power to perform it and also within my power not to perform it. According to the soft determinist, an action is free if it is such that if I wish to perform it I may, and if I wish not to perform it I also may. To highlight the difference between these definitions, consider the case of a man who has been hypnotized and rolls up the leg of his pants as if to cross a stream. Is his action free? According to the hard determinist, the man's action is not free, for it is not within his power to refrain from rolling up the leg of his pants. According to the soft determinist's definition of "freedom," the action would be considered free, for the agent desires to perform it, and if he didn't desire to, he wouldn't. But a man under hypnosis is not free. Therefore, the soft determinist's definition of "freedom" seems unsatisfactory.

   Perhaps this objection to soft determinism is unfair, since the desires of the hypnotized man are not his own but are controlled by the hypnotist. The force of the objection to soft determinism, however, is that the soft determinist overlooks whether a person's wishes or desires are themselves within that individual's control. The hard determinist emphasizes that my action is free only if it is up to me whether to perform it. But, in order for an action to be up to me, I need to have control over my own wishes or desires. If I do not, my desires might be controlled by a hypnotist, a brainwasher, my family, hereditary factors, and so on, and thus I would not be free. Soft determinists do not appear to take such possibilities seriously, since, according to them, I would be free even if my desires were not within my control, so long as I was acting according to my desires and could act differently if my desires were different. But could my desires have been different? That is the crucial question. If my desires could not have been different, then I could not have acted in any other way than I did. And that is the description of a person who is not free.

   By failing to consider the ways in which a person's desires can be controlled by external forces beyond the individual's control, soft determinists offer a definition of "freedom" that I find not in accord with our normal use of the term. They may, of course, define terms as they wish, but we are interested in the concept of freedom relevant to questions of moral responsibility. Any concept of freedom implying that hypnotized or brainwashed individuals are morally responsible for their actions is not the concept in question.

   What of the soft determinist's claim that a person's walking down the street is a paradigm case of a free action? Although I agree that the paradigm-case argument can sometimes be used effectively, the soft determinist's appeal to it does not seem convincing. To see why, imagine that we traveled to a land in which the inhabitants believed that every woman born on February 29 was a witch, and that every witch had the power to cause droughts. If we refused to believe that any woman was a witch, the philo-

sophically sophisticated inhabitants might try to convince us by appealing to
the paradigm-case argument, claiming that anyone born on February 29 is a
paradigm case of a witch.

What would we say in response? How does this appeal to a paradigm
case differ from Susan Stebbing's appeal to a plank as a paradigm case of solidity? No one doubts that a plank can hold significant weight and is, in that
sense, solid. But, until women born on February 29 demonstrate supernatural
powers and are in that sense witches, the linguistic claim alone has no force.

Are soft determinists appealing to an indisputable instance when they
claim that a person's walking down the street is a paradigm case of a free action? Not at all, for as we saw in the trial of Leopold and Loeb, such apparently free actions may not turn out to be judged as free. By appealing to a
disputable example as a paradigm case, soft determinists are assuming what
they are supposed to be proving. They are supposed to demonstrate that actions such as walking down the street are examples of free actions. Merely
asserting that such actions are free is to overlook the hard determinist's argument that such actions are not free. No questionable instance can be used
as a paradigm case, and walking down the street is, as Darrow demonstrated, a questionable example of a free action. So soft determinism appears to
have a serious weakness.

Remember that the hard determinist argues that since premises (1) and
(2) of Darrow's argument are true, so is the conclusion. Soft determinists argue that premise (1) is false. If they are mistaken, then the only way to avoid
hard determinism is to reject premise (2). That position is known as "liber-
tarianism."

The *libertarian* agrees with the hard determinist that an action is not free
if it must occur. For the libertarian as well as for the hard determinist, I am
free with regard to a particular action only if it is within my power to perform the action and within my power not to perform it. But do persons ever
act freely? The hard determinist believes that people are never free, since in
the case of every action antecedent conditions, known or unknown, ensure
the action's occurrence. Libertarians refuse to accept this conclusion, but find
it impossible to reject premise (1) of Darrow's argument. So their only re-
course is to reject premise (2). As Sherlock Holmes noted, "When you have
eliminated the impossible, whatever remains, however improbable, must be
the truth."[10] The libertarian thus denies that every event has a cause.

But why is the libertarian so convinced that people sometimes act freely?
Consider an ordinary human action: for instance, raising your hand at a
meeting to attract the speaker's attention. If you are attending a lecture and
the time comes for questions from the audience, you believe it is within your
power to raise your hand and also within your power not to raise it. The
choice is yours. Nothing forces you to ask a question, and nothing prevents
you from asking one. What could be more obvious? If this description of the
situation is accurate, then hard determinism is incorrect, for you are free
with regard to the act of raising your hand.

The heart of the libertarian's position is that innumerable examples of this sort are conclusive evidence for free will. Indeed, we normally accept them as such. We assume on most occasions that we are free with regard to our actions, and, moreover, we assume that other persons are free with regard to theirs. If a friend agrees to meet us at six o'clock for dinner and arrives an hour late claiming to have lost track of time, we blame her for her tardiness, since we assume she had it within her power to act otherwise. All she had to do was glance at her watch, and assuming no special circumstances were involved, it was within her power to do so. She was simply negligent and deserves to be blamed, for she could have acted conscientiously. But to believe she could have acted in a way other than she did is to believe she was free.

How do hard determinists respond to such examples? They argue that such situations need to be examined in greater detail. In the case of our friend who arrives an hour late for dinner, we assume she is to blame for her actions, but the hard determinist points out that some motive impelled her to be late. Perhaps she was more interested in finishing her work at the office than in arriving on time for dinner. But why was she more interested in finishing her work than in arriving on time? Perhaps because her parents instilled in her the importance of work but not promptness. Hard determinists stress that whatever the explanation for her lateness, the motive causing it was stronger than the motive impelling her to arrive on time. She acted as she did because her strongest motive prevailed. Which motive was the strongest, however, was not within her control, and so she was not free.

The hard determinist's reply may seem persuasive. How can I deny that I am invariably caused to act by my strongest motive? But analysis reveals that the thesis is tautological, immune from refutation, and so devoid of empirical content. For no matter what example of a human action is presented, a defender of the thesis could argue that the person's action resulted from the strongest motive. If I take a swim, taking a swim must have been my strongest motive. If I decide to forgo the swim and read a book instead, then reading a book must have been my strongest motive. How do we know that my motive to read a book was stronger than my motive to take a swim? Because I read a book and did not take a swim. If this line of argument appears powerful, the illusion will last only so long as we do not ask how we are to identify a person's strongest motive. For the only possible answer appears to be that the strongest motive is the motive that prevails, the motive that causes the person to act. If the strongest motive is the motive causing the person to act, what force is there in the claim that the motive causing a person to act is causing the person to act? No insight into the complexities of human action is obtained by trumpeting such an empty redundancy.

Thus, the hard determinist does not so easily succeed in overturning the examples of free actions offered by the libertarian. But both hard and soft determinists have another argument to offer against the libertarian's position. If the libertarian is correct that free actions are uncaused, why do they occur? Are they inexplicable occurrences? If so, to act freely would be to act in a random, chaotic, unintelligible fashion. Yet it is unreasonable to hold people morally blameworthy for inexplicable actions. If you are driving a car and, to your surprise, you find yourself turning the wheel to the right, we can hardly blame you if an accident occurs, for what happened was beyond your control.

So determinists argue that libertarians are caught in a dilemma. If we are caused to do whatever we do, libertarians assert we are not morally responsible for our actions. Yet if our actions are uncaused and inexplicable, libertarians again must deny our moral responsibility. How then can libertarians claim we ever act responsibly?

To understand the libertarian response, consider the simple act of a man's picking up a telephone receiver. Suppose we want to understand what he is doing and are told he is calling his stockbroker. The man has decided to buy some stock and wishes his broker to place the appropriate order. With this explanation, we now know why this man has picked up the telephone. Although we may be interested in learning more about the man or his choice of stocks, we have a complete explanation of his action, which turns out not to be random, chaotic, or unintelligible. We may not know what, if anything, is causing the man to act, but we do know the reason for the man's action. The libertarian thus replies to the determinist's dilemma by arguing that an action can be uncaused yet understandable, explicable in terms of the agent's intentions or purposes.

Now contrast the libertarian's description of a particular action with a determinist's. Let the action be your moving of your arm to adjust your television set. A determinist claims you were caused to move your arm by your desire to adjust the set and your belief that you could make this adjustment by turning the dials. A libertarian claims you moved your arm in order to adjust the set.

Note that the libertarian explains human actions fundamentally differently from the way in which we explain the movements of rocks or rivers. If we speak of a rock's purpose in falling off a cliff or a river's purpose in flowing south, we do so only metaphorically, for we believe that rocks and rivers have no purposes of their own but are caused to do what they do. Strictly speaking, a rock does not fall in order to hit the ground, and a river does not flow in order to reach the south. But libertarians are speaking not metaphorically but literally when they say that people act in order to achieve their purposes. After all, not even the most complex machine can act as a person does. A machine can break down and fail to operate, but only a human being can protest and stop work on purpose.

Is the libertarian's view correct? I doubt anyone is justified in answering that question with certainty, but if the libertarian is right, human beings are often morally responsible for their actions. They deserve praise when acting admirably and blame when acting reprehensibly. Darrow may have been correct in arguing that Leopold and Loeb were not free agents, but if the libertarian is right, the burden of proof lay with Darrow, for he had to demonstrate that these boys were in that respect unlike the rest of us.

But what if the libertarian is not correct? What if all human actions are caused by antecedent conditions, known or unknown, that ensure their occurrence? Then moral responsibility would vanish, but even so people could be held legally responsible for their actions. Just as we need to be safeguarded against mad dogs, so we need protection from dangerous people. Thus, even if no person were morally responsible, we would still have a legal system, courts, criminals, and prisons. Remember that Darrow's eloquence did not free his clients; indeed, he did not ask that they be freed. Although he did not blame them for their actions, he did not want those actions repeated. To Darrow, Leopold and Loeb were sick men who needed the same care as sick persons with a contagious disease. After all, in a world without freedom, events need not be viewed as agreeable; they should, however, be understood as necessary.

NOTES

1. The following information is found in Irving Stone's *Clarence Darrow for the Defense* (Garden City, N.Y.: Doubleday, Doran & Co., Inc., 1941), pp. 384–391.
2. *Attorney for the Damned*, ed. Arthur Weinberg (New York: Simon and Schuster, Inc., 1957), pp. 37, 65.
3. *Ibid.*, p. 37.
4. The expressions "hard determinism" and "soft determinism" were coined by William James in his essay "The Dilemma of Determinism," reprinted in *Essays on Faith and Morals* (Cleveland and New York: The World Publishing Company, 1962).
5. *The Maxims of La Rochefoucauld,* trans. Louis Kronenberger (New York: Random House, 1959), #379.
6. John Hospers, "What Means This Freedom," *Determinism and Freedom in the Age of Modern Science,* ed. Sidney Hook (New York: Collier Books, 1961), p. 138.
7. For a detailed discussion of the philosophical implications of quantum mechanics, see Ernest Nagel's *The Structure of Science* (New York: Harcourt Brace Jovanovich, 1961), ch. 10.
8. A. S. Eddington, *The Nature of the Physical World* (New York: The Macmillan Company, 1928), p. 342.
9. L. Susan Stebbing, *Philosophy and the Physicists* (New York: Dover Publications, Inc., 1958), pp. 51–52.
10. Sir Arthur Conan Doyle, "The Sign of Four," in *The Complete Sherlock Holmes* (Garden City, N.Y.: Doubleday & Company, Inc., n. d.), p. 111.

Free Will and Determinism

W. T. STACE

> In the previous essay I argued that free will and determinism are in-
> compatible, that one or the other is false. Many philosophers, how-
> ever, believe the two theses are compatible and that both are true.
>
> These philosophers are sympathetic to the sort of argument pre-
> sented in our next selection by W. T. Stace (1886–1967), an English-
> man who became Professor of Philosophy at Princeton University
> and President of the American Philosophical Association. He main-
> tains that once we define "free will" properly, any apparent incom-
> patibility with determinism disappears. Whose position is more per-
> suasive I leave for you to decide.

[T]hose learned professors of philosophy or psychology who deny the existence of free will do so only in their professional moments and in their studies and lecture rooms. For when it comes to doing anything practical, even of
the most trivial kind, they invariably behave as if they and others were free.
They inquire from you at dinner whether you will choose this dish or that
dish. They will ask a child why he told a lie, and will punish him for not having chosen the way of truthfulness. All of which is inconsistent with a disbe-
lief in free will. This should cause us to suspect that the problem is not a real
one; and this, I believe, is the case. The dispute is merely verbal, and is due to
nothing but a confusion about the meanings of words. . . .

Throughout the modern period, until quite recently, it was assumed,
both by the philosophers who denied free will and by those who defended it,
that *determinism is inconsistent with free will.* If a man's actions were wholly
determined by chains of causes stretching back into the remote past, so that
they could be predicted beforehand by a mind which knew all the causes, it
was assumed that they could not in that case be free. This implies that a certain definition of actions done from free will was assumed, namely that they
are actions *not* wholly determined by causes or predictable beforehand. Let
us shorten this by saying that free will was defined as meaning indeterminism. This is the incorrect definition which has led to the denial of free will. As
soon as we see what the true definition is we shall find that the question
whether the world is deterministic, as Newtonian science implied, or in a

measure indeterministic, as current physics teaches, is wholly irrelevant to the problem. . . .

At a recent murder trial in Trenton some of the accused had signed confessions, but afterwards asserted that they had done so under police duress. The following exchange might have occurred:

JUDGE: Did you sign this confession of your own free will?

PRISONER: No. I signed it because the police beat me up.

Now suppose that a philosopher had been a member of the jury. We could imagine this conversation taking place in the jury room.

FOREMAN OF THE JURY: The prisoner says he signed the confession because he was beaten, and not of his own free will.

PHILOSOPHER: This is quite irrelevant to the case. There is no such thing as free will.

FOREMAN: Do you mean to say that it makes no difference whether he signed because his conscience made him want to tell the truth or because he was beaten?

PHILOSOPHER: None at all. Whether he was caused to sign by a beating or by some desire of his own—the desire to tell the truth, for example—in either case his signing was causally determined, and therefore in neither case did he act of his own free will. Since there is no such thing as free will, the question whether he signed of his own free will ought not to be discussed by us.

The foreman and the rest of the jury would rightly conclude that the philosopher must be making some mistake. What sort of a mistake could it be? There is only one possible answer. The philosopher must be using the phrase "free will" in some peculiar way of his own which is not the way in which men usually use it. . . .

What, then, is the difference between acts which are freely done and those which are not? . . . The free acts are all caused by desires, or motives, or by some sort of internal psychological states of the agent's mind. The unfree acts, on the other hand, are all caused by physical forces or physical conditions, outside the agent. . . . We may therefore frame the following rough definitions. *Acts freely done are those whose immediate causes are psychological states in the agent. Acts not freely done are those whose immediate causes are states of affairs external to the agent.*

It is plain that if we define free will in this way, then free will certainly exists, and the philosopher's denial of its existence is seen to be what it is— nonsense. For it is obvious that all those actions of men which we should ordinarily attribute to the exercise of their free will, or of which we should say that they freely chose to do them, are in fact actions which have been caused by their own desires, wishes, thoughts, emotions, impulses, or other psychological states.

In applying our definition we shall find that it usually works well, but that there are some puzzling cases which it does not seem exactly to fit. These puzzles can always be solved by paying careful attention to the ways in which words are used, and remembering that they are not always used consistently. I have space for only one example. Suppose that a thug threatens to shoot you unless you give him your wallet, and suppose that you do so. Do you, in giving him your wallet, do so of your own free will or not? If we apply our definition, we find that you acted freely, since the immediate cause of the action was not an actual outside force but the fear of death, which is a psychological cause. Most people, however, would say that you did not act of your own free will but under compulsion. Does this show that our definition is wrong? I do not think so. . . . In the case under discussion, though no actual force was used, the gun at your forehead so nearly approximated to actual force that we tend to say the case was one of compulsion. It is a borderline case.

Here is what may seem like another kind of puzzle. According to our view an action may be free though it could have been predicted beforehand with certainty. But suppose you told a lie, and it was certain beforehand that you would tell it. How could one then say, "You could have told the truth"? The answer is that it is perfectly true that you could have told the truth *if* you had wanted to. In fact you would have done so, for in that case the causes producing your action, namely your desires, would have been different, and would therefore have produced different effects. It is a delusion that predictability and free will are incompatible. This agrees with common sense. For if, knowing your character, I predict that you will act honorably, no one would say when you do act honorably, that this shows you did not do so of your own free will.

Mind and Body

$$\Phi\Phi\Phi\Phi\Phi\Phi\Phi\Phi\Phi\Phi\Phi\Phi\Phi\Phi\Phi\Phi\Phi\Phi\Phi\Phi\Phi\Phi\Phi\Phi\Phi\Phi\Phi\Phi\Phi\Phi\Phi\Phi\Phi\Phi\Phi\Phi\Phi\Phi\Phi\Phi\Phi\Phi\Phi\Phi\Phi$$

RICHARD TAYLOR

One of the central issues in metaphysics is commonly referred to by philosophers as "the mind–body problem." The difficulty is to explain how our minds, our mental processes, are related to our bod-

Metaphysics, 4th edition, by Taylor, R., © 1974. Reprinted by permission of Prentice-Hall, Inc., Upper Saddle River, NJ.

ies, our physical states, and processes. How can a physical object, a body, think, feel, desire, believe, or hope? To put the question differently, are you identical with your body, your mind, or some combination of the two? And if you are a combination of the two, how are they connected?

These issues are explored in the next article by Richard Taylor, Professor Emeritus of Philosophy at the University of Rochester. In addition to his distinguished career as a scholar and teacher of philosophy, he is also renowned internationally for his knowledge of apiculture, the keeping of bees.

1.   Persons and Bodies

However unsure I may be of the nature of myself and of the relation of myself to my body, I can hardly doubt the reality of either. Whether I am identical with my body, or whether I am a spirit, or soul, or perhaps only a collection of thoughts and feelings—whatever I am, I cannot doubt my own being, cannot doubt that I am part of the world, even prior to any philosophical reflection on the matter. For surely if I know anything at all, as presumably I do, then I know that I exist. There seems to be nothing I could possibly know any better. And this is, of course, quite consistent with my great ignorance as to the nature of that self of whose existence I feel so assured.

I know, further, that I have a body. I may have learned this from experience, in the same way that I have learned of the existence of innumerable other things, or I may not have; it is, in any case, something I surely know. I may also have only the vaguest conception, or even a totally erroneous one, of the relationship between myself and my body; I can nevertheless no more doubt the reality of the one than the other. I may also be, as I surely am, quite ignorant of the nature and workings of my body and even of many of its parts, but no such ignorance raises the slightest doubt of its reality.

Now, what is the connection between these, between myself and my body? Just what relationship am I affirming by "have," when I say with such confidence that I have a body? Abstractly, there seem to be just three general possibilities. In the first place, my having a body might consist simply in the *identity* of myself with my body, or of my *being* a body. Or, second, it might amount to *possession,* such that my having a body consists essentially in this body's being among the various other things that I own or possess, it being at the same time, perhaps, in some way unique among these. Or, finally, there may be some special, perhaps highly metaphysical relationship between the two, such as that I as a person am one thing, my body another quite different thing, the two being somehow connected to each other in a special way, appropriately expressed by the assertion that the one *has* the other.

Now there are great difficulties in all these suggestions. . . . We had best, however, begin with the simplest view, to see, then, whether any of the others are any better.

Materialism

I know that I have a body, and that this is a material thing, though a somewhat unusual and highly complicated one. There would, in fact, be no other reason for calling it my body, except to affirm that it is entirely material, for nothing that is not matter could possibly be a part of my body. Now if my having a body consists simply in the identity of myself with my body, then it follows that I *am* this body, and nothing more. Nor would the affirmation of the identity of myself with my body be at all inconsistent with saying that I have a body, for we often express the relationship of identity in just this way. Thus, one might correctly say of a table that it *has* four legs and a top, or of a bicycle that it *has* two wheels, a frame, a seat, and handlebars. In such cases, no one would suppose that the table or the bicycle is one thing, and its parts or "body" another, the two being somehow mysteriously connected. The table or the bicycle just *is* its parts, suitably related. So likewise, I might just *be* the totality of my bodily parts, suitably related and all functioning together in the manner expressed by saying that I am a living body, or a living, material animal organism.

This materialistic conception of a person has the great advantage of simplicity. We do know that there are bodies, that there are living animal bodies, and that some of these are in common speech called *people*. A person is, then, on this view, nothing mysterious or metaphysical, at least as regards the *kind* of thing he or she is.

A consequence of this simplicity is that we need not speculate upon the relationship between one's body and one's mind, or ask how the two are connected, or how one can act upon the other, all such questions being rendered senseless within the framework of this view, which in the first place denies that we are dealing with two things. The death of the animal organism—which is, of course, an empirical fact and not subject to speculation—will, moreover, be equivalent to the destruction of the person, consisting simply in the cessation of those functions that together constitute one's being alive. Hence, the fate of a person is simply, on this view, the fate of his body, which is ultimately a return to the dust whence he sprang. This alleged identity of oneself with one's body accounts, moreover, for the solicitude every person has for his body, and for its health and well-being. If a person is identical with his body, then any threat to the latter is a threat to himself, and he must view the destruction of it as the destruction of himself. And such, in fact, does seem to be everyone's attitude, whatever may be their philosophical or religious opinions. Again, the distinction that everyone draws between himself and other people, or himself and other things, need be no more than the distinction between one body and others. When I declare that some foreign object—a doorknob, for instance, or a shoe—is no part of myself, I may be merely making the point that it is no part of my body. I would, surely, be more hesitant in declaring that my hand, or my brain and nervous system, which are physical objects, are no parts of me.

Such a conception has nevertheless always presented enormous difficulties, and these have seemed so grave to most philosophers that almost any theory, however absurd when examined closely, has at one time or another seemed to them preferable to materialism. Indeed, the difficulties of materialism are so grave that, for some persons, they need only to be mentioned to render the theory unworthy of discussion.

The Meaning of "Identity"

By "identity" the materialist must mean a strict and total identity of himself and his body, nothing less. Now to say of anything, X, and anything, Y, that X and Y are identical, or that they are really one and the same thing, one must be willing to assert of X anything whatever that he asserts of Y, and vice versa. This is simply a consequence of their identity, for if there is anything whatever that can be truly asserted of any object X but cannot be truly asserted of some object Y, then it logically follows that X and Y are two different things, and not the same thing. In saying, for instance, that the British wartime prime minister and Winston Churchill are one and the same person, one commits himself to saying of either whatever he is willing to say of the other—such as that he lived to a great age, smoked cigars, was a resolute leader, was born at Blenheim Palace, and so on. If there were any statement whatever that was true of, say, Mr. Churchill, but not true of the wartime prime minister, then it would follow that Mr. Churchill was not the wartime prime minister, that we are here referring to two different men.

The question can now be asked, then, whether there is anything true of me that is not true of my body, and vice versa. There are, of course, ever so many things that can be asserted indifferently of both me and my body without absurdity. For instance, we can say that I was born at such and such place and time, and it is not the least odd to say this of my body as well. Or we can say that my body now weighs exactly so many pounds, and it would be just as correct to give this as my weight; and so on.

But now consider more problematical assertions. It might, for instance, be true of me at a certain time that I am morally blameworthy or praiseworthy. Can we then say that my body or some part of it, such as my brain, is in exactly the same sense blameworthy or praiseworthy? Can moral predicates be applied without gross incongruity to any physical object at all? Or suppose I have some profound wish or desire, or some thought—the desire, say, to be in some foreign land at a given moment, or to have the thoughts of the Homeric gods. It seems at least odd to assert that my body, or some part of it, wishes that it were elsewhere, or has thoughts of the gods. How, indeed, can any purely physical state of any purely physical object ever be a state that is *for* something, or *of* something, in the way that my desires and thoughts are such? And how, in particular, could a purely physical state be in this sense *for* or *of* something that is not real? Or again, suppose that I am religious and can truly say that I love God and neighbor, for instance. Can I without absurdity say that my body or some part of it, such as my foot or brain, is religious, and loves God and neighbor? Or can one suppose that my being religious, or having such love, consists simply in my body's being in a certain state, or behaving in a certain way? If I claim the identity of myself with my body, I must say all these odd things; that is, I must be willing to assert of my body, or some part of it, everything I assert of myself. There is perhaps no logical absurdity or clear falseness in speaking thus of one's corporeal frame, but such assertions as these are at least strange, and it can be questioned whether, as applied to the body, they are even still meaningful.

The disparity between bodily and personal predicates becomes even more apparent, however, if we consider epistemological predicates involved in statements about belief and knowledge. Thus, if I believe something—believe, for instance, that today is February 31—then I am in a certain state; the state, namely, of having a certain belief, which is in this case necessarily a false one. Now, how can a physical state of any physical object be identical with that? And how, in particular, can anything be a *false* physical state of an object? The physical states of things, it would seem, just *are*, and one cannot even think of anything that could ever distinguish one such state from another as being either true or false. Physiologists might give a complete physical description of a brain and nervous system at a particular time, but they could never distinguish some of those states as true and others as false, nor would they have any idea what to look for if they were asked to do this. At least, so it would certainly seem.

Platonic Dualism

It is this sort of reflection that has always led metaphysicians and theologians to distinguish radically between the mind or soul of a man and his body, ascribing properties to the mind that are utterly different in kind from those exhibited by the body; properties that, it is supposed, could not be possessed by any body, just because of its nature as a physical object.

The simplest and most radical of such views *identifies* the person or self with a soul or mind and declares its relationship to the body to be the almost accidental one of mere occupancy, possession, or use. Thus Plato, and many mystical philosophers before and after him, thought of the body as a veritable prison of the soul, a gross thing of clay from which the soul one day gladly escapes, to live its own independent and untrammeled existence, much as a bird flees its cage or a snake sheds its skin. A person, thus conceived, is a nonmaterial substance—a *spirit*, in the strictest sense—related to an animal body as possessor to thing possessed, tenant to abode, or user to thing used. A person *has* a body only in the sense that he, perhaps temporarily, occupies, owns, or uses a body, being all the while something quite distinct from it and having, perhaps, a destiny quite different from the melancholy one that is known sooner or later to overtake the body.

This dualism of mind and body has been, and always is, firmly received by millions of unthinking people partly because it is congenial to the religious framework in which their everyday metaphysical opinions are formed, and partly, no doubt, because everyone wishes to think of himself as something more than just one more item of matter in the world. Wise philosophers, too, speak easily of the attributes of the mind as distinct from those of the body, thereby sundering the two once and for all. Some form of dualism seems, in fact, indicated by the metaphysical, moral, and epistemological difficulties of materialism, which are, it must be confessed, formidable indeed.

But whatever difficulties such simple dualism may resolve, it appears to raise others equally grave. For one thing, it is not nearly as simple as it seems. Whatever a partisan of such a view might say of the simplicity of the mind or soul, a *person* is nonetheless, on this view, *two* quite disparate things, a mind and a body, each having almost nothing in common and only the flimsiest connection with the other. This difficulty, once it is acutely felt, is usually minimized by conceiving of a person in his true self as nothing but a mind, and representing his body as something ancillary to this true self, something that is not really any part of him at all but only one among the many physical objects that he happens to possess, use, or what not, much as he possesses and uses various other things in life. His body does, to be sure, occupy a preeminent place among such things, for it is something without which he would be quite helpless; but this renders it no more a part or whole of his true self or person than any other of the world's physical things.

Possession, however, is essentially a social concept, and sometimes a strictly legal one. Something counts as one of my possessions by virtue of my title to it, and this is something conferred in accordance with conventions and laws. Thus does a field or a building count as one of my possessions. But a certain animal body, which I identify as mine, is not mine in any sense such as this. My dominion over my body arises from no human conventions or laws and is not alterable by them. The body of a slave, though it may be owned by another man in the fullest sense of ownership that is reflected in the idea of possession, is nevertheless the slave's body in a metaphysical sense. And, in this sense, it could not possibly be the body of his master. One has, moreover, a solicitude for his body wholly incommensurate with his concern for any treasure, however dear. The loss of the latter is regarded as no more than a loss, though perhaps a grave one, while the abolition of one's body cannot be regarded as the mere loss of something dearly held, but is contemplated as an appalling and total calamity.

The ideas of occupancy or use do not express the relation of mind and body any better. *Occupancy,* for instance, is a physical concept; one thing occupies another by being in or upon it. But the mind, on this view, is no physical thing, and no sense can be attached to its resting within or upon any body; the conception is simply ridiculous. Nor do you simply *use* your body the way you use implements and tools. You do, to be sure, sometimes use your limbs and other parts, over which you have voluntary control, in somewhat the manner in which you use tools; but many of your bodily parts, including some that are vital, the very existence of which may be unknown to you, are not within your control at all. They are nonetheless parts of your body. Artificial devices, too, like hearing aids, eyeglasses, and the like, do not in the least become parts of one's body merely by being used, even in the case of someone who can barely do without them. They are merely things worn or used. Nor can you say that your body is that physical being in the world upon which you absolutely depend for your continuing life, for there are many such things. You depend on the sun, for instance, and the air you breathe, and without these you would perish as certainly as if deprived of your heart. Yet no one regards the sun or the air around him as any part of his body.

A person does not, then, *have* a body in the way in which he has anything else at all, and any comparison of the body to a material possession or instrument is about as misleading as likening it to a chamber in which one is more or less temporarily closeted. The connection between yourself and your body is far more intimate and metaphysical than anything else you can think of. One's body is at least a part of himself, and is so regarded by everyone. Yet it is not merely a part, as the arm is part of the body; and we are so far without any hint of how the mind and the body are connected. . . .

2. Interactionism

Because I can hardly deny that I exist, and that I have a body which is at least a part of myself, then I must either affirm the identity of myself with my body, according to the materialistic conception described earlier, or else affirm that I am two things—a mind that has a body and, equally, a body that has a mind. Nothing else is consistent with the data with which we began.

Now, the simplest and most common way of expressing the relation between a body and a mind, so that they together constitute a person, is to say that they interact; that is, they causally act, each upon the other. More fully we can say that while the mind of a person is not a physical thing, events that transpire within it sometimes have causal consequences or effects within the body. Conversely, although the body of a person is clearly not a mental or nonphysical thing, the events that occur within it, particularly within the nervous system and brain, sometimes have causal consequences or effects within the mind or consciousness. The body and mind of an individual person, accordingly, are whatever body and mind are so related. *My* body is that physical object that is within my immediate control, that is, that physical object, alone among all the others in the universe, that events within my mind are capable of affecting directly; and similarly, *my* mind is that mind, among all the others in the universe, that events within my body are capable of affecting directly. This, according to the view we are now considering, is what is meant by saying of a given body that it is mine, or that I *have* a certain body. What *I* am, accordingly, is a certain composite of body and mind that thus interact with each other.

Now, this conception of a person, which is very old and familiar, appears in some measure confirmed by the manner in which we often describe certain of our experiences. Thus, when there is some disorder in my body, such as a severely decayed tooth, or a laceration in the skin, it appears clearly to be the *cause* of a purely subjective, unobservable state called *pain*. And the fact that such a pain is subjective and unobservable to anyone else suggests that it is not, like the decay or the laceration, a state of my body at all, but rather something mental. Thus a dentist can observe the decay, and a physiologist can describe in some detail the changes within my nerves, which are further bodily changes, that this decay gives rise to; but both the dentist and physiologist are necessarily barred from ever observing the pain that is the ultimate effect of these bodily changes, just because it is not, like these, a bodily change at all. Instruments of increasing refinement, such as microscopes and the like, can pick out more and more bodily changes hitherto unobserved. Their inability ever to pick out a pain for observation does not result from their inadequacy as instruments of observation but from metaphysical considerations. A pain cannot, along with physical changes of whatever minuteness, be observed by any devices whatsoever, simply because it is not a physical change at all but a mental one, and for that reason unobservable. The only person who can become aware of a pain or any other state of mind or mental event is that person in whose mind it occurs, and his awareness of it is, of course, immediate. Even he cannot observe it in the same way that he observes any physical object, state, or change, whether in his own body or some other.

Similarly, it is not uncommon to think of purely mental changes having observable effects within the body. Fear, for example, is a subjective mental state that produces perspiration and other bodily changes. Again, the mere thought of food sometimes produces salivation, and some persons' hands can be made to perspire by the mere thought of high places and precarious situations. Voluntary activity, moreover, is often represented as bodily behavior having among its causes one's choices, decisions, intentions, or volitions, and these are psychological in nature and hence unobservable by any outsider. Though someone were able to witness *all* the inner and outer workings of my body, in all its minutest parts, and accurately describe *all* the physical and chemical changes occurring therein, that person could not, it is often alleged, ever pick out one of my volitions or choices. He could see the *effects* of these in the form of gross and subtle bodily changes; but he could not *see* the choices or volitions that cause these effects, simply because they are not bodily changes to begin with. They are changes within the mind, and for that reason metaphysically incapable of being observed.

The Refutation of This

However natural it may seem to conceive a person in such terms, as a dual complex of two wholly disparate things, body and mind, it is nonetheless an impossible conception, on the simplest metaphysical grounds. For on this view, the body and the mind *are* wholly disparate things, so that any bodily change wrought by the mind or by some nonphysical occurrence transpiring therein is a change that lies quite outside the realm of physical law. This means that human behavior is veritably miraculous. Now, some people, reflecting on the old dictum that anything, after all, can cause anything, might be willing to accept this consequence, thus broadly stated, pointing out at the same time that human nature is, after all, somewhat mysterious. Nevertheless, when we come to some precise instance of the alleged interaction of body and mind, as conceived by this theory, we find that we are dealing with something that is not merely mysterious but wholly unintelligible.

Consider some clear and simple case of what would on this theory constitute the action of the mind upon the body. Suppose, for example, that I am dwelling in my thought upon high and precarious places, all the while knowing that I am really safely ensconced in my armchair. I imagine, perhaps, that I am picking my way along a precipice and visualize the destruction that awaits me far below in case I make the smallest slip. Soon, simply as the result of these thoughts and images, which are not for a moment attended by any belief that I am in the slightest danger, perspiration appears on the palms of my hands. Now here is surely a case, if there is any, of something purely mental, unobservable, and wholly outside the realm of physical nature bringing about observable physical changes. We do not have in this situation an instance of physical stimuli from the environment causing physical reactions in the organism, for the actual stimuli are the normal ones of my room and armchair, and these do not change. The only significant change is in my thoughts and images, which are directly in the control of my will and are followed by the physical effect on my hands. Here, then, one wants to say, the mind acts upon the body, producing perspiration.

But what actually happens, alas, is not nearly so simple as this. . . . What is involved is an enormously complex causal chain of physical processes. For each part of this causal chain that is understood, there are doubtless a hundred that are not. The important point, however, is that in describing it as best we can, there is no need, at any stage, to introduce mental or nonphysical substances or reactions. . . .

We know the end result of this chain of physical processes; it is the secretion of perspiration on the hands. We know, more or less, a good many of the intermediate processes. The baffling question that now arises, however, is how such a complex series gets *started*. . . . Presumably, thoughts—that is, ideas or images—occur "within the mind." This must not for a moment be thought to mean that these occur within the brain or any part of it, for they are, according to the view we have been considering, strictly nonphysical entities having no location in space, either within the head or elsewhere, and no physical property whatever that would ever render them susceptible to observation or even to any detection by microscopes, probes, or any other physical apparatus. Yet these nonphysical things do, according to this view, act upon a physical object: the brain. What we must conceive, then, is a physical change within the brain, this change being wrought not by some other physical change in the brain or elsewhere but by an *idea*. We do not know what that physical change in the brain is, but that does not matter so long as it is clearly understood that it is a change of a physical substance, the brain. We can suppose, then, just to get some sort of picture before us, that it is a change consisting of the diffusion of sodium ions into certain of the brain's cells. Conceive, then, if possible, how an *idea* can effect such a change as this, how an idea can render more permeable the membranes of certain brain cells, how an idea can enter into a chemical reaction whose effect is the diffusion of sodium ions at a certain place, or how an idea can move the particles of the cortical cells or otherwise aid or inhibit chemical reactions occurring therein. Try, I say, to form a conception of this, and then confess that, as soon as the smallest attempt at any description is made, the description becomes unintelligible and the conception an impossible one. That compounds should be constituted and decomposed by physical forces and according to physical law, that minute particles of matter should be moved hither or thither by the action upon them of other particles, that a substance should be ionized by an electrical current or by the action of another physical substance—all this is clearly intelligible. But that these same things should be made to happen without any physical substances or physical processes among their causal antecedents, that they should be wrought by something so nebulous as an idea or mental image, by something having no physical property and not even a location, by something that could never enter into the physical description of anything, or into any chemical equation, and in violation of the very physical laws and principles according to which all physical objects such as the brain and its parts operate—that anything like this should happen seems quite unintelligible. It is one thing to say that the mind acts upon the body. But it is quite another thing to give some clear instance of a bodily change and then try to imagine how the mind, or any thought or idea, could in any way be involved in any such change as that. To say that a diffusion of sodium ions was caused by an "idea" is not to give any causal explanation at all. It is, rather, to confess that the explanation of that diffusion is simply not known. . . .

3.   The Mind as a Function of the Body

One thing should by now seem quite plain . . . and that is that the difficulties of simple materialism are not overcome by any form of dualism. There is, therefore, no point in recommending dualism as an improvement over materialism. To assert that a person is both body *and* mind—that is, two things rather than one—not only does not remove any problem involved in saying that he is one thing only, namely, a body, but also introduces all the problems of describing the connection between those two things. We are led to conclude, then, that a metaphysical understanding of human nature must be sought within the framework of materialism, according to which a person is entirely identical with his body.

All forms of dualism arise from the alleged disparity between persons and physical objects. People, it is rightly noted, are capable of thinking, believing, feeling, wishing, and so on, but bodies, it is claimed, are capable of none of these things, and the conclusion is drawn that people are not bodies. Yet it cannot be denied that they *have* bodies; hence, it is decided that a person is a nonphysical entity, somehow more or less intimately related to a body. But here it is rarely noted that whatever difficulties there may be in applying personal and psychological predicates and descriptions to bodies, precisely the same difficulties are involved in applying such predicates and descriptions to *anything whatever,* including spirits or souls. If, for example, a philosopher reasons that a body cannot think and thereby affirms that, since a person thinks, a person is a soul or spirit or mind rather than a body, we are entitled to ask how a spirit can think. For surely if a spirit or soul can think, we can affirm that a body can do so; and if we are asked *how* a body can think, our reply can be that it thinks in precisely the manner in which the dualist supposes a soul thinks. The difficulty of imagining how a body thinks is not in the least lessened by asserting that something else, which is not a body, thinks. And so it is with every other personal predicate or description. Whenever faced with the dualist's challenge to explain how a body can have desires, wishes, how it can deliberate, choose, repent, how it can be intelligent or stupid, virtuous or wicked, and so on, our reply can always be: The body can do these things, and be these things, in whatever manner one imagines the soul can do these things and be these things. For to repeat, the difficulty here is in seeing how *anything at all* can deliberate, choose, repent, think, be virtuous or wicked, and so on, and *that* difficulty is not removed but simply glossed over by the invention of some new thing, henceforth to be called the "mind" or "soul."

It becomes quite obvious what is the source of dualistic metaphysics when the dualist or soul philosopher is pressed for some description of the mind or soul. The mind or soul, it turns out in such descriptions, is just whatever it is that thinks, reasons, deliberates, chooses, feels, and so on. But the fact with which we began was that *human beings* think, reason, deliberate, choose, feel, and so on. And we do in fact have some fairly clear notion of what we mean by a human being, for we think of an individual person as existing in space and time, having a certain height and weight—as a being, in short, having many things in common with other objects in space and time, and particularly with those that are living, i.e., with other animals. But the dualist, noting that a human being is significantly different from other beings, insofar as he, unlike most of them, is capable of thinking, deliberating, choosing, and so on, suddenly asserts that it is not a person, as previously conceived, that does these things at all, but something else, namely, a mind or soul, or something that does not exist in space and time nor have any height and weight, nor have, in fact, any material properties at all. And then when we seek some understanding of what this mind or soul is, we find it simply described as a thing that thinks, deliberates, feels, and so on. But surely the proper inference should have been that people are like all other physical objects in some respects—e.g., in having size, mass, and location in space and time; that they are like some physical objects but unlike others in certain further respects—e.g., in being living, sentient, and so on; and like no other physical objects at all in still other respects—e.g., in being rational, deliberative, and so on. And of course none of this suggests that people are not physical objects, but rather that they are precisely physical objects, like other bodies in some ways, unlike many other bodies in other ways, and unlike any other bodies in still other respects.

The dualist or soul philosopher reasons that since people think, feel, desire, choose, and so on, and since such things cannot be asserted of bodies, then people are not bodies. Reasoning in this fashion, we are forced to the conclusion that people are not bodies—though it is a stubborn fact that they nevertheless *have* bodies. So the great problem then is to connect people, now conceived as souls or minds, to their bodies. But philosophically, it is just exactly as good to reason that, since people think, feel, desire, choose, etc., and since people are bodies—i.e., are living animal organisms having the essential material attributes of weight, size, and so on—then *some* bodies think, feel, desire, choose, etc. This argument is just as good as the dualist's argument and does not lead us into a morass of problems concerning the connection between soul and body.

Death

◈◈◈

THOMAS NAGEL

Many who approach the study of philosophy for the first time assume that the subject will focus on such overarching themes as the meaning of life or the inevitability of tragedy. These readers may be disappointed to find that most often philosophers concentrate on far more specific and technical issues, seemingly remote from personal outlooks on the human condition.

But from time to time philosophers do address questions of ultimate concern, and what follows is an example. The author is Thomas Nagel (no relation to Ernest Nagel), Professor of Philosophy at New York University. He considers how the mind–body problem relates to a matter that concerns each of us deeply: the nature and significance of death.

Everybody dies, but not everybody agrees about what death is. Some believe they will survive after the death of their bodies, going to Heaven or Hell or somewhere else, becoming a ghost, or returning to Earth in a different body, perhaps not even as a human being. Others believe they will cease to exist—that the self is snuffed out when the body dies. And among those who believe they will cease to exist, some think this is a terrible fact, and others don't.

It is sometimes said that no one can conceive of his own nonexistence, and that therefore we can't really believe that our existence will come to an end with our deaths. But this doesn't *seem true*. Of course you can't conceive of your own nonexistence *from the inside*. You can't conceive of what it would be like to be totally annihilated, because there's nothing it would be like, from the inside. But in that sense, you can't conceive of what it would be like to be completely unconscious, even temporarily. The fact that you can't conceive of that from the inside doesn't mean you can't conceive of it at all: you just have to think of yourself from the outside, having been knocked out, or in a deep sleep. And even though you have to be conscious to *think* that, it doesn't mean that you're thinking *of* yourself as conscious.

It's the same with death. To imagine your own annihilation you have to think of it from the outside—think about the body of the person you are, with all the life and experience gone from it. To imagine something it is not necessary to imagine how it would feel for *you* to experience it. When you imagine your own funeral, you are not imagining the impossible situation of being *present* at your own funeral: you're imagining how it would look through someone else's eyes. Of course you are alive while you think of your own death, but that is no more of a problem than being conscious while imagining yourself unconscious.

The question of survival after death is related to the mind–body problem. . . . If dualism is true, and each person consists of a soul and a body connected together, we can understand how life after death might be possible. The soul would have to be able to exist on its own and have a mental life without the help of the body: then it might leave the body when the body dies, instead of being destroyed. It wouldn't be able to have the kind of mental life of action and sensory perception that depends on being attached to the body (unless it got attached to a new body), but it might have a different sort of inner life, perhaps depending on different causes and influences—direct communication with other souls, for instance.

I say life after death *might* be possible if dualism were true. It also might not be possible, because the survival of the soul, and its continued consciousness, might depend entirely on the support and stimulation it gets from the body in which it is housed—and it might not be able to switch bodies.

But if dualism is not true, and mental processes go on in the brain and are entirely dependent on the biological functioning of the brain and the rest of the organism, then life after death of the body is not possible. Or to put it more exactly, mental life after death would require the restoration of biological, physical life: it would require that the *body* come to life again. This might become technically possible some day: It may become possible to freeze people's bodies when they die, and then later on by advanced medical procedures to fix whatever was the matter with them, and bring them back to life.

Even if this became possible, there would still be a question whether the person who was brought to life several centuries later would be you or somebody else. Maybe if you were frozen after death and your body was later revived, *you* wouldn't wake up, but only someone very like you, with memories of your past life. But even if revival after death of the same you in the same body should become possible, that's not what's ordinarily meant by life after death. Life after death usually means life without your old body.

It's hard to know how we could decide whether we have separable souls. All the evidence is that *before* death, conscious life depends entirely on what happens in the nervous system. If we go only by ordinary observation, rather than religious doctrines or spiritualist claims to communicate with the dead, there is no reason to believe in an afterlife. Is that, however, a reason to believe that there is *not* an afterlife? I think so, but others may prefer to remain neutral.

Still others may believe in an afterlife on the basis of faith, in the absence of evidence. I myself don't fully understand how this kind of faith-inspired belief is possible, but evidently some people can manage it, and even find it natural.

Let me turn to the other part of the problem: how we ought to *feel* about death. Is it a good thing, a bad thing, or neutral? I am talking about how it's reasonable to feel about your own death—not so much about other people's. Should you look forward to the prospect of death with terror, sorrow, indifference, or relief?

Obviously it depends on what death is. If there is life after death, the prospect will be grim or happy depending on where your soul will end up. But the difficult and most philosophically interesting question is how we should feel about death if it's the end. Is it a terrible thing to go out of existence?

People differ about this. Some say that non-existence, being nothing at all, can't possibly be either good or bad for the dead person. Others say that to be annihilated, to have the possible future course of your life cut off completely, is the ultimate evil, even if we all have to face it. Still others say death is a blessing—not of course if it comes too early, but eventually—because it would be unbearably boring to live forever.

If death without anything after it is either a good or a bad thing for the person who dies, it must be a *negative* good or evil. Since in itself it is nothing, it can't be either pleasant or unpleasant. If it's good, that must be because it is the absence of something bad (like boredom or pain); if it's bad, that must be because it is the absence of something good (like interesting or pleasant experiences).

Now it might seem that death can't have any value, positive or negative, because someone who doesn't exist can't be either benefited or harmed: after all, even a *negative* good or evil has to happen to *somebody*. But on reflection, this is not really a problem. We can say that the person who *used* to exist has been benefited or harmed by death. For instance, suppose he is trapped in a burning building, and a beam falls on his head, killing him instantly. As a result, he doesn't suffer the agony of being burned to death. It seems that in that case we can say he was lucky to be killed painlessly, because it avoided something worse. Death at that time was a negative good, because it saved him from the positive evil he would otherwise have suffered for the next five minutes. And the fact that he's not around to enjoy that negative good doesn't mean it's not a good for him at all. "Him" means the person who was alive, and who would have suffered if he hadn't died.

The same kind of thing could be said about death as a negative evil. When you die, all the good things in your life come to a stop: no more meals, movies, travel, conversation, love, work, books, music, or anything else. If those things would be good, their absence is bad. Of course you won't *miss* them: death is not like being locked up in solitary confinement. But the ending of everything good in life, because of the stopping of life itself, seems clearly to be a negative evil for the person who was alive and is now dead. When someone we know dies, we feel sorry not only for ourselves but for him, because he can't see the sun shine today, or smell the bread in the toaster.

When you think of your own death, the fact that all the good things in life will come to an end is certainly a reason for regret. But that doesn't seem to be the whole story. Most people want there to be more of what they enjoy in life, but for some people, the prospect of nonexistence is itself frightening, in a way that isn't adequately explained by what has been said so far. The thought that the world will go on without you, that you will become *nothing*, is very hard to take in.

It's not clear why. We all accept the fact that there was a time before we were born, when we didn't yet exist—so why should we be so disturbed at the prospect of nonexistence after our death? But somehow it doesn't feel the same. The prospect of nonexistence is frightening, at least to many people, in a way that past nonexistence cannot be.

The fear of death is very puzzling, in a way that regret about the end of life is not. It's easy to understand that we might want to have more life, more of the things it contains, so that we see death as a negative evil. But how can the *prospect* of your own nonexistence be alarming in a positive way? If we really cease to exist at death, there's nothing to look forward to, so how can there be anything to be afraid of? If one thinks about it logically, it seems as though death should be something to be afraid of only if we *will* survive it, and perhaps undergo some terrifying transformation. But that doesn't prevent many people from thinking that annihilation is one of the worst things that could happen to them.

Meno

❖❖

PLATO

Plato was an Athenian, born into an aristocratic family. After coming under the influence of Socrates, Plato gave up his ambition for a career in politics and devoted himself to philosophy. When Socrates was executed, Plato withdrew from Athens, traveled in Italy, Sicily, and perhaps Egypt, and eventually returned home to found his Academy, the school where he lectured and wrote for nearly forty years.

Plato's works consist entirely of dialogues, commonly classified as early, middle, and late, although the chronology is open to scholarly disagreement. The *Meno,* which is usually considered to be from the middle period, serves as an excellent introduction to Plato's thought, combining many Platonic themes in accessible form. Indeed, our translator, W. K. C. Guthrie, who taught at the University of Cambridge, refers to the *Meno* as "a microcosm of the whole series of Plato's dialogues."

The extent to which the historical Socrates espoused the views attributed to the character "Socrates" in Plato's dialogues is a matter of long-standing controversy. What is widely agreed is that the historical Socrates was concerned with the search for definitions of such concepts as "virtue" and "piety," and that he defended the thesis that those who know what is good will do what is good. However, the immortality of the soul as well as other positive metaphysical and epistemological doctrines found in the middle and late dialogues appear Platonic rather than Socratic in origin.

As you read the dialogue, you may become impatient with Meno's replies and wonder why he doesn't give better answers to Socrates' questions. I like to suppose that when Plato heard Socrates' questions to such as Meno, Plato, too, thought better answers could be given and proposed his own. When Socrates raised difficulties with them, Plato offered further responses, and soon he had joined his teacher in the search for wisdom. By ourselves suggesting improvements in Meno's replies, we thereby extend the tradition of philosophical inquiry that is Socrates' greatest legacy.

MENO: Can you tell me, Socrates—is virtue something that can be taught? Or does it come by practice? Or is it neither teaching nor practice that gives it to a man but natural aptitude or something else?[1]

SOCRATES: Well, Meno, in the old days the Thessalians had a great reputation among the Greeks for their wealth and their horsemanship. Now it seems they are philosophers as well—especially the men of Larissa, where your friend Aristippus comes from. It is Gorgias[2] who has done it. He went to that city and captured the hearts of the foremost of the Aleuadae for his wisdom (among them your own admirer Aristippus), not to speak of other leading Thessalians. In particular he got you into the habit of answering any question you might be asked, with the confidence and dignity appropriate to those who know the answers, just as he himself invites questions of every kind from anyone in the Greek world who wishes to ask, and never fails to answer them. But here at Athens, my dear Meno, it is just the reverse. There is a dearth of wisdom, and it looks as if it had migrated from our part of the country to yours. At any rate if you put your question to any of our people, they will all alike laugh and say: "You must think I am singularly fortunate, to know whether virtue can be taught or how it is acquired. The fact is that far from knowing whether it can be taught, I have no idea what virtue itself is."

That is my own case. I share the poverty of my fellow-countrymen in this respect, and confess to my shame that I have no knowledge about virtue at all. And how can I know a property of something when I don't even know what it is? Do you suppose that somebody entirely ignorant who Meno is could say whether he is handsome and rich and well-born or the reverse? Is that possible, do you think?

MENO: No. But is this true about yourself, Socrates, that you don't even know what virtue is? Is this the report that we are to take home about you?

SOCRATES: Not only that; you may say also that, to the best of my belief, I have never yet met anyone who did know.

MENO: What! Didn't you meet Gorgias when he was here?

SOCRATES: Yes.

MENO: And you still didn't think he knew?

SOCRATES: I'm a forgetful sort of person, and I can't say just now what I thought at the time. Probably he did know, and I expect you know what he used to say about it. So remind me what it was, or tell me yourself if you will. No doubt you agree with him.

MENO: Yes I do.

SOCRATES: Then let's leave him out of it, since after all he isn't here. What do you yourself say virtue is? I do ask you in all earnestness not to refuse me, but to speak out. I shall be only too happy to be proved wrong if you and Gorgias turn out to know this, although I said I had never met anyone who did.

MENO: But there is no difficulty about it. First of all, if it is manly virtue you are after, it is easy to see that the virtue of a man consists in managing the city's affairs capably, and so that he will help his friends and injure his foes while taking care to come to no harm himself. Or if you want a woman's virtue, that is easily described. She must be a good housewife, careful with her stores and obedient to her husband. Then there is another virtue for a child, male or female, and another for an old man, free or slave as you like; and a great many more kinds of virtue, so that no one need be at a loss to say what it is. For every act and every time of life, with reference to each separate function, there is a virtue for each one of us, and similarly, I should say, a vice.

SOCRATES: I seem to be in luck. I wanted one virtue and I find that you have a whole swarm of virtues to offer. But seriously, to carry on this metaphor of the swarm, suppose I asked you what a bee is, what is its essential nature, and you replied that bees were of many different kinds, what would you say if I went on to ask: "And is it in being bees that they are many and various and different from one another? Or would you agree that it is not in this respect that they differ, but in something else, some other quality like size or beauty?"

MENO: I should say that in so far as they are bees, they don't differ from one another at all.

SOCRATES: Suppose I then continued: "Well, this is just what I want you to tell me. What is that character in respect of which they don't differ at all, but are all the same?" I presume you would have something to say?

MENO: I should.

SOCRATES: Then do the same with the virtues. Even if they are many and various, yet at least they all have some common character which makes them virtues. That is what ought to be kept in view by anyone who answers the question: "What is virtue?" Do you follow me?

MENO: I think I do, but I don't yet really grasp the question as I should wish.

SOCRATES: Well, does this apply in your mind only to virtue, that there is a different one for a man and a woman and the rest? Is it the same with health and size and strength, or has health the same character everywhere, if it is health, whether it be in a man or any other creature?

MENO: I agree that health is the same in a man or in a woman.

SOCRATES: And what about size and strength? If a woman is strong, will it be the same thing, the same strength, that makes her strong? My meaning is that in its character as strength, it is no different, whether it be in a man or in a woman. Or do you think it is?

MENO: No.

SOCRATES: And will virtue differ, in its character as virtue, whether it be in a child or an old man, a woman or a man?

MENO: I somehow feel that this is not on the same level as the other cases.

SOCRATES: Well then, didn't you say that a man's virtue lay in directing the city well, and a woman's in directing her household well?

MENO: Yes.

SOCRATES: And is it possible to direct anything well—city or household or anything else—if not temperately and justly?

MENO: Certainly not.

SOCRATES: And that means with temperance and justice?

MENO: Of course.

SOCRATES: Then both man and woman need the same qualities, justice and temperance, if they are going to be good.

MENO: It looks like it.

SOCRATES: And what about your child and old man? Could they be good if they were incontinent and unjust?

MENO: Of course not.

SOCRATES: They must be temperate and just?

MENO: Yes.

SOCRATES: So everyone is good in the same way, since they become good by possessing the same qualities.

MENO: So it seems.

SOCRATES: And if they did not share the same virtue, they would not be good in the same way.

MENO: No.

SOCRATES: Seeing then that they all have the same virtue, try to remember and tell me what Gorgias, and you who share his opinion, say it is.

MENO: It must be simply the capacity to govern men, if you are looking for one quality to cover all the instances.

SOCRATES: Indeed I am. But does this virtue apply to a child or a slave? Should a slave be capable of governing his master, and if he does, is he still a slave?

MENO: I hardly think so.

SOCRATES: It certainly doesn't sound likely. And here is another point. You speak of "capacity to govern." Shall we not add "justly but not otherwise"?

MENO: I think we should, for justice is virtue.

SOCRATES: Virtue, do you say, or *a* virtue?

MENO: What do you mean?

SOCRATES: Something quite general. Take roundness, for instance. I should say that it is a shape, not simply that it is shape, my reason being that there are other shapes as well.

MENO: I see your point, and I agree that there are other virtues besides justice.

SOCRATES: Tell me what they are. Just as I could name other shapes if you told me to, in the same way mention some other virtues.

MENO: In my opinion then courage is a virtue and temperance and wisdom and dignity and many other things.

SOCRATES: This puts us back where we were. In a different way we have discovered a number of virtues when we were looking for one only. This single virtue, which permeates each of them, we cannot find.

MENO: No, I cannot yet grasp it as you want, a single virtue covering them all, as I do in other instances.

SOCRATES: I'm not surprised, but I shall do my best to get us a bit further if I can. You understand, I expect, that the question applies to everything. If someone took the example I mentioned just now, and asked you: "What is shape?" and you replied that roundness is shape, and he then asked you as I did, "Do you mean it is shape or *a* shape?" you would reply of course that it is *a* shape.

MENO: Certainly.

SOCRATES: Your reason being that there are other shapes as well.

MENO: Yes.

SOCRATES: And if he went on to ask you what they were, you would tell him.

MENO: Yes.

SOCRATES: And the same with colour—if he asked you what it is, and on your replying "White," took you up with: "Is white colour or *a* colour?" you would say that it is *a* colour, because there are other colours as well.

MENO: I should.

SOCRATES: And if he asked you to, you would mention other colours which are just as much colours as white is.

MENO: Yes.

SOCRATES: Suppose then he pursued the question as I did, and objected: "We always arrive at a plurality, but that is not the kind of answer I want. Seeing that you call these many particulars by one and the same name, and say that every one of them is a shape, even though they are the contrary of each other, tell me what this is which embraces round as well as straight, and what you mean by shape when you say that straightness is a shape as much as roundness. You do say that?"

MENO: Yes.

SOCRATES: "And in saying it, do you mean that roundness is no more round than straight, and straightness no more straight than round?"

MENO: Of course not.

SOCRATES: "Yet you do say that roundness is no more a shape than straightness, and the other way about."

MENO: Quite true.

SOCRATES: "Then what is this thing which is called 'shape'? Try to tell me." If when asked this question either about shape or colour you said: "But I don't understand what you want, or what you mean," your questioner would perhaps be surprised and say: "Don't you see that I am looking for what is the same in all of them?" Would you even so be unable to reply, if the question was: "What is it that is common to roundness and straightness and the other things which you call shapes?" Do your best to answer, as practice for the question about virtue.

MENO: No, you do it, Socrates.

SOCRATES: Do you want me to give in to you?

MENO: Yes.

SOCRATES: And will you in your turn give me an answer about virtue?

MENO: I will.

SOCRATES: In that case I must do my best. It's in a good cause.

MENO: Certainly.

SOCRATES: Well now, let's try to tell you what shape is. See if you accept this definition. Let us define it as the only thing which always accompanies colour. Does that satisfy you, or do you want it in some other way? I should be content if your definition of virtue were on similar lines.

MENO: But that's a naïve sort of definition, Socrates.

SOCRATES: How?

MENO: Shape, if I understand what you say, is what always accompanies colour. Well and good—but if somebody says that he doesn't know what colour is, but is no better off with it than he is with shape, what sort of answer have you given him, do you think?

SOCRATES: A true one; and if my questioner were one of the clever, disputatious and quarrelsome kind, I should say to him: "You have heard my answer. If it is wrong, it is for you to take up the argument and refute it." However, when friendly people, like you and me, want to converse with each other, one's reply must be milder and more conducive to discussion. By that I mean that it must not only be true, but must employ terms with which the questioner admits he is familiar. So I will try to answer you like that. Tell me therefore, whether you recognize the term "end"; I mean limit or boundary—all these words I use in the same sense. Prodicus[3] might perhaps quarrel with us, but I assume you speak of something being bounded or coming to an end. That is all I mean, nothing subtle.

MENO: I admit the notion, and believe I understand your meaning.

SOCRATES: And again, you recognize "surface" and "solid," as they are used in geometry?

MENO: Yes.

SOCRATES: Then with these you should by this time understand my definition of shape. To cover all its instances, I say that shape is that in which a solid terminates, or more briefly, it is the limit of a solid.

MENO: And how do you define colour?

SOCRATES: What a shameless fellow you are, Meno. You keep bothering an old man to answer, but refuse to exercise your memory and tell me what was Gorgias's definition of virtue.

MENO: I will, Socrates, as soon as you tell me this.

SOCRATES: Anyone talking to you could tell blindfold that you are a handsome man and still have your admirers.

MENO: Why so?

SOCRATES: Because you are for ever laying down the law as spoilt boys do, who act the tyrant as long as their youth lasts. No doubt you have discovered that I can never resist good looks. Well, I will give in and let you have your answer.

MENO: Do by all means.

SOCRATES: Would you like an answer à la Gorgias, such as you would most readily follow?

MENO: Of course I should.

SOCRATES: You and he believe in Empedocles's theory of effluences, do you not?[4]

MENO: Whole-heartedly.

SOCRATES: And passages to which and through which the effluences make their way?

MENO: Yes.

SOCRATES: Some of the effluences fit into some of the passages, whereas others are too coarse or too fine.

MENO: That is right.

SOCRATES: Now you recognize the term "sight"?

MENO: Yes.

SOCRATES: From these notions, then, "grasp what I would tell," as Pindar says.[5] Colour is an effluence from shapes commensurate with sight and perceptible by it.

MENO: That seems to me an excellent answer.

SOCRATES: No doubt it is the sort you are used to. And you probably see that it provides a way to define sound and smell and many similar things.

MENO: So it does.

SOCRATES: Yes, it's a high-sounding answer, so you like it better than the one on shape.

MENO: I do.

SOCRATES: Nevertheless, son of Alexidemus, I am convinced that the other is better; and I believe you would agree with me if you had not, as you told me yesterday, to leave before the mysteries, but could stay and be initiated.[6]

MENO: I would stay, Socrates, if you gave me more answers like this.

SOCRATES: You may be sure I shan't be lacking in keenness to do so, both for your sake and mine; but I'm afraid I may not be able to do it often. However, now it is your turn to do as you promised, and try to tell me the general nature of virtue. Stop making many out of one, as the humorists say when somebody breaks a plate. Just leave virtue whole and sound and tell me what it is, as in the examples I have given you.

MENO: It seems to me then, Socrates, that virtue is, in the words of the poet, "to rejoice in the fine and have power," and I define it as desiring fine things and being able to acquire them.

SOCRATES: When you speak of a man desiring fine things, do you mean it is good things he desires?

MENO: Certainly.

SOCRATES: Then do you think some men desire evil and others good? Doesn't everyone, in your opinion, desire good things?

MENO: No.

SOCRATES: And would you say that the others suppose evils to be good, or do they still desire them although they recognize them as evil?

MENO: Both, I should say.

SOCRATES: What? Do you really think that anyone who recognizes evils for what they are, nevertheless desires them?

MENO: Yes.

SOCRATES: Desires in what way? To possess them?

MENO: Of course.

SOCRATES: In the belief that evil things bring advantage to their possessor, or harm?

MENO: Some in the first belief, but some also in the second.

SOCRATES: And do you believe that those who suppose evil things bring advantage understand that they are evil?

MENO: No, that I can't really believe.

SOCRATES: Isn't it clear then this class, who don't recognize evils for what they are, don't desire evil but what they think is good, though in fact it is evil; those who through ignorance mistake bad things for good obviously desire the good.

MENO: For them I suppose that is true.

SOCRATES: Now as for those whom you speak of as desiring evils in the belief that they do harm to their possessor, these presumably know that they will be injured by them?

MENO: They must.

SOCRATES: And don't they believe that whoever is injured is, insofar as he is injured, unhappy?

MENO: That too they must believe.

SOCRATES: And unfortunate?

MENO: Yes.

SOCRATES: Well, does anybody want to be unhappy and unfortunate?

MENO: I suppose not.

SOCRATES: Then if not, nobody desires what is evil; for what else is unhappiness but desiring evil things and getting them?

MENO: It looks as if you are right, Socrates, and nobody desires what is evil.

SOCRATES: Now you have just said that virtue consists in a wish for good things plus the power to acquire them. In this definition the wish is common to everyone, and in that respect no one is better than his neighbour.

MENO: So it appears.

SOCRATES: So if one man is better than another, it must evidently be in respect of the power, and virtue, according to your account, is the power of acquiring good things.

MENO: Yes, my opinion is exactly as you now express it.

SOCRATES: Let us see whether you have hit the truth this time. You may well be right. The power of acquiring good things, you say, is virtue?

MENO: Yes.

SOCRATES: And by good do you mean such things as health and wealth?

MENO: I include the gaining both of gold and silver and of high and honourable office in the State.

SOCRATES: Are these the only classes of goods that you recognize?

MENO: Yes, I mean everything of that sort.

SOCRATES: Right. In the definition of Meno, hereditary guest-friend of the great king, the acquisition of gold and silver is virtue. Do you add "just and righteous" to the word "acquisition," or doesn't it make any difference to you? Do you call it virtue all the same even if they are unjustly acquired?

MENO: Certainly not.

SOCRATES: Vice then?

MENO: Most certainly.

SOCRATES: So it seems that justice or temperance or piety, or some other part of virtue, must attach to the acquisition. Otherwise, although it is a means to good things, it will not be virtue.

MENO: No, how could you have virtue without these?

SOCRATES: In fact lack of gold and silver, if it results from failure to acquire it—either for oneself or another—in circumstances which would have made its acquisition unjust, it itself virtue.

MENO: It would seem so.

SOCRATES: Then to have such goods is no more virtue than to lack them. Rather we may say that whatever is accompanied by justice is virtue, whatever is without qualities of that sort is vice.

MENO: I agree that your conclusion seems inescapable.

SOCRATES: But a few minutes ago we called each of these—justice, temperance, and the rest—a part of virtue?

MENO: Yes, we did.

SOCRATES: So it seems you are making a fool of me.

MENO: How so, Socrates?

SOCRATES: I have just asked you not to break virtue up into fragments, and given you models of the type of answer I wanted, but taking no notice of this you tell me that virtue consists in the acquisition of good things with justice; and justice, you agree, is a part of virtue.

MENO: True.

SOCRATES: So it follows from your own statements that to act with a part of virtue is virtue, if you call justice and all the rest parts of virtue. The point I want to make is that whereas I asked you to give me an account of virtue as a whole, far from telling me what it is itself you say that every action is virtue which exhibits a part of virtue as if you had already told me what the whole is, so that I should recognize it even if you chop it up into bits. It seems to me that we must put the same old question to you, my dear Meno—the question: "What is virtue?"—if every act becomes virtue when combined with a part of virtue. That is, after all, what it means to say that every act performed with justice is virtue. Don't you agree that the same question needs to be put? Does anyone know what a part of virtue is, without knowing the whole?

MENO: I suppose not.

SOCRATES: No, and if you remember, when I replied to you about shape just now, I believe we rejected the type of answer that employs terms which are still in question and not yet agreed upon.

MENO: We did, and rightly.

SOCRATES: Then please do the same. While the nature of virtue as a whole is still under question, don't suppose that you can explain it to anyone in terms of its parts, or by any similar type of explanation. Understand rather that the same question remains to be answered; you say this and that about virtue, but what *is* it? Does this seem nonsense to you?

MENO: No, to me it seems right enough.

SOCRATES: Then go back to the beginning and answer my question. What do you and your friend say that virtue is?

MENO: Socrates, even before I met you they told me that in plain truth you are a perplexed man yourself and reduce others to perplexity. At this moment I feel you are exercising magic and witchcraft upon me and positively laying me under your spell until I am just a mass of helplessness. If I may be flippant, I think that not only in outward appearance but in other respects as well you are exactly like the flat sting-ray that one meets in the sea.[7] Whenever anyone comes into contact with it, it numbs him, and that is the sort of thing that you seem to be doing to me now. My mind and my lips are literally numb, and I have nothing to reply to you. Yet I have spoken about virtue hundreds of times, held forth often on the subject in front of large audiences, and very well too, or so I thought. Now I can't even say what it is. In my opinion you are well advised not to leave Athens and live abroad. If you behaved like this as a foreigner in another country, you would most likely be arrested as a wizard.

SOCRATES: You're a real rascal, Meno. You nearly took me in.

MENO: Just what do you mean?

SOCRATES: I see why you used a simile about me.

MENO: Why, do you think?

SOCRATES: To be compared to something in return. All good-looking people, I know perfectly well, enjoy a game of comparisons. They get the best of it, for naturally handsome folk provoke handsome similes. But

I'm not going to oblige you. As for myself, if the sting-ray paralyses others only through being paralysed itself, then the comparison is just, but not otherwise. It isn't that, knowing the answers myself, I perplex other people. The truth is rather that I infect them also with the perplexity I feel myself. So with virtue now. I don't know what it is. You may have known before you came into contact with me, but now you look as if you don't. Nevertheless I am ready to carry out, together with you, a joint investigation and inquiry into what it is.

MENO: But how will you look for something when you don't in the least know what it is? How on earth are you going to set up something you don't know as the object of your search? To put it another way, even if you come right up against it, how will you know that what you have found is the thing you didn't know?

SOCRATES: I know what you mean. Do you realize that what you are bringing up is the trick argument that a man cannot try to discover either what he knows or what he does not know? He would not seek what he knows, for since he knows it there is no need of the inquiry, nor what he does not know, for in that case he does not even know what he is to look for.

MENO: Well, do you think it a good argument?

SOCRATES: No.

MENO: Can you explain how it fails?

SOCRATES: I can. I have heard from men and women who understand the truths of religion—

[*Here he presumably pauses to emphasize the solemn change of tone which the dialogue undergoes at this point.*]

MENO: What did they say?

SOCRATES: Something true, I thought, and fine.

MENO: What was it, and who were they?

SOCRATES: Those who tell it are priests and priestesses of the sort who make it their business to be able to account for the functions which they perform. Pindar speaks of it too, and many another of the poets who are divinely inspired. What they say is this—see whether you think they are speaking the truth. They say that the soul of man is immortal: at one time it comes to an end—that which is called death—and at another is born again, but is never finally exterminated. On these grounds a man must live all his days as righteously as possible. For those from whom

Persephone receives requital for ancient doom,
In the ninth year she restores again
Their souls to the sun above.
From whom rise noble kings

And the swift in strength and greatest in wisdom;
And for the rest of time
They are called heroes and sanctified by men.[8]

Thus the soul, since it is immortal and has been born many times, and has seen all things both here and in the other world, has learned everything that is. So we need not be surprised if it can recall the knowledge of virtue or anything else which, as we see, it once possessed. All nature is akin, and the soul has learned everything, so that when a man has recalled a single piece of knowledge—*learned* it, in ordinary language—there is no reason why he should not find out all the rest, if he keeps a stout heart and does not grow weary of the search; for seeking and learning are in fact nothing but recollection.[9]

We ought not then to be led astray by the contentious argument you quoted. It would make us lazy, and is music in the ears of weaklings. The other doctrine produces energetic seekers after knowledge; and being convinced of its truth, I am ready, with your help, to inquire into the nature of virtue.

MENO: I see, Socrates. But what do you mean when you say that we don't learn anything, but that what we call learning is recollection? Can you teach me that it is so?

SOCRATES: I have just said that you're a rascal, and now you ask me if I can teach you, when I say there is no such thing as teaching, only recollection. Evidently you want to catch me contradicting myself straight away.

MENO: No, honestly, Socrates, I wasn't thinking of that. It was just habit. If you can in any way make clear to me that what you say is true, please do.

SOCRATES: It isn't an easy thing, but still I should like to do what I can since you ask me. I see you have a large number of retainers here. Call one of them, anyone you like, and I will use him to demonstrate it to you.

MENO: Certainly. (*To a slave-boy.*) Come here.

SOCRATES: He is a Greek and speaks our language?

MENO: Indeed yes—born and bred in the house.

SOCRATES: Listen carefully then, and see whether it seems to you that he is learning from me or simply being reminded.

MENO: I will.

SOCRATES: Now boy, you know that a square is a figure like this?

(*Socrates begins to draw figures in the sand at his feet. He points to the square* ABCD.)

BOY: Yes.

SOCRATES: It has all these four sides equal?

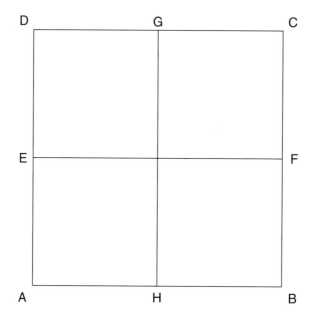

BOY: Yes.

SOCRATES: And these lines which go through the middle of it are also equal? (The lines EF, GH.)

BOY: Yes.

SOCRATES: Such a figure could be either larger or smaller, could it not?

BOY: Yes.

SOCRATES: Now if this side is two feet long, and this side the same, how many feet will the whole be? Put it this way. If it were two feet in this direction and only one in that, must not the area be two feet taken once?

BOY: Yes.

SOCRATES: But since it is two feet this way also, does it not become twice two feet?

BOY: Yes.

SOCRATES: And how many feet is twice two? Work it out and tell me.

BOY: Yes.

SOCRATES: Now could one draw another figure double the size of this, but similar, that is, with all its sides equal like this one?

BOY: Yes.

SOCRATES: How many feet will its area be?

BOY: Eight.

SOCRATES: Now then, try to tell me how long each of its sides will be. The present figure has a side of two feet. What will be the side of the double-sized one?[10]

BOY: It will be double, Socrates, obviously.

SOCRATES: You see, Meno, that I am not teaching him anything, only asking. Now he thinks he knows the length of the side of the eight-feet square.

MENO: Yes.

SOCRATES: But does he?

MENO: Certainly not.

SOCRATES: He thinks it is twice the length of the other.

MENO: Yes.

SOCRATES: Now watch how he recollects things in order—the proper way to recollect.

You say that the side of double length produces the double-sized figure? Like this I mean, not long this way and short that. It must be equal on all sides like the first figure, only twice its size, that is eight feet. Think a moment whether you still expect to get it from doubling the side.

BOY: Yes, I do.

SOCRATES: Well now, shall we have a line double the length of this (AB) if we add another the same length at this end (BJ)?

BOY: Yes.

SOCRATES: It is on this line then, according to you, that we shall make the eight-feet square, by taking four of the same length?

BOY: Yes.

SOCRATES: Let us draw in four equal lines (*i.e., counting* AJ, *and adding* JK, KL, *and* LA *made complete by drawing in its second half* LD), using the first as a base. Does this not give us what you call the eight-feet figure?

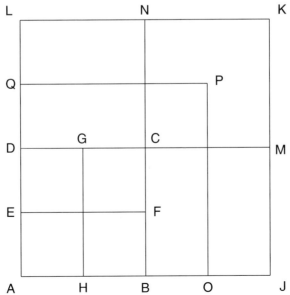

BOY: Certainly.

SOCRATES: But does it contain these four squares, each equal to the original four-feet one?

> (*Socrates has drawn in the lines* CM, CN *to complete the squares that he wishes to point out.*)

BOY: Yes.

SOCRATES: How big is it then? Won't it be four times as big?

BOY: Of course.

SOCRATES: And is four times the same as twice?

BOY: Of course not.

SOCRATES: So doubling the side has given us not a double but a fourfold figure?

BOY: True.

SOCRATES: And four times four are sixteen, are they not?

BOY: Yes.

SOCRATES: Then how big is the side of the eight-feet figure? This one has given us four times the original area, hasn't it?

BOY: Yes.

SOCRATES: And a side half the length gave us a square of four feet?

BOY: Yes.

SOCRATES: Good. And isn't a square of eight feet double this one and half that?

BOY: Yes.

SOCRATES: Will it not have a side greater than this one but less than that?

BOY: I think it will.

SOCRATES: Right. Always answer what you think. Now tell me: was not this side two feet long, and this one four?

BOY: Yes.

SOCRATES: Then the side of the eight-feet figure must be longer than two feet but shorter than four?

BOY: It must.

SOCRATES: Try to say how long you think it is.

BOY: Three feet.

SOCRATES: If so, shall we add half of this bit (BO, *half of* BJ) and make it three feet? Here are two, and this is one, and on this side similarly we have two plus one; and here is the figure you want.

> (*Socrates completes the square* AOPQ.)

BOY: Yes.

SOCRATES: If it is three feet this way and three that, will the whole area be three times three feet?

BOY: It looks like it.

SOCRATES: And that is how many?

BOY: Nine.

SOCRATES: Whereas the square double our first square had to be how many?

BOY: Eight.

SOCRATES: But we haven't yet got the square of eight feet even from a three-feet side?

BOY: No.

SOCRATES: Then what length will give it? Try to tell us exactly. If you don't want to count it up, just show us on the diagram.

BOY: It's no use, Socrates, I just don't know.

SOCRATES: Observe, Meno, the stage he has reached on the path of recollection. At the beginning he did not know the side of the square of eight feet. Nor indeed does he know it now, but then he thought he knew it and answered boldly, as was appropriate—he felt no perplexity. Now however he does feel perplexed. Not only does he not know the answer; he doesn't even think he knows.

MENO: Quite true.

SOCRATES: Isn't he in a better position now in relation to what he didn't know?

MENO: I admit that too.

SOCRATES: So in perplexing him and numbing him like the sting-ray, have we done him any harm?

MENO: I think not.

SOCRATES: In fact we have helped him to some extent towards finding out the right answer, for now not only is he ignorant of it but he will be quite glad to look for it. Up to now, he thought he could speak well and fluently, on many occasions and before large audiences, on the subject of a square double the size of a given square, maintaining that it must have a side of double the length.

MENO: No doubt.

SOCRATES: Do you suppose then that he would have attempted to look for, or learn, what he thought he knew (though he did not), before he was thrown into perplexity, became aware of his ignorance, and felt a desire to know?

MENO: No.

SOCRATES: Then the numbing process was good for him?

MENO: I agree.

SOCRATES: Now notice what, starting from this state of perplexity, he will discover by seeking the truth in company with me, though I simply ask him questions without teaching him. Be ready to catch me if I give him any instruction or explanation instead of simply interrogating him on his own opinions.

(Socrates here rubs out the previous figures and starts again.)

Tell me, boy, is not this our square of four feet? (ABCD.) You understand?

BOY: Yes.

SOCRATES: Now we can add another equal to it like this? (BCEF.)

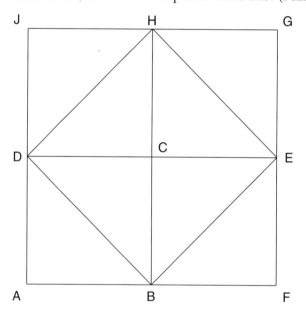

BOY: Yes.

SOCRATES: And a third here, equal to each of the others? (CEGH.)

BOY: Yes.

SOCRATES: And then we can fill in this one in the corner? (DCHJ.)

BOY: Yes.

SOCRATES: Then here we have four equal squares?

BOY: Yes.

SOCRATES: And how many times the size of the first square is the whole?

BOY: Four times.

SOCRATES: And we want one double the size. You remember?

BOY: Yes.

SOCRATES: Now does this line going from corner to corner cut each of these squares in half?

BOY: Yes.

SOCRATES: And these are four equal lines enclosing this area? (BEHD.)

BOY: They are.

SOCRATES: Now think. How big is this area?

BOY: I don't understand.

SOCRATES: Here are four squares. Has not each line cut off the inner half of each of them?

BOY: Yes.

SOCRATES: And how many such halves are there in this figure? (BEHD.)

BOY: Four.

SOCRATES: And how many in this one? (ABCD.)

BOY: Two.

SOCRATES: And what is the relation of four to two?

BOY: Double.

SOCRATES: How big is this figure then?

BOY: Eight feet.

SOCRATES: On what base?

BOY: This one.

SOCRATES: The line which goes from corner to corner of the square of four feet?

BOY: Yes.

SOCRATES: The technical name for it is "diagonal" so if we use that name, it is your personal opinion that the square on the diagonal of the original square is double its area.

BOY: That is so, Socrates.

SOCRATES: What do you think, Meno? Has he answered with any opinions that were not his own?

MENO: No, they were all his.

SOCRATES: Yet he did not know, as we agreed a few minutes ago.

MENO: True.

SOCRATES: But these opinions were somewhere in him, were they not?

MENO: Yes.

SOCRATES: So a man who does not know has in himself true opinions on a subject without having knowledge.

MENO: It would appear so.

SOCRATES: At present these opinions, being newly aroused, have a dream-like quality. But if the same questions are put to him on many occasions and in different ways, you can see that in the end he will have a knowledge on the subject as accurate as anybody's.

MENO: Probably.

SOCRATES: This knowledge will not come from teaching but from questioning. He will recover it for himself.

MENO: Yes.

SOCRATES: And the spontaneous recovery of knowledge that is in him is recollection, isn't it?

MENO: Yes.

SOCRATES: Either then he has at some time acquired the knowledge which he now has, or he has always possessed it. If he always possessed it, he must always have known; if on the other hand he acquired it at some previous time, it cannot have been in this life, unless somebody has taught him geometry. He will behave in the same way with all geometrical knowledge, and every other subject. Has anyone taught him all these? You ought to know, especially as he has been brought up in your household.

MENO: Yes, I know that no one ever taught him.

SOCRATES: And has he these opinions, or hasn't he?

MENO: It seems we can't deny it.

SOCRATES: Then if he did not acquire them in this life, isn't it immediately clear that he possessed and had learned them during some other period?

MENO: It seems so.

SOCRATES: When he was not in human shape?

MENO: Yes.

SOCRATES: If then there are going to exist in him, both while he is and while he is not a man, true opinions which can be aroused by questioning and turned into knowledge, may we say that his soul has been for ever in a state of knowledge? Clearly he always either is or is not a man.

MENO: Clearly.

SOCRATES: And if the truth about reality is always in our soul, the soul must be immortal, and one must take courage and try to discover—that is, to recollect—what one doesn't happen to know, or (more correctly) remember, at the moment.

MENO: Somehow or other I believe you are right.

SOCRATES: I think I am. I shouldn't like to take my oath on the whole story, but one thing I am ready to fight for as long as I can, in word and act:

that is, that we shall be better, braver and more active men if we believe it right to look for what we don't know than if we believe there is no point in looking because what we don't know we can never discover.

MENO: There too I am sure you are right.

SOCRATES: Then since we are agreed that it is right to inquire into something that one does not know, are you ready to face with me the question: what is virtue?

MENO: Quite ready. All the same, I would rather consider the question as I put it at the beginning, and hear your views on it; that is, are we to pursue virtue as something that can be taught, or do men have it as a gift of nature or how?

SOCRATES: If I were your master as well as my own, Meno, we should not have inquired whether or not virtue can be taught until we had first asked the main question—what it is; but not only do you make no attempt to govern your own actions—you prize your freedom, I suppose—but you attempt to govern mine. And you succeed too, so I shall let you have your way. There's nothing else for it, and it seems we must inquire into a single property of something about whose essential nature we are still in the dark. Just grant me one small relaxation of your sway, and allow me, in considering whether or not it can be taught, to make use of a hypothesis—the sort of thing, I mean, that geometers often use in their inquiries. When they are asked, for example, about a given area, whether it is possible for this area to be inscribed as a triangle in a given circle, they will probably reply: "I don't know yet whether it fulfils the conditions, but I think I have a hypothesis which will help us in the matter. It is this. If the area is such that, when one has applied it [*namely, as a rectangle*] to the given line [*i.e., the diameter*] of the circle, it is deficient by another rectangle similar to the one which is applied, then, I should say, one result follows; if not, the result is different. If you ask me, then, about the inscription of the figure in the circle—whether it is possible or not—I am ready to answer you in this hypothetical way."[11]

Let us do the same about virtue. Since we don't know what it is or what it resembles, let us use a hypothesis in investigating whether it is teachable or not. We shall say: "What attribute of the soul must virtue be, if it is to be teachable or otherwise?" Well, in the first place, if it is anything else but knowledge, is there a possibility of anyone teaching it—or, in the language we used just now, reminding someone of it? We needn't worry about which name we are to give to the process, but simply ask: will it be teachable? Isn't it plain to everyone that a man is not taught anything except knowledge?

MENO: That would be my view.

SOCRATES: If on the other hand virtue is some sort of knowledge, clearly it could be taught.

MENO: Certainly.

SOCRATES: So that question is easily settled; I mean, on what condition virtue would be teachable.

MENO: Yes.

SOCRATES: The next point then, I suppose, is to find out whether virtue is knowledge or something different.

MENO: That is the next question, I agree.

SOCRATES: Well then, do we assert that virtue is something good? Is that assumption a firm one for us?

MENO: Undoubtedly.

SOCRATES: That being so, if there exists any good thing different from, and not associated with, knowledge, virtue will not necessarily be any form of knowledge. If on the other hand knowledge embraces everything that is good, we shall be right to suspect that virtue is knowledge.

MENO: Agreed.

SOCRATES: First then is it virtue which makes us good?

MENO: Yes.

SOCRATES: And if good, then advantageous. All good things are advantageous, are they not?

MENO: Yes.

SOCRATES: So virtue itself must be something advantageous?

MENO: That follows also.

SOCRATES: Now suppose we consider what are the sort of things that profit us. Take them in a list. Health, we may say, and strength and good looks, and wealth—these and their like we call advantageous, you agree?

MENO: Yes.

SOCRATES: Yet we also speak of these things as sometimes doing harm. Would you object to that statement?

MENO: No, it is so.

SOCRATES: Now look here: what is the controlling factor which determines whether each of these is advantageous or harmful? Isn't it right use which makes them advantageous, and lack of it, harmful?

MENO: Certainly.

SOCRATES: We must also take spiritual qualities into consideration. You recognize such things as temperance, justice, courage, quickness of mind, memory, nobility of character, and others?

MENO: Yes of course I do.

SOCRATES: Then take any such qualities which in your view are not knowledge but something different. Don't you think they may be harmful as well as advantageous? Courage for instance, if it is something thoughtless, just a sort of confidence. Isn't it true that to be confident without reason does a man harm, whereas a reasoned confidence profits him?

MENO: Yes.

SOCRATES: Temperance and quickness of mind are no different. Learning and discipline are profitable in conjunction with wisdom, but without it harmful.

MENO: That is emphatically true.

SOCRATES: In short, everything that the human spirit undertakes or suffers will lead to happiness when it is guided by wisdom, but to the opposite, when guided by folly.

MENO: A reasonable conclusion.

SOCRATES: If then virtue is an attribute of the spirit, and one which cannot fail to be beneficial, it must be wisdom; for all spiritual qualities in and by themselves are neither advantageous nor harmful, but become advantageous or harmful by the presence with them of wisdom or folly. If we accept this argument, then virtue, to be something advantageous, must be a sort of wisdom.

MENO: I agree.

SOCRATES: To go back to the other class of things, wealth and the like, of which we said just now that they are sometimes good and sometimes harmful, isn't it the same with them? Just as wisdom when it governs our other psychological impulses turns them to advantage, and folly turns them to harm, so the mind by its right use and control of these material assets makes them profitable and by wrong use renders them harmful.

MENO: Certainly.

SOCRATES: And the right user is the mind of the wise man, the wrong user the mind of the foolish.

MENO: That is so.

SOCRATES: So we may say in general that the goodness of non-spiritual assets depends on our spiritual character, and the goodness of that on wisdom. This argument shows that the advantageous element must be wisdom; and virtue, we agree, is advantageous, so that amounts to saying that virtue is wisdom, either the whole or a part of it.

MENO: The argument seems to me fair enough.

SOCRATES: If so, good men cannot be good by nature.

MENO: I suppose not.

SOCRATES: There is another point. If they were, there would probably be experts among us who could recognize the naturally good at an early stage. They would point them out to us and we should take them and shut them away safely in the Acropolis, sealing them up more carefully than bullion to protect them from corruption and ensure that when they came to maturity they would be of use to the State.

MENO: It would be likely enough.

SOCRATES: Since then goodness does not come by nature, is it got by learning?

MENO: I don't see how we can escape the conclusion. Indeed it is obvious on our assumption that, if virtue is knowledge, it is teachable.

SOCRATES: I suppose so. But I wonder if we were right to bind ourselves to that.

MENO: Well, it seemed all right just now.

SOCRATES: Yes, but to be sound it has got to seem all right not only "just now" but at this moment and in the future.

MENO: Of course. But what has occurred to you to make you turn against it and suspect that virtue may not be knowledge?

SOCRATES: I'll tell you. I don't withdraw from the position that if it is knowledge, it must be teachable; but as for its being knowledge, see whether you think my doubts on this point are well founded. If anything—not virtue only—is a possible subject of instruction, must there not be teachers and students of it?

MENO: Surely.

SOCRATES: And what of the converse, that if there are neither teachers nor students of a subject, we may safely infer that it cannot be taught?

MENO: That is true. But don't you think there are teachers of virtue?

SOCRATES: All I can say is that I have often looked to see if there are any, and in spite of all my efforts I cannot find them, though I have had plenty of fellow-searchers, the kind of men especially whom I believe to have most experience in such matters. But look Meno, here's a piece of luck. Anytus has just sat down beside us.[12] We couldn't do better than make him a partner in our inquiry. In the first place he is the son of Anthemion, a man of property and good sense, who didn't get his money out of the blue or as a gift—like Ismenias of Thebes, who has just come into the fortune of a Croesus[13]—but earned it by his own brains and hard work. Besides this he shows himself a decent, modest citizen with no arrogance or bombast or offensiveness about him. Also he brought up his son well and had him properly educated, as the Athenian people appreciate: look how they elect him into the highest offices in the State. This is certainly the right sort of man with whom to inquire whether there are any teachers of virtue, and if so who they are.

Please help us, Anytus—Meno, who is a friend of your family, and myself—to find out who may be the teachers of this subject. Look at it like this. If we wanted Meno to become a good doctor, shouldn't we send him to the doctors to be taught?

ANYTUS: Of course.

SOCRATES: And if we wanted him to become a shoemaker, to the shoe-makers?

ANYTUS: Yes.

SOCRATES: And so on with other trades?

ANYTUS: Yes.

SOCRATES: Now another relevant question. When we say that to make Meno a doctor we should be right in sending him to the doctors, have we in mind that the sensible thing is to send him to those who profess the subject rather than to those who don't, men who charge a fee as pro-fessionals, having announced that they are prepared to teach whoever likes to come and learn?

ANYTUS: Yes.

SOCRATES: The same is surely true of flute-playing and other accomplish-ments. If you want to make someone a performer on the flute it would be very foolish to refuse to send him to those who undertake to teach the art and are paid for it, but to go and bother other people instead and have him try to learn from them—people who don't set up to be teachers or take any pupils in the subject which we want our young man to learn. Doesn't that sound very unreasonable?

ANYTUS: Sheer stupidity I should say.

SOCRATES: I agree. And now we can both consult together about our visi-tor Meno. He has been telling me all this while that he longs to acquire the kind of wisdom and virtue which fits men to manage an estate or govern a city, to look after their parents, and to entertain and send off guests in proper style, both their own countrymen and foreigners. With this in mind, to whom would it be right to send him? What we have just said seems to show that the right people are those who profess to be teachers of virtue and offer their services freely to any Greek who wish-es to learn, charging a fixed fee for their instruction.

ANYTUS: Whom do you mean by that, Socrates?

SOCRATES: Surely you know yourself that they are the men called Sophists.

ANYTUS: Good heavens, what a thing to say! I hope no relative of mine or any of my friends, Athenian or foreign, would be so mad as to go and let himself be ruined by those people. That's what they are, the manifest ruin and corruption of anyone who comes into contact with them.

SOCRATES: What, Anytus? Can they be so different from other claimants to useful knowledge that they not only don't do good, like the rest, to the material that one puts in their charge, but on the contrary spoil it—and have the effrontery to take money for doing so? I for one find it difficult to believe you. I know that one of them alone, Protagoras,[14] earned more money from being a Sophist than an outstandingly fine craftsman like Phidias[15] and ten other sculptors put together. A man who mends old shoes or restores coats couldn't get away with it for a month if he gave them back in worse condition than he received them; he would soon find himself starving. Surely it is incredible that Protagoras took in the whole of Greece, corrupting his pupils and sending them away worse than when they came to him, for more than forty years. I believe he was nearly seventy when he died, and had been practising for forty years, and all that time—indeed to this very day—his reputation has been consistently high; and there are plenty of others besides Protagoras, some before his time and others still alive. Are we to suppose from your remark that they consciously deceive and ruin young men, or are they unaware of it themselves? Can these remarkably clever men—as some regard them—be mad enough for that?

ANYTUS: Far from it, Socrates. It isn't they who are mad, but rather the young men who hand over their money, and those responsible for them, who let them get into the Sophists' hands, are even worse. Worst of all are the cities who allow them in, or don't expel them, whether it be a foreigner or one of themselves who tries that sort of game.

SOCRATES: Has one of the Sophists done you a personal injury, or why are you so hard on them?

ANYTUS: Heavens, no! I've never in my life had anything to do with a single one of them, nor would I hear of any of my family doing so.

SOCRATES: So you've had no experience of them at all?

ANYTUS: And don't want any either.

SOCRATES: You surprise me. How can you know what is good or bad in something when you have no experience of it?

ANYTUS: Quite easily. At any rate I know *their* kind, whether I've had experience or not.

SOCRATES: It must be second sight, I suppose; for how else you know about them, judging from what you tell me yourself, I can't imagine. However, we are not asking whose instruction it is that would ruin Meno's character. Let us say that those are the Sophists if you like, and tell us instead about the ones we want. You can do a good turn to a friend of your father's house if you will let him know to whom in our great city he should apply for proficiency in the kind of virtue I have just described.

ANYTUS: Why not tell him yourself?

SOCRATES: Well, I did mention the men who in my opinion teach these things, but apparently I was talking nonsense. So you say, and you may well be right. Now it is your turn to direct him; mention the name of any Athenian you like.

ANYTUS: But why mention a particular individual? Any decent Athenian gentleman whom he happens to meet, if he follows his advice, will make him a better man than the Sophists would.

SOCRATES: And did these gentlemen get their fine qualities spontaneously—self-taught, as it were, and yet able to teach this untaught virtue to others?

ANYTUS: I suppose they in their turn learned it from forebears who were gentlemen like themselves. Would you deny that there have been many good men in our city?

SOCRATES: On the contrary, there are plenty of good statesmen here in Athens and have been as good in the past. The question is, have they also been good teachers of their own virtue? That is the point we are discussing now—not whether or not there are good men in Athens or whether there have been in past times, but whether virtue can be taught. It amounts to the question whether the good men of this and former times have known how to hand on to someone else the goodness that was in themselves, or whether on the contrary it is not something that can be handed over, or that one man can receive from another. That is what Meno and I have long been puzzling over. Look at it from your own point of view. You would say that Themistocles was a good man?[16]

ANYTUS: Yes, none better.

SOCRATES: And that he, if anyone, must have been a good teacher of his own virtue?

ANYTUS: I suppose so, if he wanted to be.

SOCRATES: But don't you think he must have wanted others to become worthy men—above all, surely, his own son? Do you suppose he grudged him this and purposely didn't pass on his own virtue to him? You must have heard that he had his son Cleophantus so well trained in horsemanship that he could stand upright on horseback and throw a javelin from that position; and many other wonderful accomplishments the young man had, for his father had him taught and made expert in every skill that a good instructor could impart. You must have heard this from older people?

ANYTUS: Yes.

SOCRATES: No one, then, could say that there was anything wrong with the boy's natural powers?

ANYTUS: Perhaps not.

SOCRATES: But have you ever heard anyone, young or old, say that Cleophantus the son of Themistocles was a good and wise man in the way that his father was?

ANYTUS: Certainly not.

SOCRATES: Must we conclude then that Themistocles's aim was to educate his son in other accomplishments, but not to make him any better than his neighbours in his own type of wisdom—that is, supposing that virtue could be taught?

ANYTUS: I hardly think we can.

SOCRATES: So much then for Themistocles as a teacher of virtue, whom you yourself agree to have been one of the best men of former times. Take another example, Aristides son of Lysimachus.[17] You accept him as a good man?

ANYTUS: Surely.

SOCRATES: He too gave his son Lysimachus the best education in Athens, in all subjects where a teacher could help; but did he make him a better man than his neighbour? You know him, I think, and can say what he is like. Or again there is Pericles, that great and wise man.[18] He brought up two sons, Paralus and Xanthippus, and had them taught riding, music, athletics, and all the other skilled pursuits till they were as good as any in Athens. Did he then not want to make them good men? Yes, he wanted that, no doubt, but I am afraid it is something that cannot be done by teaching. And in case you should think that only very few, and those the most insignificant, lacked this power, consider that Thucydides also had two sons, Melesias and Stephanus, to whom he gave an excellent education. Among other things they were the best wrestlers in Athens, for he gave one to Xanthias to train and the other to Eudoxus—the two who, I understand, were considered the finest wrestlers of their time. You remember?

ANYTUS: I have heard of them.

SOCRATES: Surely then he would never have had his children taught these expensive pursuits and yet refused to teach them to be good men—which would have cost nothing at all—if virtue could have been taught? You are not going to tell me that Thucydides was a man of no account, or that he had not plenty of friends both at Athens and among the allies? He came of an influential family and was a great power both here and in the rest of Greece. If virtue could have been taught, he would have found the man to make his sons good, either among our own citizens or abroad, supposing his political duties left him no time to do it himself. No, my dear Anytus, it looks as if it cannot be taught.

ANYTUS: You seem to me, Socrates, to be too ready to run people down. My advice to you, if you will listen to it, is to be careful. I dare say that in all cities it is easier to do a man harm than good, and it is certainly so here, as I expect you know yourself.

SOCRATES: Anytus seems angry, Meno, and I am not surprised. He thinks I am slandering our statesmen, and moreover he believes himself to be one of them. He doesn't know what slander really is: if he ever finds out, he will forgive me.

However, tell me this yourself: are there not similar fine characters in your country?

MENO: Yes certainly.

SOCRATES: Do they come forward of their own accord to teach the young? Do they agree that they are teachers and that virtue can be taught?

MENO: No indeed, they don't agree on it at all. Sometimes you will hear them say that it can be taught, sometimes that it cannot.

SOCRATES: Ought we then to class as teachers of it men who are not even agreed that it can be taught?

MENO: Hardly, I think.

SOCRATES: And what about the Sophists, the only people who profess to teach it? Do you think they do?

MENO: The thing I particularly admire about Gorgias, Socrates, is that you will never hear him make this claim; indeed he laughs at the others when he hears them do so. In his view his job is to make clever speakers.

SOCRATES: So you too don't think the Sophists are teachers?

MENO: I really can't say. Like most people I waver—sometimes I think they are and sometimes I think they are not.

SOCRATES: Has it ever occurred to you that you and our statesmen are not alone in this? The poet Theognis[19] likewise says in one place that virtue is teachable and in another that it is not.

MENO: Really? Where?

SOCRATES: In the elegiacs in which he writes:

Eat, drink, and sit with men of power and weight,
Nor scorn to gain the favour of the great.
For fine men's teaching to fine ways will win thee:
Low company destroys what wit is in thee.

There he speaks as if virtue can be taught, doesn't he?

MENO: Clearly.

SOCRATES: But elsewhere he changes his ground a little

Were mind by art created and instilled
Immense rewards had soon the pockets filled

of the people who could do this. Moreover

No good man's son would ever worthless be,
Taught by wise counsel. But no teacher's skill
Can turn to good what is created ill.

Do you see how he contradicts himself?

MENO: Plainly.

SOCRATES: Can you name any other subject, in which the professed teachers are not only not recognized as teachers of others, but are thought to have no understanding of it themselves, and to be no good at the very subject they profess to teach; whereas those who are acknowledged to be the best at it are in two minds whether it can be taught or not? When people are so confused about a subject, can you say that they are in a true sense teachers?

MENO: Certainly not.

SOCRATES: Well, if neither the Sophists nor those who display fine qualities themselves are teachers of virtue, I am sure no one else can be, and if there are no teachers, there can be no students either.

MENO: I quite agree.

SOCRATES: And we have also agreed that a subject of which there were neither teachers nor students was not one which could be taught.

MENO: That is so.

SOCRATES: Now there turn out to be neither teachers nor students of virtue, so it would appear that virtue cannot be taught.

MENO: So it seems, if we have made no mistake; and it makes me wonder, Socrates, whether there are in fact no good men at all, or how they are produced when they do appear.

SOCRATES: I have a suspicion, Meno, that you and I are not much good. Our masters Gorgias and Prodicus have not trained us properly. We must certainly take ourselves in hand, and try to find someone who will improve us by hook or by crook. I say this with our recent discussion in mind, for absurdly enough we failed to perceive that it is not only under the guidance of knowledge that human action is well and rightly conducted. I believe that may be what prevents us from seeing how it is that men are made good.

MENO: What do you mean?

SOCRATES: This. We were correct, were we not, in agreeing that good men must be profitable or useful? It cannot be otherwise, can it?

MENO: No.

SOCRATES: And again that they will be of some use if they conduct our affairs aright—that also was correct?

MENO: Yes.

SOCRATES: But in insisting that knowledge was a *sine qua non* for right leadership, we look like being mistaken.

MENO: How so?

SOCRATES: Let me explain. If someone knows the way to Larissa,[20] or anywhere else you like, then when he goes there and takes others with him he will be a good and capable guide, you would agree?

MENO: Of course.

SOCRATES: But if a man judges correctly which is the road, though he has never been there and doesn't know it, will he not also guide others aright?

MENO: Yes, he will.

SOCRATES: And as long as he has a correct opinion on the points about which the other has knowledge, he will be just as good a guide, believing the truth but not knowing it.

MENO: Just as good.

SOCRATES: Therefore true opinion is as good a guide as knowledge for the purpose of acting rightly. That is what we left out just now in our discussion of the nature of virtue, when we said that knowledge is the only guide to right action. There was also, it seems, true opinion.

MENO: It seems so.

SOCRATES: So right opinion is something no less useful than knowledge.

MENO: Except that the man with knowledge will always be successful, and the man with right opinion only sometimes.

SOCRATES: What? Will he not always be successful so long as he has the right opinion?

MENO: That must be so, I suppose. In that case, I wonder why knowledge should be so much more prized than right opinion, and indeed how there is any difference between them.

SOCRATES: Shall I tell you the reason for your surprise, or do you know it?

MENO: No, tell me.

SOCRATES: It is because you have not observed the statues of Daedalus.[21] Perhaps you don't have them in your country.

MENO: What makes you say that?

SOCRATES: They too, if no one ties them down, run away and escape. If tied, they stay where they are put.

MENO: What of it?

SOCRATES: If you have one of his works untethered, it is not worth much: it gives you the slip like a runaway slave. But a tethered specimen is very valuable, for they are magnificent creations. And that, I may say, has a bearing on the matter of true opinions. True opinions are a fine thing and do all sorts of good so long as they stay in their place; but they will not stay long. They run away from a man's mind, so they are not worth much until you tether them by working out the reason. That process, my dear Meno, is recollection, as we agreed earlier. Once they are tied down, they become knowledge, and are stable. That is why knowledge is something more valuable than right opinion. What distinguishes one from the other is the tether.

MENO: It does seem something like that, certainly.

SOCRATES: Well of course, I have only been using an analogy myself, not knowledge. But it is not, I am sure, a mere guess to say that right opinion and knowledge are different. There are few things that I should claim to know, but that at least is among them, whatever else is.

MENO: You are quite right.

SOCRATES: And is this right too, that true opinion when it governs any course of action produces as good a result as knowledge?

MENO: Yes, that too is right, I think.

SOCRATES: So that for practical purposes right opinion is no less useful than knowledge, and the man who has it is no less useful than the one who knows.

MENO: That is so.

SOCRATES: Now we have agreed that the good man is useful.

MENO: Yes.

SOCRATES: To recapitulate then: assuming that there are men good and useful to the community, it is not only knowledge that makes them so, but also right opinion, and neither of these comes by nature but both are acquired—or do you think either of them *is* natural?

MENO: No.

SOCRATES: So if both are acquired, good men themselves are not good by nature.

MENO: No.

SOCRATES: That being so, the next thing we inquired was whether their goodness was a matter of teaching, and we decided that it would be, if virtue were knowledge, and conversely, that if it could be taught, it would be knowledge.

MENO: Yes.

SOCRATES: Next, that if there were teachers of it, it could be taught, but not if there were none.

MENO: That was so.

SOCRATES: But we have agreed that there are no teachers of it, and so that it cannot be taught and is not knowledge.

MENO: We did.

SOCRATES: At the same time we agreed that it is something good, and that to be useful and good consists in giving right guidance.

MENO: Yes.

SOCRATES: And that these two, true opinion and knowledge, are the only things which direct us aright and the possession of which makes a man a true guide. We may except chance, because what turns out right by chance is not due to human direction, and say that where human control leads to right ends, these two principles are directive, true opinion and knowledge.

MENO: Yes, I agree.

SOCRATES: Now since virtue cannot be taught, we can no longer believe it to be knowledge, so that one of our two good and useful principles is excluded, and knowledge is not the guide in public life.

MENO: No.

SOCRATES: It is not then by the possession of any wisdom that such men as Themistocles, and the others whom Anytus mentioned just now, became leaders in their cities. This fact, that they do not owe their eminence to knowledge, will explain why they are unable to make others like themselves.

MENO: No doubt it is as you say.

SOCRATES: That leaves us with the other alternative, that it is well-aimed conjecture which statesmen employ in upholding their countries' welfare. Their position in relation to knowledge is no different from that of prophets and tellers of oracles, who under divine inspiration utter many truths, but have no knowledge of what they are saying.

MENO: It must be something like that.

SOCRATES: And ought we not to reckon those men divine who with no conscious thought are repeatedly and outstandingly successful in what they do or say?

MENO: Certainly.

SOCRATES: We are right therefore to give this title to the oracular priests and the prophets that I mentioned, and to poets of every description. Statesmen too, when by their speeches they get great things done yet know nothing of what they are saying, are to be considered as acting no less under divine influence, inspired and possessed by the divinity.

MENO: Certainly.

SOCRATES: Women, you know, Meno, do call good men "divine," and the Spartans too, when they are singing a good man's praises, say "He is divine."

MENO: And it looks as if they are right—though our friend Anytus may be annoyed with you for saying so.

SOCRATES: I can't help that. We will talk to him some other time. If all we have said in this discussion, and the questions we have asked, have been right, virtue will be acquired neither by nature nor by teaching. Whoever has it gets it by divine dispensation without taking thought, unless he be the kind of statesman who can create another like himself. Should there be such a man, he would be among the living practically what Homer said Tiresias[22] was among the dead, when he described him as the only one in the underworld who kept his wits—"the others are mere flitting shades." Where virtue is concerned such a man would be just like that, a solid reality among shadows.

MENO: That is finely put, Socrates.

SOCRATES: On our present reasoning then, whoever has virtue gets it by divine dispensation. But we shall not understand the truth of the matter until, before asking how men get virtue, we try to discover what virtue is in and by itself. Now it is time for me to go; and my request to you is that you will allay the anger of your friend Anytus by convincing him that what you now believe is true. If you succeed, the Athenians may have cause to thank you.

NOTES

(prepared by Andrea Tschemplik)

1. Meno, a mercenary soldier, was a person of dubious character; hence, his questions carry a touch of irony.
2. Gorgias was one of the most famous of the Sophists, itinerant teachers of oratory who were paid for their services.
3. Prodicus was a Sophist, best known for his precision in drawing verbal distinctions.
4. Empedocles (c. 493–c. 433 B.C.E.) was a pre-Socratic philosopher, who thought that our perceptions are the result of effluences from physical objects entering our sense organs.
5. Pindar (518–438 B.C.E.) was a celebrated lyric poet.
6. Evidently the Athenians are about to celebrate the famous rites of the Eleusinian Mysteries, but Meno has to return to Thessaly before they fall due. Plato frequently plays upon the analogy between religious initiation, which bestowed a revelation of divine secrets, and the insight which comes from initiation into the truths of philosophy (translator's note).
7. The sting-ray, which paralyzed its victims, was a danger to Mediterranean swimmers.
8. The quotation is from Pindar (translator's note).
9. Recollection is related to, but not identical with, memory. A distinction between the two may be that knowledge based on experience is remembered, whereas knowledge not based on experience is recollected.
10. Socrates asks the slave boy to find a line whose length is the square root of eight, an irrational number.

11. The geometrical illustration here adduced by Socrates is very loosely and ob-
    scurely expressed. Fortunately it is not necessary to understand the example in
    order to grasp the hypothetical method which Socrates is expounding (transla-
    tor's note). A cogent explanation of the mathematics that may be involved is pro-
    vided by Judith I. Meyers in "Plato's Geometric Hypothesis: *Meno* 86E–87B,"
    Apeiron 21 (Fall 1988), pp. 173–180.
12. Anytus, who helped restore Athenian democracy, was one of the three accusers
    of Socrates at his trial.
13. Ismenias (d. 382 B.C.E.) was a noted statesman. Croesus was a legendary man of
    wealth, not specifically mentioned in the original Greek text.
14. Protagoras (c. 490–c. 420 B.C.E.) was one of the most prominent Sophists.
15. Phidias, active in the mid-fifth century B.C.E., was the most famous Athenian
    sculptor.
16. Themistocles (528–462 B.C.E.) was an Athenian statesman and general who helped
    defeat the Persians.
17. Aristides was an Athenian statesman and hero of the Persian War, renowned for
    his honesty.
18. Pericles (c. 495–429 B.C.E.), the most famous leader of democratic Athens, was cel-
    ebrated for his incorruptible character.
19. Theognis was a sixth-century B.C.E. elegaic poet from Megara.
20. Larissa was the principal city of Thessaly, the region of Meno's birth.
21. Daedalus, a legendary artist, craftsman, and inventor, made lifelike figures that
    moved.
22. Tiresias was a legendary blind Theban, gifted with the power of prophecy.

Meditations on First Philosophy

RENÉ DESCARTES

The Frenchman René Descartes (1596–1650), mathematician, scientist, and philosopher, wrote one of the most influential of all
philosophical works, his *Meditations on First Philosophy,* published
in Latin in 1641. Its combination of personal narrative and rigorous
argument is highly unusual.

Descartes is driven by his desire to place philosophy on a reliable foundation that cannot be shaken. He searches for a starting

point that can withstand all doubt. After considering and rejecting various possibilities, he arrives at the principle he believes he is seeking, best known as formulated in another of his works as, "I think; therefore, I am," in Latin "Cogito, ergo sum." According to Descartes, the Cogito, as it is called by philosophers, is undeniable, since, in the act of attempting to deny one is thinking, one thinks and so renders the denial false.

Using the Cogito as the premise of his philosophical system, Descartes argues that since he is certain he is thinking but not certain of the existence of anything other than his own mind, therefore, he is to be identified with his mind. And he claims that it is by relying on the judgements of his mind rather than the evidence of his senses he can attain knowledge.

The *Meditations* is universally regarded as a philosophical classic, even by the many who do not accept its conclusions. What continues to fascinate philosophers is the provocative manner in which Descartes formulated and pursued such a variety of crucial issues. To meditate along with him is as good a way as any to come to an understanding of philosophical inquiry.

What follows are the first two of Descartes' six meditations. An excerpt from the fifth appears in the next section of the book (pp. 233–235).

First Meditation

What Can Be Called into Doubt

Some years ago I was struck by the large number of falsehoods that I had accepted as true in my childhood, and by the highly doubtful nature of the whole edifice that I had subsequently based on them. I realized that it was necessary, once in the course of my life, to demolish everything completely and start again right from the foundations if I wanted to establish anything at all in the sciences that was stable and likely to last. But the task looked an enormous one, and I began to wait until I should reach a mature enough age to ensure that no subsequent time of life would be more suitable for tackling such inquiries. This led me to put the project off for so long that I would now be to blame if by pondering over it any further I wasted the time still left for carrying it out. So today I have expressly rid my mind of all worries and arranged for myself a clear stretch of free time. I am here quite alone, and at last I will devote myself sincerely and without reservation to the general demolition of my opinions.

But to accomplish this, it will not be necessary for me to show that all my opinions are false, which is something I could perhaps never manage. Reason now leads me to think that I should hold back my assent from opinions which are not completely certain and indubitable just as carefully as I do from those which are patently false. So, for the purpose of rejecting all my opinions, it will be enough if I find in each of them at least some reason for doubt. And to do this I will not need to run through them all individually, which would be an endless task. Once the foundations of a building are undermined, anything built on them collapses of its own accord; so I will go straight for the basic principles on which all my former beliefs rested.

Whatever I have up till now accepted as most true I have acquired either from the senses or through the senses. But from time to time I have found that the senses deceive, and it is prudent never to trust completely those who have deceived us even once.

Yet although the senses occasionally deceive us with respect to objects which are very small or in the distance, there are many other beliefs about which doubt is quite impossible, even though they are derived from the senses—for example, that I am here, sitting by the fire, wearing a winter dressing-gown, holding this piece of paper in my hands, and so on. Again, how could it be denied that these hands or this whole body are mine? Unless perhaps I were to liken myself to madmen, whose brains are so damaged by the persistent vapours of melancholia that they firmly maintain they are kings when they are paupers, or say they are dressed in purple when they are naked, or that their heads are made of earthenware, or that they are pumpkins, or made of glass. But such people are insane, and I would be thought equally mad if I took anything from them as a model for myself.

A brilliant piece of reasoning! As if I were not a man who sleeps at night, and regularly has all the same experiences while asleep as madmen do when awake—indeed sometimes even more improbable ones. How often, asleep at night, am I convinced of just such familiar events—that I am here in my dressing-gown, sitting by the fire—when in fact I am lying undressed in bed! Yet at the moment my eyes are certainly wide awake when I look at this piece of paper; I shake my head and it is not asleep; as I stretch out and feel my hand I do so deliberately, and I know what I am doing. All this would not happen with such distinctness to someone asleep. Indeed! As if I did not remember other occasions when I have been tricked by exactly similar thoughts while asleep! As I think about this more carefully, I see plainly that there are never any sure signs by means of which being awake can be distinguished from being asleep. The result is that I begin to feel dazed, and this very feeling only reinforces the notion that I may be asleep.

Suppose then that I am dreaming, and that these particulars—that my eyes are open, that I am moving my head and stretching out my hands—are not true. Perhaps, indeed, I do not even have such hands or such a body at all. Nonetheless, it must surely be admitted that the visions which come in sleep are like paintings, which must have been fashioned in the likeness of things that are real, and hence that at least these general kinds of things—eyes, head, hands, and the body as a whole—are things which are not imaginary but are real and exist. For even when painters try to create sirens and satyrs with the most extraordinary bodies, they cannot give them natures which are new in all respects; they simply jumble up the limbs of different animals. Or if perhaps they manage to think up something so new that nothing remotely similar has ever been seen before—something which is therefore completely fictitious and unreal—at least the colours used in the composition must be real. By similar reasoning, although these general kinds of things—eyes, head, hands and so on—could be imaginary, it must at least be admitted that certain other even simpler and more universal things are real. These are as it were the real colours from which we form all the images of things, whether true or false, that occur in our thought.

This class appears to include corporeal nature in general, and its extension; the shape of extended things; the quantity, or size and number of these things; the place in which they may exist, the time through which they may endure, and so on.

So a reasonable conclusion from this might be that physics, astronomy, medicine, and all other disciplines which depend on the study of composite things, are doubtful; while arithmetic, geometry, and other subjects of this kind, which deal only with the simplest and most general things, regardless of whether they really exist in nature or not, contain something certain and indubitable. For whether I am awake or asleep, two and three added together are five, and a square has no more than four sides. It seems impossible that such transparent truths should incur any suspicion of being false.

And yet firmly rooted in my mind is the long-standing opinion that there is an omnipotent God who made me the kind of creature that I am. How do I know that he has not brought it about that there is no earth, no sky, no extended thing, no shape, no size, no place, while at the same time ensuring that all these things appear to me to exist just as they do now? What is more, just as I consider that others sometimes go astray in cases where they think they have the most perfect knowledge, how do I know that God has not brought it about that I too go wrong every time I add two and three or count the sides of a square, or in some even simpler matter, if that is imaginable? But perhaps God would not have allowed me to be deceived in this way, since he is said to be supremely good. But if it were inconsistent with his goodness to have created me such that I am deceived all the time, it would seem equally foreign to his goodness to allow me to be deceived even occasionally; yet this last assertion cannot be made.

Perhaps there may be some who would prefer to deny the existence of so powerful a God rather than believe that everything else is uncertain. Let us not argue with them, but grant them that everything said about God is a fiction. According to their supposition, then, I have arrived at my present state by fate or chance or a continuous chain of events, or by some other means;

yet since deception and error seem to be imperfections, the less powerful they make my original cause, the more likely it is that I am so imperfect as to be deceived all the time. I have no answer to these arguments, but am finally compelled to admit that there is not one of my former beliefs about which a doubt may not properly be raised; and this is not a flippant or ill-considered conclusion, but is based on powerful and well thought-out reasons. So in future I must withhold my assent from these former beliefs just as carefully as I would from obvious falsehoods, if I want to discover any certainty.

But it is not enough merely to have noticed this; I must make an effort to remember it. My habitual opinions keep coming back, and, despite my wishes, they capture my belief, which is as it were bound over to them as a result of long occupation and the law of custom. I shall never get out of the habit of confidently assenting to these opinions, so long as I suppose them to be what in fact they are, namely, highly probable opinions—opinions which, despite the fact that they are in a sense doubtful, as has just been shown, it is still much more reasonable to believe than to deny. In view of this, I think it will be a good plan to turn my will in completely the opposite direction and deceive myself, by pretending for a time that these former opinions are utterly false and imaginary. I shall do this until the weight of preconceived opinion is counter-balanced and the distorting influence of habit no longer prevents my judgement from perceiving things correctly. In the meantime, I know that no danger or error will result from my plan, and that I cannot possibly go too far in my distrustful attitude. This is because the task now in hand does not involve action but merely the acquisition of knowledge.

I will suppose therefore that not God, who is supremely good and the source of truth, but rather some malicious demon of the utmost power and cunning has employed all his energies in order to deceive me. I shall think that the sky, the air, the earth, colours, shapes, sounds, and all external things are merely the delusions of dreams which he has devised to ensnare my judgement. I shall consider myself as not having hands or eyes, or flesh, or blood or senses, but as falsely believing that I have all these things. I shall stubbornly and firmly persist in this mediation; and, even if it is not in my power to know any truth, I shall at least do what is in my power, that is, resolutely guard against assenting to any falsehoods, so that the deceiver, however powerful and cunning he may be, will be unable to impose on me in the slightest degree. But this is an arduous undertaking, and a kind of laziness brings me back to normal life. I am like a prisoner who is enjoying an imaginary freedom while asleep; as he begins to suspect that he is asleep, he dreads being woken up, and goes along with the pleasant illusion as long as he can. In the same way, I happily slide back into my old opinions and dread being shaken out of them, for fear that my peaceful sleep may be followed by hard labour when I wake, and that I shall have to toil not in the light, but amid the inextricable darkness of the problems I have now raised.

Second Meditation

The Nature of the Human Mind, and How It Is Better Known Than the Body

So serious are the doubts into which I have been thrown as a result of yesterday's mediation that I can neither put them out of my mind nor see any way of resolving them. It feels as if I have fallen unexpectedly into a deep whirlpool which tumbles me around so that I can neither stand on the bottom nor swim up to the top. Nevertheless I will make an effort and once more attempt the same path which I started on yesterday. Anything which admits of the slightest doubt I will set aside just as if I had found it to be wholly false; and I will proceed in this way until I recognize something certain, or, if nothing else, until I at least recognize for certain that there is no certainty. Archimedes used to demand just one firm and immovable point in order to shift the entire earth; so I too can hope for great things if I manage to find just one thing, however slight, that is certain and unshakeable.

I will suppose then, that everything I see is spurious. I will believe that my memory tells me lies, and that none of the things that it reports ever happened. I have no senses. Body, shape, extension, movement, and place are chimeras. So what remains true? Perhaps just the one fact that nothing is certain.

Yet apart from everything I have just listed, how do I know that there is not something else which does not allow even the slightest occasion for doubt? Is there not a God, or whatever I may call him, who puts into me the thoughts I am now having? But why do I think this, since I myself may perhaps be the author of these thoughts? In that case am not I, at least, something? But I have just said that I have no senses and no body. This is the sticking point: what follows from this? Am I not so bound up with a body and with senses that I cannot exist without them? But I have convinced myself that there is absolutely nothing in the world, no sky, no earth, no minds, no bodies. Does it now follow that I too do not exist? No: if I convinced myself of something then I certainly existed. But there is a deceiver of supreme power and cunning who is deliberately and constantly deceiving me. In that case I too undoubtedly exist, if he is deceiving me; and let him deceive me as much as he can, he will never bring it about that I am nothing so long as I think that I am something. So after considering everything very thoroughly, I must finally conclude that this proposition, *I am, I exist*, is necessarily true whenever it is put forward by me or conceived in my mind.

But I do not yet have a sufficient understanding of what this "I" is, that now necessarily exists. So I must be on my guard against carelessly taking something else to be this "I," and so making a mistake in the very item of knowledge that I maintain is the most certain and evident of all. I will therefore go back and meditate on what I originally believed myself to be, before I embarked on this present train of thought. I will then subtract anything capable of being weakened, even minimally, by the arguments now introduced, so that what is left at the end may be exactly and only what is certain and unshakeable.

What then did I formerly think I was? A man. But what is a man? Shall I say "a rational animal"? No; for then I should have to inquire what an animal is, what rationality is, and in this way one question would lead me down the slope to other harder ones, and I do not now have the time to waste on subtleties of this kind. Instead I propose to concentrate on what came into my thoughts spontaneously and quite naturally whenever I used to consider what I was. Well, the first thought to come to mind was that I had a face, hands, arms, and the whole mechanical structure of limbs which can be seen in a corpse, and which I called the body. The next thought was that I was nourished, that I moved about, and that I engaged in sense-perception and thinking; and these actions I attributed to the soul. But as to the nature of this soul, either I did not think about this or else I imagined it to be something tenuous, like a wind or fire or ether, which permeated my more solid parts. As to the body, however, I had no doubts about it, but thought I knew its nature distinctly. If I had tried to describe the mental conception I had of it, I would have expressed it as follows: by a body I understand whatever has a determinable shape and a definable location and can occupy a space in such a way as to exclude any other body; it can be perceived by touch, sight, hearing, taste, or smell, and can be moved in various ways, not by itself but by whatever else comes into contact with it. For, according to my judgement, the power of self-movement, like the power of sensation or of thought, was quite foreign to the nature of a body; indeed, it was a source of wonder to me that certain bodies were found to contain faculties of this kind.

But what shall I now say that I am, when I am supposing that there is some supremely powerful and, if it is permissible to say so, malicious deceiver, who is deliberately trying to trick me in every way he can? Can I now assert that I possess even the most insignificant of all the attributes which I have just said belong to the nature of a body? I scrutinize them, think about them, go over them again, but nothing suggests itself; it is tiresome and pointless to go through the list once more. But what about the attributes I assigned to the soul? Nutrition or movement? Since now I do not have a body, these are mere fabrications. Sense-perception? This surely does not occur without a body, and besides, when asleep I have appeared to perceive through the senses many things which I afterwards realized I did not perceive through the senses at all. Thinking? At last I have discovered it— thought; this alone is inseparable from me. I am, I exist—that is certain. But for how long? For as long as I am thinking. For it could be that were I totally to cease from thinking, I should totally cease to exist. At present I am not admitting anything except what is necessarily true. I am, then, in the strict sense only a thing that thinks; that is, I am a mind, or intelligence, or intellect, or reason—words whose meaning I have been ignorant of until now.

But for all that I am a thing which is real and which truly exists. But what kind of a thing? As I have just said—a thinking thing.

What else am I? I will use my imagination. I am not that structure of limbs which is called a human body. I am not even some thin vapour which permeates the limbs—a wind, fire, air, breath, or whatever I depict in my imagination; for these are things which I have supposed to be nothing. Let this supposition stand; for all that I am still something. And yet may it not perhaps be the case that these very things which I am supposing to be nothing, because they are unknown to me, are in reality identical with the "I" of which I am aware? I do not know, and for the moment I shall not argue the point, since I can make judgements only about things which are known to me. I know that I exist; the question is, what is this "I" that I know? If the "I" is understood strictly as we have been taking it, then it is quite certain that knowledge of it does not depend on things of whose existence I am as yet unaware; so it cannot depend on any of the things which I invent in my imagination. And this very word "invent" shows me my mistake. It would indeed be a case of fictitious invention if I used my imagination to establish that I was something or other; for imagining is simply contemplating the shape or image of a corporeal thing. Yet now I know for certain both that I exist and at the same time that all such images and, in general, everything relating to the nature of body, could be mere dreams ⟨and chimeras⟩. Once this point has been grasped, to say "I will use my imagination to get to know more distinctly what I am" would seem to be as silly as saying "I am now awake, and see some truth; but since my vision is not yet clear enough, I will deliberately fall asleep so that my dreams may provide a truer and clearer representation." I thus realize that none of the things that the imagination enables me to grasp is at all relevant to this knowledge of myself which I possess, and that the mind must therefore be most carefully diverted from such things if it is to perceive its own nature as distinctly as possible.

But what then am I? A thing that thinks. What is that? A thing that doubts, understands, affirms, denies, is willing, is unwilling, and also imagines and has sensory perceptions.

This is a considerable list, if everything on it belongs to me. But does it? Is it not one and the same "I" who is now doubting almost everything, who nonetheless understands some things, who affirms that this one thing is true, denies everything else, desires to know more, is unwilling to be deceived, imagines many things even involuntarily, and is aware of many things which apparently come from the senses? Are not all these things just as true as the fact that I exist, even if I am asleep all the time, and even if he who created me is doing all he can to deceive me? Which of all these activities is distinct from my thinking? Which of them can be said to be separate from myself? The fact that it is I who am doubting and understanding and willing is so evident that I see no way of making it any clearer. But it is also the case that the "I" who imagines is the same "I." For even if, as I have supposed, none of the objects of imagination are real, the power of imagination is something which really exists and is part of my thinking. Lastly, it is also the same "I" who has sensory perceptions, or is aware of bodily things as it were through the senses. For example, I am now seeing light, hearing a noise, feeling heat. But I am asleep, so all this is false. Yet I certainly *seem* to see, to hear, and to be warmed. This cannot be false; what is called "having a sensory perception" is strictly just this, and in this restricted sense of the term it is simply thinking.

From all this I am beginning to have a rather better understanding of what I am. But it still appears—and I cannot stop thinking this—that the corporeal things of which images are formed in my thought, and which the senses investigate, are known with much more distinctness than this puzzling "I" which cannot be pictured in the imagination. And yet it is surely surprising that I should have a more distinct grasp of things which I realize are doubtful, unknown, and foreign to me, than I have of that which is true and known—my own self. But I see what it is: my mind enjoys wandering off and will not yet submit to being restrained within the bounds of truth. Very well then; just this once let us give it a completely free rein, so that after a while, when it is time to tighten the reins, it may more readily submit to being curbed.

Let us consider the things which people commonly think they understand most distinctly of all; that is, the bodies which we touch and see. I do not mean bodies in general—for general perceptions are apt to be somewhat more confused—but one particular body. Let us take, for example, this piece of wax. It has just been taken from the honeycomb; it has not yet quite lost the taste of the honey; it retains some of the scent of the flowers from which it was gathered; its colour, shape, and size are plain to see; it is hard, cold and can be handled without difficulty; if you rap it with your knuckle, it makes a sound. In short, it has everything which appears necessary to enable a body to be known as distinctly as possible. But even as I speak, I put the wax by the fire, and look: the residual taste is eliminated, the smell goes away, the colour changes, the shape is lost, the size increases; it becomes liquid and hot; you can hardly touch it, and if you strike it, it no longer makes a sound. But does the same wax remain? It must be admitted that it does; no one denies it, no one thinks otherwise. So what was it in the wax that I understood with such distinctness? Evidently none of the features which I arrived at by means of the senses; for whatever came under taste, smell, sight, touch, or hearing has now altered—yet the wax remains.

Perhaps the answer lies in the thought which now comes to my mind; namely, the wax was not after all the sweetness of the honey, or the fragrance of the flowers, or the whiteness, or the shape, or the sound, but was rather a body which presented itself to me in these various forms a little while ago, but which now exhibits different ones. But what exactly is it that I am now imagining? Let us concentrate, take away everything which does not belong to the wax, and see what is left: merely something extended, flexible, and changeable. But what is meant here by "flexible" and "changeable"? Is it

what I picture in my imagination: that this piece of wax is capable of changing from a round shape to a square shape, or from a square shape to a trian-
gular shape? Not at all; for I can grasp that the wax is capable of countless
changes of this kind, yet I am unable to run through this immeasurable number of changes in my imagination, from which it follows that it is not the faculty of imagination that gives me my grasp of the wax as flexible and
changeable. And what is meant by "extended"? Is the extension of the wax
also unknown? For it increases if the wax melts, increases again if it boils,
and is greater still if the heat is increased. I would not be making a correct
judgement about the nature of wax unless I believed it capable of being extended in many more different ways than I will ever encompass in my imagination. I must therefore admit that the nature of this piece of wax is in no
way revealed by my imagination, but is perceived by the mind alone. (I am
speaking of this particular piece of wax; the point is even clearer with regard
to wax in general.) But what is this wax which is perceived by the mind
alone? It is of course the same wax which I see, which I touch, which I picture in my imagination, in short the same wax which I thought it to be from
the start. And yet, and here is the point, the perception I have of it is a case
not of vision or touch or imagination—nor has it ever been, despite previous
appearances—but of purely mental scrutiny; and this can be imperfect and
confused, as it was before, or clear and distinct as it is now, depending on
how carefully I concentrate on what the wax consists in.

But as I reach this conclusion I am amazed at how ⟨weak and⟩ prone to
error my mind is. For although I am thinking about these matters within
myself, silently and without speaking, nonetheless the actual words bring
me up short, and I am almost tricked by ordinary ways of talking. We say
that we see the wax itself, if it is there before us, not that we judge it to be
there from its colour or shape; and this might lead me to conclude without
more ado that knowledge of the wax comes from what the eye sees, and not
from the scrutiny of the mind alone. But then if I look out of the window and
see men crossing the square, as I just happen to have done, I normally say
that I see the men themselves, just as I say that I see the wax. Yet do I see any
more than hats and coats which could conceal automatons? I *judge* that they
are men. And so something which I thought I was seeing with my eyes is in
fact grasped solely by the faculty of judgement which is in my mind.

However, one who wants to achieve knowledge above the ordinary level should feel ashamed at having taken ordinary ways of talking as a basis
for doubt. So let us proceed, and consider on which occasion my perception
of the nature of the wax was more perfect and evident. Was it when I first
looked at it, and believed I knew it by my external senses, or at least by what
they call the "common" sense—that is, the power of imagination? Or is my
knowledge more perfect now, after a more careful investigation of the nature
of the wax and of the means by which it is known? Any doubt on this issue
would clearly be foolish; for what distinctness was there in my earlier perception? Was there anything in it which an animal could not possess? But

when I distinguish the wax from its outward forms—take the clothes off, as it were, and consider it naked—then although my judgement may still contain errors, at least my perception now requires a human mind.

But what am I to say about this mind, or about myself? (So far, remember, I am not admitting that there is anything else in me except a mind.) What, I ask, is this "I" which seems to perceive the wax so distinctly? Surely my awareness of my own self is not merely much truer and more certain than my awareness of the wax, but also much more distinct and evident. For if I judge that the wax exists from the fact that I see it, clearly this same fact entails much more evidently that I myself also exist. It is possible that what I see is not really the wax; it is possible that I do not even have eyes with which to see anything. But when I see, or think I see (I am not here distinguishing the two), it is simply not possible that I who am now thinking am not something. By the same token, if I judge that the wax exists from the fact that I touch it, the same result follows, namely, that I exist. If I judge that it exists from the fact that I imagine it, or for any other reason, exactly the same thing follows. And the result that I have grasped in the case of the wax may be applied to everything else located outside me. Moreover, if my perception of the wax seemed more distinct after it was established not just by sight or touch but by many other considerations, it must be admitted that I now know myself even more distinctly. This is because every consideration whatsoever which contributes to my perception of the wax, or of any other body, cannot but establish even more effectively the nature of my own mind. But besides this, there is so much else in the mind itself which can serve to make my knowledge of it more distinct, that it scarcely seems worth going through the contributions made by considering bodily things.

I see that without any effort I have now finally got back to where I wanted. I now know that even bodies are not strictly perceived by the senses or the faculty of imagination but by the intellect alone, and that this perception derives not from their being touched or seen but from their being understood; and in view of this I know plainly that I can achieve an easier and more evident perception of my own mind than of anything else. But since the habit of holding on to old opinions cannot be set aside so quickly, I should like to stop here and mediate for some time on this new knowledge I have gained, so as to fix it more deeply in my memory.

An Enquiry Concerning Human Understanding

DAVID HUME

The Scotsman David Hume (1711–1776), essayist, historian, and philosopher, developed one of the most influential of all philosophical systems. He presented it first in his monumental *Treatise of Human Nature,* published when he was twenty-eight years old. Later he reworked the material to make it more accessible, and the selection that follows is from *An Enquiry Concerning Human Understanding,* which appeared in 1748.

The fundamental principle of Hume's philosophy is that our knowledge of the world depends entirely on the evidence provided by our senses. While this premise may appear uncontroversial, as developed by Hume it has startling consequences.

To use an example he offers, suppose you see one billiard ball hit a second and then the second moves. You would say the first made the second move. But Hume points out that all you see is one event followed by another; you do not actually see any connection between them. You assume the connection, but the force of Hume's argument is that your assumption violates the principle that our knowledge rests only on the evidence of our senses. For you did not sense any necessary connection between the two events but presumed it anyway.

Hume extends this reasoning and argues that so far as we know, the world consists of entirely separate events, some regularly following others but all unconnected. He concludes that our beliefs about the necessity of causation are instinctive, not rational.

Hume's arguments are among the most challenging in the history of philosophy, and we shall read more of his work in our next section.

Of the Origin of Ideas

Everyone will readily allow that there is a considerable difference between the perceptions of the mind, when a man feels the pain of excessive heat, or the pleasure of moderate warmth, and when he afterwards recalls to his memory this sensation, or anticipates it by his imagination. These faculties may mimic or copy the perceptions of the senses; but they never can entirely reach the force and vivacity of the original sentiment. The utmost we say of them, even when they operate with greatest vigor, is that they represent their object in so lively a manner, that we could *almost* say we feel or see it: But, except the mind be disordered by disease or madness, they never can arrive at such a pitch of vivacity, as to render these perceptions altogether undistinguishable. All the colors of poetry, however splendid, can never paint natural objects in such a manner as to make the description be taken for a real landscape. The most lively thought is still inferior to the dullest sensation.

We may observe a like distinction to run through all the other perceptions of the mind. A man in a fit of anger is actuated in a very different manner from one who only thinks of that emotion. If you tell me, that any person is in love, I easily understand your meaning, and form a just conception of his situation; but never can mistake that conception for the real disorders and agitations of the passion. When we reflect on our past sentiments and affections, our thought is a faithful mirror, and copies its objects truly; but the colors which it employs are faint and dull, in comparison of those in which our original perceptions were clothed. It requires no nice discernment or metaphysical head to mark the distinction between them.

Here therefore we may divide all the perceptions of the mind into two classes or species, which are distinguished by their different degrees of force and vivacity. The less forcible and lively are commonly denominated *thoughts* or *ideas.* The other species want a name in our language, and in most others; I suppose, because it was not requisite for any, but philosophical purposes, to rank them under a general term or appellation. Let us, therefore, use a little freedom, and call them *impressions;* employing that word in a sense somewhat different from the usual. By the term *impression,* then, I mean all our more lively perceptions, when we hear, or see, or feel, or love, or hate, or desire, or will. And impressions are distinguished from ideas, which are the less lively perceptions, of which we are conscious, when we reflect on any of those sensations or movements above mentioned.

Nothing, at first view, may seem more unbounded than the thought of man, which not only escapes all human power and authority, but is not even restrained within the limits of nature and reality. To form monsters, and join incongruous shapes and appearances, costs the imagination no more trouble than to conceive the most natural and familiar objects. And while the body is confined to one planet, along which it creeps with pain and difficulty; the thought can in an instant transport us into the most distant regions of the universe; or even beyond the universe, into the unbounded chaos, where nature is supposed to lie in total confusion. What never was seen, or heard of, may yet be conceived; nor is anything beyond the power of thought, except what implies an absolute contradiction.

But though our thought seems to possess this unbounded liberty, we shall find, upon a nearer examination, that it is really confined within very narrow limits, and that all this creative power of the mind amounts to no more than the faculty of compounding, transposing, augmenting, or diminishing the materials afforded us by the senses and experience. When we think of a golden mountain, we only join two consistent ideas, *gold,* and *mountain,* with which we were formerly acquainted. A virtuous horse we can conceive; because, from our own feeling, we can conceive virtue; and this we may unite to the figure and shape of a horse, which is an animal familiar to us. In short, all the materials of thinking are derived either from our outward or inward sentiment: the mixture and composition of these belongs alone to the mind and will. Or, to express myself in philosophical language, all our ideas or more feeble perceptions are copies of our impressions or more lively ones.

To prove this, the two following arguments will, I hope, be sufficient. First, when we analyze our thoughts or ideas, however compounded or sublime, we always find that they resolve themselves into such simple ideas as were copied from a precedent feeling or sentiment. Even those ideas, which, at first view, seem the most wide of this origin, are found, upon a nearer scrutiny, to be derived from it. The idea of God, as meaning an infinitely intelligent, wise, and good Being, arises from reflecting on the operations of our own mind, and augmenting, without limit, those qualities of goodness and wisdom. We may prosecute this inquiry to what length we please; where we shall always find, that every idea which we examine is copied from a similar impression. Those who would assert that this position is not universally true nor without exception, have only one, and that an easy method of refuting it; by producing that idea, which, in their opinion, is not derived from this source. It will then be incumbent on us, if we would maintain our doctrine, to produce the impression, or lively perception, which corresponds to it.

Secondly. If it happen, from a defect of the organ, that a man is not susceptible of any species of sensation, we always find that he is as little susceptible of the correspondent ideas. A blind man can form no notion of colors; a deaf man of sounds. Restore either of them that sense in which he is deficient; by opening this new inlet for his sensations, you also open an inlet for the ideas; and he finds no difficulty in conceiving these objects. . . . When we entertain, therefore, any suspicion that a philosophical term is employed without any meaning or idea (as is but too frequent), we need but inquire, *from what impression is that supposed idea derived?* And if it be impossible to assign any, this will serve to confirm our suspicion. By bringing ideas into so clear a light we may reasonably hope to remove all dispute, which may arise, concerning their nature and reality. . . .

Sceptical Doubts Concerning the Operations of the Understanding

Part I

All the objects of human reason or inquiry may naturally be divided into two kinds, to wit, *relations of ideas*, and *matters of fact*. Of the first kind are the sciences of geometry, algebra, and arithmetic; and in short, every affirmation which is either intuitively or demonstratively certain. *That the square of the hypothenuse is equal to the squares of the two sides*, is a proposition which expresses a relation between these figures. *That three times five is equal to the half of thirty*, expresses a relation between these numbers. Propositions of this kind are discoverable by the mere operation of thought, without dependence on what is anywhere existent in the universe. Though there never was a circle or triangle in nature, the truths demonstrated by Euclid would for ever retain their certainty and evidence.

Matters of fact, which are the second objects of human reason, are not ascertained in the same manner; nor is our evidence of their truth, however great, of a like nature with the foregoing. The contrary of every matter of fact is still possible; because it can never imply a contradiction, and is conceived by the mind with the same facility and distinctness, as if ever so conformable to reality. *That the sun will not rise tomorrow* is no less intelligible a proposition, and implies no more contradiction than the affirmation, *that it will rise.* We should in vain, therefore, attempt to demonstrate its falsehood. Were it demonstratively false, it would imply a contradiction, and could never be distinctly conceived by the mind.

It may, therefore, be a subject worthy of curiosity, to inquire what is the nature of that evidence which assures us of any real existence and matter of fact, beyond the present testimony of our senses, or the records of our memory. This part of philosophy, it is observable, has been little cultivated, either by the ancients or moderns; and therefore our doubts and errors, in the prosecution of so important an inquiry, may be the more excusable; while we march through such difficult paths without any guide or direction. They may even prove useful, by exciting curiosity, and destroying that implicit faith and security, which is the bane of all reasoning and free inquiry. The discovery of defects in the common philosophy, if any such there be, will not, I presume, be a discouragement, but rather an incitment, as is usual, to attempt something more full and satisfactory than has yet been proposed to the public.

All reasonings concerning matter of fact seem to be founded on the relation of *cause and effect*. By means of that relation alone we can go beyond the evidence of our memory and senses. If you were to ask a man, why he believes any matter of fact, which is absent; for instance, that his friend is in the country, or in France; he would give you a reason; and this reason would be some other fact; as a letter received from him, or the knowledge of his former resolutions and promises. A man finding a watch or any other machine in a desert island, would conclude that there had once been men in that island. All our reasonings concerning fact are of the same nature. And here it is constantly supposed that there is a connection between the present fact and that which is inferred from it. Were there nothing to bind them together, the inference would be entirely precarious. The hearing of an articulate voice and rational discourse in the dark assures us of the presence of some person: Why? because these are the effects of the human make and fabric, and closely connected with it. If we anatomize all the other reasonings of this nature, we shall find that they are founded on the relation of cause and effect, and that this relation is either near or remote, direct or collateral. Heat and light are collateral effects of fire, and the one effect may justly be inferred from the other.

If we would satisfy ourselves, therefore, concerning the nature of that evidence, which assures us of matters of fact, we must inquire how we arrive at the knowledge of cause and effect.

I shall venture to affirm, as a general proposition, which admits of no exception, that the knowledge of this relation is not, in any instance, attained by reasonings a priori; but arises entirely from experience, when we find that any particular objects are constantly conjoined with each other. Let an object be presented to a man of ever so strong natural reason and abilities; if that object be entirely new to him, he will not be able, by the most accurate examination of its sensible qualities, to discover any of its causes or effects. Adam, though his rational faculties be supposed, at the very first, entirely perfect, could not have inferred from the fluidity and transparency of water that it would suffocate him, or from the light and warmth of fire that it would consume him. No object ever discovers, by the qualities which appear to the senses, either the causes which produced it, or the effects which will arise from it; nor can our reason, unassisted by experience, ever draw any inference concerning real existence and matter of fact.

This proposition, *that causes and effects are discoverable, not by reason but by experience,* will readily be admitted with regard to such objects, as we remember to have once been altogether unknown to us; since we must be conscious of the utter inability, which we then lay under, of foretelling what would arise from them. Present two smooth pieces of marble to a man who has no tincture of natural philosophy; he will never discover that they will adhere together in such a manner as to require great force to separate them in a direct line, while they make so small a resistance to a lateral pressure. Such events, as bear little analogy to the common course of nature, are also readily confessed to be known only by experience; nor does any man imagine that the explosion of gunpowder, or the attraction of a loadstone, could ever be discovered by arguments a priori. In like manner, when an effect is supposed to depend upon an intricate machinery or secret structure of parts, we make no difficulty in attributing all our knowledge of it to experience. Who will assert that he can give the ultimate reason, why milk or bread is proper nourishment for a man, not for a lion or a tiger?

But the same truth may not appear, at first sight, to have the same evidence with regard to events, which have become familiar to us from our first appearance in the world, which bear a close analogy to the whole course of nature, and which are supposed to depend on the simple qualities of objects, without any secret structure of parts. We are apt to imagine that we could discover these effects by the mere operation of our reason, without experience. We fancy, that were we brought on a sudden into this world, we could at first have inferred that one billiard ball would communicate motion to another upon impulse; and that we needed not to have waited for the event, in order to pronounce with certainty concerning it. Such is the influence of custom, that, where it is strongest, it not only covers our natural ignorance, but even conceals itself, and seems not to take place, merely because it is found in the highest degree.

But to convince us that all the laws of nature, and all the operations of bodies without exception, are known only by experience, the following reflections may, perhaps, suffice. Were any object presented to us, and were we required to pronounce concerning the effect, which will result from it, without consulting past observation; after what manner, I beseech you, must the mind proceed in this operation? It must invent or imagine some event, which it ascribes to the object as its effect; and it is plain that this invention must be entirely arbitrary. The mind can never possibly find the effect in the supposed cause, by the most accurate scrutiny and examination. For the effect is totally different from the cause, and consequently can never be discovered in it. Motion in the second billiard ball is a quite distinct event from motion in the first: nor is there anything in the one to suggest the smallest hint of the other. A stone or piece of metal raised into the air, and left without any support, immediately falls: but to consider the matter a priori, is there anything we discover in this situation which can beget the idea of a downward, rather than an upward, or any other motion, in the stone or metal?

And as the first imagination or invention of a particular effect, in all natural operations, is arbitrary, where we consult not experience; so must we also esteem the supposed tie or connection between the cause and effect, which binds them together, and renders it impossible that any other effect could result from the operation of that cause. When I see, for instance, a billiard ball moving in a straight line towards another; even suppose motion in the second ball should by accident be suggested to me, as the result of their contact or impulse; may I not conceive, that a hundred different events might as well follow from that cause? May not both these balls remain at absolute rest? May not the first ball return in a straight line, or leap off from the second in any line or direction? All these suppositions are consistent and conceivable. Why then should we give the preference to one, which is no more consistent or conceivable than the rest? All our reasonings a priori, will never be able to show us any foundation for this preference.

In a word, then, every effect is a distinct event from its cause. It could not, therefore, be discovered in the cause, and the first invention or conception of it, a priori, must be entirely arbitrary. And even after it is suggested, the conjunction of it with the cause must appear equally arbitrary; since there are always many other effects, which, to reason, must seem fully as consistent and natural. In vain, therefore, should we pretend to determine any single event, or infer any cause or effect, without the assistance of observation and experience. . . .

Part II

But we have not yet attained any tolerable satisfaction with regard to the question first proposed. Each solution still gives rise to a new question as difficult as the foregoing, and leads us on to farther inquiries. When it is asked, *What is the nature of all our reasonings concerning matter of fact?* the proper answer seems to be, that they are founded on the relation of cause and effect. When again it is asked, *What is the foundation of all our reasonings and conclusions concerning that relation?* it may be replied in one word, *experience*. But if we still carry on our sifting humor, and ask, *What is the foundation of all conclusions from experience?* this implies a new question, which may be of more difficult solution and explication. Philosophers, that give themselves airs of superior wisdom and sufficiency, have a hard task when they encounter persons of inquisitive dispositions, who push them from every corner to which they retreat, and who are sure at last to bring them to some dangerous dilemma. The best expedient to prevent this confusion, is to be modest in our pretensions; and even to discover the difficulty ourselves before it is objected to us. By this means, we may make a kind of merit of our very ignorance.

I shall content myself, in this section, with an easy task, and shall pretend only to give a negative answer to the question here proposed. I say then, that, even after we have experience of the operations of cause and effect, our conclusions from that experience are *not* founded on reasoning, or any process of the understanding. This answer we must endeavor both to explain and to defend.

It must certainly be allowed, that nature has kept us at a great distance from all her secrets, and has afforded us only the knowledge of a few superficial qualities of objects; while she conceals from us those powers and principles on which the influence of those objects entirely depends. Our senses inform us of the color, weight, and consistence of bread; but neither sense nor reason can ever inform us of those qualities which fit it for the nourishment and support of a human body. Sight or feeling conveys an idea of the actual motion of bodies; but as to that wonderful force or power, which would carry on a moving body forever in a continued change of place, and which bodies never lose but by communicating it to others; of this we cannot form the most distant conception. But notwithstanding this ignorance of natural powers and principles, we always presume, when we see like sensible qualities, that they have like secret powers, and expect that effects, similar to those which we have experienced, will follow from them. If a body of like color and consistence with that bread, which we have formerly eat, be presented to us, we make no scruple of repeating the experiment, and foresee, with certainty, like nourishment and support. Now this is a process of the mind or thought, of which I would willingly know the foundation. It is allowed on all hands that there is no known connection between the sensible qualities and the secret powers; and consequently, that the mind is not led to form such a conclusion concerning their constant and regular conjunction, by anything which it knows of their nature. As to past *experience,* it can be allowed to give *direct* and *certain* information of those precise objects only, and that precise period of time, which fell under its cognizance: but why this experience should be extended to future times, and to other objects, which, for aught we know, may be only in appearance similar; this is the main question on which I would insist. The bread, which I formerly eat, nourished me; that is, a body of such sensible qualities was, at that time, endued with such secret powers: but does it follow, that other bread must also nourish me at another time, and that like sensible qualities must always be attended with like secret powers? The consequence seems no wise necessary. At least, it must be acknowledged that there is here a consequence drawn by the mind; that there is a certain step taken; a process of thought, and an inference, which wants to be explained. These two propositions are far from being the same, *I have found that such an object has always been attended with such an effect,* and *I foresee, that other objects, which are, in appearance, similar, will be attended with similar effects.* I shall allow, if you please, that the one proposition may justly be inferred from the other; I know, in fact, that it always is inferred. But if you insist that the inference is made by a chain of reasoning, I desire you to produce that reasoning. . . .

To say it is experimental is begging the question. For all inferences from experience suppose, as their foundation, that the future will resemble the past, and that similar powers will be conjoined with similar sensible qualities. If there be any suspicion that the course of nature may change, and that the past may be no rule for the future, all experience becomes useless, and can give rise to no inference or conclusion. It is impossible, therefore, that any arguments from experience can prove this resemblance of the past to the future; since all these arguments are founded on the supposition of that resemblance. Let the course of things be allowed hitherto ever so regular; that alone, without some new argument or inference, proves not that, for the future, it will continue so. In vain do you pretend to have learned the nature of bodies from your past experience. Their secret nature, and consequently all their effects and influence, may change, without any change in their sensible qualities. This happens sometimes, and with regard to some objects: Why may it not happen always, and with regard to all objects? What logic, what process of argument secures you against this supposition? My practice, you say, refutes my doubts. But you mistake the purport of my question. As an agent, I am quite satisfied in the point; but as a philosopher, who has some share of curiosity, I will not say scepticism, I want to learn the foundation of this inference. No reading, no inquiry has yet been able to remove my difficulty, or give me satisfaction in a matter of such importance. Can I do better than propose the difficulty to the public, even though, perhaps, I have small hopes of obtaining a solution? We shall, at least, by this means, be sensible of our ignorance, if we do not augment our knowledge . . .

Sceptical Solution of These Doubts

Suppose a person, though endowed with the strongest faculties of reason and reflection, to be brought on a sudden into this world; he would, indeed, immediately observe a continual succession of objects, and one event following another; but he would not be able to discover anything farther. He would not, at first, by any reasoning, be able to reach the idea of cause and effect; since the particular powers, by which all natural operations are performed, never appear to the senses; nor is it reasonable to conclude, merely because one event, in one instance, precedes another, that therefore the one is the cause, the other the effect. Their conjunction may be arbitrary and casual. There may be no reason to infer the existence of one from the appearance of the other. And in a word, such a person, without more experience, could never employ his conjecture or reasoning concerning any matter of fact, or be assured of anything beyond what was immediately present to his memory and senses.

Suppose, again, that he has acquired more experience, and has lived so long in the world as to have observed familiar objects or events to be constantly conjoined together; what is the consequence of this experience? He immediately infers the existence of one object from the appearance of the other. Yet he has not, by all his experience, acquired any idea or knowledge of the secret power by which the one object produces the other; nor is it, by any process of reasoning, he is engaged to draw this inference. But still he finds himself determined to draw it: And though he should be convinced that his understanding has no part in the operation, he would nevertheless continue in the same course of thinking. There is some other principle which determines him to form such a conclusion.

This principle is *custom* or *habit*. For wherever the repetition of any particular act or operation produces a propensity to renew the same act or operation, without being impelled by any reasoning or process of the understanding, we always say, that this propensity is the effect of *custom*. By employing that word, we pretend not to have given the ultimate reason of such a propensity. We only point out a principle of human nature, which is universally acknowledged, and which is well known by its effects. Perhaps we can push our inquiries no farther, or pretend to give the cause of this cause; but must rest contented with it as the ultimate principle, which we can assign, of all our conclusions from experience. . . .

Custom, then, is the great guide of human life. It is that principle alone which renders our experience useful to us, and makes us expect, for the future, a similar train of events with those which have appeared in the past. Without the influence of custom, we should be entirely ignorant of every matter of fact beyond what is immediately present to the memory and senses. We should never know how to adjust means to ends, or to employ our natural powers in the production of any effect. There would be an end at once of all action, as well as of the chief part of speculation. . . .

What, then, is the conclusion of the whole matter? A simple one; though, it must be confessed, pretty remote from the common theories of philosophy. All belief of matter of fact or real existence is derived merely from some object, present to the memory or senses, and a customary conjunction between that and some other object. Or in other words; having found, in many instances, that any two kinds of objects—flame and heat, snow and cold—have always been conjoined together; if flame or snow be presented anew to the senses, the mind is carried by custom to expect heat or cold, and to *believe* that such a quality does exist, and will discover itself upon a nearer approach. This belief is the necessary result of placing the mind in such circumstances. It is an operation of the soul, when we are so situated, as unavoidable as to feel the passion of love, when we receive benefits; or hatred, when we meet with injuries. All these operations are a species of natural instincts, which no reasoning or process of the thought and understanding is able either to produce or to prevent.

PART 4

GOD

Does God Exist?

ERNEST NAGEL

One metaphysical issue that interests us all is whether God exists. A theist believes God does exist. An atheist believes God does not exist. An agnostic believes the available evidence is insufficient to decide the matter. Which of these positions is the most reasonable?

The first step in answering this question is to determine what is meant by the term "God." Let us adopt a view common to many religious believers that "God" refers to an all-good, all-powerful, eternal Creator of the world. The question then is whether a Being of that description exists.

Throughout the centuries various arguments have been put forth to prove the existence of God. One of the best known is referred to as the "cosmological argument." It rests on the assumption that everything that exists is caused to exist by something else. For example, a house is caused to exist by its builder, and rain is caused by certain meteorological conditions. But if everything that exists is caused to exist by something else, then the world must be caused to exist by something else. This "something else" is God.

A second classic proof for the existence of God is called the "ontological argument." Since God is defined as a Being who possesses every perfection, and assuming that to exist is more perfect than not to exist, it follows that God, a perfect Being, must exist.

While the ontological argument is abstruse, the next argument, called the "teleological argument," is easily understood and highly plausible.

Look around at the world in which we live. It possesses a highly ordered structure, just like an extraordinarily complex machine. Each part of the machine is adjusted to all the other parts with wondrous precision, and the more we investigate the working of the world, the more we are amazed at its intricate patterns. For instance, the human eye, which so many of us take for granted, is a mechanism of such enormous complexity that its design is breathtaking. But doesn't a design require a designer? The magnificent order of our world cannot be a result of pure chance but must be the work of a Supreme Mind that is responsible for the order. That Supreme Mind is God. So argue defenders of the teleological argument.

From *Basic Beliefs*, ed. J. E. Fairchild. Copyright © 1959 by Sheridan House, Inc.

Just as some arguments support the existence of God, other arguments reach an opposing conclusion. One well-known challenge to theism is "the problem of evil." It rests on the observation that the world is not perfect. Consider droughts, floods, famines, hurricanes, tornadoes, earthquakes, and the innumerable varieties of disease that plague us. And what of the evils people cause each other? The savageries of war, the indignities of slavery, and the torments of injustice and treachery extend far beyond the limits of our imagination.

But why should we suffer ills if our world was created by an all-good, all-powerful Being? An all-good Being would do everything possible to abolish evil. An all-powerful Being would be able to abolish evil. So if an all-good, all-powerful Being existed, evil would not. But evil exists. Therefore, an all-good, all-powerful Being doesn't.

The next essay considers various arguments for and against the existence of God. The author is Ernest Nagel, whose work in philosophy of science we read previously (pp. 63–68).

1

I want now to discuss three classical arguments for the existence of God, arguments which have constituted at least a partial basis for theistic commitments. As long as theism is defended simply as a dogma, asserted as a matter of direct revelation or as the deliverance of authority, belief in the dogma is impregnable to rational argument. In fact, however, reasons are frequently advanced in support of the theistic creed, and these reasons have been the subject of acute philosophical critiques.

One of the oldest intellectual defenses of theism is the cosmological argument, also known as the argument from a first cause. Briefly put, the argument runs as follows. Every event must have a cause. Hence an event A must have as cause some event B, which in turn must have a cause C, and so on. But if there is no end to this backward progression of causes, the progression will be infinite; and in the opinion of those who use this argument, an infinite series of actual events is unintelligible and absurd. Hence there must be a first cause, and this first cause is God, the initiator of all change in the universe.

The argument is an ancient one, and . . . it has impressed many generations of exceptionally keen minds. The argument is nonetheless a weak reed on which to rest the theistic thesis. Let us waive any question concerning the validity of the principle that every event has a cause, for though the question is important, its discussion would lead us far afield. However, if the principle is assumed, it is surely incongruous to postulate a first cause as a way of escaping from the coils of an infinite series. For if everything must have a cause, why does not God require one for His own existence? The standard answer is that He does not need any, because He is self-caused. But if God can be self-caused, why cannot the world itself be self-caused? Why do we require a God transcending the world to bring the world into existence and to initiate changes in it? On the other hand, the supposed inconceivability and absurdity of an infinite series of regressive causes will be admitted by no one who has competent familiarity with the modern mathematical analysis of infinity. The cosmological argument does not stand up under scrutiny.

The second "proof" of God's existence is usually called the ontological argument. It too has a long history going back to early Christian days, though it acquired great prominence only in medieval times. The argument can be stated in several ways, one of which is the following. Since God is conceived to be omnipotent, he is a perfect being. A perfect being is defined as one whose essence or nature lacks no attributes (or properties) whatsoever, one whose nature is complete in every respect. But it is evident that we have an idea of a perfect being, for we have just defined the idea; and since this is so, the argument continues, God who is the perfect being must exist. Why must he? Because his existence follows from his defined nature. For if God lacked the attribute of existence, he would be lacking at least one attribute, and would therefore not be perfect. To sum up, since we have an idea of God as a perfect being, God must exist.

There are several ways of approaching this argument, but I shall consider only one. The argument was exploded by the eighteenth century philosopher Immanuel Kant. The substance of Kant's criticism is that it is just a confusion to say that existence is an attribute, and that though the *word* "existence" may occur as the grammatical predicate in a sentence, no attribute is being predicated of a thing when we say that the thing exists or has existence. Thus, to use Kant's example, when we think of $100 we are thinking of the nature of this sum of money; but the nature of $100 remains the same whether we have $100 in our pockets or not. Accordingly, we are confounding grammar with logic if we suppose that some characteristic is being attributed to the nature of $100 when we say that a hundred dollar bill exists in someone's pocket.

To make the point clearer, consider another example. When we say that a lion has a tawny color, we are predicating a certain attribute of the animal, and similarly when we say that the lion is fierce or is hungry. But when we say the lion exists, all that we are saying is that something is (or has the nature of) a lion; we are not specifying an attribute which belongs to the nature of anything that is a lion. In short, the word "existence" does not signify any attribute, and in consequence no attribute that belongs to the nature of anything. Accordingly, it does not follow from the assumption that we have an idea of a perfect being that such a being exists. For the idea of a perfect being does not involve the attribute of existence as a constituent of that idea, since there is no such attribute. The ontological argument thus has a serious leak, and it can hold no water.

2

The two arguments discussed thus far are purely dialectical, and attempt to establish God's existence without any appeal to empirical data. The next argument, called the argument from design, is different in character, for it is based on what purports to be empirical evidence. I wish to examine two forms of this argument.

One variant of it calls attention to the remarkable way in which different things and processes in the world are integrated with each other, and concludes that this mutual "fitness" of things can be explained only by the assumption of a divine architect who planned the world and everything in it. For example, living organisms can maintain themselves in a variety of environments, and do so in virtue of their delicate mechanisms which adapt the organisms to all sorts of environmental changes. There is thus an intricate pattern of means and ends throughout the animate world. But the existence of this pattern is unintelligible, so the argument runs, except on the hypothesis that the pattern has been deliberately instituted by a Supreme Designer. If we find a watch in some deserted spot, we do not think it came into existence by chance, and we do not hesitate to conclude that an intelligent creature designed and made it. But the world and all its contents exhibit mechanisms and mutual adjustments that are far more complicated and subtle than are those of a watch. Must we not therefore conclude that these things too have a Creator?

The conclusion of this argument is based on an inference from analogy: the watch and the world are alike in possessing a congruence of parts and an adjustment of means to ends; the watch has a watch-maker; hence the world has a world-maker. But is the analogy a good one? Let us once more waive some important issues, in particular the issue whether the universe is the unified system such as the watch admittedly is. And let us concentrate on the question what is the ground for our assurance that watches do not come into existence except through the operations of intelligent manufacturers. The answer is plain. We have never run across a watch which has not been deliberately made by someone. But the situation is nothing like this in the case of the innumerable animate and inanimate systems with which we are familiar. Even in the case of living organisms, though they are generated by their parent organisms, the parents do not "make" their progeny in the same sense in which watch-makers make watches. And once this point is clear, the inference from the existence of living organisms to the existence of a supreme designer no longer appears credible.

Moreover, the argument loses all its force if the facts which the hypothesis of a divine designer is supposed to explain can be understood on the ba-

sis of a better supported assumption. And indeed, such an alternative explanation is one of the achievements of Darwinian biology. For Darwin showed
that one can account for the variety of biological species, as well as for their
adaptations to their environments, without invoking a divine creator and
acts of special creation. The Darwinian theory explains the diversity of biological species in terms of chance variations in the structure of organisms,
and of a mechanism of selection which retains those variant forms that possess some advantages for survival. The evidence for these assumptions is
considerable; and developments subsequent to Darwin have only strength-
ened the case for a thoroughly naturalistic explanation of the facts of biological adaptation. In any event, this version of the argument from design has
nothing to recommend it.

A second form of this argument has been recently revived in the specu-
lations of some modern physicists. No one who is familiar with the facts can
fail to be impressed by the success with which the use of mathematical methods has enabled us to obtain intellectual mastery of many parts of nature.
But some thinkers have therefore concluded that since the book of nature is
ostensibly written in mathematical language, nature must be the creation of
a divine mathematician. However, the argument is most dubious. For it
rests, among other things, on the assumption that mathematical tools can be
successfully used only if the events of nature exhibit some *special* kind of order, and on the further assumption that if the structure of things were different from what they are, mathematical language would be inadequate for describing such structure. But it can be shown that no matter what the world
were like—even if it impressed us as being utterly chaotic—it would still
possess some order, and would in principle be amenable to a mathematical
description. In point of fact, it makes no sense to say that there is absolutely
no pattern in any conceivable subject matter. To be sure, there are differences
in complexities of structure, and if the patterns of events were sufficiently
complex, we might not be able to unravel them. But however that may be,
the success of mathematical physics in giving us some understanding of the
world around us does not yield the conclusion that only a mathematician
could have devised the patterns of order we have discovered in nature.

3

The inconclusiveness of the three classical arguments for the existence of
God was already made evident by Kant, in a manner substantially not different from the above discussion. There are, however, other types of arguments for theism that have been influential in the history of thought, two of
which I wish to consider, even if only briefly.

Indeed, though Kant destroyed the classical intellectual foundations for
theism, he himself invented a fresh argument for it. Kant's attempted proof
is not intended to be a purely theoretical demonstration, and is based on the

supposed facts of our moral nature. It has exerted an enormous influence on subsequent theological speculation. In barest outline, the argument is as follows. According to Kant, we are subject not only to physical laws like the rest of nature, but also to moral ones. These moral laws are categorical imperatives, which we must heed not because of their utilitarian consequences, but simply because as autonomous moral agents it is our duty to accept them as binding. However, Kant was keenly aware that though virtue may be its reward, the virtuous man (that is, the man who acts out of a sense of duty and in conformity with the moral law) does not always receive his just desserts in this world; nor did he shut his eyes to the fact that evil men frequently enjoy the best things this world has to offer. In short, virtue does not always reap happiness. Nevertheless, the highest human good is the realization of happiness commensurate with one's virtue; and Kant believed that it is a practical postulate of the moral life to promote this good. But what can guarantee that the highest good is realizable? Such a guarantee can be found only in God, who must therefore exist if the highest good is not to be a fatuous ideal. The existence of an omnipotent, omniscient, and omnibenevolent God is thus postulated as a necessary condition for the possibility of a moral life.

Despite the prestige this argument has acquired, it is difficult to grant it any force. It is easy enough to postulate God's existence. But as Bertrand Russell observed in another connection, postulation has all the advantages of theft over honest toil. No postulation carries with it any assurance that what is postulated is actually the case. And though we may postulate God's existence as a means to guaranteeing the possibility of realizing happiness together with virtue, the postulation establishes neither the actual realizability of this ideal nor the fact of his existence. Moreover, the argument is not made more cogent when we recognize that it is based squarely on the highly dubious conception that considerations of utility and human happiness must not enter into the determination of what is morally obligatory. Having built his moral theory on a radical separation of means from ends, Kant was driven to the desperate postulation of God's existence in order to relate them again. The argument is thus at best a *tour de force*, contrived to remedy a fatal flaw in Kant's initial moral assumptions. It carries no conviction to anyone who does not commit Kant's initial blunder.

One further type of argument, pervasive in much Protestant theological literature, deserves brief mention. Arguments of this type take their point of departure from the psychology of religious and mystical experience. Those who have undergone such experiences often report that during the experience they feel themselves to be in the presence of the divine and holy, that they lose their sense of self-identity and become merged with some fundamental reality, or that they enjoy a feeling of total dependence upon some ultimate power. The overwhelming sense of transcending one's finitude which characterizes such vivid periods of life, and of coalescing with some ultimate source of all existence, is then taken to be compelling evidence for the existence of a supreme being. In a variant form of this argument, other theologians have identified God as the object which satisfies the commonly experienced need for integrating one's scattered and conflicting impulses into a coherent unity, or as the subject which is of ultimate concern to us. In short, a proof of God's existence is found in the occurrence of certain distinctive experiences.

It would be flying in the face of well-attested facts were one to deny that such experiences frequently occur. But do these facts constitute evidence for the conclusion based on them? Does the fact, for example, that an individual experiences a profound sense of direct contact with an alleged transcendent ground of all reality constitute competent evidence for the claim that there is such a ground and that it is the immediate cause of the experience? If well-established canons for evaluating evidence are accepted, the answer is surely negative. No one will dispute that many men do have vivid experiences in which such things as ghosts or pink elephants appear before them; but only the hopelessly credulous will without further ado count such experiences as establishing the existence of ghosts and pink elephants. To establish the existence of such things, evidence is required that is obtained under controlled conditions and that can be confirmed by independent inquirers. Again, though a man's report that he is suffering pain may be taken at face value, one cannot take at face value the claim, were he to make it, that it is the food he ate which is the cause (or a contributory cause) of his felt pain—not even if the man were to report a vivid feeling of abdominal disturbance. And similarly, an overwhelming feeling of being in the presence of the Divine is evidence enough for admitting the genuineness of such feeling; it is no evidence for the claim that a supreme being with a substantial existence independent of the experience is the cause of the experience.

4

Thus far the discussion has been concerned with noting inadequacies in various arguments widely used to support theism. However, much atheistic criticism is also directed toward exposing incoherencies in the very thesis of theism. I want therefore to consider this aspect of the atheistic critique, though I will restrict myself to the central difficulty in the theistic position which arises from the simultaneous attribution of omnipotence, omniscience, and omnibenevolence to the Deity. The difficulty is that of reconciling these attributes with the occurrence of evil in the world. Accordingly, the question to which I now turn is whether, despite the existence of evil, it is possible to construct a theodicy which will justify the ways of an infinitely powerful and just God to man.

Two main types of solutions have been proposed for this problem. One way that is frequently used is to maintain that what is commonly called evil is only an illusion, or at worst only the "privation" or absence of good. Accordingly, evil is not "really real," it is only the "negative" side of God's beneficence, it is only the product of our limited intelligence which fails to plumb the true character of God's creative bounty. A sufficient comment on this proposed solution is that facts are not altered or abolished by rebaptizing them. Evil may indeed be only an appearance and not genuine. But this does not eliminate from the realm of appearance the tragedies, the sufferings, and the iniquities which men so frequently endure. And it raises once more, though on another level, the problem of reconciling the fact that there is evil in the realm of appearance with God's alleged omnibenevolence. In any event, it is small comfort to anyone suffering a cruel misfortune for which he is in no way responsible, to be told that what he is undergoing is only the absence of good. It is a gratuitous insult to mankind, a symptom of insensitivity and indifference to human suffering, to be assured that all the miseries and agonies men experience are only illusory.

Another gambit often played in attempting to justify the ways of God to man is to argue that the things called evil are evil only because they are viewed in isolation; they are not evil when viewed in proper perspective and in relation to the rest of creation. Thus, if one attends to but a single instrument in an orchestra, the sounds issuing from it may indeed be harsh and discordant. But if one is placed at a proper distance from the whole orchestra, the sounds of that single instrument will mingle with the sounds issuing from the other players to produce a marvellous bit of symphonic music. Analogously, experiences we call painful undoubtedly occur and are real enough. But the pain is judged to be an evil only because it is experienced in a limited perspective—the pain is there for the sake of a more inclusive good, whose reality eludes us because our intelligences are too weak to apprehend things in their entirety.

It is an appropriate retort to this argument that of course we judge things to be evil in a human perspective, but that since we are not God this is the only proper perspective in which to judge them. It may indeed be the case that what is evil for us is not evil for some other part of creation. However, we are not this other part of creation, and it is irrelevant to argue that were we something other than what we are, our evaluations of what is good and bad would be different. Moreover, the worthlessness of the argument becomes even more evident if we remind ourselves that it is unsupported speculation to suppose that whatever is evil in a finite perspective is good from the purported perspective of the totality of things. For the argument can be turned around: what we judge to be a good is a good only because it is viewed in isolation; when it is viewed in proper perspective, and in relation to the entire scheme of things, it is an evil. This is in fact a standard form of the argument for a universal pessimism. Is it any worse than the similar argument for a universal optimism? The very raising of this question is a *reductio ad absurdum* of the proposed solution to the ancient problem of evil.

I do not believe it is possible to reconcile the alleged omnipotence and omnibenevolence of God with the unvarnished facts of human existence. In point of fact, many theologians have concurred in this conclusion; for in order to escape from the difficulty which the traditional attributes of God present, they have assumed that God is not all powerful, and that there are limits as to what He can do in his efforts to establish a righteous order in the universe. But whether such a modified theology is better off is doubtful; and in any event, the question still remains whether the facts of human life support the claim that an omnibenevolent Deity, though limited in power, is revealed in the ordering of human history. It is pertinent to note in this connection that though there have been many historians who have made the effort, no historian has yet succeeded in showing to the satisfaction of his professional colleagues that the hypothesis of a Divine Providence is capable of explaining anything which cannot be explained just as well without this hypothesis.

Why God Allows Evil

❖❖

RICHARD SWINBURNE

> Richard Swinburne, who holds a professorship at the University of Oxford, is a leading proponent of theism and other tenets of Christianity. In our next selection he seeks to explain why an all-good God who had the power to eliminate evil might choose not to do so.
>
> Swinburne's clear arguments provide an excellent opportunity for you to test your philosophical skills. After reading the article, ask yourself whether he has offered a plausible account of why God might allow evil. If Swinburne has not persuaded you, try to spell out your dissatisfactions with his view. If he has convinced you, consider why others might disagree with him and how you would answer their possible objections. Such critical thinking is the appropriate way to respond to a philosophical essay.

The world . . . contains much evil. An omnipotent God could have prevented this evil, and surely a perfectly good and omnipotent God would have done so. So why is there this evil? Is not its existence strong evidence against the existence of God? It would be unless we can construct what is known as a

theodicy, an explanation of why God would allow such evil to occur. I believe that that can be done, and I shall outline a theodicy. . . . I emphasize that
. . . in writing that God would do this or that, I am not taking for granted the
existence of God, but merely claiming that, if there is a God, it is to be expected that he would do certain things, including allowing the occurrence of
certain evils; and so, I am claiming, their occurrence is not evidence against
his existence.

It is inevitable that any attempt by myself or anyone else to construct a
theodicy will sound callous, indeed totally insensitive to human suffering.
Many theists, as well as atheists, have felt that any attempt to construct a
theodicy evinces an immoral approach to suffering. I can only ask the reader
to believe that I am not totally insensitive to human suffering, and that I do
mind about the agony of poisoning, child abuse, bereavement, solitary imprisonment, and marital infidelity as much as anyone else. True, I would not
in most cases recommend that a pastor give this chapter to victims of sudden
distress at their worst moment to read for consolation. But this is not because
its arguments are unsound; it is simply that most people in deep distress
need comfort, not argument. Yet there is a problem about why God allows
evil, and, if the theist does not have (in a cool moment) a satisfactory answer
to it, then his belief in God is less than rational, and there is no reason why
the atheist should share it. To appreciate the argument of this chapter, each
of us needs to stand back a bit from the particular situation of his or her own
life and that of close relatives and friends (which can so easily seem the only
important thing in the world), and ask very generally what good things
would a generous and everlasting God give to human beings in the course of
a short earthly life. Of course thrills of pleasure and periods of contentment
are good things, and—other things being equal—God would certainly seek
to provide plenty of those. But a generous God will seek to give deeper good
things than these. He will seek to give us great responsibility for ourselves,
each other, and the world, and thus a share in his own creative activity of determining what sort of world it is to be. And he will seek to make our lives
valuable, of great use to ourselves and each other. The problem is that God
cannot give us these goods in full measure without allowing much evil on
the way. . . .

[T]here are plenty of evils, positive bad states, which God could if he
chose remove. I divide these into moral evils and natural evils. I understand
by "natural evil" all evil which is not deliberately produced by human beings and which is not allowed by human beings to occur as a result of their
negligence. Natural evil includes both physical suffering and mental suffering, of animals as well as humans; all the trial of suffering which disease,
natural disasters, and accidents unpredictable by humans bring in their
train. "Moral evil" I understand as including all evil caused deliberately by
humans doing what they ought not to do (or allowed to occur by humans
negligently failing to do what they ought to do) *and* also the evil constituted
by such deliberate actions or negligent failure. It includes the sensory pain of

the blow inflicted by the bad parent on his child, the mental pain of the parent depriving the child of love, the starvation allowed to occur in Africa because of negligence by members of foreign governments who could have prevented it, and also the evil of the parent or politician deliberately bringing about the pain or not trying to prevent the starvation.

Moral Evil

The central core of any theodicy must, I believe, be the "free-will defence," which deals—to start with—with moral evil, but can be extended to deal with much natural evil as well. The free-will defence claims that it is a great good that humans have a certain sort of free will which I shall call free and responsible choice, but that, if they do, then necessarily there will be the natural possibility of moral evil. (By the "natural possibility" I mean that it will not be determined in advance whether or not the evil will occur.) A God who gives humans such free will necessarily brings about the possibility, and puts outside his own control whether or not that evil occurs. It is not logically possible—that is, it would be self-contradictory to suppose—that God could give us such free will and yet ensure that we always use it in the right way.

Free and responsible choice is not just free will in the narrow sense of being able to choose between alternative actions, without our choice being causally necessitated by some prior cause. . . . [H]umans could have that kind of free will merely in virtue of being able to choose freely between two equally good and unimportant alternatives. Free and responsible choice is rather free will (of the kind discussed) to make significant choices between good and evil, which make a big difference to the agent, to others, and to the world.

Given that we have free will, we certainly have free and responsible choice. Let us remind ourselves of the difference that humans can make to themselves, others, and the world. Humans have opportunities to give themselves and others pleasurable sensations, and to pursue worthwhile activities—to play tennis or the piano, to acquire knowledge of history and science and philosophy, and to help others to do so, and thereby to build deep personal relations founded upon such sensations and activities. And humans are so made that they can form their characters. Aristotle famously remarked: "we become just by doing just acts, prudent by doing prudent acts, brave by doing brave acts." That is, by doing a just act when it is difficult—when it goes against our natural inclinations (which is what I understand by desires)—we make it easier to do a just act next time. We can gradually change our desires, so that—for example—doing just acts becomes natural. Thereby we can free ourselves from the power of the less good desires to which we are subject. And, by choosing to acquire knowledge and to use it to build machines of various sorts, humans can extend the range of the differences they can make to the world—they can build universities to last for centuries, or save energy for the next generation; and by cooperative effort over many decades they can eliminate poverty. The possibilities for free and responsible choice are enormous.

It is good that the free choices of humans should include *genuine* responsibility for other humans, and that involves the opportunity to benefit *or* harm them. God has the power to benefit or to harm humans. If other agents are to be given a share in his creative work, it is good that they have that power too (although perhaps to a lesser degree). A world in which agents can benefit each other but not do each other harm is one where they have only very limited responsibility for each other. If my responsibility for you is limited to whether or not to give you a camcorder, but I cannot cause you pain, stunt your growth, or limit your education, then I do not have a great deal of responsibility for you. A God who gave agents only such limited responsibilities for their fellows would not have given much. God would have reserved for himself the all-important choice of the kind of world it was to be, while simply allowing humans the minor choice of filling in the details. He would be like a father asking his elder son to look after the younger son, and adding that he would be watching the elder son's every move and would intervene the moment the elder did a thing wrong. The elder son might justly retort that, while he would be happy to share his father's work, he could really do so only if he were left to make his own judgements as to what to do within a significant range of the options available to the father. A good God, like a good father, will delegate responsibility. In order to allow creatures a share in creation, he will allow them the choice of hurting and maiming, of frustrating the divine plan. Our world is one where creatures have just such deep responsibility for each other. I cannot only benefit my children, but harm them. One way in which I can harm them is that I can inflict physical pain on them. But there are much more damaging things which I can do to them. Above all I can stop them growing into creatures with significant knowledge, power, and freedom; I can determine whether they come to have the kind of free and responsible choice which I have. The possibility of humans bringing about significant evil is a logical consequence of their having this free and responsible choice. Not even God could give us this choice without the possibility of resulting evil.

Now . . . an action would not be intentional unless it was done for a reason—that is, seen as in some way a good thing (either in itself or because of its consequences). And, if reasons alone influence actions, that regarded by the subject as most important will determine what is done; an agent under the influence of reason alone will inevitably do the action which he regards as overall the best. If an agent does not do the action which he regards as overall the best, he must have allowed factors other than reason to exert an influence on him. In other words, he must have allowed desires for what he regards as good only in a certain respect, but not overall, to influence his conduct. So, in order to have a choice between good and evil, agents need already a certain depravity, in the sense of a system of desires for what they correctly believe to be evil. I need to *want* to overeat, get more than my fair share of money or power, indulge my sexual appetites even by deceiving my spouse or partner, want to see you hurt, if I am to have choice between good and evil. This depravity is itself an evil which is a necessary condition of a greater good. It makes possible a choice made seriously and deliberately, because made in the face of a genuine alternative. I stress that, according to the free-will defence, it is the natural possibility of moral evil which is the necessary condition of the great good, not the actual evil itself. Whether that occurs is (through God's choice) outside God's control and up to us.

Note further and crucially that, if I suffer in consequence of your freely chosen bad action, that is not by any means pure loss for me. In a certain respect it is a good for *me.* My suffering would be pure loss for me if the only good thing in life was sensory pleasure, and the only bad thing sensory pain; and it is because the modern world tends to think in those terms that the problem of evil seems so acute. If these were the only good and bad things, the occurrence of suffering would indeed be a conclusive objection to the existence of God. But we have already noted the great good of freely choosing and influencing our future, that of our fellows, and that of the world. And now note another great good—the good of our life serving a purpose, of being of use to ourselves and others. Recall the words of Christ, "it is more blessed to give than to receive" (as quoted by St. Paul (Acts 20: 35)). We tend to think, when the beggar appears on our doorstep and we feel obliged to give and do give, that that was lucky for him but not for us who happened to be at home. That is not what Christ's words say. They say that *we* are the lucky ones, not just because we have a lot, out of which we can give a little, but because we are privileged to contribute to the beggar's happiness—and that privilege is worth a lot more than money. And, just as it is a great good freely to choose to do good, so it is also a good to be used by someone else for a worthy purpose (so long, that is, that he or she has the right, the authority, to use us in this way). Being allowed to suffer to make possible a great good is a privilege, even if the privilege is forced upon you. Those who are allowed to die for their country and thereby save their country from foreign oppression are privileged. Cultures less obsessed than our own by the evil of purely physical pain have always recognized that. And they have recognized that it is still a blessing, even if the one who died had been conscripted to fight.

And even twentieth-century man can begin to see that—sometimes—when he seeks to help prisoners, not by giving them more comfortable quarters, but by letting them help the handicapped; or when he pities rather than envies the "poor little rich girl" who has everything and does nothing for anyone else. And one phenomenon prevalent in end-of-century Britain draws this especially to our attention—the evil of unemployment. Because of our system of Social Security, the unemployed on the whole have enough money to live without too much discomfort; certainly they are a lot better off than are many employed in Africa or Asia or Victorian Britain. What is evil about unemployment is not so much any resulting poverty but the uselessness of the unemployed. They often report feeling unvalued by society, of no use, "on the scrap heap." They rightly think it would be a good for them to contribute; but they cannot. Many of them would welcome a system where they were obliged to do useful work in preference to one where society has no use for them.

It follows from that fact that being of use is a benefit for him who is of use, and that those who suffer at the hands of others, and thereby make possible the good of those others who have free and responsible choice, are themselves benefited in this respect. I am fortunate if the natural possibility of my suffering if you choose to hurt me is the vehicle which makes your choice really matter. My vulnerability, my openness to suffering (which necessarily involves my actually suffering if you make the wrong choice), means that you are not just like a pilot in a simulator, where it does not matter if mistakes are made. That our choices matter tremendously, that we can make great differences to things for good or ill, is one of the greatest gifts a creator can give us. And if my suffering is the means by which he can give you that choice, I too am in this respect fortunate. Though of course suffering is in itself a bad thing, my good fortune is that the suffering is not random, pointless suffering. It is suffering which is a consequence of my vulnerability which makes me of such use.

Someone may object that the only good thing is not *being* of use (dying for one's country or being vulnerable to suffering at your hands), but *believing* that one is of use—believing that one is dying for one's country and that this is of use; the "feel-good" experience. But that cannot be correct. Having comforting beliefs is only a good thing if they are true beliefs. It is not a good thing to believe that things are going well when they are not, or that your life is of use when it is not. Getting pleasure out of a comforting falsehood is a cheat. But if I get pleasure out of a true belief, it must be that I regard the state of things which I believe to hold to be a good thing. If I get pleasure out of the true belief that my daughter is doing well at school, it must be that I regard it as a good thing that my daughter does well at school (whether or not I believe that she is doing well). If I did not think the latter, I would not get any pleasure out of believing that she is doing well. Likewise, the belief that I am vulnerable to suffering at your hands, and that that is a good thing, can only be a good thing if being vulnerable to suffering at your hands is itself a good thing (independently of whether I believe it or not). Certainly, when my life is of use and that is a good for me, it is even better if I believe it and get comfort therefrom; but it can only be even better if it is already a good for me whether I believe it or not.

But though suffering may in these ways serve good purposes, does God have the right to allow me to suffer for your benefit, without asking my permission? For surely, an objector will say, no one has the right to allow one person A to suffer for the benefit of another one B without A's consent. We judge that doctors who use patients as involuntary objects of experimentation in medical experiments which they hope will produce results which can be used to benefit others are doing something wrong. After all, if my arguments about the utility of suffering are sound, ought we not all to be causing suffering to others in order that those others may have the opportunity to react in the right way?

There are, however, crucial differences between God and the doctors. The first is that God as the author of our being has certain rights, a certain authority over us, which we do not have over our fellow humans. He is the cause of our existence at each moment of our existence and sustains the laws of nature which give us everything we are and have. To allow someone to suffer for his own good or that of others, one has to stand in some kind of parental relationship towards him. I do not have the right to let some stranger suffer for the sake of some good, when I could easily prevent this, but I do have *some* right of this kind in respect of my own children. I may let the younger son suffer *somewhat* for his own good or that of his brother. I have this right because in small part I am responsible for the younger son's existence, his beginning and continuance. If I have begotten him, nourished, and educated him, I have some limited rights over him in return; to a *very limited* extent I can use him for some worthy purpose. If this is correct, then a God who is so much more the author of our being than are our parents has so much more right in this respect. Doctors do have over us even the rights of parents.

But secondly and all-importantly, the doctors *could* have asked the patients for permission; and the patients, being free agents of some power and knowledge, could have made an informed choice of whether or not to allow themselves to be used. By contrast, God's choice is not about how to use already existing agents, but about the sort of agents to make and the sort of world into which to put them. In God's situation there are no agents to be asked. I am arguing that it is good that one agent A should have deep responsibility for another B (who in turn could have deep responsibility for another C). It is not logically possible for God to have asked B if he wanted things thus, for, if A is to be responsible for B's growth in freedom, knowledge, and power, there will not be a B with enough freedom and knowledge to make any choice, before God has to choose whether or not to give A responsibility for him. One cannot ask a baby into which sort of world he or she wishes to be born. The creator has to make the choice independently of his creatures. He will seek on balance to benefit them—all of them. And, in giving them the gift of life—whatever suffering goes with it—that is a substantial benefit. But when one suffers at the hands of another, often perhaps it is not enough of a benefit to outweigh the suffering. Here is the point to recall that it is an additional benefit to the sufferer that his suffering is the means whereby the one who hurt him had the opportunity to make a significant choice between good and evil which otherwise he would not have had.

Although for these reasons, as I have been urging, God has the right to allow humans to cause each other to suffer, there must be a limit to the amount of suffering which he has the right to allow a human being to suffer for the sake of a great good. A parent may allow an elder child to have the power to do some harm to a younger child for the sake of the responsibility given to the elder child; but there are limits. And there are limits even to the moral right of God, our creator and sustainer, to use free sentient beings as pawns in a greater game. Yet, if these limits were too narrow, God would be unable to give humans much real responsibility; he would be able to allow them only to play a toy game. Still, limits there must be to God's rights to allow humans to hurt each other; and limits there are in the world to the extent to which they can hurt each other, provided above all by the short finite life enjoyed by humans and other creatures—one human can hurt another for no more than eighty years or so. And there are a number of other safety-devices in-built into our physiology and psychology, limiting the amount of pain we can suffer. But the primary safety limit is that provided by the shortness of our finite life. Unending, unchosen suffering would indeed to my mind provide a very strong argument against the existence of God. But that is not the human situation.

So then God, without asking humans, has to choose for them between the kinds of world in which they can live—basically either a world in which there is very little opportunity for humans to benefit or harm each other, or a world in which there is considerable opportunity. How shall he choose? There are clearly reasons for both choices. But it seems to me (just, on balance) that his choosing to create the world in which we have considerable opportunity to benefit or harm each other is to bring about a good at least as great as the evil which he thereby allows to occur. *Of course* the suffering he allows is a bad thing; and, other things being equal, to be avoided. But having the natural possibility of causing suffering makes possible a greater good. God, in creating humans who (of logical necessity) cannot choose for themselves the kind of world into which they are to come, plausibly exhibits his goodness in making for them the heroic choice that they come into a risky world where they may have to suffer for the good of others.

Natural Evil

Natural evil is not to be accounted for along the same lines as moral evil. Its main role rather, I suggest, is to make it possible for humans to have the kind of choice which the free-will defence extols, and to make available to humans specially worthwhile kinds of choice.

There are two ways in which natural evil operates to give humans those choices. First, the operation of natural laws producing evils gives humans knowledge (if they choose to seek it) of how to bring about such evils themselves. Observing you catch some disease by the operation of natural processes gives me the power either to use those processes to give that disease to other people, or through negligence to allow others to catch it, or to take measures to prevent others from catching the disease. Study of the mechanisms of nature producing various evils (and goods) opens up for humans a wide range of choice. This is the way in which in fact we learn how to bring about (good and) evil. But could not God give us the requisite knowledge (of how to bring about good or evil) which we need in order to have free and responsible choice by a less costly means? Could he not just whisper in our ears from time to time what are the different consequences of different actions of ours? Yes. But anyone who believed that an action of his would have some effect because he believed that God had told him so would see all his actions as done under the all-watchful eye of God. He would not merely believe strongly that there was a God, but would know it with real certainty. That knowledge would greatly inhibit his freedom of choice, would make it very difficult for him to choose to do evil. This is because we all have a natural inclination to wish to be thought well of by everyone, and above all by an all-good God; that we have such an inclination is a very good feature of humans, without which we would be less than human. Also, if we were directly informed of the consequences of our actions, we would be deprived of the choice whether to seek to discover what the consequences were through experiment and hard cooperative work. Knowledge would be available on tap. Natural processes alone give humans knowledge of the effects of their actions without inhibiting their freedom, and if evil is to be a possibility for them they must know how to allow it to occur.

The other way in which natural evil operates to give humans their freedom is that it makes possible certain kinds of action towards it between which agents can choose. It increases the range of significant choice. A particular natural evil, such as physical pain, gives to the sufferer a choice—whether to endure it with patience, or to bemoan his lot. His friend can choose whether to show compassion towards the sufferer, or to be callous. The pain makes possible these choices, which would not otherwise exist. There is no guarantee that our actions in response to the pain will be good ones, but the pain gives us the opportunity to perform good actions. The good or bad actions which we perform in the face of natural evil themselves provide opportunities for further choice—of good or evil stances towards the former actions. If I am patient with my suffering, you can choose whether to encourage or laugh at my patience; if I bemoan my lot, you can teach me by word and example what a good thing patience is. If you are sympathetic, I have then the opportunity to show gratitude for the sympathy; or to be so self-involved that I ignore it. If you are callous, I can choose whether to ignore this or to resent it for life. And so on. I do not think that there can be much doubt that natural evil, such as physical pain, makes available these sorts of choice. The actions which natural evil makes possible are ones which allow us to perform at our best and interact with our fellows at the deepest level.

It may, however, be suggested that adequate opportunity for these great good actions would be provided by the occurrence of moral evil without any need for suffering to be caused by natural processes. You can show courage when threatened by a gunman, as well as when threatened by cancer; and show sympathy to those likely to be killed by gunmen as well as to those likely to die of cancer. But just imagine all the suffering of mind and body caused by disease, earthquake, and accident unpreventable by humans removed at a stroke from our society. No sickness, no bereavement in consequence of the untimely death of the young. Many of us would then have such an easy life that we simply would not have much opportunity to show courage or, indeed, manifest much in the way of great goodness at all. We need those insidious processes of decay and dissolution which money and strength cannot ward off for long to give us the opportunities, so easy otherwise to avoid, to become heroes.

God has the right to allow natural evils to occur (for the same reason as he has the right to allow moral evils to occur)—up to a limit. It would, of course, be crazy for God to multiply evils more and more in order to give endless opportunity for heroism, but to have *some* significant opportunity for real heroism and consequent character formation is a benefit for the person to whom it is given. Natural evils give to us the knowledge to make a range of choices between good and evil, and the opportunity to perform actions of especially valuable kinds.

There is, however, no reason to suppose that animals have free will. So what about their suffering? Animals had been suffering for a long time before humans appeared on this planet—just how long depends on which animals are conscious beings. The first thing to take into account here is that, while the higher animals, at any rate the vertebrates, suffer, it is most unlikely that they suffer nearly as much as humans do. Given that suffering depends directly on brain events (in turn caused by events in other parts of the body), then, since the lower animals do not suffer at all and humans suffer a lot, animals of intermediate complexity (it is reasonable to suppose) suffer only a moderate amount. So, while one does need a theodicy to account for why God allows animals to suffer, one does not need as powerful a theodicy as one does in respect of humans. One only needs reasons adequate to account for God allowing an amount of suffering much less than that of humans. That said, there is, I believe, available for animals parts of the theodicy which I have outlined above for humans.

The good of animals, like that of humans, does not consist solely in thrills of pleasure. For animals, too, there are more worthwhile things, and in particular intentional actions, and among them serious significant intentional actions. The life of animals involves many serious significant intentional actions. Animals look for a mate, despite being tired and failing to find one. They take great trouble to build nests and feed their young, to decoy predators and explore. But all this inevitably involves pain (going on despite being tired) and danger. An animal cannot intentionally avoid forest fires, or take trouble to rescue its offspring from forest fires, unless there exists a serious danger of getting caught in a forest fire. The action of rescuing despite danger simply cannot be done unless the danger exists—and the danger will not exist unless there is a significant natural probability of being caught in the fire. Animals do not choose freely to do such actions, but the actions are nevertheless worthwhile. It is great that animals feed their young, not just themselves; that animals explore when they know it to be dangerous; that animals save each other from predators, and so on. These are the things that give the lives of animals their value. But they do often involve some suffering to some creature.

To return to the central case of humans—the reader will agree with me to the extent to which he or she values responsibility, free choice, and being of use very much more than thrills of pleasure or absence of pain. There is no other way to get the evils of this world into the right perspective, except to reflect at length on innumerable very detailed thought experiments (in addition to actual experiences of life) in which we postulate very different sorts of worlds from our own, and then ask ourselves whether the perfect goodness of God would require him to create one of these (or no world at all) rather than our own. But I conclude with a very small thought experiment, which may help to begin this process. Suppose that you exist in another world before your birth in this one, and are given a choice as to the sort of life you are to have in this one. You are told that you are to have only a short life, maybe of only a few minutes, although it will be an adult life in the sense that you will have the richness of sensation and belief characteristic of adults. You have a choice as to the sort of life you will have. You can have either a few minutes of very considerable pleasure, of the kind produced by some drug such as heroin, which you will experience by yourself and which will have no effects at all in the world (for example, no one else will know about it); or you can have a few minutes of considerable pain, such as the pain of childbirth, which will have (unknown to you at the time of pain) considerable good effects on others over a few years. You are told that, if you do not make the second choice, those others will never exist—and so you are under no moral obligation to make the second choice. But you seek to make the choice which will make *your* own life the best life for *you* to have led. How will you choose? The choice is, I hope, obvious. You should choose the second alternative.

For someone who remains unconvinced by my claims about the relative strengths of the good and evils involved—holding that, great though the goods are, they do not justify the evils which they involve—there is a fallback position. My arguments may have convinced you of the greatness of the goods involved sufficiently for you to allow that a perfectly good God would be justified in bringing about the evils for the sake of the good which they make possible, if and only if God also provided compensation in the form of happiness after death to the victims whose sufferings make possible the goods. . . . While believing that God does provide at any rate for many humans such life after death, I have expounded a theodicy without relying on this assumption. But I can understand someone thinking that the assumption is needed, especially when we are considering the worst evils.

(This compensatory afterlife need not necessarily be the everlasting life of Heaven.)

It remains the case, however, that evil is evil, and there is a substantial price to pay for the goods of our world which it makes possible. God would not be less than perfectly good if he created instead a world without pain and suffering, and so without the particular goods which those evils make possible. Christian, Islamic, and much Jewish tradition claims that God has created worlds of both kinds—our world, and the Heaven of the blessed. The latter is a marvellous world with a vast range of possible deep goods, but it lacks a few goods which our world contains, including the good of being able to reject the good. A generous God might well choose to give some of us the choice of rejecting the good in a world like ours before giving to those who embrace it a wonderful world in which the former possibility no longer exists.

Theology and Falsification

Antony Flew and Basil Mitchell

Suppose a friend tells you that he possesses a radio with a magnificent sound system. But when he turns the radio on, you hear a tinny tone and much static. You would expect your friend to withdraw, or at least modify, his statement in the face of such evidence to the contrary. If he refuses to do so, insisting that what you heard does not conflict with his claim, then you could no longer make sense of what he had said. In short, for a statement of fact to maintain its meaning requires that evidence against it be taken seriously.

In our next selection Antony Flew, a professor at the University of Reading in England, challenges the theist to explain the conceivable evidence that could count against the existence of God. If the theist refuses to acknowledge that any possible events could ever conflict with theism, then Flew claims that theism has become meaningless.

To see the force of his point, consider the assertion that God loves us. Is His love consistent with our suffering the most horrendous evils? If not, then the presence of such evils would constitute strong evidence against God's love for us. But suppose the theist refuses to grant that any evils, no matter how terrible, would be evidence against God's love. In that case, what meaning or comfort could be found in such a love?

An intriguing reply to Flew's argument is offered by Basil Mitchell, a professor at the University of Oxford. He believes evils do count against the existence of God but not decisively. Whether his answer is satisfactory I leave for you to consider.

Antony Flew

Let us begin with a parable. . . . Once upon a time two explorers came upon a clearing in the jungle. In the clearing were growing many flowers and many weeds. One explorer says, "Some gardener must tend this plot." The other disagrees, "There is no gardener." So they pitch their tents and set a watch. No gardener is ever seen. "But perhaps he is an invisible gardener." So they set up a barbed-wire fence. They electrify it. They patrol with bloodhounds. . . . But no shrieks ever suggest that some intruder has received a shock. No movements of the wire ever betray an invisible climber. The bloodhounds never give cry. Yet still the Believer is not convinced. "But there is a gardener, invisible, intangible, insensible to electric shocks, a gardener who has no scent and makes no sound, a gardener who comes secretly to look after the garden which he loves." At last the Sceptic despairs, "But what remains of your original assertion? Just how does what you call an invisible, intangible, eternally elusive gardener differ from an imaginary gardener or even from no gardener at all?"

In this parable we can see how what starts as an assertion . . . may be reduced step by step to an altogether different status, to an expression perhaps of a "picture preference." . . . A fine brash hypothesis may thus be killed by inches, the death by a thousand qualifications.

And in this, it seems to me, lies the peculiar danger, the endemic evil, of theological utterance. Take such utterances as "God has a plan," "God created the world," "God loves us as a father loves his children." They look at first sight very much like assertions, vast cosmological assertions. Of course, this is no sure sign that they either are, or are intended to be, assertions. But let us confine ourselves to the cases where those who utter such sentences intend them to express assertions. . . .

Now to assert that such and such is the case is necessarily equivalent to denying that such and such is not the case. Suppose then that we are in doubt as to what someone who gives vent to an utterance is asserting, or suppose that, more radically, we are sceptical as to whether he is really asserting anything at all, one way of trying to understand (or perhaps it will be to expose) his utterance is to attempt to find what he would regard as counting against, or as being incompatible with, its truth. . . . [I]f there is nothing which a putative assertion denies, then there is nothing which it asserts either: and so it is not really an assertion. When the Sceptic in the parable asked the Believer, "Just how does what you call an invisible, intangible, eternally elusive gardener differ from an imaginary gardener or even from no gardener at all?" he was suggesting that the Believer's earlier statement had been so eroded by qualification that it was no longer an assertion at all.

Now it often seems to people who are not religious as if there was no conceivable event or series of events the occurrence of which would be admitted by sophisticated religious people to be a sufficient reason for conceding "There wasn't a God after all" or "God does not really love us then." Someone tells us that God loves us as a father loves his children. We are reassured. But then we see a child dying of inoperable cancer of the throat. His earthly father is driven frantic in his efforts to help, but his Heavenly Father reveals no obvious sign of concern. Some qualification is made—God's love is "not a merely human love" or it is "an inscrutable love," perhaps—and we realize that such sufferings are quite compatible with the truth of the assertion that "God loves us as a father. . . ." We are reassured again. But then perhaps we ask: what is this assurance of God's (appropriately qualified) love worth, what is this apparent guarantee really a guarantee against? Just what would have to happen . . . to entitle us to say "God does not love us" or even "God does not exist?" I therefore put . . . the simple central questions, "What would have to occur or to have occurred to constitute for you a disproof of the love of, or of the existence of, God?"

Basil Mitchell

Flew's article is searching and perceptive, but there is, I think, something odd about his conduct of the theologian's case. The theologian surely would not deny that the fact of pain counts against the assertion that God loves men. This very incompatibility generates the most intractable of theological problems—the problem of evil. So the theologian *does* recognize the fact of pain as counting against Christian doctrine. But it is true that he will not allow it—or anything—to count decisively against it; for he is committed by his faith to trust in God. His attitude is not that of the detached observer, but of the believer.

Perhaps this can be brought out by yet another parable. In time of war in an occupied country, a member of the resistance meets one night a stranger who deeply impresses him. They spend that night together in conversation. The Stranger tells the partisan that he himself is on the side of the resistance—indeed that he is in command of it, and urges the partisan to have faith in him no matter what happens. The partisan is utterly convinced at that meeting of the Stranger's sincerity and constancy and undertakes to trust him.

They never meet in conditions of intimacy again. But sometimes the Stranger is seen helping members of the resistance, and the partisan is grateful and says to his friends, "He is on our side."

Sometimes he is seen in the uniform of the police handing over patriots to the occupying power. On these occasions his friends murmur against him: but the partisan still says, "He is on our side." He still believes that, in spite of appearances, the Stranger did not deceive him. Sometimes he asks the Stranger for help and receives it. He is then thankful. Sometimes he asks and does not receive it. Then he says, "The Stranger knows best." Sometimes his friends, in exasperation, say, "Well, what *would* he have to do for you to admit that you were wrong and that he is not on our side?" But the partisan refuses to answer. He will not consent to put the Stranger to the test. And sometimes his friends complain, "Well, if *that's* what you mean by his being on our side, the sooner he goes over to the other side the better."

The partisan of the parable does not allow anything to count decisively against the proposition "The Stranger is on our side." This is because he has committed himself to trust the Stranger. But he of course recognizes that the Stranger's ambiguous behaviour *does* count against what he believes about him. It is precisely this situation which constitutes the trial of his faith.

When the partisan asks for help and doesn't get it, what can he do? He can (a) conclude that the stranger is not on our side or; (b) maintain that he is on our side, but that he has reasons for withholding help.

The first he will refuse to do. How long can he uphold the second position without its becoming just silly?

I don't think one can say in advance. It will depend on the nature of the impression created by the Stranger in the first place. It will depend, too, on the manner in which he takes the Stranger's behaviour. If he blandly dismisses it as of no consequence, as having no bearing upon his belief, it will be assumed that he is thoughtless or insane. And it quite obviously won't do for him to say easily, "Oh, when used of the Stranger the phrase 'is on our side' *means* ambiguous behaviour of this sort." In that case he would be like the religious man who says blandly of a terrible disaster "It is God's will." No, he will only be regarded as sane and reasonable in his belief, if he experiences in himself the full force of the conflict. . . .

Do I want to say that the partisan's belief about the Stranger is, in any sense, an explanation? I think I do. It explains and makes sense of the Stranger's behaviour: it helps to explain also the resistance movement in the context of which he appears. In each case it differs from the interpretation which the others put upon the same facts.

"God loves men" resembles "the Stranger is on our side" (and many other significant statements, e.g., historical ones) in not being conclusively falsifiable. They can both be treated in at least three different ways: (1) as provisional hypotheses to be discarded if experience tells against them; (2) as significant articles of faith; (3) as vacuous formulae (expressing, perhaps, a desire for reassurance) to which experience makes no difference and which make no difference to life.

The Christian, once he has committed himself, is precluded by his faith from taking up the first attitude. . . . He is in constant danger, as Flew has observed, of slipping into the third. But he need not; and, if he does, it is a failure in faith as well as in logic.

Do Miracles Occur?

MONROE C. BEARDSLEY AND ELIZABETH LANE BEARDSLEY

If theists are asked for a proof of the existence of God, they may not offer a philosophical argument but instead appeal to the evidence of miracles, God's interventions in the natural order of the world. But do we know that any miracles have occurred? This question is discussed in our next essay. Its authors, already familiar to us (pp. 3–12), are Monroe C. Beardsley and Elizabeth Lane Beardsley.

The less you know about an object, the less it can surprise you by the way it behaves. If you see a fisherman casting his line into waters that are utterly strange to you, you have no more reason to expect him to catch one kind of fish than any other kind. But an ichthyologist can make predictions about the catch, and can be startled if it turns out to include fish that, in his experience, usually frequent waters that are warmer, or calmer, or saltier.

Surprise and puzzlement appear when our expectations are not fulfilled. And expectations are based upon the regularities we have already become adjusted to, or at least resigned to, in the course of nature. It was the *ir*regularities in the orbit of Uranus that led to the discovery of Neptune. It is when our faithful old car suddenly refuses to start one morning, for the first time, that we are presented with a problem. Now such irregularities as these, such apparent exceptions to the usual pattern of events, are ordinarily accepted only as provisional. The astronomers were not prepared to abandon Newton's laws of motion because of the eccentricities of Uranus; they merely concluded that there was another planet in the vicinity whose presence must be taken into consideration. And though you may, in moments of stress, address your car in personal terms with accusations of sheer willful perversity, you really know that the car isn't trying to be mean, and that the failure to start has a perfectly sensible and no doubt discoverable explanation—a lack of current in the battery, of gas in the tank, of air in the carburetor, etc.

When something goes wrong in this way, and there seems to be a sudden breakdown in what we have come to accept as the prevailing laws of nature, two fundamental ways of restoring order are generally open to us. . . . Basically, we are surprised by Situation S' because it is different from Situation S, which is what we were expecting. And we expected Situation S because we observed Conditions C, and we knew that (generally or always) Conditions C are followed by Situation S. A proposition like "Conditions C are followed by Situation S" is a *law,* or description of a regularity. Now when S' turns up instead of S, we have to make our choice. Maybe the law we thought was true is really not true. Or maybe the conditions present were really different from what we thought.

Suppose a man wishes water to turn into wine, and the pitcher of water on the table does turn into wine. One moment it tastes like water, and passes the relevant chemical tests; the next moment it tastes like wine, and its color and chemical properties have also changed. The law involved here (not a very technical one, to be sure, but it will serve as illustration) is that water left alone in a pitcher will remain water. (Or the law could be that wine is produced only by the fermentation of fruit.) So we take our choice. Are we mistaken in accepting this law—is there perhaps a kind of water in the world that, when left by itself for a certain time, turns into wine? Or are we mistaken in thinking that this is a case of water being left by itself? In other words, could the original tests have been faked, or wine surreptitiously introduced? Now suppose we could assure ourselves in some way that *both* of these possibilities are mistaken. The law holds good; we were not wrong there. And there really was no trickery. In that case we would have an event that occurred in clear violation of a law of nature. Such an event is, by this definition, a miraculous event, or *miracle.* And since it could not be explained by any natural causes, would it not have to be explained as a supernatural intervention in the course of nature? If so, it would be evidence for the existence of God. This is the gist of the argument from miracles.

It is interesting to note that this argument, which has played and still plays an important part in the teaching of some major religions, goes in the opposite direction from the argument from design. There it was the order in the world, here an alleged break in the order, that counts as evidence of God. There is something odd about using both arguments together, as some philosophers and theologians do. For if the order of nature is supposed to show God's power and goodness, it seems like a weakening of this claim to admit that he finds it desirable to make adjustments from time to time by suspending that order. But the two arguments don't seem to be really contradictory. There could not be miracles at all unless there were general laws to be violated by supernatural intervention; and conceivably both the general lawfulness and the specific interventions (when they have certain beneficial effects, such as mass conversions) could be part of the divine plan.

For a more careful analysis of the problem of miracles, let us consider a person suffering from a disease, like leukemia, that is believed to be incurable; everyone who has had this disease, however ministered to, has died from it. He kneels before a shrine and prays, and rises and departs. Within a few weeks the very doctors who had pronounced him fatally ill now unanimously find him perfectly well. And they can think of absolutely no medical explanation of this cure. What can be said about this kind of case?

Dr. A may say that the cure simply cannot be explained at this time, but that of course it must have a natural explanation which will one day be found. The assumed law about the incurability of leukemia must be too simple; there must have been something this patient did, or ate, or breathed, that did the trick, although he was unaware of it. Suppose he was accidentally exposed to some strange radiation. Then the true law is not that leukemia is fatal, but that leukemia without exposure to that radiation is fatal. The lawfulness of the situation is preserved by dissolving the apparent irregularity into a higher regularity.

Dr. A, in other words, agrees that the cure really occurred, but denies that it was miraculous. Dr. B, on the other hand, believes that a mistake has been made in thinking that the patient is now cured. Something could conceivably have gone wrong with the tests, however carefully they were made. Though he does not look it, the patient is still ill, and will soon die. Dr. C thinks it was not the later, but the original, diagnosis that must have been mistaken. Perhaps the trouble was not leukemia but a hitherto undiscovered disease that acts very much like leukemia, and is hard to distinguish from it at one stage of development, but is not fatal. Since the symptoms have now disappeared, it is too late to run further tests on them. But other doctors should be warned to watch out for cases of pseudoleukemia in the future.

So Dr. B and Dr. C deny that a cure has taken place at all. And that leaves Dr. D (this one a Doctor of Divinity), who takes a different line. He is convinced that there was a genuine cure, and that no strictly medical explanation ever will, or can, even in principle, be given. It was therefore a miracle, and a sign from God. Now the first thing to notice is that this is claiming a great deal. To show that the event is a miracle it is not enough to show that it cannot be explained by any known laws—heaven knows that is true of many things. You must show that it can *never* be so explained—and that seems an impossible task.

To prove that a particular event is a miracle, then, you must prove (a) that there actually is a law governing this sort of event, that is, a true proposition of the form "Whenever Conditions C occur, X occurs"; and (b) that the law was violated in this case, in other words that C occurred, but X did not. At Fatima, Portugal, on Oct. 13, 1917, seventy thousand people saw the sun turn into a silver disc that whirled about, plunged toward the crowd, and rose again to its proper place in the heavens. What they saw, if it happened, was almost certainly a miracle, for this behavior of the sun appears to be utterly inconsistent with the known laws governing the motions of stars and planets. Seventy thousand people is a huge body of witnesses—few of the events of history whose occurrence we regard as well established can boast so large a testimony. Yet many philosophers would maintain—with David Hume—that this testimony cannot make it more probable that the miraculous event occurred than that it did not—even if we discount the pious witnesses' strong desire to see what they saw, the atmosphere of emotionalism, and the absence of scientifically trained observers. To say that the occurrence of this event would violate a physical law is to admit that the more probable, the better established, the law, the more improbable the event. For every bit of evidence that the law holds true is evidence that no event has violated it. So the testimony of the witnesses must be weighed against all the mountains of evidence that go to support Newton's laws of motion—and that evidence includes the combined daily experience of all humanity, plus the controlled experimental inquiries of physicists.

Another way to sharpen this issue might be to imagine someone coming to you and saying, "At midnight last night a perfect murder was committed in this room." You reply, "I hardly think so; there are no signs of a struggle, no blood, no powder marks." "You are thinking of an imperfect crime," he says. "A perfect crime leaves absolutely no trace at all. Nothing is disturbed; there can be no clues. In this instance, the victim was a hermit who has lived by himself for forty years and is absolutely unknown to anyone else. And the murderer bumped his head afterward with such force as to cause complete amnesia for the crime. There is no way it can be detected."

Now, there doesn't seem to be any way of disproving the statement that the perfect murder was committed. We can't say that it is impossible. On the other hand, we have no good reason to believe it, either, for the very hypothesis is that no evidence can ever be found. Even the person telling us about it is in a peculiar position, for if what he says is true, then he has no way of knowing it. Of course, in this case it would be irrational to believe him. Now compare the perfect crime with the miraculous event. Any particular event *could* be miraculous—though of course no one is likely to call it so unless it is especially significant. Even if your car starts as usual in the morning, that may be a miracle—the battery went dead in the night and was restored to life just as you pushed the starter, contrary to all electrochemical laws. But the question is whether we ever have a good reason to believe that a particular event is miraculous—or whether it is always more probable either that the event really didn't occur, or that it was different from what it seemed to be and did not really violate the law, or that there is some other (as yet undiscovered) law that would explain it.

This, perhaps, is the central question about miracles. And with it we end this discussion.

Faith

❖❖

RICHARD TAYLOR

In the essay that follows, Richard Taylor, whose work we read previously (pp. 101–112), accepts as obvious the claim that Christianity is not reasonable. But rather than concluding that Christian belief should be abandoned, he urges that reason should give way to faith. Such an approach has strong appeal to many firm believers, and Taylor's defense of the appropriateness of their religious devotion is uncompromising and unapologetic.

"Our most holy religion," David Hume said, "is founded on *faith*, not on reason." (All quotations are from the last two paragraphs of Hume's essay "Of Miracles.") He did not then conclude that it ought, therefore, to be rejected by reasonable men. On the contrary, he suggests that rational evaluation has no proper place in this realm to begin with, that a religious man need not feel in the least compelled to put his religion "to such a trial as it is, by no means, fitted to endure, " and he brands as "dangerous friends or disguised enemies" of religion those "who have undertaken to defend it by the principles of human reason."

I want to defend Hume's suggestion, and go a bit farther by eliciting some things that seem uniquely characteristic of *Christian* faith, in order to show what it has, and what it has not, in common with other things to which it is often compared. I limited myself to Christian faith, because I know rather little of any other, and faith is, with love and hope, supposed to be a uniquely Christian virtue.

Faith and Reason

Faith is not reason, else religion would be, along with logic and metaphysics, a part of philosophy, which it assuredly is not. Nor is faith belief resting on scientific or historical inquiry, else religion would be part of the corpus of human knowledge, which it clearly is not. More than that, it seems evident that by the normal, common-sense criteria of what is reasonable, the content of Christian faith is *un*reasonable. This, I believe, should be the starting

From *Religious Experience and Truth,* New York University Press, 1961. Reprinted by permission of Ernest B. Hook.

point, the *datum,* of any discussion of faith and reason. It is, for instance, an essential content of the Christian faith that, at a certain quite recent time, God became man, dwelt among us in the person of a humble servant, and then, for a sacred purpose, died, to live again. Now, apologetics usually addresses itself to the *details* of this story, to show that they are not inherently incredible, but this is to miss the point. It is indeed *possible* to believe it, and in the strict sense the story is credible. Millions of people do most deeply and firmly believe it. But even the barest statement of the content of that belief makes it manifest that it does not and, I think, could not, ever result from rational inquiry. "Mere reason," Hume said, "is insufficient to convince us of its veracity." The Christian begins the recital of his faith with the words, "I believe," and it would be an utter distortion to construe this as anything like "I have inquired, and found it reasonable to conclude." If there were a man who could say that in honesty, as I think there is not, then he would, in a clear and ordinary sense, believe, but he would have no religious faith whatsoever, and his beliefs themselves would be robbed of what would make them religious.

Now if this essential and (it seems to me) obvious unreasonableness of Christian belief could be recognized at the outset of any discussion of religion, involving rationalists on the one hand and believers on the other, we would be spared the tiresome attack and apologetics upon which nothing ultimately turns, the believer would be spared what is, in fact, an uncalled-for task of reducing his faith to reason or science, which can, as Hume noted, result only in "exposing" it as neither, and the rationalist would be granted his main point, not as a conclusion triumphantly extracted, but as a datum too obvious to labor.

Faith and Certainty

Why, then, does a devout Christian embrace these beliefs? Now this very question, on the lips of a philosopher, is wrongly expressed, for he invariably intends it as a request for reasons, as a means of putting the beliefs to that unfair "trial" of which Hume spoke. Yet there is a clear and definite answer to this question, which has the merit of being true and evident to anyone who has known intimately those who dwell in the atmosphere of faith. The reason the Christian believes that story around which his whole life turns is, simply, that he cannot help it. If he is trapped into eliciting grounds for it, they are grounds given after the fact of conviction. . . . One neither seeks nor needs grounds for the acceptance of what he cannot help believing. "Whoever is moved by *faith* to assent," Hume wrote, "is conscious of a continued miracle in his own person, which subverts all the principles of his understanding, and gives him a determination to believe. . . ." It is this fact of faith which drives philosophers to such exasperation, in the face of which the believer is nonetheless so utterly unmoved.

The believer sees his life as a gift of God, the world as the creation of God, his own purposes, insofar as they are noble, as the purposes of God, and history as exhibiting a divine plan, made known to him through the Christian story. He sees things this way, just because they do seem so, and he cannot help it. This is why, for him, faith is so "easy," and secular arguments to the contrary so beside the point. No one seeks evidence for that of which he is entirely convinced, or regards as relevant what seems to others to cast doubt. The believer is like a child who recoils from danger, as exhibited, for instance, in what he for the first time sees as a fierce animal; the child has no difficultly *believing* he is in peril, just because he cannot help believing it, yet his belief results not at all from induction based on past experience with fierce animals, and no reassurances, garnered from *our* past experience, relieve his terror at all.

Some Confusions

If this is what religious faith essentially is—if, as a believer might poetically but, I think, correctly describe it, faith is an involuntary conviction, often regarded as a "gift," on the part of one who has voluntarily opened his mind and heart to receive it—then certain common misunderstandings can be removed.

In the first place, faith should never be likened to an *assumption,* such as the scientist's assumption of the uniformity of nature, or what not. An assumption is an intellectual device for furthering inquiry. It need not be a conviction nor, indeed, even a belief. But a half-hearted faith is no religious faith. Faith thus has that much, at least, in common with knowledge, that it is a *conviction,* and its subjective state is *certainty.* One thus wholly distorts faith if he represents the believer as just "taking" certain things "on faith," and then reasons, like a philosopher, from these beginnings, as though what were thus "taken" could, like an assumption, be rejected at will.

Again, it is a misunderstanding to represent faith as "mere tenacity." Tenacity consists in stubbornly clinging to what one hopes, but of which one is not fully convinced. The child who is instantly convinced of danger in the presence of an animal is not being tenacious or stubborn, even in the face of verbal reassurances, and no more is the Christian whose acts are moved by faith. The believer does not so much *shun* evidence as something that might *shake* his faith, but rather regards it as not to the point. In this he may appear to philosophers to be mistaken, but only if one supposes, as he need not, that one should hold only such beliefs as are rational.

Again, it is misleading to refer to any set of propositions, such as those embodied in a creed, as being this or that person's "faith." Concerning that content of belief in which one is convinced by faith, it is logically (though I think not otherwise) possible that one might be convinced by evidence, in which case it would have no more to do with faith or religion than do the statements in a newspaper. This observation has this practical importance, that it is quite possible—in fact, common—for the faith of different believers to be one and the same, despite creedal differences.

And finally, both "faith" (or "fideism") and "reason" (or "rationalism") can be, and often are, used as pejorative terms, and as terms of commendation. Which side one takes here is arbitrary, for there is no non-question-begging way of deciding. A rationalist can perhaps find reasons for being a rationalist, though this is doubtful; but in any case it would betray a basic misunderstanding to expect a fideist to do likewise. This is brought out quite clearly by the direction that discussions of religion usually take. A philosophical teacher will often, for instance, labor long to persuade his audience that the content of Christian faith is unreasonable, which is a shamefully easy task for him, unworthy of his learning. Then suddenly, the underlying assumption comes to light that Christian beliefs ought, therefore, to be abandoned by rational people! A religious hearer of this discourse might well reply that, religion being unreasonable but nonetheless manifestly worthy of belief, we should conclude with Hume that reason, in this realm at least, ought to be rejected. Now, one can decide *that* issue by any light that is granted him, but it is worth stressing that the believer's position on it is just exactly as good, and just as bad, as the rational sceptic's.

Faith and Reason

❖❖❖

Michael Scriven

In the previous selection Richard Taylor maintained that in deciding matters of religious belief the appeal to faith is as appropriate as the use of reason. According to him, the choice between the two approaches is arbitrary.

The next essay argues against this view. The author is Michael Scriven, Professor of Philosophy at Claremont Graduate University. He claims that reason and faith are not on a par, since reason has passed tests of effectiveness that faith has not. His approach is rem-

From *Primary Philosophy*, by Michael Scriven. Copyright © 1966 by McGraw-Hill. Reprinted by permission of The McGraw-Hill Companies.

iniscent of the strategy used earlier in the book by Cohen and Nagel (pp. 56–59), when they defended the scientific method of fixing belief against the competing claims of the methods of tenacity, authority, and intuition.

We must now contend with the suggestion that reason is irrelevant to the commitment to theism because this territory is the domain of another faculty: the faculty of faith. It is sometimes even hinted that it is morally wrong and certainly foolish to suggest we should be reasoning about God. For this is the domain of faith or of the "venture of faith," of the "knowledge that passeth understanding," of religious experience and mystic insight.

Now the normal meaning of *faith* is simply "confidence"; we say that we have great faith in someone or in some claim or product, meaning that we believe and act as if they were very reliable. Of such faith we can properly say that it is well founded or not, depending on the evidence for whatever it is in which we have faith. So there is no incompatibility between this kind of faith and reason; the two are from different families and can make a very good marriage. Indeed if they do not join forces, then the resulting ill-based or inadequate confidence will probably lead to disaster. So faith, in this sense, means only a high degree of belief and may be reasonable or unreasonable.

But the term is sometimes used to mean an *alternative to reason* instead of something that should be founded on reason. Unfortunately, the mere use of the term in this way does not demonstrate that faith is a possible route to truth. It is like using the term "winning" as a synonym for "playing" instead of one possible outcome of playing. This is quaint, but it could hardly be called a satisfactory way of proving that we are winning; any time we "win" by changing the meaning of winning, the victory is merely illusory. And so it proves in this case. To use "faith" *as if* it were an alternative way to the truth cannot by-pass the crucial question whether such results really have any likelihood of being true. A rose by any other name will smell the same, and the inescapable facts about "faith" in the new sense are that it is still *applied to* a belief and is still supposed to imply *confidence in* that belief: the belief in the existence and goodness of God. So we can still ask the same old question about that belief: Is the confidence justified or misplaced? To say we "take it on faith" does not get it off parole.

Suppose someone replies that theism is a kind of belief that does not need justification by evidence. This means either that no one cares whether it is correct or not or that there is some other way of checking that it is correct besides looking at the evidence for it, i.e., giving reasons for believing it. But the first alternative is false since very many people care whether there is a God or not; and the second alternative is false because any method of showing that belief is likely to be true is, by definition, a justification of that belief, i.e., an appeal to reason. You certainly cannot show that a belief in God is likely to be true just by having confidence in it and by saying this is a case of knowledge "based on" faith, any more than you can win a game just by playing it and by calling that winning.

It is psychologically possible to have faith in something without any basis in fact, and once in a while you will turn out to be lucky and to have backed the right belief. This does not show you "really knew all along"; it only shows you cannot be unlucky all the time. . . . But, in general, beliefs without foundations lead to an early grave or to an accumulation of superstitions, which are usually troublesome and always false beliefs. It is hardly possible to defend this approach just by *saying* that you have decided that in this area confidence is its own justification.

Of course, you might try to *prove* that a feeling of great confidence about certain types of propositions is a reliable indication of their truth. If you succeeded, you would indeed have shown that the belief was justified; you would have done *this* by justifying it. To do this you would have to show what the real facts were and show that when someone had the kind of faith we are now talking about, it usually turned out that the facts were as he believed, just as we might justify the claims of a telepath. The catch in all this is simply that you have got to show what the real facts are in some way *other* than by appealing to faith, since that would simply be assuming what you are trying to prove. And if you can show what the facts are in this other way, you do not need faith in any new sense at all; you are already perfectly entitled to confidence in any belief that you have shown to be well supported.

How are you going to show what the real facts are? You show this by any method of investigation that has itself been tested, the testing being done by still another tested method, etc., through a series of tested connections that eventually terminates in our ordinary everyday reasoning and testing procedures of logic and observation.

Is it not prejudiced to require that the validation of beliefs always involve ultimate reference to our ordinary logic and everyday-plus-scientific knowledge? May not faith (religious experience, mystic insight) give us access to some new domain of truth? It is certainly possible that it does this. But, of course, it is also possible that it lies. One can hardly accept the reports of those with faith or, indeed, the apparent revelations of one's own religious experiences on the ground that they *might* be right. So *might* be a fervent materialist who saw his interpretation as a revelation. Possibility is not veracity. Is it not of the very greatest importance that we should try to find out whether we really can justify the use of the term "truth" or "knowledge" in describing the content of faith? If it is, then we must find something in that content that is known to be true in some other way, because to get off the ground we must first push off against the ground—we cannot lift ourselves by our shoelaces. If the new realm of knowledge is to be a realm of knowledge and not mythology, then it must tell us something which relates it to the kind of case that gives meaning to the term "truth." If you want to use the old word for the new events, you must show that it is applicable.

Could not the validating experience, which religious experience must have if it is to be called true, be the experience of others who also have or have had religious experiences? The religious community could, surely, provide a basis of agreement analogous to that which ultimately underlies scientific truth. Unfortunately, agreement is not the only requirement for avoiding error, for all may be in error. The difficulty for the religious community is to show that its agreement is not simply agreement about a shared mistake. If agreement were the only criterion of truth, there could never be a shared mistake; but clearly either the atheist group or the theist group shares a mistake. To decide which is wrong must involve appeal to something other than mere agreement. And, of course, it is clear that particular religious beliefs are mistaken, since religious groups do not all agree and they cannot all be right.

Might not some or all scientific beliefs be wrong, too? This is conceivable, but there are crucial differences between the two kinds of belief. In the first place, any commonly agreed religious beliefs concern only one or a few entities and their properties and histories. What for convenience we are here calling "scientific belief" is actually the sum total of all conventionally founded human knowledge, much of it not part of any science, and it embraces billions upon billions of facts, each of them perpetually or frequently subject to checking by independent means, each connected with a million others. The success of *this* system of knowledge shows up every day in everything that we do: we eat, and the food is not poison; we read, and the pages do not turn to dust; we slip, and gravity does not fail to pull us down. We are not just relying on the existence of agreement about the interpretation of a certain experience among a small part of the population. We are relying directly on our extremely reliable, nearly universal, and independently tested senses, and each of us is constantly obtaining independent confirmation for claims based on these, many of these confirmations being obtained for many claims, independently of each other. It is the wildest flight of fancy to suppose that there is a body of common religious beliefs which can be set out to exhibit this degree of repeated checking by religious experiences. In fact, there is not only gross disagreement on even the most fundamental claims in the creeds of different churches, each of which is supported by appeal to religious experience or faith, but where there is agreement by many people, it is all too easily open to the criticism that it arises from the common cultural exposure of the child or the adult convert and hence is not independent in the required way.

This claim that the agreement between judges is spurious in a particular case because it only reflects previous common indoctrination of those in agreement is a serious one. It must always be met by direct disproof whenever agreement is appealed to in science, and it is. The claim that the food is not poison cannot be explained away as a myth of some subculture, for anyone, even if told nothing about the eaters in advance, will judge that the people who ate it are still well. The whole methodology of testing is committed to the doctrine that any judges who could have learned what they are expected to say about the matter they are judging are completely valueless. Now anyone exposed to religious teaching, whether a believer or not, has long known the standard for such experiences, the usual symbols, the appropriate circumstances, and so on. These suggestions are usually very deeply implanted, so that they cannot be avoided by good intentions, and consequently members of our culture are rendered entirely incapable *of* being independent observers. Whenever observers are not free from previous contamination in this manner, the only way to support their claims is to examine independently testable *consequences* of the novel claims, such as predictions about the future. In the absence of these, the religious-experience gambit, whether involving literal or analogical claims, is wholly abortive.

A still more fundamental point counts against the idea that agreement among the religious can help support the idea of faith as an alternative path to truth. It is that every sane theist also believes in the claims of ordinary experience, while the reverse is not the case. Hence, the burden of proof is on the theist to show that the *further step* he wishes to take will not take him beyond the realm of truth. The two positions, of science and religion, are not symmetrical; the adherent of one of them suggests that we extend the range of allowable beliefs and yet is unable to produce the same degree of acceptance or "proving out" in the ordinary field of human activities that he insists on before believing in a new instrument or source of information. The atheist obviously cannot be shown his error in the way someone who thinks that there are no electrons can be shown his, *unless some of the arguments for the existence of God are sound.* . . . If some of them work, the position of religious knowledge is secure; if they do not, nothing else will make it secure.

In sum, the idea of separating religious from scientific knowledge and making each an independent realm with its own basis in experience of quite different kinds is a counsel of despair and not a product of true sophistication, for one cannot break the connection between everyday experience and religious claims, for purposes of defending the latter, without eliminating the consequences of religion for everyday life. There is no way out of this inexorable contract: if you want to support your beliefs, you must produce some experience which can be shown to be a reliable indicator of truth, and that can be done only by showing a connection between the experience and what we know to be true in a previously established way.

So, if the criteria of religious truth are not connected with the criteria of everyday truth, then they are not criteria of truth at all and the beliefs they "establish" have no essential bearing on our lives, constitute no explanation of what we see around us, and provide no guidance for our course through time.

Euthyphro

❖❖

PLATO

The *Euthyphro* is generally considered to be among Plato's earlier dialogues. The setting is shortly before Socrates' trial. The dramatic intensity is high, since Socrates has been charged with impiety, and Euthyphro, who is accusing his own father of homicide, claims to be acting in accord with piety.

But what is piety? Euthyphro is sure he knows but finds himself unable to maintain a consistent position in the face of Socrates' insistent questioning. When the dialogue ends, the definition remains undetermined.

The *Euthyphro* contains many points of philosophical interest, but the work is best known for its challenge to the view that morality rests on theism. Socrates asks the following question: Are actions right because God says they are right, or does God say actions are right because they are right? This question is not a verbal trick; on the contrary, it poses a serious dilemma for those who believe in the existence of God.

Socrates is inquiring whether actions are right due to God's fiat or whether God Himself is subject to moral standards. If actions are right due solely to God's command, then the discomforting conclusion is that anything God commands is right, even if He should command torture or murder. Furthermore, accepting this view removes any significance from the claim that God issues good commands. For if the good is whatever God commands, then to say God commands rightly is simply to say that He commands as He commands, a statement that is uninformative.

To avoid these unwanted implications, we are led to the view that actions are not right because God commands them; on the contrary, God commands them because they are right. In other words, what God commands conforms to a standard that is independent of God's will. But then one can oneself act in accord with that standard, thereby doing what is right, without necessarily believing in the existence of God.

Our translator is again David Gallop, and the notes are his. The

From *Defence of Socrates, Euthyphro, and Crito,* translated by David Gallop. Copyright © 1997 by Oxford University Press. Reprinted by permission of the publisher and translator.

Index of Names he prepared can be found at the end of the *Defence of Socrates* in Part I (pp. 38–40).

Why does the *Euthyphro* conclude without a resolution of its central question? A compelling reply is offered by Gallop, who explains that the dialogue

> aims for the same effect upon its readers as Socrates vainly tries to produce upon Euthyphro. It does not expressly tell us what holiness is, but it makes us recognize that we do not know, and provokes us into trying to find out. That is a task in which all readers of the *Euthyphro* must engage for themselves.

And so we turn to the text itself.

EUTHYPHRO: What trouble has arisen, Socrates, to make you leave your haunts in the Lyceum,[1] and spend your time here today at the Porch of the King Archon?[2] Surely you of all people don't have some sort of lawsuit before him, as I do?

SOCRATES: Well no; Athenians, at any rate, don't call it a lawsuit, Euthyphro—they call it an indictment.

EUTHYPHRO: What's that you say? Somebody must have indicted you, since I can't imagine your doing that to anyone else.

SOCRATES: No, I haven't.

EUTHYPHRO: But someone else has indicted you?

SOCRATES: Exactly.

EUTHYPHRO: Who is he?

SOCRATES: I hardly even know the man myself, Euthyphro; I gather he's young and unknown—but I believe he's named Meletus. He belongs to the Pitthean deme—can you picture a Meletus from that deme, with straight hair, not much of a beard, and a rather aquiline nose?

EUTHYPHRO: No, I can't picture him, Socrates. But tell me, what is this indictment he's brought against you?

SOCRATES: The indictment? I think it does him credit. To have made such a major discovery is no mean achievement for one so young: he claims to know how the young people are being corrupted, and who are corrupting them. He's probably a smart fellow; and noticing that in my ignorance I'm corrupting his contemporaries, he is going to denounce me to the city, as if to his mother.

Actually, he seems to me to be the only one who's making the right start in politics: it *is* right to make it one's first concern that the young should be as good as possible, just as a good farmer is likely to care first for the young plants, and only later for the others. And so Meletus is no doubt first weeding out those of us who are "ruining the shoots of youth," as he puts it. Next after this, he'll take care of the older people, and will obviously bring many great blessings to the city: at least that would be the natural outcome after such a start.

EUTHYPHRO: So I could wish, Socrates, but I'm afraid the opposite may happen: in trying to injure you, I really think he's making a good start at damaging the city. Tell me, what does he claim you are actually doing to corrupt the young?

SOCRATES: Absurd things, by the sound of them, my admirable friend: he says that I'm an inventor of gods; and for inventing strange gods, while failing to recognize the gods of old, he's indicted me on their behalf, so he says.

EUTHYPHRO: I see, Socrates; it's because you say that your spiritual sign visits you now and then. So he's brought this indictment against you as a religious innovator, and he's going to court to misrepresent you, knowing that such things are easily misrepresented before the public. Why, it's just the same with me: whenever I speak in the Assembly[4] on religious matters and predict the future for them, they laugh at me as if I were crazy; and yet not one of my predictions has failed to come true. Even so, they always envy people like ourselves. We mustn't worry about them, though—we must face up to them.

SOCRATES: Yes, my dear Euthyphro, being laughed at is probably not important. You know, Athenians don't much care, it seems to me, if they think someone clever, so long as he's not imparting his wisdom to others; but once they think he's making other people clever, then they get angry—whether from envy, as you say, or for some other reason.

EUTHYPHRO: In that case I don't much want to test their feelings towards me.

SOCRATES: Well, they probably think you give sparingly of yourself, and aren't willing to impart your wisdom. But in my case, I fear my benevolence makes them think I give all that I have, by speaking without reserve to every comer; not only do I speak without charge, but I'd gladly be out of pocket if anyone cares to listen to me. So, as I was just saying, if they were only going to laugh at me, as you say they laugh at you, it wouldn't be bad sport if they passed the time joking and laughing in the courtroom. But if they're going to be serious, then there's no knowing how things will turn out—except for you prophets.

EUTHYPHRO: Well, I dare say it will come to nothing, Socrates. No doubt you'll handle your case with intelligence, as I think I shall handle mine.

SOCRATES: And what is this case of yours, Euthyphro? Are you defending or prosecuting?

EUTHYPHRO: Prosecuting.

SOCRATES: Whom?

EUTHYPHRO: Once again, someone whom I'm thought crazy to be prosecuting.

SOCRATES: How's that? Are you chasing a bird on the wing?

EUTHYPHRO: The bird is long past flying: in fact, he's now quite elderly.

SOCRATES: And who is he?

EUTHYPHRO: My father.

SOCRATES: *What?* Your own *father!*

EUTHYPHRO: Precisely.

SOCRATES: But what is the charge? What is the case about?

EUTHYPHRO: It's a case of murder, Socrates.

SOCRATES: Good heavens above! Well, Euthyphro, most people are obviously ignorant of where the right lies in such a case, since I can't imagine any ordinary person taking that action. It must need someone pretty far advanced in wisdom.

EUTHYPHRO: Goodness yes, Socrates. Far advanced indeed!

SOCRATES: And is your father's victim one of your relatives? Obviously, he must be—you'd hardly be prosecuting him for murder on behalf of a stranger.

EUTHYPHRO: It's ridiculous, Socrates, that you should think it makes any difference whether the victim was a stranger or a relative, and not see that the sole consideration is whether or not the slaying was lawful. If it was, one should leave the slayer alone; but if it wasn't, one should prosecute, even if the slayer shares one's own hearth and board—because the pollution is just the same, if you knowingly associate with such a person, and fail to cleanse yourself and him by taking legal action.

In point of fact, the victim was a day-labourer of mine: when we were farming in Naxos,[5] he was working there on our estate. He had got drunk, flown into a rage with one of our servants, and butchered him. So my father had him bound hand and foot, and flung into a ditch; he then sent a messenger here to find out from the religious authority[6] what should be done. In the meantime, he disregarded his captive, and neglected him as a murderer, thinking it wouldn't much matter even if he died. And that was just what happened: the man died of hunger and cold, and from his bonds, before the messenger got back from the authority.

That's why my father and other relatives are now upset with me, because I'm prosecuting him for murder on a murderer's behalf. According to them, he didn't even kill him. And even if he was definitely a

killer, they say that, since the victim was a murderer, I shouldn't be troubled on such a fellow's behalf—because it is unholy for a son to prosecute his father for murder. Little do they know, Socrates, of religious law
about what is holy and unholy.

SOCRATES: But heavens above, Euthyphro, do you think you have such exact knowledge of religion, of things holy and unholy? Is it so exact that
in the circumstances you describe, you aren't afraid that, by bringing
your father to trial, you might prove guilty of unholy conduct yourself?

EUTHYPHRO: Yes it is, Socrates; in fact I'd be good for nothing, and Euthyphro wouldn't differ at all from the common run of men, unless I had exact knowledge of all such matters.

SOCRATES: Why then, my admirable Euthyphro, my best course is to become your student, and to challenge Meletus on this very point before
his indictment is heard. I could say that even in the past I always used to
set a high value upon religious knowledge; and that now, because he
says I've gone astray by free-thinking and religious innovation, I have
become your student.

　　"Meletus," I could say: "if you agree that Euthyphro is an expert on
such matters, then you should regard me as orthodox too, and drop the
case. But if you don't admit that, then proceed against that teacher of
mine, not me, for corrupting the elderly—namely, myself and his own
father—myself by his teaching, and his father by admonition and punishment."

　　Then, if he didn't comply and drop the charge, or indict you in my
place, couldn't I repeat in court the very points on which I'd already
challenged him?

EUTHYPHRO: By God, Socrates, if he tried indicting me, I fancy I'd soon
find his weak spots; and we'd have _him_ being discussed in the courtroom long before I was.

SOCRATES: Why yes, dear friend, I realize that, and that's why I'm eager to
become your student. I know that this Meletus, amongst others no
doubt, doesn't even seem to notice you; it's me he's detected so keenly
and so readily that he can charge me with impiety.

　　So now, for goodness' sake, tell me what you were just maintaining
you knew for sure. What sort of thing would you say that the pious and
the impious are, whether in murder or in other matters? Isn't the holy itself the same as itself in every action? And conversely, isn't the unholy[7]
the exact opposite of the holy, in itself similar to itself, or possessed of a
single character,[8] in anything at all that is going to be unholy?

EUTHYPHRO: Indeed it is, Socrates.

SOCRATES: Tell me, then, what do you say that the holy is? And the unholy?

EUTHYPHRO: All right, I'd say that the holy is just what I'm doing now:

prosecuting wrongdoers, whether in cases of murder or temple-robbery, or those guilty of any other such offence, be they one's father or mother or anyone else whatever; and failing to prosecute is unholy.

See how strong my evidence is, Socrates, that this is the law—evidence I've already given others that my conduct was correct: one must not tolerate an impious man, no matter who he may happen to be. The very people who recognize Zeus as best and most righteous of the gods admit that he put his father in bonds for wrongfully gobbling up his children; and that that father in turn castrated *his* father for similar misdeeds. And yet they are angry with me, because I'm prosecuting *my* father as a wrongdoer. Thus, they contradict themselves in what they say about the gods and about me.

SOCRATES: Could this be the reason why I'm facing indictment, Euthyphro? Is it because when people tell such stories of the gods, I somehow find them hard to accept? That, I suppose, is why some will say that I've gone astray. But now, if these stories convince you—with your great knowledge of such matters—then it seems that the rest of us must accept them as well. What can we possibly say, when by our own admission we know nothing of these matters? But tell me, in the name of friendship, do you really believe that those things happened as described?

EUTHYPHRO: Yes, and even more remarkable things, Socrates, of which most people are ignorant.

SOCRATES: And do you believe that the gods actually make war upon one another?[9] That they have terrible feuds and fights, and much more of the sort related by our poets, and depicted by our able painters, to adorn our temples—especially the robe which is covered with such adornments, and gets carried up to the Acropolis at the great Panathenaean festival?[10] Are we to say that those stories are true, Euthyphro?

EUTHYPHRO: Not only those, Socrates, but as I was just saying, I'll explain to you many further points about religion, if you'd like, which I'm sure you'll be astonished to hear.

SOCRATES: I shouldn't be surprised. But explain them to me at leisure some other time. For now, please try to tell me more clearly what I was just asking. You see, my friend, you didn't instruct me properly when I asked my earlier question: I asked what the holy might be, but you told me that the holy was what you are now doing, prosecuting your father for murder.

EUTHYPHRO: Yes, and there I was right, Socrates.

SOCRATES: Maybe. Yet surely, Euthyphro, there are many other things you call holy as well.

EUTHYPHRO: So there are.

SOCRATES: And do you recall that I wasn't urging you to teach me about one or two of those many things that are holy, but rather about the form itself[11] whereby all holy things are holy? Because you said, I think, that it was by virtue of a single character that unholy things are unholy, and holy things are holy. Don't you remember?

EUTHYPHRO: Yes, I do.

SOCRATES: Then teach me about that character, about what it might be, so that by fixing my eye upon it and using it as a model, I may call holy any action of yours or another's, which conforms to it, and may deny to be holy whatever does not.

EUTHYPHRO: All right, if that's what you want, Socrates, that's what I'll tell you.

SOCRATES: Yes, that *is* what I want.

EUTHYPHRO: In that case, what is agreeable to the gods is holy, and what is not agreeable to them is unholy.

SOCRATES: Splendid, Euthyphro!—You've given just the sort of answer I was looking for. Mind you, I don't yet know whether it's correct, but obviously you will go on to show that what you say is true.

EUTHYPHRO: I certainly will.

SOCRATES: All right then, let's consider what it is we're saying. A thing or a person loved-by-the-gods is holy, whereas something or someone hated-by-the-gods is unholy; and the holy isn't the same as the unholy, but is the direct opposite of it. Isn't that what we're saying?

EUTHYPHRO: Exactly.

SOCRATES: And does it seem well put?

EUTHYPHRO: I think so, Socrates.

SOCRATES: And again, Euthyphro, the gods quarrel and have their differences, and there is mutual hostility amongst them. Hasn't that been said as well?

EUTHYPHRO: Yes, it has.

SOCRATES: Well, on what matters do their differences produce hostility and anger, my good friend? Let's look at it this way. If we differed, you and I, about which of two things was more numerous, would our difference on these questions make us angry and hostile towards one another? Or would we resort to counting in such disputes, and soon be rid of them?

EUTHYPHRO: We certainly would.

SOCRATES: Again, if we differed about which was larger and smaller, we'd soon put an end to our difference by resorting to measurement, wouldn't we?

EUTHYPHRO: That's right.

SOCRATES: And we would decide a dispute about which was heavier and lighter, presumably, by resorting to weighing.

EUTHYPHRO: Of course.

SOCRATES: Then what sorts of questions would make us angry and hostile towards one another, if we differed about them and were unable to reach a decision? Perhaps you can't say offhand. But consider my suggestion, that they are questions of what is just and unjust,[12] honourable and dishonourable, good and bad. Aren't those the matters on which our disagreement and our inability to reach a satisfactory decision occasionally make enemies of us, of you and me, and of people in general?

EUTHYPHRO: Those are the differences, Socrates, and that's what they're about.

SOCRATES: And what about the gods, Euthyphro? If they really do differ, mustn't they differ about those same things?

EUTHYPHRO: They certainly must.

SOCRATES: Then, by your account, noble Euthyphro, different gods also regard different things as just, or as honourable and dishonourable, good and bad; because unless they differed on those matters, they wouldn't quarrel, would they?

EUTHYPHRO: Correct.

SOCRATES: And again, the things each of them regards as honourable, good, or just, are also the things they love, while it's the opposites of those things that they hate.

EUTHYPHRO: Indeed.

SOCRATES: And yet it's the same things, according to you, that some gods consider just, and others unjust, about which their disputes lead them to quarrel and make war upon one another. Isn't that right?

EUTHYPHRO: It is.

SOCRATES: Then the same things, it appears, are both hated and loved by the gods, and thus the same things would be both hated-by-the-gods and loved-by-the-gods.

EUTHYPHRO: It does appear so.

SOCRATES: So by this argument, Euthyphro, the same things would be both holy and unholy.

EUTHYPHRO: It looks that way.

SOCRATES: So then you haven't answered my question, my admirable friend. You see, I wasn't asking what self-same thing proves to be at once holy and unholy. And yet something which is loved-by-the-gods is apparently also hated-by-the-gods. Hence, as regards your present action in punishing your father, Euthyphro, it wouldn't be at all surprising if you were thereby doing something agreeable to Zeus but odious to Cronus and Uranus, or pleasing to Hephaestus but odious to Hera; and likewise for any other gods who may differ from one another on the matter.

EUTHYPHRO: Yes, Socrates, but I don't think any of the gods do differ from one another on this point, at least: whoever has unjustly killed another should be punished.

SOCRATES: Really? Well, what about human beings, Euthyphro? Have you never heard any of them arguing that someone who has killed unjustly, or acted unjustly in some other way, should not be punished?

EUTHYPHRO: Why yes, they are constantly arguing that way, in the law-courts as well as elsewhere: people who act unjustly in all sorts of ways will do or say anything to escape punishment.

SOCRATES: But do they admit acting unjustly, Euthyphro, yet still say, despite that admission, that they shouldn't be punished?

EUTHYPHRO: No, they don't say that at all.

SOCRATES: So it isn't just anything that they will say or do. This much, I imagine, they don't dare to say or argue: if they act unjustly, they should not be punished. Rather, I imagine, they deny acting unjustly, don't they?

EUTHYPHRO: True.

SOCRATES: Then they don't argue that one who acts unjustly should not be punished; but they do argue, maybe, about who it was that acted unjustly, and what he did, and when.

EUTHYPHRO: True.

SOCRATES: Then doesn't the very same thing also apply to the gods—if they really do quarrel about just and unjust actions, as your account suggests, and if each party says that the other acts unjustly, while the other denies it? Because surely, my admirable friend, no one among gods or men dares to claim that anyone should go unpunished who *has* acted unjustly.

EUTHYPHRO: Yes, what you say is true, Socrates, at least on the whole.

SOCRATES: Rather, Euthyphro, I think it is the individual act that causes arguments among gods as well as human beings—if gods really do argue: it is with regard to some particular action that they differ, some saying it was done justly, while others say it was unjust. Isn't that so?

EUTHYPHRO: Indeed.

SOCRATES: Then please, my dear Euthyphro, instruct me too, that I may grow wiser. When a hired man has committed murder, has been put in bonds by the master of his victim, and has died from those bonds before his captor can find out from the authorities what to do about him, what proof have you that all gods regard that man as having met an unjust death? Or that it is right for a son to prosecute his father and press a charge of murder on behalf of such a man? Please try to show me plainly that all gods undoubtedly regard that action in those circumstances as right. If you can show that to my satisfaction, I'll never stop singing the praises of your wisdom.

EUTHYPHRO: Well, that may be no small task, Socrates, though I *could* of course prove it to you quite plainly.

SOCRATES: I see. You must think me a slower learner than the jury, because obviously you will show them that the acts in question were unjust, and that all the gods hate such things.

EUTHYPHRO: I will show that very clearly, Socrates, provided they listen while I'm talking.

SOCRATES: They'll listen all right, so long as they approve of what you're saying.

But while you were talking, I reflected and put to myself this question: "Even suppose Euthyphro were to instruct me beyond any doubt that the gods all do regard such a death as unjust, what more have I learnt from him about what the holy and the unholy might be? This particular deed would be hated-by-the-gods, apparently; yet it became evident just now that the holy and unholy were not defined in that way, since what is hated-by-the-gods proved to be loved-by-the-gods as well."

So I'll let you off on that point, Euthyphro; let *all* the gods consider it unjust, if you like, and let *all* of them hate it. Is this the correction we are now making in our account: whatever *all* the gods hate is unholy, and whatever they *all* love is holy; and whatever some gods love but others hate is neither or both? Is that how you would now have us define the holy and the unholy?

EUTHYPHRO: What objection could there be, Socrates?

SOCRATES: None on my part, Euthyphro. But consider your own view, and see whether, by making that suggestion, you will most easily teach me what you promised.

EUTHYPHRO: Very well, I would say that the holy is whatever all the gods love; and its opposite, whatever all the gods hate, is unholy.

SOCRATES: Then shall we examine that in turn, Euthyphro, and see whether it is well put? Or shall we let it pass, and accept it from ourselves and others? Are we to agree with a position merely on the strength of someone's say so, or should we examine what the speaker is saying?

EUTHYPHRO: We should examine it. Even so, for my part I believe that this time our account is well put.

SOCRATES: We shall soon be better able to tell, sir. Just consider the following question: is the holy loved by the gods because it is holy? Or is it holy because it is loved?

EUTHYPHRO: I don't know what you mean, Socrates.

SOCRATES: All right, I'll try to put it more clearly. We speak of a thing's "being carried" or "carrying," of its "being led" or "leading," of its "being seen" or "seeing." And you understand, don't you, that all such things are different from each other, and how they differ?[13]

EUTHYPHRO: Yes, I think I understand.

SOCRATES: And again, isn't there something that is "being loved," while that which loves is different from it?

EUTHYPHRO: Of course.

SOCRATES: Then tell me whether something in a state of "being carried" is in that state because someone is carrying it, or for some other reason.

EUTHYPHRO: No, that is the reason.

SOCRATES: And something in a state of "being led" is so because someone is leading it, and something in a state of "being seen" is so because someone is seeing it?

EUTHYPHRO: Certainly.

SOCRATES: Then someone does not see a thing because it is in a state of "being seen," but on the contrary, it is in that state because someone is seeing it; nor does someone lead a thing because it is in a state of "being led," but rather it is in that state because someone is leading it; nor does someone carry a thing because it is in a state of "being carried," but it is in that state because someone is carrying it. Is my meaning quite clear, Euthyphro? What I mean is this: if something gets into a certain state or is affected in a certain way, it does not get into that state because it possesses it; rather, it possesses that state because it gets into it; nor is it thus affected because it is in that condition; rather, it is in that condition because it is thus affected. Don't you agree with that?

EUTHYPHRO: Yes, I do.

SOCRATES: Again, "being loved" is a case of either being in a certain state or being in a certain condition because of some agent?

EUTHYPHRO: Certainly.

SOCRATES: Then this case is similar to our previous examples: it is not because it is in a state of "being loved" that an object is loved by those who love it; rather, it is in that state because it is loved by them. Isn't that right?

EUTHYPHRO: It must be.

SOCRATES: Now what are we saying about the holy, Euthyphro? On your account, doesn't it consist in being loved by all the gods?

EUTHYPHRO: Yes.

SOCRATES: Is that because it is holy, or for some other reason?

EUTHYPHRO: No, that is the reason.

SOCRATES: So it is loved because it is holy, not holy because it is loved.

EUTHYPHRO: So it seems.

SOCRATES: By contrast, what is loved-by-the-gods is in that state—namely, being loved-by-the-gods—because the gods love it.

EUTHYPHRO: Of course.

SOCRATES: Then what is loved-by-the-gods is not the holy, Euthyphro, nor is the holy what is loved-by-the-gods, as you say, but they differ from each other.

EUTHYPHRO: How so, Socrates?

SOCRATES: Because we are agreed, aren't we, that the holy is loved because it is holy, not holy because it is loved?

EUTHYPHRO: Yes.

SOCRATES: Whereas what is loved-by-the-gods is so because the gods love it. It is loved-by-the-gods by virtue of their loving it; it is not because it is in that state that they love it.

EUTHYPHRO: That's true.

SOCRATES: But if what is loved-by-the-gods and the holy were the same thing, Euthyphro, then if the holy were loved because it is holy, what is loved-by-the-gods would be loved because it is loved-by-the-gods; and again, if what is loved-by-the-gods were loved-by-the-gods because they love it, then the holy would be holy because they love it. In actual fact, however, you can see that the two of them are related in just the opposite way, as two entirely different things: one of them is lovable because they love it, whereas the other they love for the reason that it is lovable.

And so, Euthyphro, when you are asked what the holy might be, it looks as if you'd prefer not to explain its essence to me, but would rather tell me one of its properties—namely, that the holy has the property of being loved by all the gods; but you still haven't told me what it *is*.

So please don't hide it from me, but start again and tell me what the holy might be—whether it is loved by the gods or possesses any other property, since we won't disagree about that.[14] Out with it now, and tell me what the holy and the unholy are.

EUTHYPHRO: The trouble is, Socrates, that I can't tell you what I have in mind, because whatever we suggest keeps moving around somehow, and refuses to stay put where we established it.

SOCRATES: My ancestor Daedalus seems to be the author of your words, Euthyphro. Indeed, if they were my own words and suggestions, you might make fun of me, and say that it's because of my kinship with him that my works of art in conversation run away from me too, and won't stay where they're placed. But in fact those suggestions are your own; and so you need a different joke, because you're the one for whom they won't stay put—as you realize yourself.

EUTHYPHRO: No, I think it's much the same joke that is called for by what we said, Socrates: I'm not the one who makes them move around and not stay put. I think you're the Daedalus because, as far as I'm concerned, they would have kept still.

SOCRATES: It looks then, my friend, as if I've grown this much more accomplished at my craft than Daedalus himself: he made only his own works move around, whereas I do it, apparently, to those of others besides my own. And indeed the really remarkable feature of my craft is that I'm an expert at it without even wanting to be. You see, I'd prefer to have words stay put for me, immovably established, than to acquire the wealth of Tantalus and the skill of Daedalus combined.

But enough of this. Since I think you are being feeble, I'll join you myself in an effort to help you instruct me about the holy. Don't give up too soon, now. Just consider whether you think that everything that is holy must be just.

EUTHYPHRO: Yes, I do.

SOCRATES: Well then, is everything that is just holy? Or is everything that is holy just, but not everything that is just holy? Is part of it holy, and part of it something else?

EUTHYPHRO: I can't follow what you're saying, Socrates.

SOCRATES: And yet you are as much my superior in youth as you are in wisdom. But as I say, your wealth of wisdom has enfeebled you. So pull yourself together, my dear sir—it really isn't hard to see what I mean: it's just the opposite of what the poet meant who composed these verses:

With Zeus, who wrought it and who generated all these things,
You cannot quarrel; for where there is fear, there is also shame.

I disagree with that poet. Shall I tell you where?

EUTHYPHRO: By all means.

SOCRATES: I don't think that "where there is fear, there is also shame"; because many people, I take it, dread illnesses, poverty, and many other such things. Yet although they dread them, they are not ashamed of what they fear. Don't you agree?

EUTHYPHRO: Certainly.

SOCRATES: On the other hand, where there is shame, there is also fear: doesn't anyone who is ashamed and embarrassed by a certain action both fear and dread a reputation for wickedness?

EUTHYPHRO: Indeed he does.

SOCRATES: Then it isn't right to say that "where there is fear, there is also shame"; nevertheless, where there is shame there is also fear, even though shame is not found everywhere there is fear. Fear is broader than shame, I think, since shame is one kind of fear, just as odd is one kind of number. Thus, it is not true that wherever there is number there is also odd, although it is true that where there is odd, there is also number. You follow me now, presumably?

EUTHYPHRO: Perfectly.

SOCRATES: Well, that's the sort of thing I meant just now: I was asking, "Is it true that wherever a thing is just, it is also holy? Or is a thing just wherever it is holy, but not holy wherever it is just?" In other words, isn't the holy part of what is just? Is that what we're to say, or do you disagree?

EUTHYPHRO: No, let's say that: your point strikes me as correct.

SOCRATES: Then consider the next point: if the holy is one part of what is just, it would seem that we need to find out which part it might be. Now, if you asked me about one of the things just mentioned, for example, which kind of number is even, and what sort of number it might be, I'd say that it's any number which is not scalene but isosceles.[15] Would you agree?

EUTHYPHRO: I would.

SOCRATES: Now you try to instruct me, likewise, which part of what is just is holy. Then we'll be able to tell Meletus not to treat us unjustly any longer, or indict us for impiety, because I've now had proper tuition from you about what things are pious or holy, and what are not.

EUTHYPHRO: Well then, in my view, the part of what is just that is pious or holy has to do with ministering to the gods, while the rest of it has to do with ministering to human beings.

SOCRATES: Yes, I think you put that very well, Euthyphro. I am still missing one small detail, however. You see, I don't yet understand this "ministering" of which you speak. You surely don't mean "ministering" to the gods in the same sense as "ministering" to other things. That's how we talk, isn't it? We say, for example, that not everyone understands how to minister to horses, but only the horse-trainer. Isn't that right?

EUTHYPHRO: Certainly.

SOCRATES: Because, surely, horse-training is ministering to horses.

EUTHYPHRO: Yes.

SOCRATES: Nor, again, does everyone know how to minister to dogs, but only the dog-trainer.

EUTHYPHRO: Just so.

SOCRATES: Because, of course, dog-training is ministering to dogs.

EUTHYPHRO: Yes.

SOCRATES: And again, cattle-farming is ministering to cattle.

EUTHYPHRO: Certainly.

SOCRATES: And holiness or piety is ministering to the gods, Euthyphro? Is that what you're saying?

EUTHYPHRO: It is.

SOCRATES: Well, doesn't all ministering achieve the same thing? I mean something like this: it aims at some good or benefit for its object. Thus, you may see that horses, when they are being ministered to by horse-training, are benefited and improved. Or don't you think they are?

EUTHYPHRO: Yes, I do.

SOCRATES: And dogs, of course, are benefited by dog-training, and cattle by cattle-farming, and the rest likewise. Or do you suppose that ministering is for harming its objects?

EUTHYPHRO: Goodness, no!

SOCRATES: So it's for their benefit?

EUTHYPHRO: Of course.

SOCRATES: Then, if holiness is ministering to the gods, does it benefit the gods and make them better? And would you grant that whenever you do something holy, you're making some god better?

EUTHYPHRO: Heavens, no!

SOCRATES: No, I didn't think you meant that, Euthyphro—far from it—but that was the reason why I asked what sort of ministering to the gods you did mean. I didn't think you meant that sort.

EUTHYPHRO: Quite right, Socrates: that's not the sort of thing I mean.

SOCRATES: Very well, but then what sort of ministering to the gods would holiness be?

EUTHYPHRO: The sort which slaves give to their masters, Socrates.

SOCRATES: I see. Then it would appear to be some sort of service to the gods.

EUTHYPHRO: Exactly.

SOCRATES: Now could you tell me what result is achieved by service to doctors? It would be health, wouldn't it?

EUTHYPHRO: It would.

SOCRATES: And what about service to shipwrights? What result is achieved in their service?

EUTHYPHRO: Obviously, Socrates, the construction of ships.

SOCRATES: And service to builders, of course, achieves the construction of houses.

EUTHYPHRO: Yes.

SOCRATES: Then tell me, good fellow, what product would be achieved by service to the gods? You obviously know, since you claim religious knowledge superior to any man's.

EUTHYPHRO: Yes, and there I'm right, Socrates.

SOCRATES: Then tell me, for goodness' sake, just what that splendid task is which the gods accomplish by using our services?

EUTHYPHRO: They achieve many fine things, Socrates.

SOCRATES: Yes, and so do generals, my friend. Yet you could easily sum up their achievement as the winning of victory in war, couldn't you?

EUTHYPHRO: Of course.

SOCRATES: And farmers too. They achieve many fine things, I believe. Yet they can be summed up as the production of food from the earth.

EUTHYPHRO: Certainly.

SOCRATES: And now how about the many fine achievements of the gods? How can their work be summed up?

EUTHYPHRO: I've already told you a little while ago, Socrates, that it's a pretty big job to learn the exact truth on all these matters. But I will simply tell you this much: if one has expert knowledge of the words and deeds that gratify the gods through prayer and sacrifice, those are the ones that are holy: such practices are the salvation of individual families, along with the common good of cities; whereas practices that are the opposite of gratifying are impious ones, which of course upset and ruin everything.

SOCRATES: I'm sure you could have given a summary answer to my question far more briefly, Euthyphro, if you'd wanted to. But you're not eager to teach me—that's clear because you've turned aside just when you were on the very brink of the answer. If you'd given it, I would have learnt properly from you about holiness by now. But as it is, the questioner must follow wherever the person questioned may lead him. So, once again, what are you saying that the holy or holiness is? Didn't you say it was some sort of expertise in sacrifice and prayer?

EUTHYPHRO: Yes, I did.

SOCRATES: And sacrifice is giving things to the gods, while prayer is asking things of them?

EUTHYPHRO: Exactly, Socrates.

SOCRATES: So, by that account, holiness will be expertise in asking from the gods and giving to them.

EUTHYPHRO: You've gathered my meaning beautifully, Socrates.

SOCRATES: Yes, my friend, that's because I'm greedy for your wisdom, and apply my intelligence to it, so that what you say won't fall wasted to the ground. But tell me, what is this service to the gods? You say it is asking from them, and giving to them?

EUTHYPHRO: I do.

SOCRATES: Well, would asking rightly be asking for things we need from them?

EUTHYPHRO: Why, what else could it be?

SOCRATES: And conversely, giving rightly would be giving them in return things that they do, in fact, need from us. Surely it would be inept to give anybody things he didn't need, wouldn't it?

EUTHYPHRO: True, Socrates.

SOCRATES: So then holiness would be a sort of skill in mutual trading between gods and mankind?

EUTHYPHRO: Trading, yes, if that's what you prefer to call it.

SOCRATES: I don't prefer anything unless it is actually true. But tell me, what benefit do the gods derive from the gifts they receive from us? What they give, of course, is obvious to anyone—since we possess nothing good which they don't give us. But how are they benefited by what they receive from us? Do we get so much the better bargain in our trade with them that we receive all the good things from them, while they receive none from us?

EUTHYPHRO: Come, Socrates, do you really suppose that the gods are benefited by what they receive from us?

SOCRATES: Well if not, Euthyphro, what ever would they be, these gifts of ours to the gods?

EUTHYPHRO: What else do you suppose but honour and reverence, and—as I said just now—what is gratifying to them?

SOCRATES: So the holy is gratifying, but not beneficial or loved by the gods?

EUTHYPHRO: I imagine it is the most loved of all things.

SOCRATES: Then, once again, it seems that this is what the holy is: what is loved by the gods.

EUTHYPHRO: Absolutely.

SOCRATES: Well now, if you say that, can you wonder if you find that words won't keep still for you, but walk about? And will you blame me as the Daedalus who makes them walk, when you're far more skilled than Daedalus yourself at making them go round in a circle? Don't you notice that our account has come full circle back to the same point? You recall, no doubt, how we found earlier that what is holy and what is loved-by-the-gods were not the same, but different from each other? Don't you remember?

EUTHYPHRO: Yes, I do.

SOCRATES: Then don't you realize that now you're equating holy with what the gods love? But that makes it identical with loved-by-the-gods, doesn't it?

EUTHYPHRO: Indeed.

SOCRATES: So either our recent agreement wasn't sound; or else, if it was, our present suggestion is wrong.

EUTHYPHRO: So it appears.

SOCRATES: Then we must start over again, and consider what the holy is, since I shan't be willing to give up the search till I learn the answer. Please don't scorn me, but give the matter your very closest attention and tell me the truth—because you must know it, if any man does; and like Proteus you mustn't be let go until you tell it.

You see, if you didn't know for sure what is holy and what unholy, there's no way you'd ever have ventured to prosecute your elderly father for murder on behalf of a labourer. Instead, fear of the gods would have saved you from the risk of acting wrongly, and you'd have been embarrassed in front of human beings. But in fact I'm quite sure that you think you have certain knowledge of what is holy and what is not; so tell me what you believe it to be, excellent Euthyphro, and don't conceal it.

EUTHYPHRO: Some other time, Socrates: I'm hurrying somewhere just now, and it's time for me to be off.

SOCRATES: What a way to behave, my friend, going off like this, and dashing the high hopes I held! I was hoping I'd learn from you what acts are holy and what are not, and so escape Meletus' indictment, by showing him that Euthyphro had made me an expert in religion, and that my ignorance no longer made me a free-thinker or innovator on that subject: and also, of course, that I would live better for what remains of my life.

NOTES

1. A gymnasium outside the walls of Athens, and a favorite resort of Socrates, where the philosophical discussions in Plato's dialogues are sometimes set.
2. The archons were nine officials chosen annually as Athens' chief magistrates. The "King Archon" was one of their number chosen by lot, with special responsibility for religious ceremonial and ritual purification, and for cases involving offences against state religion. His Porch was in the Agora or marketplace.
3. A deme was one of the divisions, originally territorial, upon which the registration of Athenian voters was based.
4. The sovereign body of Athenian democracy. All adult male citizens were eligible to attend its meetings and to vote.
5. A large island in the Cyclades, the group of Aegean islands lying to the southeast of Attica.
6. This official was an interpreter of religious law, who gave advice upon procedures for purification in homicide cases.
7. When Socrates asks about "the pious" or "the holy," he wishes to understand more clearly what it means to ascribe that property to an action or a person, and to discover a criterion for doing so. No distinction seems intended between "pious" and "holy."
8. The word translated "character" (*idea*) is the ancestor of the English "idea." Socrates is not, however, seeking an "idea" in the sense of a subjective or mind-dependent entity. He is seeking an objective property, common to all the many holy (or unholy) items, in virtue of which they are so called.
9. Strife amongst the gods abounds in Homer's *Iliad* and *Odyssey,* and is a mainspring for the plots of both epics.
10. The Acropolis was the large rocky eminence that dominated Athens. It was the site of various temples, including the renowned Parthenon, sacred to the city's patron goddess Athena. A festival called "Panathenaea" was held annually to celebrate her birthday.
11. The role of Platonic "forms" in settling ethical disputes is explained here. The form is said to function as a "model" or "exemplar" (*paradeigma*), enabling particular items to be described as possessing or lacking a given property, according as they conform, or fail to conform, to the model. Thus one motivation for philosophical inquiry is the hope of settling disagreements by finding a *standard* to which appeal can be made in disputed cases.
12. The Greek adjectives (*dikaios* and *adikos*) can be used of both actions and persons, where as the English "right" and "wrong" belong, in their moral sense, only to actions.

13. Socrates distinguishes active from passive participles of the verbs "carry," "lead," and "see," and suggests a parallel distinction for "love." The distinction is between the agent that bestows a certain treatment on something and the recipient of that treatment.
14. The words rendered "essence" (*ousia*) and "property" (*pathos*) are used to distinguish between essential and accidental features of an item. "Being approved by the gods" is not, as we would say, an essential feature of holy actions, but one that they just happen to possess.
15. Greek mathematicians thought of numbers by analogy with geometrical figures. An isosceles triangle has two equal sides, whereas a scalene triangle has none. Hence, an even number is "isosceles," because it can be divided into two equal parts that are both whole numbers, whereas an odd number is "scalene," because it cannot be so divided.

Summa Theologiae

❖❖

Saint Thomas Aquinas

Saint Thomas Aquinas (1225–1274), born near Naples, was the most influential philosopher of the medieval period. He joined the Dominican order and taught at the University of Paris. In his vast writings, composed in Latin, he sought to demonstrate that Christian belief was consistent with the philosophy of Aristotle, whose writings had only recently been recovered in Europe and were highly esteemed. Aquinas' synthesis of Aristotelianism and Christianity was considered so successful by the Church that five hundred years later in 1879 Pope Leo XIII declared Aquinas' system to be the official Catholic philosophy.

Aquinas' greatest work was the *Summa Theologiae*, and its most famous passage, reprinted here, is the five ways to prove the existence of God. While Aquinas believed that not all the tenets of

From *The Basic Writings of St. Thomas Aquinas* (New York: Random House, 1945), trans. Anton C. Pegis, pp. 25–27. Reprinted by permission of Hackett Publishing Company, Inc. All rights reserved.

Christian doctrine could be demonstrated by reason alone without reliance on Divine revelation, he did maintain that the existence of God was provable without any appeal to faith. Thus those who consider the existence of God a mystery beyond the bounds of reason are at odds with the official philosophy of Catholicism.

In the fourth way Aquinas cites "*Metaph.* ii." The reference is to the second book of Aristotle's *Metaphysics* and serves as a reminder of Aristotle's central place in Aquinas' thought.

The existence of God can be proved in five ways.

The first and more manifest way is the argument from motion. It is certain, and evident to our senses, that in the world some things are in motion. Now whatever is moved is moved by another, for nothing can be moved except it is in potentiality to that towards which it is moved; whereas a thing moves inasmuch as it is in act. For motion is nothing else than the reduction of something from potentiality to actuality. But nothing can be reduced from potentiality to actuality, except by something in a state of actuality. Thus that which is actually hot, as fire, makes wood, which is potentially hot, to be actually hot, and thereby moves and changes it. Now it is not possible that the same thing should be at once in actuality and potentiality in the same respect, but only in different respects. For what is actually hot cannot simultaneously be potentially hot; but it is simultaneously potentially cold. It is therefore impossible that in the same respect and in the same way a thing should be both mover and moved, i.e., that it should move itself. Therefore, whatever is moved must be moved by another. If that by which it is moved be itself moved, then this also must needs be moved by another, and that by another again. But this cannot go on to infinity, because then there would be no first mover, and, consequently, no other mover, seeing that subsequent movers move only inasmuch as they are moved by the first mover; as the staff moves only because it is moved by the hand. Therefore it is necessary to arrive at a first mover, moved by no other; and this everyone understands to be God.

The second way is from the nature of efficient cause. In the world of sensible things we find there is an order of efficient causes. There is no case known (neither is it, indeed, possible) in which a thing is found to be the efficient cause of itself; for so it would be prior to itself, which is impossible. Now in efficient causes it is not possible to go on to infinity, because in all efficient causes following in order, the first is the cause of the intermediate cause, and the intermediate is the cause of the ultimate cause, whether the intermediate cause be several, or one only. Now to take away the cause is to take away the effect. Therefore, if there be no first cause among efficient causes, there will be no ultimate, nor any intermediate, cause. But if in efficient causes it is possible to go on to infinity, there will be no first efficient cause, neither will there be an ultimate effect, nor any intermediate efficient causes; all of which is plainly false. Therefore it is necessary to admit a first efficient cause, to which everyone gives the name of God.

The third way is taken from possibility and necessity, and runs thus. We find in nature things that are possible to be and not to be, since they are found to be generated, and to be corrupted, and consequently, it is possible for them to be and not to be. But it is impossible for these always to exist, for that which can not-be at some time is not. Therefore, if everything can not-be, then at one time there was nothing in existence. Now if this were true, even now there would be nothing in existence, because that which does not exist begins to exist only through something already existing. Therefore, if at one time nothing was in existence, it would have been impossible for anything to have begun to exist; and thus even now nothing would be in existence—which is absurd. Therefore, not all beings are merely possible, but there must exist something the existence of which is necessary. But every necessary thing either has its necessity caused by another, or not. Now it is impossible to go on to infinity in necessary things which have their necessity caused by another, as has been already proved in regard to efficient causes. Therefore we cannot but admit the existence of some being having of itself its own necessity, and not receiving it from another, but rather causing in others their necessity. This all men speak of as God.

The fourth way is taken from the gradation to be found in things. Among beings there are some more and some less good, true, noble, and the like. But *more* and *less* are predicated of different things according as they resemble in their different ways something which is the maximum, as a thing is said to be hotter according as it more nearly resembles that which is hottest; so that there is something which is truest, something best, something noblest, and, consequently, something which is most being, for those things that are greatest in truth are greatest in being, as it is written in *Metaph.* ii. Now the maximum in any genus is the cause of all in that genus, as fire, which is the maximum of heat, is the cause of all hot things, as is said in the same book. Therefore there must also be something which is to all beings the cause of their being, goodness, and every other perfection: and this we call God.

The fifth way is taken from the governance of the world. We see that things which lack knowledge, such as natural bodies, act for an end, and this is evident from their acting always, or nearly always, in the same way, so as to obtain the best result. Hence it is plain that they achieve their end, not fortuitously, but designedly. Now whatever lacks knowledge cannot move towards an end, unless it be directed by some being endowed with knowledge and intelligence; as the arrow is directed by the archer. Therefore some intelligent being exists by whom all natural things are directed to their end; and this being we call God.

Meditations on First Philosophy

❀❀

RENÉ DESCARTES

> We return now to Descartes' *Meditations Concerning First Philoso-*
> *phy,* in particular, a passage from his Fifth Meditation. Here he of-
> fers a proof for the existence of God now commonly known as the
> "ontological argument." Descartes' claim is that just as the essence
> of a triangle contains its three-sidedness, so the essence of God
> contains His existence. For since God is a perfect Being and exis-
> tence is a perfection, it follows that God exists. If He did not exist,
> then a perfect Being would not be perfect, which is a contradiction.
>   Not many contemporary philosophers believe that this argu-
> ment justifies theism. But all would agree that throughout the cen-
> turies the argument has shown extraordinary power to stimulate
> philosophical discussion.

Fifth Meditation

[T]he idea of God, or a supremely perfect being, is one which I find within
me just as surely as the idea of any shape or number. And my understanding
that it belongs to his nature that he always exists is no less clear and distinct
than is the case when I prove of any shape or number that some property belongs to its nature. Hence, even if it turned out that not everything on which
I have meditated in these past days is true, I ought still to regard the existence of God as having at least the same level of certainty as I have hitherto
attributed to the truths of mathematics.

At first sight, however, this is not transparently clear, but has some appearance of being a sophism. Since I have been accustomed to distinguish
between existence and essence in everything else, I find it easy to persuade
myself that existence can also be separated from the essence of God, and
hence that God can be thought of as not existing. But when I concentrate
more carefully, it is quite evident that existence can no more be separated
from the essence of God than the fact that its three angles equal two right angles can be separated from the essence of a triangle, or than the idea of a
mountain can be separated from the idea of a valley. Hence it is just as much

of a contradiction to think of God (that is, a supremely perfect being) lacking existence (that is, lacking a perfection), as it is to think of a mountain without a valley.

However, even granted that I cannot think of God except as existing, just as I cannot think of a mountain without a valley, it certainly does not follow from the fact that I think of a mountain with a valley that there is any mountain in the world; and similarly, it does not seem to follow from the fact that I think of God as existing that he does exist. For my thought does not impose any necessity on things; and just as I may imagine a winged horse even though no horse has wings, so I may be able to attach existence to God even though no God exists.

But there is a sophism concealed here. From the fact that I cannot think of a mountain without a valley, it does not follow that a mountain and valley exist anywhere, but simply that a mountain and a valley, whether they exist or not, are mutually inseparable. But from the fact that I cannot think of God except as existing, it follows that existence is inseparable from God, and hence that he really exists. It is not that my thought makes it so, or imposes any necessity on any thing; on the contrary, it is the necessity of the thing itself, namely the existence of God, which determines my thinking in this respect. For I am not free to think of God without existence (that is, a supremely perfect being without a supreme perfection) as I am free to imagine a horse with or without wings.

And it must not be objected at this point that while it is indeed necessary for me to suppose God exists, once I have made the supposition that he has all perfections (since existence is one of the perfections), nevertheless the original supposition was not necessary. Similarly, the objection would run, it is not necessary for me to think that all quadrilaterals can be inscribed in a circle; but given this supposition, it will be necessary for me to admit that a rhombus can be inscribed in a circle—which is patently false. Now admittedly, it is not necessary that I ever light upon any thought of God; but whenever I do choose to think of the first and supreme being, and bring forth the idea of God from the treasure house of my mind as it were, it is necessary that I attribute all perfections to him, even if I do not at that time enumerate them or attend to them individually. And this necessity plainly guarantees that, when I later realize that existence is a perfection, I am correct in inferring that the first and supreme being exists. In the same way, it is not necessary for me ever to imagine a triangle; but whenever I do wish to consider a rectilinear figure having just three angles, it is necessary that I attribute to it the properties which license the inference that its three angles equal no more than two right angles, even if I do not notice this at the time. By contrast, when I examine what figures can be inscribed in a circle, it is in no way necessary for me to think that this class includes all quadrilaterals. Indeed, I cannot even imagine this, so long as I am willing to admit only what I clearly and distinctly understand. So there is a great difference between this kind of false supposition and the true ideas which are innate in me, of which the first and most important is the idea of God.

An Enquiry Concerning Human Understanding

❖❖

DAVID HUME

> David Hume's *An Enquiry Concerning Human Understanding*, from which we read previously (pp. 162–171), also contains a celebrated discussion of miracles. He argues that in deciding whether to believe that a miracle has occurred, the evidence in favor needs to be weighed against the evidence on the other side. But a miracle is by definition a violation of the laws of nature, and these laws have been established on the basis of the strongest possible evidence. So to believe a miracle has occurred is to give more weight to the testimony of some limited number of observers rather than to the opposing evidence that has earned universal support. Thus, according to Hume, reason always requires that we reject any claim that a miracle has occurred. In addition, such claims are typically put forward by those whose reliability is suspect or whose propensity to believe undermines their credibility.
>
> Hume's argument by no means ended all debate about miracles. But this chapter of his *Enquiry* has been the starting point for most subsequent philosophical discussions of this intriguing topic.

Part I

I flatter myself, that I have discovered an argument . . . which, if just, will, with the wise and learned, be an everlasting check to all kinds of supersti-

From *Enquiries Concerning Human Understanding and Concerning the Principles of Morals*, edited by L. A. Selby-Bigge, 3d edition, revised by P. H. Nidditch. Copyright © 1975 by Oxford University Press. Reprinted by permission of the publisher.

tious delusion, and consequently, will be useful as long as the world en-
dures. For so long, I presume, will the accounts of miracles and prodigies be
found in all history, sacred and profane.

Though experience be our only guide in reasoning concerning matters of
fact; it must be acknowledged, that this guide is not altogether infallible, but
in some cases is apt to lead us into errors. One, who in our climate, should
expect better weather in any week of June than in one of December, would
reason justly, and comformably to experience; but it is certain, that he may
happen, in the event, to find himself mistaken. However, we may observe,
that, in such a case, he would have no cause to complain of experience; because it commonly informs us beforehand of the uncertainty, by that contra-
riety of events, which we may learn from a diligent observation. All effects
follow not with like certainty from their supposed causes. Some events are
found, in all countries and all ages, to have been constantly conjoined together. Others are found to have been more variable, and sometimes to disappoint our expectations; so that, in our reasonings concerning matter of
fact, there are all imaginable degrees of assurance, from the highest certainty
to the lowest species of moral evidence.

A wise man, therefore, proportions his belief to the evidence. In such
conclusions as are founded on an infallible experience, he expects the event
with the last degree of assurance, and regards his past experience as a full
proof of the future existence of that event. In other cases, he proceeds with
more caution; he weighs the opposite experiments; he considers which side
is supported by the greater number of experiments; to that side he inclines,
with doubt and hesitation; and when at last he fixes his judgment, the evidence exceeds not what we properly call *probability*. All probability, then,
supposes an opposition of experiments and observations, where the one
side is found to overbalance the other, and to produce a degree of evidence,
proportioned to the superiority. A hundred instances or experiments on one
side, and fifty on another, afford a double expectation of any event; though
a hundred uniform experiments, with only one that is contradictory, reasonably begets a pretty strong degree of assurance. In all cases, we must balance the opposite experiments, where they are opposite, and deduct the
smaller number from the greater, in order to know the exact force of the superior evidence. . . .

A miracle is a violation of the laws of nature; and as a firm and unalter-
able experience has established these laws, the proof against a miracle, from
the very nature of the fact, is as entire as any argument from experience can
possibly be imagined. Why is it more than probable, that all men must die;
that lead cannot, of itself, remain suspended in the air; that fire consumes
wood, and is extinguished by water; unless it be, that these events are found
agreeable to the laws of nature, and there is required a violation of these
laws, or in other words, a miracle to prevent them? Nothing is esteemed a
miracle, if it ever happen in the common course of nature. It is no miracle
that a man, seemingly in good health, should die on a sudden: because such

a kind of death, though more unusual than any other, has yet been frequently observed to happen. But it is a miracle, that a dead man should come to life; because that has never been observed in any age or country. There must, therefore, be a uniform experience against every miraculous event, otherwise the event would not merit that appellation. And as a uniform experience amounts to a proof, there is here a direct and full *proof,* from the nature of the fact, against the existence of any miracle; nor can such a proof be destroyed, or the miracle rendered credible, but by an opposite proof, which is superior.

The plain consequence is (and it is a general maxim worthy of our attention), "That no testimony is sufficient to establish a miracle, unless the testimony be of such a kind, that its falsehood would be more miraculous, than the fact, which it endeavors to establish; and even in that case there is a mutual destruction of arguments, and the superior only gives us an assurance suitable to that degree of force, which remains, after deducting the inferior." When anyone tells me, that he saw a dead man restored to life, I immediately consider with myself, whether it be more probable, that this person should either deceive or be deceived, or that the fact, which he relates, should really have happened. I weigh the one miracle against the other; and according to the superiority, which I discover, I pronounce my decision, and always reject the greater miracle. If the falsehood of his testimony would be more miraculous, than the event which he relates; then, and not till then, can he pretend to command my belief or opinion.

Part II

In the foregoing reasoning we have supposed, that the testimony, upon which a miracle is founded, may possibly amount to an entire proof, and that the falsehood of that testimony would be a real prodigy. But it is easy to show, that we have been a great deal too liberal in our concession, and that there never was a miraculous event established on so full an evidence.

For *first,* there is not to be found, in all history, any miracle attested by a sufficient number of men, of such unquestioned good sense, education, and learning, as to secure us against all delusion in themselves; of such undoubted integrity, as to place them beyond all suspicion of any design to deceive others; of such credit and reputation in the eyes of mankind, as to have a great deal to lose in case of their being detected in any falsehood; and at the same time, attesting facts performed in such a public manner and in so celebrated a part of the world, as to render the detection unavoidable: all which circumstances are requisite to give us a full assurance in the testimony of men.

Secondly. We may observe in human nature a principle which, if strictly examined, will be found to diminish extremely the assurance, which we might, from human testimony, have, in any kind of prodigy. The maxim, by which we commonly conduct ourselves in our reasonings, is, that the objects, of which we have no experience, resemble those, of which we have; that what we have found to be most usual is always most probable; and that where there is an opposition of arguments, we ought to give the preference to such as are founded on the greatest number of past observations. But though, in proceeding by this rule, we readily reject any fact which is unusual and incredible in an ordinary degree; yet in advancing farther, the mind observes not always the same rule; but when anything is affirmed utterly absurd and miraculous, it rather the more readily admits of such a fact, upon account of that very circumstance, which ought to destroy all its authority. The passion of *surprise* and *wonder,* arising from miracles, being an agreeable emotion, gives a sensible tendency towards the belief of those events, from which it is derived. And this goes so far, that even those who cannot enjoy this pleasure immediately, nor can believe those miraculous events, of which they are informed, yet love to partake of the satisfaction at second hand or by rebound, and place a pride and delight in exciting the admiration of others. . . .

The many instances of forged miracles, and prophecies, and supernatural events, which, in all ages, have either been detected by contrary evidence, or which detect themselves by their absurdity, prove sufficiently the strong propensity of mankind to the extraordinary and the marvellous, and ought reasonably to beget a suspicion against all relations of this kind. This is our natural way of thinking, even with regard to the most common and most credible events. For instance: there is no kind of report which rises so easily, and spreads so quickly, especially in country places and provincial towns, as those concerning marriages; insomuch that two young persons of equal condition never see each other twice, but the whole neighborhood immediately join them together. The pleasure of telling a piece of news so interesting, of propagating it, and of being the first reporters of it, spreads the intelligence. And this is so well known, that no man of sense gives attention to these reports, till he find them confirmed by some greater evidence. Do not the same passions, and others still stronger, incline the generality of mankind to believe and report, with the greatest vehemence and assurance, all religious miracles?

Thirdly. It forms a strong presumption against all supernatural and miraculous relations, that they are observed chiefly to abound among ignorant and barbarous nations; or if a civilized people has ever given admission to any of them, that people will be found to have received them from ignorant and barbarous ancestors, who transmitted them with that inviolable sanction and authority, which always attend received opinions. When we peruse the first histories of all nations, we are apt to imagine ourselves transported into some new world; where the whole frame of nature is disjointed, and every element performs its operations in a different manner, from what it does at present. Battles, revolutions, pestilence, famine, and death, are never the effect of those natural causes, which we experience. Prodigies, omens, oracles, judgments, quite obscure the few natural events, that are intermingled with them. But as the former grow thinner every page, in proportion as we advance nearer the enlightened ages, we soon learn, that there is nothing mysterious or supernatural in the case, but that all proceeds from the usual propensity of mankind towards the marvellous, and that, though this inclination may at intervals receive a check from sense and learning, it can never be thoroughly extirpated from human nature. . . .

I may add as a *fourth* reason, which diminishes the authority of prodigies, that there is no testimony for any, even those which have not been expressly detected, that is not opposed by an infinite number of witnesses; so that not only the miracle destroys the credit of testimony, but the testimony destroys itself. To make this the better understood, let us consider, that, in matters of religion, whatever is different is contrary; and that it is impossible the religions of ancient Rome, of Turkey, of Siam, and of China should, all of them, be established on any solid foundation. Every miracle, therefore, pretended to have been wrought in any of these religions (and all of them abound in miracles), as its direct scope is to establish the particular system to which it is attributed; so has it the same force, though more indirectly, to overthrow every other system. In destroying a rival system, it likewise destroys the credit of those miracles, on which that system was established; so that all the prodigies of different religions are to be regarded as contrary facts, and the evidences of these prodigies, whether weak or strong, as opposite to each other. . . .

Upon the whole, then, it appears, that no testimony for any kind of miracle has ever amounted to a probability, much less to a proof; and that, even supposing it amounted to a proof, it would be opposed by another proof; derived from the very nature of the fact, which it would endeavor to establish. It is experience only, which gives authority to human testimony; and it is the same experience, which assures us of the laws of nature. When, therefore, these two kinds of experience are contrary, we have nothing to do but subtract the one from the other, and embrace an opinion, either on one side or the other, with that assurance which arises from the remainder. But according to the principle here explained, this subtraction, with regard to all popular religions, amounts to an entire annihilation; and therefore we may establish it as a maxim, that no human testimony can have such force as to prove a miracle, and make it a just foundation for any such system of religion.

I beg the limitations here made may be remarked, when I say, that a miracle can never be proved, so as to be the foundation of a system of religion. For I own, that otherwise, there may possibly be miracles, or violations of the usual course of nature, of such a kind as to admit of proof from human testimony; though, perhaps, it will be impossible to find any such in all the records of history. Thus, suppose, all authors, in all languages, agree, that, from the first of January 1600, there was a total darkness over the whole earth for eight days: suppose that the tradition of this extraordinary event is still strong and lively among the people: that all travelers, who return from foreign countries, bring us accounts of the same tradition, without the least variation or contradiction: it is evident, that our present philosophers, instead of doubting the fact, ought to receive it as certain, and ought to search for the causes whence it might be derived. The decay, corruption, and dissolution of nature, is an event rendered probable by so many analogies, that any phenomenon, which seems to have a tendency towards that catastrophe, comes within the reach of human testimony, if that testimony be very extensive and uniform.

But suppose, that all the historians who treat of England, should agree, that, on the first of January 1600, Queen Elizabeth died; that both before and after her death she was seen by her physicians and the whole court, as is usual with persons of her rank; that her successor was acknowledged and proclaimed by the parliament; and that, after being interred a month, she again appeared, resumed the throne, and governed England for three years. I must confess that I should be surprised at the concurrence of so many odd circumstances, but should not have the least inclination to believe so miraculous an event. I should not doubt of her pretended death, and of those other public circumstances that followed it; I should only assert it to have been pretended, and that it neither was, nor possibly could be real. You would in vain object to me the difficulty, and almost impossibility of deceiving the world in an affair of such consequence; the wisdom and solid judgment of that renowned queen; with the little or no advantage which she could reap from so poor an artifice. All this might astonish me; but I would still reply, that the knavery and folly of men are such common phenomena, that I should rather believe the most extraordinary events to arise from their concurrence, than admit of so signal a violation of the laws of nature.

But should this miracle be ascribed to any new system of religion; men, in all ages, have been so much imposed on by ridiculous stories of that kind, that this very circumstance would be a full proof of a cheat, and sufficient, with all men of sense, not only to make them reject the fact, but even reject it without farther examination. Though the Being to whom the miracle is ascribed, be, in this case, Almighty, it does not, upon that account, become a whit more probable; since it is impossible for us to know the attributes or actions of such a Being, otherwise than from the experience which we have of his productions, in the usual course of nature. This still reduces us to past observation, and obliges us to compare the instances of the violation of truth in the testimony of men, with those of the violation of the laws of nature by miracles, in order to judge which of them is most likely and probable. As the violations of truth are more common in the testimony concerning religious miracles, than in that concerning any other matter of fact; this must diminish very much the authority of the former testimony, and make us form a general resolution, never to lend any attention to it, with whatever specious pretense it may be covered. . . .

I am the better pleased with the method of reasoning here delivered, as I

think it may serve to confound those dangerous friends or disguised enemies to the *Christian Religion,* who have undertaken to defend it by the principles of human reason. Our most holy religion is founded on *faith,* not on
reason; and it is a sure method of exposing it to put it to such a trial as it is,
by no means, fitted to endure. . . .

[T]he *Christian Religion* not only was at first attended with miracles,
but even at this day cannot be believed by any reasonable person without
one. Mere reason is insufficient to convince us of its veracity: and whoever
is moved by *faith* to assent to it, is conscious of a continued miracle in his
own person, which subverts all the principles of his understanding, and
gives him a determination to believe what is most contrary to custom and
experience.

PART 5

MORALITY

The Challenge of Cultural Relativism

◈◈

JAMES RACHELS

We turn now to that major field of philosophy known as "ethics," a term derived from the Greek word *ethos,* meaning "character." The subject, which may also be referred to as "moral philosophy," focuses on the nature of a moral judgment, the principles that ought to guide a good life, and the resolution of such thorny practical issues as abortion or euthanasia.

Some would claim, however, that the search for universal answers to moral questions is futile, since morality differs from one culture to another. This view, known as "cultural relativism," maintains that, while we can seek understanding of a particular culture's moral system, we have no basis for judging it. Morality is just a matter of custom, as suggested by the origin of the term "morality," which comes from the Latin word *moralis,* meaning "custom."

In our next selection James Rachels, Professor of Philosophy at the University of Alabama at Birmingham, examines cultural relativism and finds that it has serious shortcomings.

How Different Cultures Have Different Moral Codes

Darius, a king of ancient Persia, was intrigued by the variety of cultures he encountered in his travels. He had found, for example, that the Callatians (a tribe of Indians) customarily ate the bodies of their dead fathers. The Greeks, of course, did not do that—the Greeks practiced cremation and regarded the funeral pyre as the natural and fitting way to dispose of the dead. Darius thought that a sophisticated understanding of the world must include an appreciation of such differences between cultures. One day, to teach this lesson, he summoned some Greeks who happened to be present at his court and asked them what they would take to eat the bodies of their dead fathers. They were shocked, as Darius knew they would be, and replied that no amount of money could persuade them to do such a thing. Then Darius called in some Callatians, and while the Greeks listened asked them what they would take to burn their dead fathers' bodies. The Callatians were horrified and told Darius not even to mention such a dreadful thing.

This story, recounted by Herodotus in his *History*, illustrates a recurring theme in the literature of social science: different cultures have different moral codes. What is thought right within one group may be utterly abhorrent to the members of another group, and vice versa. Should we eat the bodies of the dead or burn them? If you were a Greek, one answer would seem obviously correct; but if you were a Callatian, the opposite would seem equally certain.

It is easy to give additional examples of the same kind. Consider the Eskimos. They are a remote and inaccessible people. Numbering only about 25,000, they live in small, isolated settlements scattered mostly along the northern fringes of North America and Greenland. Until the beginning of this century, the outside world knew little about them. Then explorers began to bring back strange tales.

Eskimo customs turned out to be very different from our own. The men often had more than one wife, and they would share their wives with guests, lending them for the night as a sign of hospitality. Moreover, within a community, a dominant male might demand—and get—regular sexual access to other men's wives. The women, however, were free to break these arrangements simply by leaving their husbands and taking up with new partners—free, that is, so long as their former husbands chose not to make trouble. All in all, the Eskimo practice was a volatile scheme that bore little resemblance to what we call marriage.

But it was not only their marriage and sexual practices that were different. The Eskimos also seemed to have less regard for human life. Infanticide, for example, was common. Knud Rasmussen, one of the most famous early explorers, reported that he met one woman who had borne twenty children but had killed ten of them at birth. Female babies, he found, were especially liable to be destroyed, and this was permitted simply at the parents' discretion, with no social stigma attached to it. Old people also, when they became too feeble to contribute to the family, were left out in the snow to die. So there seemed to be, in this society, remarkably little respect for life.

To the general public, these were disturbing revelations. Our own way of living seems so natural and right that for many of us it is hard to conceive of others living so differently. And when we do hear of such things, we tend immediately to categorize those other peoples as "backward" or "primitive." But to anthropologists and sociologists, there was nothing particularly surprising about the Eskimos. Since the time of Herodotus, enlightened observers have been accustomed to the idea that conceptions of right and wrong differ from culture to culture. If we assume that *our* ideas of right and wrong will be shared by all peoples at all times, we are merely naive.

Cultural Relativism

To many thinkers, this observation—"Different cultures have different moral codes"—has seemed to be the key to understanding morality. The idea of universal truth in ethics, they say, is a myth. The customs of different societies are all that exist. These customs cannot be said to be "correct" or "incorrect," for that implies we have an independent standard of right and wrong by which they may be judged. But there is no such independent standard; every standard is culture-bound. The great pioneering sociologist William Graham Sumner, writing in 1906, put the point like this:

> The "right" way is the way which the ancestors used and which has been handed down. The tradition is its own warrant. It is not held subject to verification by experience. The notion of right is in the folkways. It is not outside of them, of independent origin, and brought to test them. In the folkways, whatever is, is right. This is because they are traditional, and therefore contain in themselves the authority of the ancestral ghosts. When we come to the folkways we are at the end of our analysis.

This line of thought has probably persuaded more people to be skeptical about ethics than any other single thing. *Cultural Relativism,* as it has been called, challenges our ordinary belief in the objectivity and universality of moral truth. It says, in effect, that there is no such thing as universal truth in ethics; there are only the various cultural codes, and nothing more. Moreover, our own code has no special status; it is merely one among many.

As we shall see, this basic idea is really a compound of several different thoughts. It is important to separate the various elements of the theory because, on analysis, some parts of the theory turn out to be correct, whereas others seem to be mistaken. As a beginning, we may distinguish the following claims, all of which have been made by cultural relativists:

1. Different societies have different moral codes.
2. There is no objective standard that can be used to judge one societal code better than another.
3. The moral code of our own society has no special status; it is merely one among many.
4. There is no "universal truth" in ethics—that is, there are no moral truths that hold for all peoples at all times.
5. The moral code of a society determines what is right within that society; that is, if the moral code of a society says that a certain action is right, then that action *is* right, at least within that society.
6. It is mere arrogance for us to try to judge the conduct of other peoples. We should adopt an attitude of tolerance toward the practices of other cultures.

Although it may seem that these six propositions go naturally together, they are independent of one another, in the sense that some of them might be true even if others are false. In what follows, we will try to identify what is correct in Cultural Relativism, but we will also be concerned to expose what is mistaken about it.

The Cultural Differences Argument

Cultural Relativism is a theory about the nature of morality. At first blush it seems quite plausible. However, like all such theories, it may be evaluated by subjecting it to rational analysis; and when we analyze Cultural Relativism we find that it is not so plausible as it first appears to be.

The first thing we need to notice is that at the heart of Cultural Relativism there is a certain *form of argument*. The strategy used by cultural relativists is to argue from facts about the differences between cultural outlooks to a conclusion about the status of morality. Thus we are invited to accept this reasoning:

1. The Greeks believed it was wrong to eat the dead, whereas the Callatians believed it was right to eat the dead.
2. Therefore, eating the dead is neither objectively right nor objectively wrong. It is merely a matter of opinion, which varies from culture to culture.

Or, alternatively:

1. The Eskimos see nothing wrong with infanticide, whereas Americans believe infanticide is immoral.
2. Therefore, infanticide is neither objectively right nor objectively wrong. It is merely a matter of opinion, which varies from culture to culture.

Clearly, these arguments are variations of one fundamental idea. They are both special cases of a more general argument, which says:

1. Different cultures have different moral codes.
2. Therefore, there is no objective "truth" in morality. Right and wrong are only matters of opinion, and opinions vary from culture to culture.

We may call this the *Cultural Differences Argument*. To many people, it is very persuasive. But from a logical point of view, is it a *sound* argument?

It is not sound. The trouble is that the conclusion does not really follow from the premise—that is, even if the premise is true, the conclusion still might be false. The premise concerns what people *believe*: in some societies, people believe one thing; in other societies, people believe differently. The conclusion, however, concerns *what really is the case*. The trouble is that this sort of conclusion does not follow logically from this sort of premise.

Consider again the example of the Greeks and Callatians. The Greeks believed it was wrong to eat the dead; the Callatians believed it was right. Does it follow, *from the mere fact that they disagreed*, that there is no objective truth in the matter? No, it does not follow; for it *could* be that the practice was objectively right (or wrong) and that one or the other of them was simply mistaken.

To make the point clearer, consider a very different matter. In some societies, people believe the earth is flat. In other societies, such as our own, people believe the earth is (roughly) spherical. Does it follow, *from the mere fact that they disagree,* that there is no "objective truth" in geography? Of course not; we would never draw such a conclusion because we realize that, in their beliefs about the world, the members of some societies might simply be wrong. There is no reason to think that if the world is round everyone must know it. Similarly, there is no reason to think that if there is moral truth everyone must know it. The fundamental mistake in the Cultural Differences Argument is that it attempts to derive a substantive conclusion about a subject (morality) from the mere fact that people disagree about it.

It is important to understand the nature of the point that is being made here. We are *not* saying (not yet, anyway) that the conclusion of the argument is false. Insofar as anything being said here is concerned, it is still an open question whether the conclusion is true. We *are* making a purely logical point and saying that the conclusion does not *follow from* the premise. This is important, because in order to determine whether the conclusion is true, we need arguments in its support. Cultural Relativism proposes this argument, but unfortunately the argument turns out to be fallacious. So it proves nothing.

The Consequences of Taking Cultural Relativism Seriously

Even if the Cultural Differences Argument is invalid, Cultural Relativism might still be true. What would it be like if it were true?

In the passage quoted above, William Graham Sumner summarizes the essence of Cultural Relativism. He says that there is no measure of right and wrong other than the standards of one's society: "The notion of right is in the folkways. It is not outside of them, of independent origin, and brought to test them. In the folkways, whatever is, is right."

Suppose we took this seriously. What would be some of the consequences?

1. *We could no longer say that the customs of other societies are morally inferior to our own.* This, of course, is one of the main points stressed by Cultural Relativism. We would have to stop condemning other societies merely because they are "different." So long as we concentrate on certain examples, such as the funerary practices of the Greeks and Callatians, this may seem to be a sophisticated, enlightened attitude.

However, we would also be stopped from criticizing other, less benign practices. Suppose a society waged war on its neighbors for the purpose of taking slaves. Or suppose a society was violently anti-Semitic and its leaders set out to destroy the Jews. Cultural Relativism would preclude us from saying that either of these practices was wrong. We would not even be able to say that a society tolerant of Jews is *better* than the anti-Semitic society, for that would imply some sort of transcultural standard of comparison. The failure to condemn *these* practices does not seem "enlightened"; on the contrary, slavery and anti-Semitism seem wrong *wherever* they occur. Nevertheless, if we took Cultural Relativism seriously, we would have to admit that these social practices also are immune from criticism.

2. *We could decide whether actions are right or wrong just by consulting the standards of our society.* Cultural Relativism suggests a simple test for determining what is right and what is wrong: all one has to do is ask whether the action is in accordance with the code of one's society. Suppose a resident of South Africa is wondering whether his country's policy of *apartheid*—rigid racial segregation—is morally correct. All he has to do is ask whether this policy conforms to his society's moral code. If it does, there is nothing to worry about, at least from a moral point of view.

This implication of Cultural Relativism is disturbing because few of us think that our society's code is perfect—we can think of ways it might be improved. Yet Cultural Relativism would not only forbid us from criticizing the codes of *other* societies; it would stop us from criticizing our *own*. After all, if right and wrong are relative to culture, this must be true for our own culture just as much as for others.

3. *The idea of moral progress is called into doubt.* Usually, we think that at least some changes in our society have been for the better. (Some, of course, may have been changes for the worse.) Consider this example: Throughout most of Western history the place of women in society was very narrowly circumscribed. They could not own property; they could not vote or hold political office; with a few exceptions, they were not permitted to have paying jobs; and generally they were under the almost absolute control of their husbands. Recently much of this has changed, and most people think of it as progress.

If Cultural Relativism is correct, can we legitimately think of this as progress? Progress means replacing a way of doing things with a *better* way. But by what standard do we judge the new ways as better? If the old ways were in accordance with the social standards of their time, then Cultural Relativism would say it is a mistake to judge them by the standards of a different time. Eighteenth-century society was, in effect, a different society from the one we have now. To say that we have made progress implies a judgment that present-day society is better, and that is just the sort of transcultural judgment that, according to Cultural Relativism, is impermissible.

Our idea of social *reform* will also have to be reconsidered. A reformer such as Martin Luther King, Jr., seeks to change his society for the better. Within the constraints imposed by Cultural Relativism, there is one way this might be done. If a society is not living up to its own ideals, the reformer may be regarded as acting for the best: the ideals of the society are the standard by which we judge his or her proposals as worthwhile. But the "reformer" may not challenge the ideals themselves, for those ideals are by def-

inition correct. According to Cultural Relativism, then, the idea of social reform makes sense only in this very limited way.

These three consequences of Cultural Relativism have led many thinkers
to reject it as implausible on its face. It does make sense, they say, to condemn some practices, such as slavery and anti-Semitism, wherever they occur. It makes sense to think that our own society has made some moral
progress, while admitting that it is still imperfect and in need of reform. Because Cultural Relativism says that these judgments make no sense, the argument goes, it cannot be right.

Why There Is Less Disagreement Than It Seems

The original impetus for Cultural Relativism comes from the observation
that cultures differ dramatically in their views of right and wrong. But just
how much do they differ? It is true that there are differences. However, it is
easy to overestimate the extent of those differences. Often, when we examine
what *seems* to be a dramatic difference, we find that the cultures do not differ
nearly as much as it appears.

Consider a culture in which people believe it is wrong to eat cows. This
may even be a poor culture, in which there is not enough food; still, the cows
are not to be touched. Such a society would *appear* to have values very different from our own. But does it? We have not yet asked why these people will
not eat cows. Suppose it is because they believe that after death the souls of
humans inhabit the bodies of animals, especially cows, so that a cow may be
someone's grandmother. Now do we want to say that their values are different from ours? No; the difference lies elsewhere. The difference is in our belief systems, not in our values. We agree that we shouldn't eat Grandma; we
simply disagree about whether the cow *is* (or could be) Grandma.

The general point is this. Many factors work together to produce the customs of a society. The society's values are only one of them. Other matters,
such as the religious and factual beliefs held by its members and the physical
circumstances in which they must live, are also important. We cannot conclude, then, merely because customs differ, that there is a disagreement
about *values*. The difference in customs may be attributable to some other aspect of social life. Thus there may be less disagreement about values than
there appears to be.

Consider the Eskimos again. They often kill perfectly normal infants, especially girls. We do not approve of this at all; a parent who did this in our
society would be locked up. Thus there appears to be a great difference in the
values of our two cultures. But suppose we ask *why* the Eskimos do this. The
explanation is not that they have less affection for their children or less respect for human life. An Eskimo family will always protect its babies if conditions permit. But they live in a harsh environment, where food is often in
short supply. A fundamental postulate of Eskimo thought is: "Life is hard,

and the margin of safety small." A family may want to nourish its babies but be unable to do so.

As in many "primitive" societies, Eskimo mothers will nurse their infants over a much longer period of time than mothers in our culture. The child will take nourishment from its mother's breast for four years, perhaps even longer. So even in the best of times there are limits to the number of infants that one mother can sustain. Moreover, the Eskimos are a nomadic people—unable to farm, they must move about in search of food. Infants must be carried, and a mother can carry only one baby in her parka as she travels and goes about her outdoor work. Other family members can help, but this is not always possible.

Infant girls are more readily disposed of because, first, in this society the males are the primary food providers—they are the hunters, according to the traditional division of labor—and it is obviously important to maintain a sufficient number of food gatherers. But there is an important second reason as well. Because the hunters suffer a high casualty rate, the adult men who die prematurely far outnumber the women who die early. Thus if male and female infants survived in equal numbers, the female adult population would greatly outnumber the male adult population. Examining the available statistics, one writer concluded that "were it not for female infanticide . . . there would be approximately one-and-a-half times as many females in the average Eskimo local group as there are food-producing males."

So among the Eskimos, infanticide does not signal a fundamentally different attitude toward children. Instead, it is a recognition that drastic measures are sometimes needed to ensure the family's survival. Even then, however, killing the baby is not the first option considered. Adoption is common; childless couples are especially happy to take a more fertile couple's "surplus." Killing is only the last resort. I emphasize this in order to show that the raw data of the anthropologists can be misleading; it can make the differences in values between cultures appear greater than they are. The Eskimos' values are not all that different from our values. It is only that life forces upon them choices that we do not have to make.

How All Cultures Have Some Values in Common

It should not be surprising that, despite appearances, the Eskimos are protective of their children. How could it be otherwise? How could a group survive that did *not* value its young? This suggests a certain argument, one which shows that all cultural groups must be protective of their infants:

1. Human infants are helpless and cannot survive if they are not given extensive care for a period of years.

2. Therefore, if a group did not care for its young, the young would not survive, and the older members of the group would not be replaced. After a while the group would die out.
3. Therefore, any cultural group that continues to exist must care for its young. Infants that are *not* cared for must be the exception rather than the rule.

Similar reasoning shows that other values must be more or less universal. Imagine what it would be like for a society to place no value at all on truth telling. When one person spoke to another, there would be no presumption at all that he was telling the truth—for he could just as easily be speaking falsely. Within that society, there would be no reason to pay attention to what anyone says. (I ask you what time it is, and you say "Four o'clock." But there is no presumption that you are speaking truly; you could just as easily have said the first thing that came into your head. So I have no reason to pay attention to your answer—in fact, there was no point in my asking you in the first place!) Communication would then be extremely difficult, if not impossible. And because complex societies cannot exist without regular communication among their members, society would become impossible. It follows that in any complex society there *must* be a presumption in favor of truthfulness. There may of course be exceptions to this rule: there may be situations in which it is thought to be permissible to lie. Nevertheless, these will be exceptions to a rule that *is* in force in the society.

Let me give one further example of the same type. Could a society exist in which there was no prohibition on murder? What would this be like? Suppose people were free to kill other people at will, and no one thought there was anything wrong with it. In such a "society," no one could feel secure. Everyone would have to be constantly on guard. People who wanted to survive would have to avoid other people as much as possible. This would inevitably result in individuals trying to become as self-sufficient as possible—after all, associating with others would be dangerous. Society on any large scale would collapse. Of course, people might band together in smaller groups with others that they *could* trust not to harm them. But notice what this means: they would be forming smaller societies that *did* acknowledge a rule against murder. The prohibition of murder, then, is a necessary feature of all societies.

There is a general theoretical point here, namely, that *there are some moral rules that all societies will have in common, because those rules are necessary for society to exist.* The rules against lying and murder are two examples. And in fact, we do find these rules in force in all viable cultures. Cultures may differ in what they regard as legitimate exceptions to the rules, but this disagreement exists against a background of agreement on the larger issues. Therefore, it is a mistake to overestimate the amount of difference between cultures. Not *every* moral rule can vary from society to society.

What Can Be Learned from Cultural Relativism

At the outset, I said that we were going to identify both what is right and what is wrong in Cultural Relativism. Thus far I have mentioned only its mistakes: I have said that it rests on an invalid argument, that it has consequences that make it implausible on its face, and that the extent of cultural disagreement is far less than it implies. This all adds up to a pretty thorough repudiation of the theory. Nevertheless, it is still a very appealing idea, and the reader may have the feeling that all this is a little unfair. The theory *must* have something going for it, or else why has it been so influential? In fact, I think there *is* something right about Cultural Relativism, and now I want to say what that is. There are two lessons we should learn from the theory, even if we ultimately reject it.

1. Cultural Relativism warns us, quite rightly, about the danger of assuming that all our preferences are based on some absolute rational standard. They are not. Many (but not all) of our practices are merely peculiar to our society, and it is easy to lose sight of that fact. In reminding us of it, the theory does a service.

Funerary practices are one example. The Callatians, according to Herodotus, were "men who eat their fathers"—a shocking idea, to us at least. But eating the flesh of the dead could be understood as a sign of respect. It could be taken as a symbolic act that says: We wish this person's spirit to dwell within us. Perhaps this was the understanding of the Callatians. On such a way of thinking, burying the dead could be seen as an act of rejection, and burning the corpse as positively scornful. If this is hard to imagine, then we may need to have our imaginations stretched. Of course we may feel a visceral repugnance at the idea of eating human flesh in any circumstances. But what of it? This repugnance may be, as the relativists say, only a matter of what is customary in our particular society.

There are many other matters that we tend to think of in terms of objective right and wrong, but that are really nothing more than social conventions. Should women cover their breasts? A publicly exposed breast is scandalous in our society, whereas in other cultures it is unremarkable. Objectively speaking, it is neither right nor wrong—there is no objective reason why either custom is better. Cultural Relativism begins with the valuable insight that many of our practices are like this—they are only cultural products. Then it goes wrong by concluding that, because *some* practices are like this, *all* must be.

2. The second lesson has to do with keeping an open mind. In the course of growing up, each of us has acquired some strong feelings: we have learned to think of some types of conduct as acceptable, and others we have learned to regard as simply unacceptable. Occasionally, we may find those feelings challenged. We may encounter someone who claims that our feelings are mistaken. For example, we may have been taught that homosexual-

ity is immoral, and we may feel quite uncomfortable around gay people and see them as alien and "different." Now someone suggests that this may be a mere prejudice; that there is nothing evil about homosexuality; that gay people are just people, like anyone else, who happen, through no choice of their own, to be attracted to others of the same sex. But because we feel so strongly about the matter, we may find it hard to take this seriously. Even after we listen to the arguments, we may still have the unshakable feeling that homosexuals *must,* somehow, be an unsavory lot.

Cultural Relativism, by stressing that our moral views can reflect the prejudices of our society, provides an antidote for this kind of dogmatism. When he tells the story of the Greeks and Callatians, Herodotus adds:

> For if anyone, no matter who, were given the opportunity of choosing from amongst all the nations of the world the set of beliefs which he thought best, he would inevitably, after careful consideration of their relative merits, choose that of his own country. Everyone without exception believes his own native customs, and the religion he was brought up in, to be the best.

Realizing this can result in our having more open minds. We can come to understand that our feelings are not necessarily perceptions of the truth—they may be nothing more than the result of cultural conditioning. Thus when we hear it suggested that some element of our social code is *not* really the best and we find ourselves instinctively resisting the suggestion, we might stop and remember this. Then we may be more open to discovering the truth, whatever that might be.

We can understand the appeal of Cultural Relativism, then, even though the theory has serious shortcomings. It is an attractive theory because it is based on a genuine insight—that many of the practices and attitudes we think so natural are really only cultural products. Moreover, keeping this insight firmly in view is important if we want to avoid arrogance and have open minds. These are important points, not to be taken lightly. But we can accept these points without going on to accept the whole theory.

How Not to Answer Moral Questions

❖❖

TOM REGAN

> Faced with an ethical issue, some people dismiss the possibility of resolving the matter through reasoned discussion. They claim that moral judgments are merely expressions of personal preference, or matters of individual opinion, or reflections of majority will, or commands of a supposed higher authority, such as God. In any of these cases, reasoning about ethics is useless. All we can do is express our feelings, reiterate our beliefs, consult polls, or perhaps seek Divine guidance.
>
> In the following selection, Tom Regan, Professor of Philosophy at North Carolina State University, argues that none of these ways of dealing with moral questions is appropriate.

Moral Judgments and Personal Preferences

Some people like New Age music; others do not. Some people think bourbon is just great; others detest its taste. Some people will go to a lot of trouble to spend an afternoon in the hot sun at the beach; others can think of nothing worse. In all these cases disagreement in preference exists. Someone likes something; someone else does not. Are moral disagreements, disagreements over whether something is morally right or wrong, good or bad, just or unjust, the same as disagreements in preference?

It does not appear so. For one thing, when a person (say, Jack) says he likes something, he is not denying what another person (Jill) says if she says she does not like it. Suppose Jack says, "I (Jack) like the Grateful Dead," and Jill says, "I (Jill) do not like the Grateful Dead." Then clearly Jill does not deny what Jack says. To deny what Jack says, Jill would have to say, "You (Jack) do not like the Grateful Dead," which is not what she says. So, in general, when two people express different personal preferences, the one does not deny what the other affirms. It is perfectly possible for two opposing expressions of personal preference to be true at the same time.

When two people express conflicting judgments about the morality of something, however, the disagreement is importantly different. Suppose

---

Jack says, "All wars are unjust," while Jill says, "Some wars are just." Then Jill *is* denying what Jack affirms; she is *denying* that wars are always unjust, so that if what she said were true, what Jack said would have to be false. Some philosophers have denied this. They have maintained that moral judgments should be understood as expressions of personal preferences. Though this view deserves to be mentioned with respect, it is doubtful that it is correct. When people say that something is morally right or wrong, it is always appropriate to ask them to give reasons to justify their judgment, reasons for accepting their judgment as *correct*. In the case of personal preferences, however, such requests are inappropriate. If Jack says he likes to go to the beach, it hardly seems apt to press him to give reasons to *justify* what he says. If he says abortion is always wrong, however, it is highly relevant to test Jack's judgment by examining the reasons he gives for thinking what he does. In this case we want to know whether Jack's judgment is correct, not merely what Jack likes or dislikes.

This difference between expressions of differing personal preference and conflicting moral judgments points to one way not to answer moral questions. Given that moral judgments are not just expressions of personal preference, it follows that moral right and wrong cannot be determined just by finding out about someone's personal preferences. This is true even in the case of our own preferences. Our personal preferences are certainly important, but we do not answer moral questions just by saying that we like some things and dislike others.

Why Thinking It So Does Not Make It So

The same is true about what someone thinks. Quite aside from her personal preferences, Bonnie, if she is sincere, does think that we who are well off ought to make sacrifices to help feed the many starving people in the world if she says that we ought to do so. Nevertheless, if her judgment is a *moral* judgment, what she means cannot be "I (Bonnie) think we who are well off ought to make sacrifices to help feed the many starving people in the world." If it were, then she would not be affirming something that Clyde denies, when *he* says, "We who are well off ought not to make such sacrifices." Each would merely be stating that each thinks something, and it is certainly possible for it *both* to be true that Bonnie thinks that we ought to make sacrifices for those who are starving *and*, at the same time, that Clyde thinks we ought not. So if Clyde is denying what Bonnie affirms, he cannot merely be stating that *he* thinks that we ought not to make sacrifices for these people. Clearly, Clyde believes that *what* he says is *correct;* and whether it *is* correct is independent of his thinking that it is. Thus, the fact that Clyde happens to think what he does is just as irrelevant to establishing whether we ought or ought not to make sacrifices to help those who are starving as Jack's feelings about war. And the same is true concerning what *we* happen to think. Our thinking something right or wrong does not make it so.

The Irrelevance of Statistics

Someone might think that though what one person thinks or feels about moral issues does not settle matters, what all or most people think or feel does. A single individual is only one voice; what most or all people think or feel is a great deal more. There is strength in numbers. Thus, the correct method for answering questions about right and wrong is to find out what most or all people think or feel. Opinion polls should be conducted, statistics compiled. That will reveal the truth.

This approach to moral questions is deficient. All that opinion polls can reveal is what all or most people think or feel about various controversial questions—for example, "Should convicted murderers be executed?" Twenty years ago most Americans believed that capital punishment should be abolished; today most Americans believe it should be retained. This is an important, interesting change in public opinion. . . . Clearly, however, merely establishing that most Americans today favor the death penalty or, to take another example, that most favor the legalization of euthanasia, is not to establish that the majority opinion is *correct*. In times past, virtually everyone believed that the world is flat, yet this consensus did not settle the correct description of its shape. There is no compelling reason to assume that the answers to moral questions differ in this respect. Questions of moral right and wrong, in short, cannot be answered just by taking a vote and seeing what the majority favors.

The Appeal to a Moral Authority

Suppose it is conceded that we cannot answer moral questions just by finding out what Jack or Jill or Bonnie and Clyde happen to think or feel, or by finding out what all or most people happen to think or feel. After all, single individuals like Jack or Jill, or most or all people like them, might think or feel one way when they should think or feel differently. We ordinary mortals, after all, are fallible. But now suppose there is someone who *never is mistaken* when it comes to moral questions: If this person judges that something is morally right, it *is* morally right; if it is judged wrong, it is wrong. No mistakes are made. Let us call such a person a moral authority. Might appealing to the judgments of a moral authority be the correct method for answering moral questions?

Most people who think there is a moral authority think this authority is not an ordinary mortal but a god. This causes problems immediately. Whether there is a god (or gods) is a very controversial question, and to rest questions of right and wrong on what an alleged god says (or the gods say) is already to base morality on an intellectually unsettled foundation. The difficulties go deeper than this, however, since even if there is a god who is a moral authority, very serious questions arise concerning whether people always understand what this authority says. The difficulties that exist when Jews and Christians consult the Bible are illustrative. Problems of interpretation abound. Some who think that we were created to be vegetarians think they find evidence in the Bible that God thinks so too; others think they find evidence that God does not. Some who think that God allows us to exploit nature without regard to its values cite what they think are supporting chapters and verses; others cite other chapters and verses they think show that God does not allow this, or they cite the same passages and argue that they should be interpreted differently. The gravity of these and kindred problems of interpretation should not be underestimated. Even if there is a moral authority, and even if the God Jews and Christians worship should happen to be this authority, that would not make it easy to find out what is right and wrong. The problem of finding out what God thinks on these matters would still remain and would be especially acute in areas where the Bible offers very little, if any, direct guidance—on the ethics of the use of life-sustaining technology for the irreversibly comatose, for example.

Problems of interpretation aside, it is clear that the correct method for answering moral questions cannot consist merely in discovering what some alleged moral authority says. Even if there is a moral authority, those who are not moral authorities can have no good reason for thinking that there is one unless the judgments of this supposed authority can be checked for their truth or reasonableness, and it is not possible to do this unless what is true or reasonable regarding right and wrong can be known independently of what this supposed authority says. An example from another quarter might make this point clearer. A plumber proves his "authority as a plumber" not merely by what he says but by the quality of his work, which can be verified independently of what he says in any particular case. *After* we have come to know, on independent grounds, that a particular plumber's judgment is reliable, *then* we have reason to rely on his judgment in the future. The same is true of the authority of one's judgment in, say, science, economics, the law, and morality: One's "credentials" can be established in the case of moral judgments only if there are independent ways of testing the truth or reasonableness of moral judgments. Thus, because there must be some independent way of knowing what judgments are true or reasonable in order to test for the authority of another's moral judgments, to appeal to this or that "moral authority" cannot itself be the method that we seek for answering moral questions.

The Nature of Ethical Disagreement

❖❖❖

CHARLES L. STEVENSON

Can we use reason to resolve moral issues? An influential answer is provided in the next essay, written by one of the twentieth century's most important ethical theorists, Charles L. Stevenson (1908–1979), who was Professor of Philosophy at the University of Michigan and President of the American Philosophical Association.

He believes that ethical disagreements often involve factual disputes, which are open to possible resolution by the use of scientific method. Once we agree on the relevant facts, our ethical disagreement may be resolved. But which facts, if any, are at issue? We can tell only by analyzing the reasons that support our beliefs.

Stevenson offers no guarantee that factual agreement will produce moral agreement, but he considers the use of reason to be what he terms a "heuristic maxim," that is, a principle that aids problem solving. In short, he believes that reasoning with those with whom we disagree morally does not assure our agreement but renders it possible.

1

When people disagree about the value of something—one saying that it is good or right and another that it is bad or wrong—by what methods of argument or inquiry can their disagreement be resolved? Can it be resolved by the methods of science, or does it require methods of some other kind, or is it open to no rational solution at all?

The question must be clarified before it can be answered. And the word that is particularly in need of clarification, as we shall see, is the word "disagreement."

Let us begin by noting that "disagreement" has two broad senses: In the first sense it refers to what I shall call "disagreements in belief." This occurs when Mr. A believes *p*, when Mr. B believes *not-p*, or something incompatible with *p*, and when neither is content to let the belief of the other remain unchallenged. Thus doctors may disagree in belief about the causes of an illness; and friends may disagree in belief about the exact date on which they last met.

In the second sense the word refers to what I shall call "disagreement in attitude." This occurs when Mr. A has a favorable attitude to something, when Mr. B has an unfavorable or less favorable attitude to it, and when neither is content to let the other's attitude remain unchanged. The term "attitude" . . . designates any psychological disposition of being *for* or *against* something. Hence love and hate are relatively specific kinds of attitudes, as are approval and disapproval, and so on.

This second sense can be illustrated in this way: Two men are planning to have dinner together. One wants to eat at a restaurant that the other doesn't like. Temporarily, then, the men cannot "agree" on where to dine. Their argument may be trivial, and perhaps only half serious; but in any case it represents a disagreement *in attitude.* The men have divergent preferences and each is trying to redirect the preference of the other—though normally, of course, each is willing to revise his own preference in the light of what the other may say.

Further examples are readily found. Mrs. Smith wishes to cultivate only the four hundred; Mr. Smith is loyal to his old poker-playing friends. They accordingly disagree, in attitude, about whom to invite to their party. The progressive mayor wants modern school buildings and large parks; the older citizens are against these "new-fangled" ways; so they disagree on civic policy. These cases differ from the one about the restaurant only in that the clash of attitudes is more serious and may lead to more vigorous argument.

The difference between the two senses of "disagreement" is essentially this: the first involves an opposition of beliefs, both of which cannot be true, and the second involves an opposition of attitudes, both of which cannot be satisfied.

Let us apply this distinction to a case that will sharpen it. Mr. A believes that most voters will favor a proposed tax and Mr. B disagrees with him. The disagreement concerns attitudes—those of the voters—but note that A and B are *not* disagreeing in attitude. Their disagreement is *in belief about* attitudes. It is simply a special kind of disagreement in belief, differing from disagreement in belief about head colds only with regard to subject matter. It implies not an opposition of the actual attitudes of the speakers but only of their beliefs about certain attitudes. Disagreement *in* attitude, on the other hand, implies that the very attitudes of the speakers are opposed. A and B may have opposed beliefs about attitudes without having opposed attitudes, just as they may have opposed beliefs about head colds without having opposed head colds. Hence we must not, from the fact that an argument is concerned with attitudes, infer that it necessarily involves disagreement *in* attitude.

2

We may now turn more directly to disagreement about values, with particular reference to normative ethics. When people argue about what is good, do they disagree in belief, or do they disagree in attitude? . . . It must be readily granted that ethical arguments usually involve disagreement in belief; but they *also* involve disagreement in attitude. And the conspicuous role of disagreement in attitude is what we usually take, whether we realize it or not, as the distinguishing feature of ethical arguments. For example:

Suppose that the representative of a union urges that the wage level in a given company ought to be higher—that it is only right that the workers receive more pay. The company representative urges in reply that the workers ought to receive no more than they get. Such an argument clearly represents a disagreement in attitude. The union is *for* higher wages; the company is *against* them, and neither is content to let the other's attitude remain unchanged. *In addition* to this disagreement in attitude, of course, the argument may represent no little disagreement in belief. Perhaps the parties disagree about how much the cost of living has risen and how much the workers are suffering under the present wage scale. Or perhaps they disagree about the company's earnings and the extent to which the company could raise wages and still operate at a profit. Like any typical ethical argument, then, this argument involves both disagreement in attitude and disagreement in belief.

It is easy to see, however, that the disagreement in attitude plays a unifying and predominating role in the argument. This is so in two ways:

In the first place, disagreement in attitude determines what beliefs are *relevant* to the argument. Suppose that the company affirms that the wage scale of fifty years ago was far lower than it is now. The union will immediately urge that this contention, even though true, is irrelevant. And it is irrelevant simply because information about the wage level of fifty years ago, maintained under totally different circumstances, is not likely to affect the present attitudes of either party. To be relevant, any belief that is introduced into the argument must be one that is likely to lead one side or the other to have a different attitude, and so reconcile disagreement in attitude. Attitudes are often functions of beliefs. We often change our attitudes to something when we change our beliefs about it; just as a child ceases to *want* to touch a live coal when he comes to *believe* that it will burn him. Thus in the present argument any beliefs that are at all likely to alter attitudes, such as those about the increasing cost of living or the financial state of the company, will be considered by both sides to be relevant to the argument. Agreement in belief on these matters may lead to agreement in attitude toward the wage scale. But beliefs that are likely to alter the attitudes of neither side will be declared irrelevant. They will have no bearing on the disagreement in attitude, with which both parties are primarily concerned.

In the second place, ethical argument usually terminates when disagreement in attitude terminates, even though a certain amount of disagreement in belief remains. Suppose, for instance, that the company and the union continue to disagree in belief about the increasing cost of living, but that the company, even so, ends by favoring the higher wage scale. The union will then be content to end the argument and will cease to press its point about living costs. It may bring up that point again, in some future argument of the same sort, or in urging the righteousness of its victory to the newspaper columnists; but for the moment the fact that the company has agreed in attitude is sufficient to terminate the argument. On the other hand: suppose that both parties agreed on all beliefs that were introduced into the argument, but even so continued to disagree in attitude. In that case neither party would feel that their dispute had been successfully terminated. They might look for other beliefs that could be introduced into the argument. They might use words to play on each other's emotion. They might agree (in attitude) to submit the case to arbitration, both feeling that a decision, even if strongly adverse to one party or the other, would be preferable to a continued impasse. Or, perhaps, they might abandon hope of settling their dispute by any peaceable means.

In many other cases, of course, men discuss ethical topics without having the strong, uncompromising attitudes that the present example has illustrated. They are often as much concerned with redirecting their own attitudes, in the light of greater knowledge, as with redirecting the attitudes of others. And the attitudes involved are often altruistic rather than selfish. Yet the above example will serve, so long as that is understood, to suggest the nature of ethical disagreement. Both disagreement in attitude and disagreement in belief are involved, but the former predominates in that (1) it determines what sort of disagreement in belief is relevantly disputed in a given ethical argument, and (2) it determines by its continued presence or its resolution whether or not the argument has been settled. We may see further how intimately the two sorts of disagreement are related: since attitudes are often functions of beliefs, an agreement in belief may lead people, as a matter of psychological fact, to agree in attitude.

3

Having discussed disagreement, we may turn to the broad question that was first mentioned, namely: By what methods of argument or inquiry may disagreement about matters of value be resolved?

It will be obvious that to whatever extent an argument involves disagreement in belief, it is open to the usual methods of the sciences. If these methods are the *only* rational methods for supporting beliefs—as I believe to be so, but cannot now take time to discuss—then scientific methods are the only rational methods for resolving the disagreement in *belief* that arguments about values may include.

But if science is granted an undisputed sway in reconciling beliefs, it does not thereby acquire, without qualification, an undisputed sway in reconciling attitudes. We have seen that arguments about values include disagreement in attitude, no less than disagreement in belief, and that in certain ways the disagreement in attitude predominates. By what methods shall the latter sort of disagreement be resolved?

The methods of science are still available for that purpose, but only in an indirect way. Initially, these methods have only to do with establishing agreement in belief. If they serve further to establish agreement in attitude, that will be due simply to the psychological fact that altered beliefs may cause altered attitudes. Hence scientific methods are conclusive in ending arguments about values only to the extent that their success in obtaining agreement in belief will in turn lead to agreement in attitude.

In other words: the extent to which scientific methods can bring about agreement on values depends on the extent to which a commonly accepted body of scientific beliefs would cause us to have a commonly accepted set of attitudes.

How much is the development of science likely to achieve, then, with regard to values? To what extent *would* common beliefs lead to common attitudes? It is, perhaps, a pardonable enthusiasm to *hope* that science will do everything—to hope that in some rosy future, when all men know the consequences of their acts, they will all have common aspirations and live peaceably in complete moral accord. But if we speak not from our enthusiastic hopes but from our present knowledge, the answer must be far less exciting. We usually *do not know,* at the beginning of any argument about values, whether an agreement in belief, scientifically established, will lead to an agreement in attitude or not. It is logically possible, at least, that two men should continue to disagree in attitude even though they had all their beliefs in common, and even though neither had made any logical or inductive error, or omitted any relevant evidence. Differences in temperament, or in early training, or in social status, might make the men retain different attitudes even though both were possessed of the complete scientific truth. Whether this logical possibility is an empirical likelihood I shall not presume to say; but it is unquestionably a possibility that must not be left out of account.

To say that science can always settle arguments about value, we have seen, is to make this assumption: Agreement in attitude will always be consequent upon complete agreement in belief, and science can always bring about the latter. Taken as purely heuristic, this assumption has its usefulness. It leads people to discover the discrepancies in their beliefs and to prolong enlightening argument that *may* lead, as a matter of fact, from commonly accepted beliefs to commonly accepted attitudes. It leads people to reconcile their attitudes in a rational, permanent way, rather than by rhapsody or exhortation. But the assumption is *nothing more,* for present knowledge, than a heuristic maxim. It is wholly without any proper foundation of probability. I conclude, therefore, that scientific methods cannot be guaranteed the definite role in the so-called normative sciences that they may have in the natural sciences. Apart from a heuristic assumption to the contrary, it is possible that the growth of scientific knowledge may leave many disputes about values permanently unsolved. Should these disputes persist, there are nonrational methods for dealing with them, of course, such as impassioned, moving oratory. But the purely intellectual methods of science, and, indeed, *all* methods of reasoning, may be insufficient to settle disputes about values even though they may greatly help to do so.

A Supreme Moral Principle?

STEVEN M. CAHN

> The essay that follows is mine and contains a concise account and assessment of some major moral theories. Those of Kant and Mill are each the subject of a vast literature, and the short presentations and criticisms offered here are intended as an orientation. In fairness, I should emphasize that such a brief overview necessarily minimizes numerous complexities.

Many thinkers have sought one basic principle that could serve as the ultimate ethical guide, requiring us to perform all the actions we ought to perform and forbidding us from performing all the actions we ought not perform. Which are the leading candidates for such a moral touchstone?

One common to various religious traditions is the Golden Rule. Its positive formulation, attributed to Jesus, is: "whatever you wish that men would do to you, do so to them."[1] The negative formulation, which appeared five hundred years earlier, is attributed to Confucius and was later proposed by the Jewish sage Hillel. The latter put it as follows: "What is hateful to you, do not to your neighbor."[2] Is either of these the supreme moral principle?

Consider first the positive formulation. Granted, we usually ought to treat others as we would wish them to treat us. For instance, we ought to go to the aid of an injured person, just as we would wish that person to come to our aid if we were injured. But if we always followed this rule, the results would be unfortunate. Consider masochists, who derive pleasure from being hurt. Were they to act according to the principle in question, their duty would be to inflict pain, thereby doing to others as they wish done to themselves. Similarly, consider a person who enjoys receiving telephone calls, regardless of who is calling. The principle would require the individual to telephone everyone, thereby reciprocating preferred treatment. Indeed, strictly speaking, it would be impossible to fulfill the positive formulation of the Golden Rule, for we wish so many others to do so much for us, we would not have time to do all that is necessary to treat them likewise. Indeed, as the philosopher Walter Kaufmann (1921–1980) noted, "anyone who tried to live up to Jesus' rule would become an insufferable nuisance."[3]

In this respect the negative formulation of the Golden Rule is preferable, for it does not imply that we have innumerable duties toward everyone else. Neither does it imply that masochists ought to inflict pain on others, nor that those who enjoy receiving telephone calls ought themselves to make calls. However, while the negative formulation does not require these actions, neither does it forbid them. It enjoins us not to do to others what is hateful to ourselves, but pain is not hateful to the masochist and calls are not hateful to the telephone enthusiast. Thus, the negative formulation of the Golden Rule, although superior in a sense to the positive formulation, is not the supreme moral principle, since it does not prohibit actions that ought to be prohibited.

Let us next consider two other standards of conduct, each of which has sometimes been thought to be the supreme moral principle. One was originally formulated by Immanuel Kant, who argued that the moral worth of an action is to be judged not by its consequences but by the nature of the maxim (the principle) that motivates the action. Thus, right actions are not necessarily those with favorable consequences but those performed in accordance with correct maxims. But which maxims are correct? According to Kant, only those that can serve as universal laws, since they are applicable to every person at any time without exception. In other words, you should act only on a maxim that can be universalized without contradiction.

To see what Kant had in mind, consider a specific example he used to illustrate his view. Suppose you need to borrow money, but it will be lent to you only if you promise to pay it back. You realize, however, that you will not be able to honor the debt. Is it permissible for you to promise to repay the money, knowing you will not keep that promise? Kant proposed that the way to determine whether such an action is permissible is to universalize the maxim in question and see whether it leads to contradiction. The maxim is: Whenever I am short of money, I shall borrow it, promising to pay it back even if I know I shall not do so. Can this maxim be universalized without contradiction? Kant argued that it cannot.

> For supposing it to be a universal law that everyone when he thinks himself in a difficulty should be able to promise whatever he pleases, with the purpose of not keeping his promise, the promise itself would become impossible, as well as the end that one might have in view in it, since no one would consider that anything was promised to him, but would ridicule all such statements as vain pretenses.[4]

In other words, to make promises with no intention of keeping them would lead to the destruction of the practice of promising. Thus, since the maxim in question cannot be universalized without contradiction, it is not morally acceptable and, consequently, any action it motivates is immoral. According to Kant, then, the supreme moral principle is: "*Act only on that maxim whereby thou canst at the same time will that it should become a universal law.*"[5]

Unfortunately, this principle prohibits actions that ought to be permitted. Although we might agree that the maxim of making insincere promises cannot be universalized, we can easily imagine cases in which a person ought to make a promise without any intention of keeping it. Suppose, for example, you and your family will starve to death unless you obtain food immediately, and a very wealthy person offers to provide the food if you will promise repayment within twenty-four hours. Surely we would say, contrary to Kant's principle, under these circumstances you ought to act on a maxim that cannot be universalized and make a promise you have no intention of keeping.

Kant's insistence that proper maxims admit of no exceptions leads him not only to approve morally repugnant actions but also to sanction some that are inconsistent. Maxims he approves may conflict, and in that case adherence to one involves the violation of another. In the preceding case, for instance, were you to act in accord with the maxim of never making insincere promises, you would violate another maxim affirmed by Kant, that of aiding those who are in distress. He argues that both maxims admit of no exceptions, but since it is impossible always to abide by both, Kant's position appears to lead to contradiction.

Perhaps his proposal fails because it concentrates exclusively on the reason for an action and fails to take into account its results. So let us next consider a principle that focuses on consequences, one defended by John Stuart Mill. He was a leading advocate for the ethical position known as utilitarianism, according to which an action is right insofar as it promotes the happiness of mankind and wrong insofar as it promotes unhappiness. By the term "happiness" Mill means pleasure and the absence of pain. By the term "mankind" he means all persons, each valued equally. So Mill's supreme moral principle is: Act in such a way as to produce the greatest pleasure for the greatest number of people, each person's pleasure counting equally.

This principle avoids the pitfalls of Kant's view, for whereas he admitted no exceptions to moral rules and was thus led to condemn insincere promises that saved human lives, the utilitarian principle is flexible enough to allow for any exceptions that increase overall happiness. Although Mill would agree that insincere promises are usually wrong, since they are apt to cause more pain than pleasure, he would allow that in some cases, such as that of the starving family, an insincere promise is morally justifiable, for it would lead to greater overall happiness than any alternative.

The flexibility of the utilitarian principle is an advantage but also a fatal flaw, for it permits action that ought to be prohibited. Consider, for example, inhabitants of a city who each week abduct a stranger and place the unfortunate in an arena to wrestle a lion. When the inhabitants of the city are challenged to justify this practice, they reply that although one person suffers much pain, thousands of spectators obtain greater pleasure from this form of entertainment than from any other, and so the spectacle is justified on utilitarian grounds. Clearly Mill's principle here yields an unacceptable implication. And other cases along similar lines likewise illustrate the laxity of utilitarianism. The sheriff who hangs an innocent person in order to satisfy the vengeance of the townspeople may maximize pleasure but nevertheless acts irresponsibly.

One way to try to salvage the utilitarian principle is to argue that not all pleasures are of equal quality, that, for example, the pleasure of spectators at a lion arena is less valuable than that enjoyed by those at a piano recital. As Mill put it, "It is better to be a human being dissatisfied than a pig satisfied; better to be Socrates dissatisfied than a fool satisfied. And if the fool, or the pig, are of a different opinion, it is because they only know their own side of the question. The other party to the comparison knows both sides."[6]

This move is dubious, for some individuals, knowing both sides of the question, would prefer to witness a struggle between human and lion rather than between human and keyboard. And even if only one knowledgeable individual had such taste, why should that person's view be disregarded? Furthermore, Mill's principle cannot be salvaged by the claim that attendance at a piano recital develops sensitivity whereas a visit to a lion arena dulls it, for, according to utilitarianism, actions are good to the extent that they produce pleasure, not to the extent that they produce sensitivity.

Perhaps, given the complexities of the human condition, any search for a supreme moral principle is doomed to failure, but the analysis so far has at least succeeded in calling attention to one fundamental feature of morality. The positive and negative formulations of the Golden Rule, the Kantian principle, and utilitarianism all serve as reminders that a moral person is obligated to be sensitive to others. This insight motivates not only the biblical injunction to treat our fellow human beings as we wish to be treated, but also the utilitarian insistence that each person's happiness is to count neither more nor less than another's. The same theme is central to Kant's view, a point he made explicit by claiming that his supreme moral principle could be reformulated as follows: "So act as to treat humanity, whether in thine own person or in that of any other, in every case as an end and never as means only."[7]

The moral point of view thus involves taking into account interests apart from our own. Do we ever do so? According to the theory known as egoism, all human behavior is motivated only by self-interest. On this view all individuals act solely in an effort to increase their own pleasure; people are kind to others only if they believe that such kindness will eventually redound to their own benefit. Thus no person would ever be a moral agent, for no one would ever act from genuinely altruistic considerations. Is egoism correct?

On the surface the theory seems clearly mistaken. Consider, for instance, a doctor who is devoted to serving the poor and has no interest whatever in publicizing this work. Doesn't such a case refute egoism?

A defender of the theory is apt to reply that this doctor only appears to be acting altruistically but is, in fact, acting selfishly, deriving pleasure from ministering to others. The egoist claims that the doctor is as selfish as the rest of us, but whereas we enjoy owning cars and attending parties, the doctor enjoys living a simple life and providing medical aid to the poor. All of us seek to maximize our pleasure, but since we differ in what we enjoy, we act in different ways. Nevertheless, the underlying motive in every case is self-interest.

The egoistic line of argument is impervious to counterexamples, but this invulnerability reveals the theory as vacuous, a reflection not of empirical evidence but of an arbitrary decision to use words idiosyncratically. The egoist declares us selfish if we act to fulfill our own desires. How are those identified? According to the egoist, we desire to do whatever we actually do, even if we are sacrificing ourselves for others. But then to say that we act as we desire is to say merely that we act as we act, which is a tautology. If we are declared selfish simply because we act as we act, then, of course, we all act selfishly, but such a definition is obviously a misuse of the term "selfish." As James Rachels notes: "The mere fact that I am acting on *my* wants does not mean that I am acting selfishly; that depends on *what it is* that I want."[8] An unselfish person cares about the welfare of others, whereas a selfish person does not. The tautology that all of us act as we act does not obliterate the distinction between an unselfish and a selfish person, no matter how the meaning of words is distorted. Thus the egoist's challenge to morality fails.

While most of us sometimes act altruistically, why should we do so on those occasions when our self-interest dictates otherwise?

This final question rests on the dubious assumption that we can ever be sure that acting morally is contrary to our own advantage. While that is how an immoral action may at first appear, as David Hume noted, "[K]naves, with all their pretended cunning and abilities, [are] betrayed by their own maxims; and while they purpose to cheat with moderation and secrecy, a tempting incident occurs, nature is frail, and they give in to the snare; whence they can never extricate themselves, without a total loss of reputation, and the forfeiture of all future trust and confidence with mankind."[9] In short, immorality invariably threatens self-interest, and rarely, if ever, can this menace be sufficiently minimized to render the risk worthwhile.

What if someone wishes to take the chance and is unmoved by altruistic considerations? Can we reason further? Perhaps in such a case we can only repeat the words of the French maximist La Rochefoucauld (1613–1680): "To virtue's credit we must confess that our greatest misfortunes are brought about by vice."[10] In sum, when sympathy is missing, morality rests on practicality.

NOTES

1. *The Holy Bible: Revised Standard Version* (New York: Thomas Nelson and Sons, 1952), Matthew 7:12.
2. *The Babylonian Talmud* (London: The Soncino Press, 1938), Shabbath, 31a.
3. Walter Kaufmann, *The Faith of a Heretic* (New York: Doubleday & Company, Inc., 1963), p. 212.
4. Immanuel Kant, *Foundations of the Metaphysics of Morals,* trans. Lewis White Beck (New York: The Liberal Arts Press, Inc., 1959), p. 40.
5. *Ibid.,* p. 39.
6. John Stuart Mill, *Utilitarianism* (Indianapolis and Cambridge: Hackett Publishing Company, 1979), p. 10.
7. Kant, p. 47.
8. "Egoism and Moral Scepticism," in Steven M. Cahn, *A New Introduction to Philosophy* (New York: Harper & Row, 1971), p. 426.
9. David Hume, *An Enquiry Concerning the Principles of Morals* (Indianapolis: Hackett Publishing Company, 1983), p. 82.
10. *The Maxims of La Rochefoucauld,* trans. Louis Kronenberger (New York: Random House, 1959), #183.

Abortion

❖◇❖

JOEL FEINBERG

Consider the following argument:

1. A fetus is an innocent human being.
2. It is always wrong to kill an innocent human being.
3. Therefore, it is always wrong to kill a fetus.

This argument is valid, since the premises imply the conclusion. But is the argument sound? In other words, are both its premises true?

Premise (1) is open to question, since arguably the earliest embryo is not a human person. Yet some believe it is and may defend their view on religious grounds. In any case you might suppose that if premise (1) were granted, then the conclusion of the argument would follow, since premise (2) may appear uncontroversial. But, in fact, much philosophical discussion has hypothesized that premise (1) is true and still denied the argument's conclusion by claiming that premise (2) is false.

On what grounds, if any, can premise (2) be rejected? That question lies at the heart of the following essay by the eminent American moral philosopher Joel Feinberg, Professor Emeritus of Philosophy at the University of Arizona and a past President of the American Philosophical Association. This article is written in his characteristic style, which is careful and detailed, clear and non-partisan.

Even if we were to grant that the fetus is a moral person and thus has a valid claim to life, it would not follow that abortion is always wrong. For there are other moral persons, in addition to the fetus, whose interests are involved. The woman in whose uterus the fetus abides, in particular, has needs and interests that may well conflict with bringing the fetus to term. Do any of these needs and interests of the woman provide grounds for her having a genuine claim to an abortion and, if they do, which of the two conflicting claims—the woman's claim to an abortion or the fetus's claim to life—ought to be respected if they happen to conflict?. . . .

Formulation of the "Right to an Abortion"

The right to an abortion that is often claimed on behalf of all women is a *discretionary right* to be exercised or not, on a given occasion, as the woman sees fit. For that reason it is sometimes called a "right to choose." If a pregnant woman has such a right, then it is up to her, and her alone, whether to bear the child or to have it aborted. She is at liberty to bear it if she chooses and at liberty to have it aborted if she chooses. She has no duty to bear it, but neither can she have a duty, imposed from without, to abort it. In respect to the fetus, her choice is sovereign. Correlated with this liberty is a duty of others not to interfere with its exercise and not to withhold the necessary means for its exercise. These duties are owed to her if she has a discretionary right to abortion, and she can claim their discharge as her due.

As a discretionary right, a right to an abortion would resemble the "right to liberty," or the right to move about or travel as one wishes. One is under no obligation to leave or stay home or to go to one destination rather than another, so that it is one's own choice that determines one's movements. But the right to move about at will, like other discretionary rights, is subject to limits. One person's liberty of movement, for example, comes to an end at the boundary of another person's property. The discretionary right to an abortion may be limited in similar ways, so that the statement of a specific right of a particular woman in a definite set of concrete circumstances may need to be qualified by various exceptive clauses—for example, ". . . may choose to have an abortion *except* when the fetus is viable." Which exceptive clauses, if any, must be appended to the formulation of the right to an abortion depends on what the basis of this discretionary right is thought to be. For example, if a woman is thought to have a right to an abortion because she has a right to property *and* because the fetus is said to be her property, then the only exceptions there could be to exercising the right to an abortion would be those that restrict the disposing of one's property. What we must realize, then, is that the alleged right to an abortion cannot be understood in a vacuum; it is a right that can only be understood by reference to the other, more fundamental rights from which it has often been claimed to be derived. Three of these rights and their possible association with the right to an abortion deserve our closest scrutiny. These are (1) the previously mentioned property rights, (2) the right to self-defense, and (3) the right to bodily autonomy. We shall consider each in its turn.

Possible Grounds for the Woman's Right

Property Rights over One's Body

Within very wide limits any person has a right to control the uses of his or her own body. With only rare exceptions, surgeons are required to secure the consent of the patient before operating because the body to be cut open, after all, is the patient's own, and he or she has the chief interest in it, and should therefore have the chief "say" over what is done to it. If we think of a fetus as literally a "part" of a woman's body in the same sense as, say, an organ, or as a mere growth attached to a part of the body on the model of a tumor or a wart, then it would seem to follow that the woman may choose to have it removed if she wishes just as she may refuse to have it removed if she prefers. It is highly implausible, however, to think of a human fetus, even if it does fall short of moral personhood, as no more than a temporary organ or a parasitic growth. A fetus is not a constituent organ of the mother, like her vermiform appendix, but rather an independent entity temporarily growing inside the mother.

It would be still less plausible to derive a maternal right to an abortion from a characterization of the fetus as the *property* of its mother and thus in the same category as the mother's wristwatch, clothing, or jewelry. One may abandon or destroy one's personal property if one wishes; one's entitlement to do those things is one of the "property rights" that define ownership. But one would think that the father would have equal or near-equal rights of disposal if the fetus were "property." It is not in his body, to be sure, but he contributed as much genetically to its existence as did the mother and might therefore make just as strong (or just as weak) a claim to ownership over it.

But neither claim would make very good conceptual sense. If fetuses were property, we would find nothing odd in the notion that they can be bought and sold, rented out, leased, used as collateral on loans, and so on. But no one has ever seriously entertained such suggestions. Finally, we must re-member the methodological assumption that we shall make throughout this section, at least for the sake of the argument, that the fetus is a full moral per-son, with a right to life like yours and mine. On this assumption it would probably be contradictory to think of the fetus as *anyone's* property, especial-ly if property rights include what we might call "the right of disposal"—to abandon or destroy as one chooses.

It is more plausible at first sight to claim that the pregnant woman owns not the fetus but the body in which she shelters the fetus. On this analogy, she owns her body (and particularly her womb) in roughly the way an innkeeper owns a hotel or a homeowner her house and garden. These analo-gies, however, are also defective. To begin with, it is somewhat paradoxical to think of the relation between a person and her body as similar to that of ownership. Is it possible to sell or rent or lease one's body without selling, renting, or leasing oneself? If one's body were one's property, the answer would be affirmative, but in fact one's relationship to one's own body is much more intimate than the ownership model suggests. More important for our present purposes, the legal analogies to the right of innkeepers and householders will not bear scrutiny. One cannot conceive of what it would be like for a fetus to enter into a contract with a woman for the use of her womb for nine months or to fall in arrears in its payments and thus forfeit its right of occupancy. Surely that cannot be the most apt analogy on which to base the woman's abortion rights! Besides, whatever this, that, or the other legal statute may say about the matter, one is not *morally* entitled, in virtue of one's property rights, to expel a weak and helpless person from one's shelter when that is tantamount to consigning the person to a certain death, and surely one is not entitled to shoot and kill a trespasser who will not, or can-not, leave one's property. In no department of human life does the vindica-tion of property rights justify homicide. The maternal right to an abortion, therefore, cannot be founded on the more basic right to property.

Self-Defense and Proportionality

Except for the most extreme pacifists, moralists agree that killing can be justi-fied if done in self-defense. If, for example, one man (A) is attacked with a lethal weapon by another (B), we think that A has a right to defend himself against B's attack. Sometimes, in fact, we think that A would be justified in killing B if this were the only way for A to defend himself. Now, some of those who urge the maternal right to an abortion believe that this right is associated with the more basic right to self-defense. There are many difficulties standing in the way to rational acceptance of this view. In particular, the innocence and the nonaggressive nature of the fetus need our special attention. We shall turn to these matters shortly. First, though, it is important to realize what reasons would not count as morally good reasons for an abortion if the right to an abortion were supposed to be founded on the more basic right of self-defense.

All parties to the abortion dispute must agree that many women can be harmed if they are required to bring an unwanted fetus to term. Unwanted sexual intercourse imposed on a woman by a rapist can inflict on its victim severe psychological trauma of a sort deemed so serious by the law that a woman is entitled under some rules to use deadly force if necessary to prevent it. Similarly, an unwanted pregnancy in some circumstances can inflict severe psychological injury on a woman who is forced to carry her child to birth. There are various familiar examples of such harm. To borrow an example from Judith Thomson, a philosophy professor at the Massachusetts Institute of Technology: A terrified fourteen-year-old high-school girl whose pregnancy has been caused by rape has already suffered one severe trauma. If she is now required, over her protests, to carry the child to full term despite her fear, anguish, deep depression, and fancied public mortification, the harmful ramifications may be multiplied a hundredfold. The forty-year-old housewife who has exhausted herself raising a large family in unfavorable economic circumstances while dependent upon an unreliable and unsympathetic husband may find herself, to her horror, pregnant again and rightly feel that if she is forced to give birth to another child, she will forfeit her last opportunity to escape the intolerably squalid conditions of her life. A man must be morally blind not to acknowledge the severe harms that enforced continuance of unwanted pregnancies can inflict on women. An unwanted child need not literally cost the woman her life, but it can effectively ruin her life from her point of view, and it is a useful moral exercise for men to put themselves imaginatively in the woman's place to share that point of view.

At this stage in the argument the antiabortionist has a ready rejoinder. A woman need not keep her child, assume the responsibilities of raising it to adulthood, and forfeit her opportunities for self-fulfillment, he might reply, simply because she forgoes an abortion. She can always put the child up for adoption and be assured in the process that it will find loving foster parents who will give it a good upbringing. All she really has to suffer, the rejoinder concludes, is nine months of minor physical inconvenience. This is an argument that comes easily to the lips of men, but it betrays the grossest sort of masculine insensitivity. In the first place, it is not always true that a woman can have her baby adopted. If she is married, that transaction may require the consent of her husband, and the consent might not be forthcoming. But waiving that point, the possibility of adoption does not give much comfort to the unhappily pregnant woman, for it imposes on her a cruel dilemma and an anguish that far surpasses "minor inconvenience." In effect, she has two choices, both of which are intolerable to her. She can carry the child to term and keep it, thus incurring the very consequences that make her unwilling to remain pregnant, *or* she can nourish the fetus to full size, go into labor, give birth to her baby, and then have it rudely wrenched away, never to be seen by her again. Let moralistic males imagine what an emotional jolt that must be!

Still, on the scale of harms, mere traumas and frustrations are not exactly equal to death. Few women would choose their own deaths in preference to the harms that may come from producing children. According to a common interpretation of the self-defense rule, however, the harm to be averted by a violent act in self-defense need not be identical in severity to that which is inflicted upon one's assailant but only somehow "proportional" to it. Both our prevailing morality and our legal traditions permit the use of lethal force to prevent harms that are less serious than death; so it is plausible to assume that the rule of "proportionality" can be satisfied by something less than equality of harms. But how much less? The late Jane English, a philosopher from the University of North Carolina, offers an answer that, though vague, is in accordance with the moral sentiments of most people when they think of situations other than that involving abortion:

> How severe an injury may you inflict in self-defense? In part this depends upon the severity of the injury to be avoided: you may not shoot someone merely to avoid having your clothes torn. This might lead one to the mistaken conclusion that the defense may only equal the threatened injury in severity; that to avoid death you may kill, but to avoid a black eye you may only inflict a black eye or the equivalent. Rather our laws and customs seem to say that you may create an injury *somewhat but not enormously greater* than the injury to be avoided. To fend off an attack whose outcome would be as serious as rape, a severe beating, or the loss of a finger, you may shoot; to avoid having your clothes torn, you may blacken an eye.[1] [Emphasis added.]

Applying English's answer to the abortion case, and assuming that both the fetus and the woman have legitimate claims, we derive the conclusion that killing the "fetal person" would not be justified when it is done merely to prevent relatively trivial harms to the mother's interests. Not *all* cases of abortion, therefore, can morally be justified, even if there is a maternal right to abortion derived from the more basic right to self-defense.

Self-Defense: The Problem of the Innocent Aggressor

Suppose, however, that the harms that will probably be caused to the mother if the fetus is brought to term are not trivial but serious. Here we have a case where the mother's right to have her important interests respected clashes with the assumed right to life of the fetus. In these circumstances, don't the mother's claims outweigh the fetus's? Doesn't self-defense in these circumstances justify abortion?

There is a serious, previously undiscussed difficulty that calls out for attention. Consider a case where someone aggressively attacks another. The reason we think that, to use English's expression, we may in self-defense create a "somewhat but not enormously greater injury" than would have been caused by the aggressor is because we think of the aggressor as the party who is morally at fault. If he had not launched the aggression in the first place, there should have been no occasion for the use of force. Since the whole episode was the aggressor's fault, his interests should not count for as much as those of the innocent victim. It is a shame that anybody has to be seriously hurt, but if it comes down to an inescapable choice between the innocent party suffering a serious harm or the culpable party suffering a still more serious harm, then the latter is the lesser of the two evils. Aggressors of course, for all their guilt, remain human beings, and consequently they do not forfeit all their human rights in launching an attack. We still may not kill them to prevent them from stealing $10. But their culpability does cost them their right to equal consideration; we may kill them to prevent them from causing serious harm.

But now suppose that the party who threatens us, even though he is the aggressor who initiates the whole episode, is not morally at fault. Suppose the person cannot act otherwise in the circumstances and thus cannot justly be held morally responsible. For example, he was temporarily (or permanently) insane, or it was a case of mistaken identity (he mistook you for a former Gestapo agent to whom you bear a striking resemblance), or someone had drugged the person's breakfast cereal and his behavior was influenced by the drug. George Fletcher, a Columbia law professor, provides a vivid illustration of the problem in what he calls "the case of the psychotic aggressor":

> Imagine that your companion in an elevator goes berserk and attacks you with a knife. There is no escape: the only way to avoid serious bodily harm or even death is to kill him. The assailant acts purposively in the sense that his means further his aggressive end . . . [but] he does act in a frenzy or a fit . . . [and] it is clear that his conduct is non-responsible. If he were brought to trial for his attack, he would have a valid defense of insanity.[2]

The general problem, as lawyers would put it, is "whether self-defense applies against an excused but unjustified aggression."[3] To *justify* an act is to show that it was the right thing to do in the circumstances; to *excuse* an act is to show that although it was unjustified, the actor didn't mean it or couldn't help it, that it was not, properly speaking, his doing at all. In the "excused but unjustified aggression" we have a more plausible model for the application of self-defense to the problem of abortion, for the *fetus is surely innocent* (not because of insanity but because of immaturity, and because *it* did not choose to threaten its mother—it did not "ask to be born").

Upon reflection, most of us would agree, I think, that one would be justified in killing even an innocent aggressor if that seemed necessary to save one's own life or to prevent one from suffering serious bodily injury. Surely we would not judge harshly the slightly built lady who shoots the armed stranger who goes berserk in the elevator. If we were in her shoes, we too would protect ourselves at all costs to the assailant, just as we would against wild animals, runaway trucks, or impersonal forces of nature. But while the berserk assailant as well as those persons mentioned in the last paragraph, all are innocent—are not *morally* responsible for what they do—they are *all* assailants, and in this respect they differ in a quite fundamental respect from the fetus. For the fetus is not only innocent but also not an aggressor. *It* didn't start the trouble in any fashion. Thus, it would seem that while we are justified in killing an innocent assailant if this is the only way to prevent him from killing us, it does not follow that we are similarly justified in killing a fetal person, since, unlike the innocent aggressor, the fetus is not an aggressor at all.

Judith Thomson has challenged this argument. She presents the following farfetched but coherent hypothetical example:

> Aggressor is driving his tank at you. But he has taken care to arrange that a baby is strapped to the front of the tank so that if you use your anti-tank gun, you will not only kill Aggressor, you will kill the baby. Now Aggressor, admittedly, is in the process of trying to kill you; but that baby isn't. Yet you can presumably go ahead and use the gun, even though this involves killing the baby as well as Aggressor.[4]

The baby in this example is not only "innocent" but also the "innocent shield of a threat."[5] Still it is hard to quarrel with Thomson's judgment that you *may* (not that you *should*) take the baby's life if necessary to save your own, that it is morally permissible, even if it is not morally obligatory, to do so. After all, you are (by hypothesis) perfectly innocent too. This example makes a better analogy to the abortion situation than any we have considered thus far, but there are still significant dissimilarities. Unless the fetus is the product of rape, it cannot conceivably be the shield of some third-party aggressor. There is simply no interpersonal "aggression" involved at all in the normal pregnancy. There may nevertheless be a genuine *threat* to the well-being of the mother, and if that threat is to her very life, then perhaps she does have a right to kill it, if necessary, in self-defense. At any rate, if the threatened victim in Thomson's tank example is justified in killing the innocent shield, then the pregnant woman threatened with similar harm is similarly entitled. But all that this would establish is that abortion is justified only if it is probably required to save the mother's life. So not only could we not use the self-defense argument to justify abortion for trivial reasons, as was argued earlier; it appears that the only reason that authorizes its use is the one that cites the fact that the mother will probably die if the fetus is not aborted.

Bodily Autonomy: The Example of the Plugged-in Violinist

The trouble with the use of self-defense as a model for abortion rights is that none of the examples of self-defense makes an *exact* analogy to the abortion situation. The examples that come closest to providing models for justified abortion are the "innocent aggressor cases," and these would apply, as we have seen, only to abortions that are necessary to prevent death to the mother. Even these examples do not fit the abortion case exactly, since the fetus is in no way itself an aggressor, culpable or innocent, but is at most a "nonaggressive, nonculpable threat," in some respects like an innocent shield.[6] And the more we change the examples to bring them closer to the situation of the fetus, the less clear is their resemblance to the central models of self-defense. Once we are allowed to protect ourselves (and especially to protect interests less weighty than self-preservation) at the expense of nonaggressive innocents, it becomes difficult to distinguish the latter from innocent bystanders whom we kill as means to our own good, and that, in turn, begins to look like unvarnished murder. The killing of an innocent person simply because his continued existence in the circumstances would make the killer's life miserable is a homicide that cannot be justified. It is not self-defense to kill your boss because he makes your work-life intolerable and you are unable to find another job, or to kill your spouse because he or she nags you to the point of extreme misery, and will not agree to a divorce,[7] or (closer to the point) to kill your shipwrecked fellow passenger in the lifeboat because there are provisions sufficient for only one to survive and he claims half of them, or to kill your innocent rival for a position or a prize because you can win only if he is out of the running. In all these cases the victim is either innocent or relatively innocent and in no way a direct aggressor.

Partly because of deficiencies in the hypothetical examples of self-defense, Thomson invented a different sort of example intended at once to be a much closer analogy to the abortion situation and also such that the killing can be seen to be morally justified for reasons less compelling than defense of the killer's very life:

> You wake up in the morning and find yourself back to back in bed with an unconscious violinist. A famous unconscious violinist. He has been found to have a fatal kidney ailment, and the Society of Music Lovers has canvassed all the available medical records and found that you alone have the right blood type to help. They have therefore kidnapped you, and last night the violinist's circulatory system was plugged into yours, so that your kidneys can be used to extract poisons from his blood as well as your own. The director of the hospital now tells you, "Look, we're sorry the Society of Music Lovers did this to you—we would never have permitted it if we had known. But still they did it, and the violinist now is plugged into you. To unplug you would be to kill him. But never mind, it's only for nine months. By then

he will have recovered from his ailment, and can safely be unplugged from you." Is it morally incumbent on you to accede to this situation? No doubt it would be very nice of you if you did, a great kindness. But do you have to accede to it? . . . What if the director . . . says . . . "Granted you have a right to decide what happens in and to your body, but a person's right to life outweighs your right to decide what happens in and to your body. So you cannot . . . be unplugged from him." I imagine you would regard this as outrageous. . . . [8]

Suppose that you defy the director on your own, and exercise your control over your own body by unplugging the unconscious violinist, thereby causing his death. This would be to kill in defense of an interest far less important than self-preservation or the prevention of serious injury to oneself. And it would be to kill an innocent nonaggressor, indeed a victim who remains unconscious throughout the entire period during which he is a threat. We have, therefore, an example which—if it works—offers far more encouragement to the proabortion position than the model of self-defense does. We must now pose two questions: (1) Would you in fact be morally justified in unplugging the violinist? and (2) How close an analogy does this bizarre example make to the abortion situation?

There is no way to argue conclusively that unplugging the violinist would be morally justified. Thomson can only make the picture as vividly persuasive as possible and then appeal to her reader's intuitions. It is not an easy case, and neither an affirmative nor a negative judgment will seem self-evident to everyone. Still the verdict for justification seems as strong as in some of the other examples of killing innocent threats, and some additional considerations can be brought to bear in its support. There is, after all, a clear "intuition" in support of a basic right "to decide what happens in and to one's own body," even though the limits of that right are lost in a fog of controversy. So unless there is some stronger competing claim, anyone has a right to refuse to consent to surgery or to enforced attachment to a machine. Or indeed to an unconscious violinist. But what of the competing claim in this example, the violinist's right to life? That is another basic right that is vague around the edges.

In its noncontroversial core, the right to life is a right not to be killed directly (except under very special circumstances) and to be rescued from impending death whenever this can be done without unreasonable sacrifice. . . . And though we all have general duties to come to the assistance of strangers in peril, we cannot be forced to make enormous sacrifices or to run unreasonably high risks to keep people alive when we stand in no special relationship to them, like "father" or "lifeguard." The wife of the violinist perhaps would have a duty to stay plugged to him (if that would help) for nine months; but the random stranger has no such duty at all. So there is good reason to grant Thomson her claim that a stranger would have a right to unplug the violinist from herself.

But how close an analogy after all is this to the normal case of pregnancy? Several differences come immediately to mind. In the normal case of pregnancy, the woman is not confined to her bed for nine months but can continue to work and function efficiently in the world until the final trimester at least. This difference, however, is of doubtful significance, since Thomson's argument is not based on a right to the protection of one's interest in efficient mobility but rather on a right to *decide* on the uses of one's own body, which is quite another thing. Another difference is that the mother and her fetus are not exactly "random strangers" in the same sense that the woman and the violinist are. Again the relationship between the mother and fetus seems to be in a class by itself. If the person who needs to use the woman's body for nine months in order to survive is her mother, father, sister, brother, son, daughter, or close friend, then the relationship would seem close enough to establish a special obligation in the woman to permit that use. If the needy person is a total stranger, then that obligation is missing. The fetus no doubt stands somewhere between these two extremes, but it is at least as close to the "special relationship" end of the spectrum as to the "total stranger" end.

The most important difference, however, between the violinist case and the normal pregnancy is that in the former the woman had absolutely nothing to do with creating the situation from which she wishes to escape. She bears no responsibility whatever for being in a state of "plugged-in-ness" with the violinist. As many commentators have pointed out, this makes Thomson's analogy fit at most one very special class of pregnancies, namely those imposed upon a woman entirely against her will, as in rape. In the "normal case" of pregnancy, the voluntary action of the woman herself (knowingly consenting to sexual intercourse) has something to do with her becoming pregnant. So once again, we find that a proabortion argument fails to establish an *unrestricted* moral right to abortion. Just as self-defense justifies abortion at most in the case where it is necessary to save the mother's life, the Thomson defense justifies abortion only when the woman shares no responsibility for her pregnancy, as, for example, when it has been caused by rape (force or fraud).

Voluntariness and Responsibility

If we continue the line of reasoning suggested by our criticism of the violinist example, we will soon reach a general principle, namely, that whether or not a woman has a duty to continue her pregnancy depends, at least in part, on how responsible she is for being pregnant in the first place, that is, on the extent to which her pregnancy is the consequence of her own voluntary actions. This formula, in turn, seems to be an application of a still more general moral principle, one that imposes duties on one party to rescue or support another, even a stranger and even when that requires great personal sacrifice or risk, to the degree that the first party, through his own voluntary actions or omissions, was responsible for the second party's dependence on him. A late-arriving bystander at the seaside has no duty to risk life or limb to save a drowning swimmer. If, however, the swimmer is in danger only because the bystander erroneously informed him that there was no danger, then the bystander has a duty to make some effort at rescue (though not a suicidal one), dangerous as it may be. If the swimmer is in the water only because the "bystander" has pushed him out of a boat, however, then the bystander has a duty to attempt rescue at any cost to personal safety,[9] since the by- stander's own voluntary action was the whole cause of the swimmer's plight.

Since the voluntariness of an action or omission is a matter of degree, so is the responsibility that stems from it, as is the stringency of the duty that derives from that responsibility. The duty to continue a pregnancy, then, will be stronger (other things being equal) in the case where the pregnancy was entered into in a fully voluntary way than it will be in the case that fits the vi- olinist model, where the pregnancy is totally involuntary. But in between these two extremes is a whole range of cases where moral judgments are more difficult to make. We can sketch the whole spectrum as follows:

1. Pregnancy caused by rape (totally involuntary).
2. Pregnancy caused by contraceptive failure, where the fault is entirely that of the manufacturer or pharmaceutical company.
3. Pregnancy caused by contraceptive failure within the advertised 1 percent margin of error (no one's fault).
4. Pregnancy caused by the negligence of the woman (or the man, or both). They are careless in the use of the contraceptive or else fail to use it at all, being unaware of a large risk that they *ought* to have been aware of.
5. Pregnancy caused by the recklessness of the woman (or the man, or both). They think of the risk but get swept along by passion and con- sciously disregard it.
6. Pregnancy caused by intercourse between partners who are genuine- ly indifferent at the time whether or not pregnancy results.
7. Pregnancy caused by the deliberate decision of the parties to produce it (completely voluntary).

There would be a somewhat hollow ring to the claim in case 7 that one has no obligation to continue one's bodily support for a moral person whose dependence on that support one has deliberately caused. That would be like denying that one has a duty to save the drowning swimmer that one has just pushed out of the boat. The case for cessation of bodily support is hardly any stronger in 6 and 5 than in 7. Perhaps it is misleading to say of the negligence case (4) that the pregnancy is only partially involuntary, or involuntary "to a degree," since the parents did not *intentionally* produce or run the risk of producing a fetus. But there is no need to haggle over that terminological question. Whether wholly or partially involuntary, the actions of the parents in the circumstances were faulty and the pregnancy resulted from the fault (negligence); so they are to a substantial degree responsible (to blame) for it. It was within their power to be more careful or knowledgeable, and yet they were careless or avoidably ignorant. So they cannot plead, in the manner of the lady plugged to the violinist, that they had no control over their condition whatever. In failing to exercise due care, they were doing something else and doing *it* "to a degree voluntarily." In these cases—4, 5, 6, and 7—the woman and her partner are therefore responsible for the pregnancy, and on the analogy with the case of the drowning swimmer who was pushed from the boat, they have a duty not to kill the fetus or permit it to die.

Cases 2 and 3 are more perplexing. In case 2, where the fault was entirely that of the manufacturer, the woman is no more responsible for being pregnant than in case 1 where she is the unwilling victim of a rape. In neither case did she choose to become pregnant. In neither case was she reckless or negligent in respect to the possibility of becoming pregnant. So if she has no duty to continue to provide bodily support for the dependent fetus in the rape case, then equally she has no duty in the other case. To be sure, there is always *some* risk of pregnancy whenever there is intercourse, no matter how careful the partners are. There may be only 1 chance in 10,000 that a contraceptive pill has an undetectable flaw, but there is no chance whatever of pregnancy without intercourse. The woman in case 2, then, would seem to have *some* responsibility, even if vanishingly small, for her pregnancy. She could have been even more careful by abstaining from sex altogether. But notice that much the same sort of thing could be said of the rape victim. By staying home in a locked building patrolled round the clock by armed guards, she could have reduced the chances of bodily assault from, say, 1 in 50,000 to effectively nil. By staying off the dangerous streets, she would have been much more careful than she was in respect to the risk of rape. But surely that does not entitle us to say that she was "partially responsible" for the rape that made her pregnant. When a person takes all the precautions that she can *reasonably* be expected to take against a certain outcome, then that outcome cannot fairly be described as her responsibility. So in case 2, where the negligence of the manufacturer of the contraceptive is the cause of the pregnancy, the woman cannot be held responsible for her condition, and that ground for ascribing to her a duty not to abort is not present.

Case 3 brings us very close to the borderline. The couple in this example do not choose to have a baby and, indeed, they take strong precautions against pregnancy. Still they know that there is a 1 percent danger and they deliberately choose to run that risk anyway. As a result, a woman becomes pregnant against her will. Does she then have a right to abandon to a certain death a newly formed moral person who is even less responsible for his dependence on her than she is? When one looks at the problem in this way from the perspective of the fetus to whom we have suppositively ascribed full moral rights, it becomes doubtful that the pregnant woman's very minimal responsibility for her plight can permit her to abandon a being who has no responsibility for it whatever. She ran a very small risk, but the fetus ran no risk at all. Nevertheless, this is a borderline case for the following reason. If we extend to this case the rule we applied to case 2, then we might be entitled to say that the woman is no more responsible than the fetus for the pregnancy. To reach that conclusion we have to judge the 1 percent chance of pregnancy to be a *reasonable* risk for a woman to run in the circumstances. That appraisal itself is a disguised moral judgment of pivotal importance, and yet it is very difficult to know how to go about establishing it. Nevertheless, *if* it is correct, then the woman is, for all practical purposes, relieved of her responsibility for the pregnancy just as she is in cases 1 and 2, and in that event the fetus's "right to life" does not entail a duty on her part to make extreme sacrifices.

Summary and Conclusion

Assuming that the fetus is a moral person, under what conditions, if any, is abortion justifiable homicide? If the woman's right to an abortion is derived from her right to own property in her body (which is not very plausible), then abortion is never justifiable homicide. Property rights simply can't support that much moral weight. If the right is derived from self-defense, then it justifies abortion at most when necessary to save the woman from death. That is because the fetus, while sometimes a threat to the interests of the woman, is an innocent and (in a sense) nonaggressive threat. The doctrine of proportionality, which permits a person to use a degree of force in self-defense that is likely to cause the assailant harm greater (within reasonable limits) than the harm the assailant would otherwise cause the victim, has application only to the case where the assailant is culpable. One can kill an "innocent threat" in order to save one's life but not to save one's pocketbook. The right of bodily autonomy (to decide what is to be done in and to one's own body) is a much solider base for the right to abortion than either the right to property or the right to self-defense, since it permits one to kill innocent persons by depriving them of one's "life-support system," even when they are threats to interests substantially less important than self-preservation. But this justification is probably available at most to victims of rape, or contraceptive failure caused by the negligence of other parties, to the risk of which the woman has not consented. That narrow restriction on the use of this defense stems from the requirement, internal to it, that the woman be in no way responsible for her pregnancy.

It does not follow automatically that because the victim of a homicide was "innocent," the killing cannot have been justified. But abortion can plausibly be construed as justifiable homicide only on the basis of inexact analogies, and then only (1) to save the mother from the most extreme harm or else (2) to save the mother from a lesser harm when the pregnancy was the result of the wrongful acts of others for which the woman had no responsibility. Another possibility that was only suggested here is (3) when it can be claimed for a defective or diseased fetus that it has a right *not* to be born. These narrow restrictions on the right of the woman to an abortion will not satisfy many people in the proabortion camp. But if the assumption of the moral personhood of the fetus is false, . . . then the woman's right to bodily autonomy will normally prevail, and abortions at all but the later stages, at least, and for the most common reasons, at least, are morally permissible.

NOTES

1. Jane English, "Abortion and the Concept of a Person," *Canadian Journal of Philosophy* 5 (1975), p. 242.
2. George Fletcher, "Proportionality and the Psychotic Aggressor: A Vignette in Comparative Criminal Law Theory," *Israel Law Review* 8 (1973), p. 376.
3. Fletcher, *loc. cit.*
4. Judith Jarvis Thomson, "Self-Defense and Rights," The Lindley Lecture, 1976 (Lawrence, Kansas: University of Kansas Philosophy Department, 1977).
5. The term comes from Robert Nozick, *Anarchy, State, and Utopia* (New York: Basic Books, 1974), p. 35.
6. Even when self-defense is acceptable as a defense to homicide in the case of forced killings of nonaggressive innocents, that may be because it is understood in those cases to be an excuse or a mitigation rather than a justification. If a criminal terrorist from a fortified position throws a bomb at my feet, and I can escape its explosion only by quickly throwing it in the direction of a baby-buggy whose infant occupant is enjoying a nap, perhaps I can be *excused* for saving my life by taking the baby's; perhaps the duress under which I acted mitigates my guilt; perhaps the law ought not to be too severe with me. But it is not convincing to argue that I was entirely justified in what I did because I was acting in self-defense. But the problem is a difficult one, and the case may be borderline.
7. See Ludwig Lewisohn's remarkable novel, *The Case of Mr. Crump* (New York: Farrar, Straus and Co., 1947).
8. Judith Jarvis Thomson, "A Defense of Abortion," *Philosophy and Public Affairs* 1 (1971), pp. 48–49.
9. The examples are Sissela Bok's. See her article "Ethical Problems of Abortion," *Hastings Center Studies* 2 (1974), p. 35.

Giving Birth

❖❖

VIRGINIA HELD

> The author of our next selection is Virginia Held, Professor of Phi-
> losophy at Hunter College and The Graduate School of The City
> University of New York. She has been a leading proponent of ensur-
> ing that philosophy takes seriously women's interests and recog-
> nizes their distinctive experiences.
>
> Here she reflects on how little attention has been paid to choic-
> es made by women who give birth. Just as dying may sometimes be
> seen as serving a higher purpose, so may giving birth. It is some-
> thing women do, not something that happens to them.

Let us begin with the recognition that the capacity to choose . . . is an important part of what it is to be distinctively human. And let us contrast how this
capacity to choose has been emphasized with respect to death, and denied
with respect to birth. Human beings, we have often been reminded, can
choose what to die for. They can overcome their fears and die courageously.
They can die for noble causes and die heroically. They can die out of loyalty,
out of duty, out of commitment. They can die for a better future, for themselves, for their children, for humankind. They can die to give birth to nations, or democracy, to put an end to tyranny, or war. They can die for God,
for civilization, for justice, for freedom. Nonhuman animals can die for none
of these; that human beings can do so is an important part of and perhaps essential to what it is to be human.

Contrast all this, now, with what has been said about human birth. Birth
is spoken of as a natural, biological process. That women give birth is said to
make them "essentially" close to nature, resembling other mammals in this
important and possibly dominant aspect of their lives. Human mothering is
seen as a kind of extension of the "natural," biological event of childbirth. It
is thought that women engage in the activity of mothering because they
have given birth and that mothering should be incorporated into the framework of the "natural."

Until recently, childbirth has been something that has for the most part
happened to women, rather than being something chosen by women. Adrienne Rich writes: "For most women actual childbirth has involved no choice

whatever, and very little consciousness. Since prehistoric times, the anticipation of labor has been associated with fear, physical anguish or death, a stream of superstitions, misinformation, theological and medical theories—in short, all we have been taught we should feel, from willing victimization to ecstatic fulfillment."[1]

For most women most of the time, then, giving birth has represented most starkly women's lack of choice, their vulnerability to the forces of nature and male domination. With little chance to avoid pregnancy and few chances for abortion, women have experienced childbirth as something almost entirely outside their control.

But even in the most extreme situations, giving birth is not wholly outside the control of women. A human female can decide not to create another human being, even if to avoid doing so requires great risk. Women throughout history have attempted to end their pregnancies, often endangering their health and lives. A woman ultimately has the capacity to refuse to yield to the forces of nature and the demands of men, for these cannot take from her the possibility of attempting abortion, or of killing herself if no other means of ending her pregnancy are successful. Thus any woman, unlike any animal, can intentionally avoid creating another human being. And in recent years women have increasingly been able to gain control over their capacity to give birth. Through contraception and more recently legal abortion, most women in the West now have a large measure of choice over whether or not to give birth.

If a woman chooses to try to become pregnant, or to continue with a pregnancy, she makes a choice that only a conscious human being can make, and the resulting birth is radically unlike the natural event of nonhuman birth. To construe human birth as primarily biological is as misleading as to construe human life and human death as primarily biological. Of course they are all also biological, but this is only their primary attribute in certain restricted contexts, such as a medical context, or from only one among many points of view, such as that of biology. To the extent that we recognize that there is more to human life and more to human death than can be comprehended through a biological framework, so should we recognize that there is more to human birth. If anything, giving birth is more human, because we *can* choose to avoid it, whereas death, eventually, is inevitable.

No one can possibly justify being born and no one should ever be asked to. The questions "what right do you have to have come into existence?" or "why should you have been born?" make no sense applied to the child. Any argument that a child should not have been born can only be addressed to the child's parents or to those in a position, through, for instance, social policies of various kinds, to have increased or decreased the likelihood of this birth. But the questions "why should you have a child?" or "why should you refrain from having a child?" make excellent sense addressed to potential mothers. The rarity with which these questions are seen to make human birth an other than biological event indicates yet again how unaccustomed we are to viewing the world from the point of view of women.

Men often imagine themselves to have come into existence full-blown. . . . Sometimes they remember that they were once children and can think back to their own childhoods or even imagine their own births. They can recognize the inappropriateness of being asked to justify their own existence. But they rarely imagine the women who gave them existence being in a position to determine whether to give them existence or not, and to do so for reasons of which women can be conscious. To understand childbirth from the point of view of women requires a shift of perspective that seems highly unusual. And yet, we can hardly hope to gain an adequate conception of human experience without exploring human life from the point of view of those in a position to create it or not create it.

Questions of what to give birth for, like questions of what to die for, or questions of what to live for, can be asked even when women have no more control over childbirth than the possibility of refusing to give birth through extreme risk to themselves.

When women have more control over whether or not to give birth, and when they have, as many now do, almost full control, the appropriateness of the questions is even more pronounced. Any woman can ask herself: Why should I give birth? What should I create a child for? To what end should I give birth? In giving birth, to what shall I be giving human expression? The compendium of reasons for which men (and women) have wondered what to die or live for can be matched by a new and even richer compendium of reasons for which women can give birth. Men (and women) can die out of loyalty, out of duty, out of commitment, and they can die for a better future. Women can give birth, or refuse to give birth, from all these motives and others. They can give birth so that a new human being can experience joy, so that humankind can continue to exist, so that the family of which they are a member can maintain itself, so that the social movement which gives them hope may have another potential adherent, so that the love they share with another may be shared with yet another. They can give birth to express their conceptions of themselves, of humanity, and of life. And so on endlessly. That women can give birth for reasons should make clear how very *unlike* a natural, biological event a human birth is.

One should note that most women may not ask themselves why they should give birth, or what they should give birth for. But neither do most men (or women) ask themselves what they should die for, or even what they should live for. Most deaths are not the result of such deliberations; neither are the conducts of most lives. Most deaths happen to people, and most people live their lives with little reflection about the ends to which they can devote themselves. Nevertheless, that a human being can choose what to die for, and what to live for, characterizes our concepts of being human, and our concepts of dying a human death and living a human life. What we should open our eyes to is that women can choose what to give birth for, or what to refuse to give birth for, and that this characterizes human birth.

If it is inappropriate to ask what to give birth for, perhaps it is also inappropriate to ask what to die for. . . . But if we recognize the appropriateness of asking for reasons to live or die one way or another, we ought to recognize reasons for giving birth. And the possibilities of deciding what to give birth for, and of choosing how to interpret what we are doing when we give birth, should characterize our concepts of woman and birth. Our concepts of woman and birth should in turn be as much at the heart of our concept of being human as are our concepts of death and of living a distinctively human life.

NOTE

1. Adrienne Rich, *Of Women Born: Motherhood as Experience and Institution* (New York: Norton, 1976), p. 149.

Active and Passive Euthanasia

❖❖

JAMES RACHELS

> The American Medical Association endorses the doctrine that while it is permissible at a patient's request to withhold extraordinary means of prolonging the patient's life, it is impermissible, even at the patient's request, to take steps to terminate that life intentionally. Is this distinction viable? James Rachels, whose work we read previously (pp. 245–255), argues that it is not.

The distinction between active and passive euthanasia is thought to be crucial for medical ethics. The idea is that it is permissible, at least in some cases, to withhold treatment and allow a patient to die, but it is never permissible to take any direct action designed to kill the patient. This doctrine seems

From *The New England Journal of Medicine,* vol. 292, no. 2 (1975). Copyright © 1975 Massachusetts Medical Society. Reprinted by permission.

to be accepted by most doctors, and it is endorsed in a statement adopted by the House of Delegates of the American Medical Association on 4 December 1973:

> The intentional termination of the life of one human being by another—mercy killing—is contrary to that for which the medical profession stands and is contrary to the policy of the American Medical Association.
> The cessation of the employment of extraordinary means to prolong the life of the body when there is irrefutable evidence that biological death is imminent is the decision of the patient and/or his immediate family. The advice and judgement of the physician should be freely available to the patient and/or his immediate family.

However, a strong case can be made against this doctrine. In what follows I will set out some of the relevant arguments, and urge doctors to reconsider their views on this matter.

To begin with a familiar type of situation, a patient who is dying of incurable cancer of the throat is in terrible pain, which can no longer be satisfactorily alleviated. He is certain to die within a few days, even if present treatment is continued, but he does not want to go on living for those days since the pain is unbearable. So he asks the doctor for an end to it, and his family joins in the request.

Suppose the doctor agrees to withhold treatment, as the conventional doctrine says he may. The justification for his doing so is that the patient is in terrible agony, and since he is going to die anyway, it would be wrong to prolong his suffering needlessly. But now notice this. If one simply withholds treatment, it may take the patient longer to die, and so he may suffer more than he would if more direct action were taken and a lethal injection given. This fact provides strong reason for thinking that, once the initial decision not to prolong his agony has been made, active euthanasia is actually preferable to passive euthanasia, rather than the reverse. To say otherwise is to endorse the option that leads to more suffering rather than less, and is contrary to the humanitarian impulse that prompts the decision not to prolong his life in the first place.

Part of my point is that the process of being "allowed to die" can be relatively slow and painful, whereas being given a lethal injection is relatively quick and painless. Let me give a different sort of example. In the United States about one in 600 babies is born with Down's syndrome. Most of these babies are otherwise healthy—that is, with only the usual pediatric care, they will proceed to an otherwise normal infancy. Some, however, are born with congenital defects such as intestinal obstructions that require operations if they are to live. Sometimes, the parents and the doctor will decide not to operate, and let the infant die. Anthony Shaw describes what happens then:

> When surgery is denied [the doctor] must try to keep the infant from suffer-
> ing while natural forces sap the baby's life away. As a surgeon whose natu-
> ral inclination is to use the scalpel to fight off death, standing by and watch-
> ing a salvageable baby die is the most emotionally exhausting experience I
> know. It is easy at a conference, in a theoretical discussion to decide that
> such infants should be allowed to die. It is altogether different to stand by in
> the nursery and watch as dehydration and infection wither a tiny being over
> hours and days. This is a terrible ordeal for me and the hospital staff—much
> more so than for the parents who never set foot in the nursery.[1]

I can understand why some people are opposed to all euthanasia, and
insist that such infants must be allowed to live. I think I can also understand
why other people favour destroying these babies quickly and painlessly. But
why should anyone favour letting "dehydration and infection wither a tiny
being over hours and days"? The doctrine that says a baby may be allowed
to dehydrate and wither, but may not be given an injection that would end
its life without suffering, seems so patently cruel as to require no further
refutation. The strong language is not intended to offend, but only to put the
point in the clearest possible way.

My second argument is that the conventional doctrine leads to decisions
concerning life and death made on irrelevant grounds.

Consider again the case of the infants with Down's syndrome who need
operations for congenital defects unrelated to the syndrome to live. Sometimes, there is no operation, and the baby dies, but when there is no such defect, the baby lives on. Now, an operation such as that to remove an intestinal obstruction is not prohibitively difficult. The reason why such operations
are not performed in these cases is, clearly, that the child has Down's syndrome and the parents and the doctor judge that because of that fact it is better for the child to die.

But notice that this situation is absurd, no matter what view one takes of
the lives and potentials of such babies. If the life of such an infant is worth
preserving, what does it matter if it needs a simple operation? Or, if one
thinks it better that such a baby should not live on, what difference does it
make that it happens to have an unobstructed intestinal tract? In either case,
the matter of life and death is being decided on irrelevant grounds. It is the
Down's syndrome, and not the intestines, that is the issue. The matter
should be decided, if at all, on that basis, and not be allowed to depend on
the essentially irrelevant question of whether the intestinal tract is blocked.

What makes this situation possible, of course, is the idea that when there
is an intestinal blockage, one can "let the baby die," but when there is no
such defect there is nothing that can be done, for one must not "kill" it. The
fact that this idea leads to such results as deciding life or death on irrelevant
grounds is another good reason why the doctrine would be rejected.

One reason why so many people think that there is an important moral
difference between active and passive euthanasia is that they think killing

someone is morally worse than letting someone die. But is it? Is killing, in it-self, worse than letting die? To investigate this issue, two cases may be con-sidered that are exactly alike except that one involves killing whereas the other involves letting someone die. Then, it can be asked whether this differ-ence makes any difference to the moral assessments. It is important that the cases be exactly alike, except for this one difference, since otherwise one can-not be confident that it is this difference and not some other that accounts for any variation in the assessments of the two cases. So, let us consider this pair of cases:

In the first, Smith stands to gain a large inheritance if anything should happen to his six-year-old cousin. One evening while the child is taking his bath, Smith sneaks into the bathroom and drowns the child, and then arranges things so that it will look like an accident.

In the second, Jones also stands to gain if anything should happen to his six-year-old cousin. Like Smith, Jones sneaks in planning to drown the child in his bath. However, just as he enters the bathroom Jones sees the child slip and hit his head, and fall face down in the water. Jones is delighted; he stands by, ready to push the child's head back under if it is necessary, but it is not necessary. With only a little thrashing about, the child drowns all by himself, "accidentally," as Jones watches and does nothing.

Now Smith killed the child, whereas Jones "merely" let the child die. That is the only difference between them. Did either man behave better, from a moral point of view? If the difference between killing and letting die were in itself a morally important matter, one should say that Jones's behaviour was less reprehensible than Smith's. But does one really want to say that? I think not. In the first place, both men acted from the same motive, personal gain, and both had exactly the same end in view when they acted. It may be inferred from Smith's conduct that he is a bad man, although that judgement may be withdrawn or modified if certain further facts are learned about him—for example, that he is mentally deranged. But would not the very same thing be inferred about Jones from his conduct? And would not the same further considerations also be relevant to any modification of this judgement? Moreover, suppose Jones pleaded, in his own defence, "After all, I didn't do anything except just stand there and watch the child drown. I didn't kill him; I only let him die." Again, if letting die were in itself less bad than killing, this defence should have at least some weight. But it does not. Such a "defence" can only be regarded as a grotesque perversion of moral reasoning. Morally speaking, it is no defence at all.

Now, it may be pointed out, quite properly, that the cases of euthanasia with which doctors are concerned are not like this at all. They do not involve personal gain or the destruction of normal, healthy children. Doctors are concerned only with cases in which the patient's life is of no further use to him, or in which the patient's life has become or will soon become a terrible burden. However, the point is the same in these cases: the bare difference be-tween killing and letting die does not, in itself, make a moral difference. If a doctor lets a patient die, for humane reasons, he is in the same moral position as if he had given the patient a lethal injection for humane reasons. If his decision was wrong—if, for example, the patient's illness was in fact curable—the decision would be equally regrettable no matter which method was used to carry it out. And if the doctor's decision was the right one, the method used is not in itself important.

The AMA policy statement isolates the crucial issue very well; the crucial issue is "the intentional termination of the life of one human being by another." But after identifying this issue, and forbidding "mercy killing," the statement goes on to deny that the cessation of treatment is the intentional termination of a life. This is where the mistake comes in, for what is the cessation of treatment, in these circumstances, if it is not "the intentional termination of the life of one human being by another"? Of course it is exactly that, and if it were not, there would be no point to it.

Many people will find this judgement hard to accept. One reason, I think, is that it is very easy to conflate the question of whether killing is, in itself, worse than letting die, with the very different question of whether most actual cases of killing are more reprehensible than most actual cases of letting die. Most actual cases of killing are clearly terrible (think, for example, of all the murders reported in the newspapers), and one hears of such cases every day. On the other hand, one hardly ever hears of a case of letting die, except for the actions of doctors who are motivated by humanitarian reasons. So one learns to think of killing in a much worse light than of letting die. But this does not mean that there is something about killing that makes it in itself worse than letting die, for it is not the bare difference between killing and letting die that makes the difference in these cases. Rather, the other factors—the murderer's motive of personal gain, for example, contrasted with the doctor's humanitarian motivation—account for different reactions to the different cases.

I have argued that killing is not in itself any worse than letting die; if my contention is right, it follows that active euthanasia is not any worse than passive euthanasia. What arguments can be given on the other side? The most common, I believe, is the following:

> The important difference between active and passive euthanasia is that, in passive euthanasia, the doctor does not do anything to bring about the patient's death. The doctor does nothing, and the patient dies of whatever ills already afflict him. In active euthanasia, however, the doctor does something to bring about the patient's death: he kills him. The doctor who gives the patient with cancer a lethal injection has himself caused his patient's death; whereas if he merely ceases treatment, the cancer is the cause of the death.

A number of points need to be made here. The first is that it is not exactly correct to say that in passive euthanasia the doctor does nothing, for he does do one thing that is very important: he lets the patient die. "Letting someone die" is certainly different, in some respects, from other types of action—mainly in that it is a kind of action that one may perform by way of not performing certain other actions. For example, one may let a patient die by way of not giving medication, just as one may insult someone by way of not shaking his hand. But for any purpose of moral assessment, it is a type of action nonetheless. The decision to let a patient die is subject to moral appraisal in the same way that a decision to kill him would be subject to moral appraisal: it may be assessed as wise or unwise, compassionate or sadistic, right or wrong. If a doctor deliberately let a patient die who was suffering from a routinely curable illness, the doctor would certainly be to blame for what he had done, just as he would be to blame if he had needlessly killed the patient. Charges against him would then be appropriate. If so, it would be no defence at all for him to insist that he didn't "do anything." He would have done something very serious indeed, for he let his patient die.

Fixing the cause of death may be very important from a legal point of view, for it may determine whether criminal charges are brought against the doctor. But I do not think that this notion can be used to show a moral difference between active and passive euthanasia. The reason why it is considered bad to be the cause of someone's death is that death is regarded as a great evil—and so it is. However, if it has been decided that euthanasia—even passive euthanasia—is desirable in a given case, it has also been decided that in this instance death is no greater an evil than the patient's continued existence. And if this is true, the usual reason for not wanting to be the cause of someone's death simply does not apply.

Finally, doctors may think that all of this is only of academic interest—the sort of thing that philosophers may worry about but that has no practical bearing on their own work. After all, doctors must be concerned about the legal consequences of what they do, and active euthanasia is clearly forbidden by the law. But even so, doctors should also be concerned with the fact that the law is forcing upon them a moral doctrine that may be indefensible, and has a considerable effect on their practices. Of course, most doctors are not now in the position of being coerced in this matter, for they do not regard themselves as merely going along with what the law requires. Rather, in statements such as the AMA policy statement that I have quoted, they are endorsing this doctrine as a central point of medical ethics. In that statement, active euthanasia is condemned not merely as illegal but as "contrary to that for which the medical profession stands," whereas passive euthanasia is approved. However, the preceding considerations suggest that there is really no moral difference between the two, considered in themselves (there may be important moral differences in some cases in their *consequences*, but, as I pointed out, these differences may make active euthanasia, and not passive euthanasia, the morally preferable option). So, whereas doctors may have to discriminate between active and passive euthanasia to satisfy the law, they should not do any more than that. In particular, they should not give the dis-

tinction any added authority and weight by writing it into official statements
of medical ethics.

NOTE

1. Shaw, Anthony, "Doctor, Do We Have a Choice?" *The New York Times Magazine*, 30
    Jan. 1972, p. 54.

Active and Passive Euthanasia: A Reply

❖❖

THOMAS D. SULLIVAN

> The previous essay by James Rachels gave rise to this response by
> Thomas D. Sullivan, Professor of Philosophy at the College of St.
> Thomas in St. Paul, Minnesota. Here is a clear instance of two
> philosophers in direct conflict. Which one makes the better case?
> The decision is yours.

Because of recent advances in medical technology, it is today possible to save
or prolong the lives of many persons who in an earlier era would have
quickly perished. Unhappily, however, it often is impossible to do so without committing the patient and his or her family to a future filled with sorrows. Modern methods of neurosurgery can successfully close the opening
at the base of the spine of a baby born with severe myelomeningocoele, but
do nothing to relieve the paralysis that afflicts it from the waist down or to
remedy the patient's incontinence of stool and urine. Antibiotics and skin
grafts can spare the life of a victim of severe and massive burns, but fail to
eliminate the immobilizing contractions of arms and legs, the extreme pain,
and the hideous disfigurement of the face. It is not surprising, therefore, that
physicians and moralists in increasing number recommend that assistance
should not be given to such patients, and that some have even begun to ad-

From *Human Life Review*, vol. 3, no. 3 (1977), by permission of the author.

vocate the deliberate hastening of death by medical means, provided informed consent has been given by the appropriate parties.

The latter recommendation consciously and directly conflicts with what might be called the "traditional" view of the physician's role. The traditional view, as articulated, for example, by the House of Delegates of the American Medical Association in 1973, declared:

> The intentional termination of the life of one human being by another—
> mercy killing—is contrary to that for which the medical profession stands
> and is contrary to the policy of the American Medical Association.
>
> The cessation of the employment of extraordinary means to prolong the
> life of the body when there is irrefutable evidence that biological death is
> imminent is the decision of the patient and/or his immediate family. The
> advice and judgement of the physician should be freely available to the pa-
> tient and/or his immediate family.

Basically this view involves two points: (1) that it is impermissible for the doctor or anyone else to terminate intentionally the life of a patient, but (2) that it is permissible in some cases to cease the employment of "extraordinary means" of preserving life, even though the death of the patient is a foreseeable consequence.

Does this position really make sense? Recent criticism charges that it does not. The heart of the complaint is that the traditional view arbitrarily rules out all cases of intentionally acting to terminate life, but permits what is in fact the moral equivalent, letting patients die. This accusation has been clearly articulated by James Rachels in a widely read article that appeared in a recent issue of the *New England Journal of Medicine,* entitled "Active and Passive Euthanasia."[1] By "active euthanasia" Rachels seems to mean *doing something* to bring about a patient's death, and by "passive euthanasia" not doing anything, i.e., just letting the patient die. Referring to the A.M.A. statement, Rachels sees the traditional position as always forbidding active euthanasia but permitting passive euthanasia. Yet, he argues, passive euthanasia may be in some cases morally indistinguishable from active euthanasia, and in other cases even worse. To make his point he asks his readers to consider the case of a Down's syndrome baby with an intestinal obstruction that easily could be remedied through routine surgery. Rachels comments:

> I can understand why some people are opposed to all euthanasia, and insist
> that such infants must be allowed to live. I think I can also understand why
> other people favor destroying these babies quickly and painlessly. But why
> should anyone favor letting "dehydration and infection wither a tiny being
> over hours and days"? The doctrine that says that a baby may be allowed to
> dehydrate and wither, but may not be given an injection that would end

its life without suffering, seems so patently cruel as to require no further refutation.[2]

Rachels' point is that decisions such as the one he describes as "patently cruel" arise out of a misconceived moral distinction between active and passive euthanasia, which in turn rests upon a distinction between killing and letting die that itself has no moral importance.

> One reason why so many people think that there is an important moral difference between active and passive euthanasia is that they think killing someone is morally worse than letting someone die. But is it? . . . To investigate this issue, two cases may be considered that are exactly alike except that one involves killing whereas the other involves letting someone die. Then, it can be asked whether this difference makes any difference to the moral assessments. . . .
>
> In the first, Smith stands to gain a large inheritance if anything should happen to his six-year-old cousin. One evening while the child is taking his bath, Smith sneaks into the bathroom and drowns the child, and then arranges things so that it will look like an accident.
>
> In the second, Jones also stands to gain if anything should happen to his six-year-old cousin. Like Smith, Jones sneaks in planning to drown the child in his bath. However, just as he enters the bathroom Jones sees the child slip and hit his head, and fall face down in the water. Jones is delighted: he stands by, ready to push the child's head back under if it is necessary, but it is not necessary. With only a little thrashing about the child drowns all by himself, "accidentally," as Jones watches and does nothing.[3]

Rachels observes that Smith killed the child, whereas Jones "merely" let the child die. If there's an important moral distinction between killing and letting die, then, we should say that Jones' behavior from a moral point of view is less reprehensible than Smith's. But while the law might draw some distinctions here, it seems clear that the acts of Jones and Smith are not different in any important way, or, if there is a difference, Jones' action is even worse.

In essence, then, the objection to the position adopted by the A.M.A. of Rachels and those who argue like him is that it endorses a highly questionable moral distinction between killing and letting die, which, if accepted, leads to indefensible medical decisions. Nowhere does Rachels quite come out and say that he favors active euthanasia in some cases, but the implication is clear. Nearly everyone holds that it is sometimes pointless to prolong the process of dying and that in those cases it is morally permissible to let a patient die even though a few hours or days could be salvaged by procedures that would also increase the agonies of the dying. But if it is impossible to defend a general distinction between letting people die and acting to terminate their lives directly, then it would seem that active euthanasia also may be morally permissible.

Now what shall we make of all this? It *is* cruel to stand by and watch a Down's baby die an agonizing death when a simple operation would remove the intestinal obstruction, but to offer the excuse that in failing to operate we didn't *do* anything to bring about death is an example of moral evasiveness comparable to the excuse Jones would offer for his action of "merely" letting his cousin die. Furthermore, it is true that if someone is trying to bring about the death of another human being, then it makes little difference from the moral point of view if his purpose is achieved by action or by malevolent omission, as in the cases of Jones and Smith.

But if we acknowledge this, are we obliged to give up the traditional view expressed by the A.M.A. statement? Of course not. To begin with, we are hardly obliged to assume the Jones-like role Rachels assigns the defender of the traditional view. We have the option of operating on the Down's baby and saving its life. Rachels mentions that possibility only to hurry past it as if that is not what his opposition would do. But, of course, that is precisely the course of action most defenders of the traditional position would choose.

Secondly, while it may be that the reason some rather confused people give for upholding the traditional view is that they think killing someone is always worse than letting them die, nobody who gives the matter much thought puts it that way. Rather they say that killing someone is clearly morally worse than not killing them, and killing them can be done by acting to bring about their death or by refusing ordinary means to keep them alive in order to bring about the same goal.

What I am suggesting is that Rachels' objections leave the position he sets out to criticize untouched. It is worth noting that the jargon of active and passive euthanasia—and it is jargon—does not appear in the resolution. Nor does the resolution state or imply the distinction Rachels attacks, a distinction that puts a moral premium on overt behavior—moving or not moving one's parts—while totally ignoring the intentions of the agent. That no such distinction is being drawn seems clear from the fact that the A.M.A. resolution speaks approvingly of ceasing to use extraordinary means in certain cases, and such withdrawals might easily involve bodily movement, for example unplugging an oxygen machine.

In addition to saddling his opposition with an indefensible distinction it doesn't make, Rachels proceeds to ignore one that it does make—one that is crucial to a just interpretation of the view. Recall the A.M.A. allows the withdrawal of what it calls extraordinary means of preserving life; clearly the contrast here is with ordinary means. Though in its short statement those expressions are not defined, the definition Paul Ramsey refers to as standard in his book, *The Patient As Person*, seems to fit.

> Ordinary means of preserving life are all medicines, treatments, and operations, which offer a reasonable hope of benefit for the patient and which can be obtained and used without excessive expense, pain, and other inconveniences.

> Extra-ordinary means of preserving life are all those medicines, treat-
> ments, and operations which cannot be obtained without excessive expense,
> pain, or other inconvenience, or which, if used, would not offer a reasonable
> hope of benefit.[4]

Now with this distinction in mind, we can see how the traditional view differs from the position Rachels mistakes for it. The traditional view is that the intentional termination of human life is impermissible, irrespective of whether this goal is brought about by action or inaction. Is the action or refraining *aimed* at producing a death? Is the termination of life *sought, chosen or planned*? Is the intention deadly? If so, the act or omission is wrong.

But we all know it is entirely possible that the unwillingness of a physician to use extraordinary means for preserving life may be prompted not by a determination to bring about death, but by other motives. For example, he may realize that further treatment may offer little hope of reversing the dying process and/or be excruciating, as in the case when a massively necrotic bowel condition in a neonate is out of control. The doctor who does what he can to comfort the infant but does not submit it to further treatment or surgery may foresee that the decision will hasten death, but it certainly doesn't follow from that fact that he intends to bring about its death. It is, after all, entirely possible to foresee that something will come about as a result of one's conduct without intending the consequence or side effect. If I drive downtown, I can foresee that I'll wear out my tires a little, but I don't drive downtown with the intention of wearing out my tires. And if I choose to forego my exercises for a few days, I may think that as a result my physical condition will deteriorate a little, but I don't omit my exercise with a view to running myself down. And if you have to fill a position and select Green, who is better qualified for the post than her rival Brown, you needn't appoint Mrs. Green with the intention of hurting Mr. Brown, though you may foresee that Mr. Brown will feel hurt. And if a country extends its general education programs to its illiterate masses, it is predictable the suicide rate will go up, but even if the public officials are aware of this fact, it doesn't follow that they initiate the program with a view to making the suicide rate go up. In general, then, it is not the case that all the foreseeable consequences and side effects of our conduct are necessarily intended. And it is because the physician's withdrawal of extraordinary means can be otherwise motivated than by a desire to bring about the predictable death of the patient that such action cannot categorically be ruled out as wrong.

But the refusal to use ordinary means is an altogether different matter. After all, what is the point of refusing assistance which offers reasonable hope of benefit to the patient without involving excessive pain or other inconvenience? How could it be plausibly maintained that the refusal is not motivated by a desire to bring about the death of the patient? The traditional position, therefore, rules out not only direct actions to bring about death, such as giving a patient a lethal injection, but malevolent omissions as well, such as not providing minimum care for the newborn.

The reason the A.M.A. position sounds so silly when one listens to arguments such as Rachels' is that he slights the distinction between ordinary and extraordinary means and then drums on cases where *ordinary* means are refused. The impression is thereby conveyed that the traditional doctrine sanctions omissions that are morally indistinguishable in a substantive way from direct killings, but then incomprehensibly refuses to permit quick and painless termination of life. If the traditional doctrine would approve of Jones' standing by with a grin on his face while his young cousin drowned in a tub, or letting a Down's baby wither and die when ordinary means are available to preserve its life, it would indeed be difficult to see how anyone could defend it. But so to conceive the traditional doctrine is simply to misunderstand it. It is not a doctrine that rests on some supposed distinction between "active" and "passive euthanasia," whatever those words are supposed to mean, nor on a distinction between moving and not moving our bodies. It is simply a prohibition against intentional killing, which includes both direct actions and malevolent omissions.

To summarize—the traditional position represented by the A.M.A. statement is not incoherent. It acknowledges, or more accurately, insists upon the fact that withholding ordinary means to sustain life may be tantamount to killing. The traditional position can be made to appear incoherent only by imposing upon it a crude idea of killing held by none of its more articulate advocates.

Thus the criticism of Rachels and other reformers, misapprehending its target, leaves the traditional position untouched. That position is simply a prohibition of murder. And it is good to remember, as C. S. Lewis once pointed out:

> No man, perhaps, ever at first described to himself the act he was about to do as Murder, or Adultery, or Fraud, or Treachery. . . . And when he hears it so described by other men he is (in a way) sincerely shocked and surprised. Those others "don't understand." If they knew what it had really been like for him, they would not use those crude "stock" names. With a wink or a titter, or a cloud of muddy emotion, the thing has slipped into his will as something not very extraordinary, something of which, rightly understood in all of his peculiar circumstances, he may even feel proud.[5]

I fully realize that there are times when those who have the noble duty to tend the sick and the dying are deeply moved by the sufferings of their patients, especially of the very young and the very old, and desperately wish they could do more than comfort and companion them. Then, perhaps, it seems that universal moral principles are mere abstractions having little to do with the agony of the dying. But of course we do not see best when our eyes are filled with tears.

NOTES

1. *The New England Journal of Medicine,* 292 (January 9, 1975), pp. 78–80.
2. Ibid., pp. 78–79.
3. Ibid., p. 79.
4. Paul Ramsey, *The Patient As Person* (New Haven and London: Yale University Press, 1970), p. 122. Ramsey abbreviates the definition first given by Gerald Kelly, S. J., *Medico-Moral Problems* (St. Louis, Mo.: The Catholic Hospital Association, 1958), p. 129.
5. C. S. Lewis, *A Preface to Paradise Lost* (London and New York: Oxford University Press, 1970), p. 126.

Choosing Death

❖❖❖

SIDNEY HOOK

Sidney Hook (1902–1989), a prolific and vigorous contributor to the intellectual debates of his time, was Professor of Philosophy at New York University and President of the American Philosophical Association. The provocative essay that follows was met by strong reactions, both for and against.

The distinction that he makes at one point between doing something "eventful" or "event-making" is drawn from one of his best-known books, *The Hero in History,* in which he distinguished "the eventful man," whose actions influence history, even if by chance, and "the event-making man," an eventful person of outstanding ability whose historical influence results from personal skill rather than historical accident.

Seneca (c. 3 B.C.E.–65 C.E.), whom Hook quotes, was a Roman philosopher, dramatist, and statesman. After his retirement he was accused, perhaps unjustly, of conspiracy and forced to commit suicide, which he did with remarkable dignity.

Hook refers in passing to his own autobiography. Titled *Out of Step,* it was published to acclaim about the same time this article appeared, just two years before his death.

A few short years ago, I lay at the point of death. A congestive heart failure was treated for diagnostic purposes by an angiogram that triggered a stroke.

Violent and painful hiccups, uninterrupted for several days and nights, prevented the ingestion of food. My left side and one of my vocal cords became paralyzed. Some form of pleurisy set in, and I felt I was drowning in a sea of slime. At one point, my heart stopped beating; just as I lost consciousness, it was thumped back into action again. In one of my lucid intervals during those days of agony, I asked my physician to discontinue all life-supporting services or show me how to do it. He refused and predicted that someday I would appreciate the unwisdom of my request.

A month later, I was discharged from the hospital. In six months, I regained the use of my limbs, and although my voice still lacks its old resonance and carrying power I no longer croak like a frog. There remain some minor disabilities and I am restricted to a rigorous, low sodium diet. I have resumed my writing and research.

My experience can be and has been cited as an argument against honoring requests of stricken patients to be gently eased out of their pain and life. I cannot agree. There are two main reasons. As an octogenarian, there is a reasonable likelihood that I may suffer another "cardiovascular accident" or worse. I may not even be in a position to ask for the surcease of pain. It seems to me that I have already paid my dues to death—indeed, although time has softened my memories they are vivid enough to justify my saying that I suffered enough to warrant dying several times over. Why run the risk of more?

Secondly, I dread imposing on my family and friends another grim round of misery similar to the one my first attack occasioned.

My wife and children endured enough for one lifetime. I know that for them the long days and nights of waiting, the disruption of their professional duties and their own familial responsibilities counted for nothing in their anxiety for me. In their joy at my recovery they have been forgotten. Nonetheless, to visit another prolonged spell of helpless suffering on them as my life ebbs away, or even worse, if I linger on into a comatose senility, seems altogether gratuitous.

But what, it may be asked, of the joy and satisfaction of living, of basking in the sunshine, listening to music, watching one's grandchildren growing into adolescence, following the news about the fate of freedom in a troubled world, playing with ideas, writing one's testament of wisdom and folly for prosperity? Is not all that one endured, together with the risk of its recurrence, an acceptable price for the multiple satisfactions that are still open even to a person of advanced years?

Apparently those who cling to life no matter what, think so. I do not.

The zest and intensity of these experiences are no longer what they used to be. I am not vain enough to delude myself that I can in the few remaining years make an important discovery useful for mankind or can lead a social movement or do anything that will be historically eventful, no less event-making. My autobiography, which describes a record of intellectual and political experiences of some historical value, already much too long, could be posthumously published. I have had my fill of joys and sorrows and am not greedy for more life. I have always thought that a test of whether one had found happiness in one's life is whether one would be willing to relive it—whether, if it were possible, one would accept the opportunity to be born again.

Having lived a full and relatively happy life, I would cheerfully accept the chance to be reborn, but certainly not to be reborn again as an infirm octogenarian. To some extent, my views reflect what I have seen happen to the aged and stricken who have been so unfortunate as to survive crippling paralysis. They suffer, and impose suffering on others, unable even to make a request that their torment be ended.

I am mindful too of the burdens placed upon the community, with its rapidly diminishing resources, to provide the adequate and costly services necessary to sustain the lives of those whose days and nights are spent on mattress graves of pain. A better use could be made of these resources to increase the opportunities and qualities of life for the young. I am not denying the moral obligation the community has to look after its disabled and aged. There are times, however, when an individual may find it pointless to insist on the fulfillment of a legal and moral right.

What is required is no great revolution in morals but an enlargement of imagination and an intelligent evaluation of alternative uses of community resources.

Long ago, Seneca observed that "the wise man will live as long as he ought, not as long as he can." One can envisage hypothetical circumstances in which one has a duty to prolong one's life despite its costs for the sake of others, but such circumstances are far removed from the ordinary prospects we are considering. If wisdom is rooted in knowledge of the alternatives of choice, it must be reliably informed of the state one is in and its likely outcome. Scientific medicine is not infallible, but it is the best we have. Should a rational person be willing to endure acute suffering merely on the chance that a miraculous cure might presently be at hand? Each one should be permitted to make his own choice—especially when no one else is harmed by it.

The responsibility for the decision, whether deemed wise or foolish, must be with the chooser.

Nicomachean Ethics

❖◈

ARISTOTLE

Aristotle (384–322 B.C.E.) was born in Macedonia, located between the Balkans and the Greek peninsula. At the age of eighteen he entered Plato's Academy, where he remained for two decades until Plato's death. He then taught outside Athens, including service as tutor to the young prince who later became known as Alexander the Great. Subsequently, Aristotle returned to Athens and founded his own school, the Lyceum. A dozen years later, when an outbreak of anti-Macedonian feeling swept Athens, Aristotle left the city, "lest," he reportedly said, "the Athenians should sin twice against philosophy," referring, of course, to the case of Socrates.

One distinguished historian of philosophy called Aristotle "the greatest mind produced by the Greeks," and a strong case can be made in support of this assessment. Virtually singlehandedly, he founded the study of logic. His philosophical treatise on metaphysics, mind, ethics, politics, and art remain more than two thousand years later among the most profound works ever written on these subjects. His scientific studies produced groundbreaking results in biology, psychology, zoology, meteorology, and astronomy. Indeed, his later influence was so profound that during the Middle Ages he was often referred to simply as "the Philosopher."

The *Nicomachean Ethics,* named after Aristotle's son Nicomachus, is widely regarded as one of the great books of moral philosophy. It includes Aristotle's answer to the question, raised at the opening of Plato's *Meno,* of whether virtue can be taught. Aristotle's answer depends on his distinction between moral and intellectual virtue. Moral virtue, which we might call "goodness of character," is formed by habit. One becomes good by doing good. Repeated acts of justice and self-control result in a just, self-controlled person who not only performs just, self-controlled actions but does so from a fixed character. Intellectual virtue, on the other hand, which we might refer to as "wisdom," requires sophisticated intelligence and is acquired by teaching.

Virtuous activities are those that avoid the two extremes of excess and deficiency. For example, if you fear too much, you be-

From *The Nicomachean Ethics,* translated by David Ross, revised by J. L. Ackrill and J. O. Urmson. Reprinted by permission of Oxford University Press.

come cowardly; if you fear too little, you become rash. The mean is courage.

To achieve the mean, you need to make a special effort to avoid that extreme to which you happen to be prone. Thus, if you tend to be foolhardy, aim at timidity, and you will achieve the right measure of boldness.

The translation is by Sir David Ross (1877–1971) and is updated by J. L. Ackrill and J. O. Urmson, all of Oxford University.

Book II

Virtue, then, being of two kinds, intellectual and moral, intellectual virtue in the main owes both its birth and its growth to teaching (for which reason it requires experience and time), while moral virtue comes about as a result of habit. . . . From this it is also plain that none of the moral virtues arises in us by nature; for nothing that exists by nature can form a habit contrary to its nature. For instance the stone which by nature moves downwards cannot be habituated to move upwards, not even if one tries to train it by throwing it up ten thousand times; nor can fire be habituated to move downwards, nor can anything else that by nature behaves in one way be trained to behave in another. Neither by nature, then, nor contrary to nature do the virtues arise in us; rather we are adapted by nature to receive them, and are made perfect by habit.

Again, of all the things that come to us by nature we first acquire the potentiality and later exhibit the activity (this is plain in the case of the senses; for it was not by often seeing or often hearing that we got these senses, but on the contrary we had them before we used them, and did not come to have them by using them); but the virtues we get by first exercising them, as also happens in the case of the arts as well. For the things we have to learn before we can do them, we learn by doing them, e.g., men become builders by building and lyre-players by playing the lyre; so too we become just by doing just acts, temperate by doing temperate acts, brave by doing brave acts. . . .

It makes no small difference, then, whether we form habits of one kind or of another from our very youth; it makes a very great difference, or rather all the difference.

Since, then, the present inquiry does not aim at theoretical knowledge like the others (for we are inquiring not in order to know what virtue is, but in order to become good, since otherwise our inquiry would have been of no use), we must examine the nature of actions, namely how we ought to do them; for these determine also the nature of the states of character that are produced, as we have said. . . .

First, then, let us consider this, that it is the nature of such things to be destroyed by defect and excess, as we see in the case of strength and of health (for to gain light on things imperceptible we must use the evidence of sensible things); exercise either excessive or defective destroys the strength, and similarly drink or food which is above or below a certain amount destroys the health, while that which is proportionate both produces and increases and preserves it. So too is it, then, in the case of temperance and courage and the other virtues. For the man who flies from and fears everything and does not stand his ground against anything becomes a coward, and the man who fears nothing at all but goes to meet every danger becomes rash; and similarly the man who indulges in every pleasure and abstains from none becomes self-indulgent, while the man who shuns every pleasure, as boors do, becomes in a way insensible; temperance and courage, then, are destroyed by excess and defect, and preserved by the mean.

But not only are the sources and causes of their origination and growth the same as those of their destruction, but also the sphere of their actualization will be the same; for this is also true of the things which are more evident to sense, e.g., of strength; it is produced by taking much food and undergoing much exertion, and it is the strong man that will be most able to do these things. So too is it with the virtues; by abstaining from pleasures we become temperate, and it is when we have become so that we are most able to abstain from them; and similarly too in the case of courage; for by being habituated to despise things that are fearful and to stand our ground against them we become brave, and it is when we have become so that we shall be most able to stand our ground against them. . . .

The question might be asked, what we mean by saying that we must become just by doing just acts, and temperate by doing temperate acts; for if men do just and temperate acts, they are already just and temperate, exactly as, if they do what is in accordance with the laws of grammar and of music, they are grammarians and musicians.

Or is this not true even of the arts? It is possible to do something that is in accordance with the laws of grammar, either by chance or under the guidance of another. A man will be a grammarian, then, only when he has both said something grammatical and said it grammatically; and this means doing it in accordance with the grammatical knowledge in himself.

Again, the case of the arts and that of the virtues are not similar; for the products of the arts have their goodness in themselves, so that it is enough that they should have a certain character, but if the acts that are in accordance with the virtues have themselves a certain character it does not follow that they are done justly or temperately. The agent also must be in a certain condition when he does them; in the first place he must have knowledge, secondly he must choose the acts, and choose them for their own sakes, and thirdly his action must proceed from a firm and unchangeable character. These are not reckoned in as conditions of the possession of the arts, except the bare knowledge; but as a condition of the possession of the virtues knowledge has little or no weight, while the other conditions count not for a little but for everything, i.e., the very conditions which result from often doing just and temperate acts.

Actions, then, are called just and temperate when they are such as the just or the temperate man would do; but it is not the man who does these that is just and temperate, but the man who also does them *as* just and temperate men do them. It is well said, then, that it is by doing just acts that the just man is produced, and by doing temperate acts the temperate man; without doing these no one would have even a prospect of becoming good.

But most people do not do these, but take refuge in theory and think they are being philosophers and will become good in this way, behaving somewhat like patients who listen attentively to their doctors, but do none of the things they are ordered to do. As the latter will not be made well in body by such a course of treatment, the former will not be made well in soul by such a course of philosophy. . . .

[E]very virtue or excellence both brings into good condition the thing of which it is the excellence and makes the work of that thing be done well; e.g., the excellence of the eye makes both the eye and its work good; for it is by the excellence of the eye that we see well. Similarly the excellence of the horse makes a horse both good in itself and good at running and at carrying its rider and at awaiting the attack of the enemy. Therefore, if this is true in every case, the virtue of man also will be the state of character which makes a man good and which makes him do his own work well.

How this is to happen we have stated already, but it will be made plain also by the following consideration of the specific nature of virtue. In everything that is continuous and divisible it is possible to take more, less, or an equal amount, and that either in terms of the thing itself or relatively to us; and the equal is an intermediate between excess and defect. By the intermediate in the object I mean that which is equidistant from each of the extremes, which is one and the same for all men; by the intermediate relatively to us that which is neither too much nor too little—and this is not one, nor the same for all. For instance, if ten is many and two is few, six is the intermediate, taken in terms of the object; for it exceeds and is exceeded by an equal amount; this is intermediate according to arithmetical proportion. But the intermediate relatively to us is not to be taken so; if ten pounds are too much for a particular person to eat and two too little, it does not follow that the trainer will order six pounds; for this also is perhaps too much for the person who is to take it, or too little—too little for Milo, too much for the beginner in athletic exercises. The same is true of running and wrestling. Thus a master of any art avoids excess and defect, but seeks the intermediate and chooses this—the intermediate not in the object but relatively to us.

If it is thus, then, that every art does its work well—by looking to the intermediate and judging its works by this standard (so that we often say of good works of art that it is not possible either to take away or to add anything, implying that excess and defect destroy the goodness of works of art, while the mean preserves it; and good artists, as we say, look to this in their work), and if, further, virtue is more exact and better than any art, as nature also is, then virtue must have the quality of aiming at the intermediate. I mean moral virtue; for it is this that is concerned with passions and actions, and in these there is excess, defect, and the intermediate. For instance, both fear and confidence and appetite and anger and pity and in general pleasure and pain may be felt both too much and too little, and in both cases not well; but to feel them at the right times, with reference to the right objects, towards the right people, with the right motive, and in the right way, is what is both intermediate and best, and this is characteristic of virtue. Similarly with regard to actions also there is excess, defect, and the intermediate. Now virtue is concerned with passions and actions, in which excess is a form of failure, and so is defect, while the intermediate is praised and is a form of success; and being praised and being successful are both characteristics of virtue. Therefore virtue is a kind of mean, since, as we have seen, it aims at what is intermediate. . . .

But not every action nor every passion admits of a mean; for some have names that already imply badness, e.g., spite, shamelessness, envy, and in the case of actions adultery, theft, murder; for all of these and suchlike things imply by their names that they are themselves bad, and not the excesses or deficiencies of them. It is not possible, then, ever to be right with regard to them; one must always be wrong. Nor does goodness or badness with regard to such things depend on committing adultery with the right woman, at the right time, and in the right way, but simply to do any of them is to go wrong. . . .

That moral virtue is a mean, then, and in what sense it is so, and that it is a mean between two vices, the one involving excess, the other deficiency, and that it is such because its character is to aim at what is intermediate in passions and in actions, has been sufficiently stated. Hence also it is no easy task to be good. For in everything it is no easy task to find the middle, e.g., to find the middle of a circle is not for everyone but for him who knows; so, too, anyone can get angry—that is easy—or give or spend money; but to do this to the right person, to the right extent, at the right time, with the right motive, and in the right way, *that* is not for everyone, nor is it easy; wherefore goodness is both rare and laudable and noble. . . .

But we must consider the things towards which we ourselves also are easily carried away; for some of us tend to one thing, some to another; and this will be recognizable from the pleasure and the pain we feel. We must drag ourselves away to the contrary extreme; for we shall get into the intermediate state by drawing well away from error. . . .

So much, then, is plain, that the intermediate state is in all things to be praised, but that we must incline sometimes towards the excess, sometimes towards the deficiency; for so shall we most easily hit the mean and what is right.

Foundations of the Metaphysics of Morals

❖❖❖

Iᴍᴍᴀɴᴜᴇʟ Kᴀɴᴛ

Immanuel Kant (1724–1804) is a preeminent figure in the history of philosophy. Born and raised in the Prussian town of Königsberg (now Kaliningrad), he attended its University and was eventually appointed to its chair of logic and metaphysics. Although he never traveled beyond the environs of his home city, his intellectual scope was far-ranging. Beginning in his early years with studies in physics and astronomy, he eventually made numerous ground-breaking contributions to all the major fields of philosophy.

The selection that follows comes from a short work of Kant's, which although intended only as a preliminary presentation of the main themes of his moral philosophy, has become the most widely read of all his ethical writings. By the "metaphysics of morals" Kant means the philosophical study of moral principles, as opposed to the anthropological survey of moral practices.

Our translator is the renowned Kant scholar Lewis White Beck (1913–1997), who was Professor of Philosophy at the University of Rochester and President of the American Philosophical Association.

A brief discussion of the fundamental principle of Kant's moral philosophy is contained in my essay "A Supreme Moral Principle?," found earlier in this section (pp. 265–270).

Everything in nature works according to laws. Only a rational being has the capacity of acting according to the conception of laws, i.e., according to principles. This capacity is will. . . .

The conception of an objective principle, so far as it constrains a will, is a command (of reason), and the formula of this command is called an *imperative*. . . .

All imperatives command either hypothetically or categorically. The former present the practical necessity of a possible action as a means to achieving something else which one desires (or which one may possibly desire). The categorical imperative would be one which presented an action as of itself objectively necessary, without regard to any other end. . . .

Foundations of the Metaphysics of Morals, 2d edition, by Kant (trans. by L. W. Beck). Reprinted by permission of Prentice-Hall, Inc., Upper Saddle River, NJ.

If the action is good only as a means to something else, the imperative is hypothetical; but if it is thought of as good in itself, and hence as necessary in a will which of itself conforms to reason as the principle of this will, the imperative is categorical. . . .

If I think of a hypothetical imperative as such, I do not know what it will contain until the condition is stated [under which it is an imperative]. But if I think of a categorical imperative, I know immediately what it contains. For since the imperative contains besides the law only the necessity that the maxim[1] should accord with this law, while the law contains no condition to which it is restricted, there is nothing remaining in it except the universality of law as such to which the maxim of the action should conform; and in effect this conformity alone is represented as necessary by the imperative.

There is, therefore, only one categorical imperative. It is: Act only according to that maxim by which you can at the same time will that it should become a universal law. . . .

We shall now enumerate some duties. . . .

1. A man who is reduced to despair by a series of evils feels a weariness with life but is still in possession of his reason sufficiently to ask whether it would not be contrary to his duty to himself to take his own life. Now he asks whether the maxim of his action could become a universal law of nature. His maxim, however, is: For love of myself, I make it my principle to shorten my life when by a longer duration it threatens more evil than satisfaction. But it is questionable whether this principle of self-love could become a universal law of nature. One immediately sees a contradiction in a system of nature whose law would be to destroy life by the feeling whose special office is to impel the improvement of life. In this case it would not exist as nature; hence that maxim cannot obtain as a law of nature, and thus it wholly contradicts the supreme principle of all duty.

2. Another man finds himself forced by need to borrow money. He well knows that he will not be able to repay it, but he also sees that nothing will be loaned him if he does not firmly promise to repay it at a certain time. He desires to make such a promise, but he has enough conscience to ask himself whether it is not improper and opposed to duty to relieve his distress in such a way. Now, assuming he does decide to do so, the maxim of his action would be as follows: When I believe myself to be in need of money, I will borrow money and promise to repay it, although I know I shall never do so. Now this principle of self-love or of his own benefit may very well be compatible with his whole future welfare, but the question is whether it is right. He changes the pretension of self-love into a universal law and then puts the question: How would it be if my maxim became a universal law? He immediately sees that it could never hold as a universal law of nature and be consistent with itself; rather it must necessarily contradict itself. For the universality of a law which says that anyone who believes himself to be in need could promise what he pleased with the intention of not fulfilling it would make the promise itself and the end to be accomplished by it impossible; no

one would believe what was promised to him but would only laugh at any such assertion as vain pretense.

3. A third finds in himself a talent which could, by means of some cultivation, make him in many respects a useful man. But he finds himself in comfortable circumstances and prefers indulgence in pleasure to troubling himself with broadening and improving his fortunate natural gifts. Now, however, let him ask whether his maxim of neglecting his gifts, besides agreeing with his propensity to idle amusement, agrees also with what is called duty. He sees that a system of nature could indeed exist in accordance with such a law, even though man (like the inhabitants of the South Sea Islands) should let his talents rust and resolve to devote his life merely to idleness, indulgence, and propagation—in a word, to pleasure. But he cannot possibly will that this should become a universal law of nature or that it should be implanted in us by a natural instinct. For, as a rational being, he necessarily wills that all his faculties should be developed, inasmuch as they are given to him for all sorts of possible purposes.

4. A fourth man, for whom things are going well, sees that others (whom he could help) have to struggle with great hardships, and he asks, "What concern of mine is it? Let each one be as happy as heaven wills, or as he can make himself; I will not take anything from him or even envy him; but to his welfare or to his assistance in time of need I have no desire to contribute." If such a way of thinking were a universal law of nature, certainly the human race could exist, and without doubt even better than in a state where everyone talks of sympathy and good will, or even exerts himself occasionally to practice them while, on the other hand, he cheats when he can and betrays or otherwise violates the rights of man. Now although it is possible that a universal law of nature according to that maxim could exist, it is nevertheless impossible to will that such a principle should hold everywhere as a law of nature. For a will which resolved this would conflict with itself, since instances can often arise in which he would need the love and sympathy of others, and in which he would have robbed himself, by such a law of nature springing from his own will, of all hope of the aid he desires.

The foregoing are a few of the many actual duties, or at least of duties we hold to be actual, whose derivation from the one stated principle is clear. We must be able to will that a maxim of our action become a universal law; this is the canon of the moral estimation of our action generally. Some actions are of such a nature that their maxim cannot even be *thought* as a universal law of nature without contradiction, far from it being possible that one could will that it should be such. In others this internal impossibility is not found, though it is still impossible to *will* that their maxim should be raised to the universality of a law of nature, because such a will would contradict itself. . . .

When we observe ourselves in any transgression of a duty, we find that we do not actually will that our maxim should become a universal law. That is impossible for us; rather, the contrary of this maxim should remain as a law generally, and we only take the liberty of making an exception to it for ourselves or for the sake of our inclination, and for this one occasion. Consequently, if we weighed everything from one and the same standpoint, namely, reason, we would come upon a contradiction in our own will, viz., that a certain principle is objectively necessary as a universal law and yet subjectively does not hold universally but rather admits exceptions. . . .

[S]uppose that there were something the existence of which in itself had absolute worth, something which, as an end in itself, could be a ground of definite laws. In it and only in it could lie the ground of a possible categorical imperative, i.e., of a practical law.

Now, I say, man and, in general, every rational being exists as an end in himself and not merely as a means to be arbitrarily used by this or that will. In all his actions, whether they are directed to himself or to other rational beings, he must always be regarded at the same time as an end. . . .

Beings whose existence does not depend on our will but on nature, if they are not rational beings, have only a relative worth as means and are therefore called "things"; on the other hand, rational beings are designated "persons" because their nature indicates that they are ends in themselves, i.e., things which may not be used merely as means. Such a being is thus an object of respect and, so far, restricts all [arbitrary] choice. Such beings are not merely subjective ends whose existence as a result of our action has a worth for us, but are objective ends, i.e., beings whose existence in itself is an end. Such an end is one for which no other end can be substituted, to which these beings should serve merely as means. For, without them, nothing of absolute worth could be found, and if all worth is conditional and thus contingent, no supreme practical principle for reason could be found anywhere.

Thus if there is to be a supreme practical principle and a categorical imperative for the human will, it must be one that forms an objective principle of the will from the conception of that which is necessarily an end for everyone because it is an end in itself. Hence this objective principle can serve as a universal practical law. The ground of this principle is: rational nature exists as an end in itself. Man necessarily thinks of his own existence in this way; thus far it is a subjective principle of human actions. Also every other rational being thinks of his existence by means of the same rational ground which holds also for myself; thus it is at the same time an objective principle from which, as a supreme practical ground, it must be possible to derive all laws of the will. The practical imperative, therefore, is the following: Act so that you treat humanity, whether in your own person or in that of another, always as an end and never as a means only. Let us now see whether this can be achieved.

To return to our previous examples:

First, . . . he who contemplates suicide will ask himself whether his action can be consistent with the idea of humanity as an end in itself. If, in order to escape from burdensome circumstances, he destroys himself, he uses a person merely as a means to maintain a tolerable condition up to the end of life. Man, however, is not a thing, and thus not something to be used merely as a means; he must always be regarded in all his actions as an end in himself. Therefore, I cannot dispose of man in my own person so as to mutilate, corrupt, or kill him. . . .

Second, . . . he who intends a deceitful promise to others sees immediately that he intends to use another man merely as a means, without the latter containing the end in himself at the same time. For he whom I want to use for my own purposes by means of such a promise cannot possibly assent to my mode of acting against him and cannot contain the end of this action in himself. This conflict against the principle of other men is even clearer if we cite examples of attacks on their freedom and property. For then it is clear that he who transgresses the rights of men intends to make use of the persons of others merely as a means, without considering that, as rational beings, they must always be esteemed at the same time as ends, i.e., only as beings who must be able to contain in themselves the end of the very same action.

Third, . . . it is not sufficient that the action not conflict with humanity in our person as an end in itself; it must also harmonize with it. Now in humanity there are capacities for greater perfection which belong to the end of nature with respect to humanity in our own person; to neglect these might perhaps be consistent with the preservation of humanity as an end in itself but not with the furtherance of that end.

Fourth, ... [h]umanity might indeed exist if no one contributed to the happiness of others, provided he did not intentionally detract from it; but this harmony with humanity as an end in itself is only negative rather than positive if everyone does not also endeavor, so far as he can, to further the ends of others. For the ends of any person, who is an end in himself, must as far as possible also be my end, if that conception of an end in itself is to have its full effect on me.

NOTE

1. A maxim is . . . the principle according to which the subject acts. The law, on the other hand, is the objective principle valid for every rational being, and the principle by which it ought to act, i.e., an imperative.

Utilitarianism

✿✿✿

JOHN STUART MILL

John Stuart Mill (1806–1873) was the leading British philosopher of the nineteenth century. Born in London, he received an intense early education from his father, James Mill, a philosophical and political writer. While pursuing a career in the East India Company, John Stuart Mill published widely in philosophy, political theory, and economics. A strong influence on his life and thought was Harriet Taylor, whom he met in 1831 and married two decades later following the death of her husband. She herself died seven years afterwards. Subsequently, Mill served as a member of Parliament, then retired and spent much of his time in Avignon, France, where his wife was buried.

The best known of his ethical writings is *Utilitarianism*, originally published in three installments in *Fraser's Magazine* of 1861. More than a century later, the work remains enormously influential. As a concise, yet comprehensive, presentation of its subject, it has never been equalled.

A brief discussion of the fundamental principle of utilitarianism is contained in my essay "A Supreme Moral Principle?," found earlier in this section (pp. 265–270).

The creed which accepts as the foundation of morals "utility" or the "greatest happiness principle" holds that actions are right in proportion as they tend to promote happiness; wrong as they tend to produce the reverse of happiness. By happiness is intended pleasure and the absence of pain; by unhappiness, pain and the privation of pleasure. To give a clear view of the moral standard set up by the theory, much more requires to be said; in particular, what things it includes in the ideas of pain and pleasure, and to what extent this is left an open question. But these supplementary explanations do not affect the theory of life on which this theory of morality is grounded—namely, that pleasure and freedom from pain are the only things desirable as ends; and that all desirable things (which are as numerous in the utilitarian as in any other scheme) are desirable either for pleasure inherent in themselves or as means to the promotion of pleasure and the prevention of pain. . . .

From *Utilitarianism* (1863).

It is quite compatible with the principle of utility to recognize the fact that some kinds of pleasure are more desirable and more valuable than others. It would be absurd that, while in estimating all other things quality is considered as well as quantity, the estimation of pleasure should be supposed to depend on quantity alone.

If I am asked what I mean by difference of quality in pleasures, or what makes one pleasure more valuable than another, merely as a pleasure, except its being greater in amount, there is but one possible answer. Of two pleasures, if there be one to which all or almost all who have experience of both give a decided preference, irrespective of any feeling of moral obligation to prefer it, that is the more desirable pleasure. If one of the two is, by those who are competently acquainted with both, placed so far above the other that they prefer it, even though knowing it to be attended with a greater amount of discontent, and would not resign it for any quantity of the other pleasure which their nature is capable of, we are justified in ascribing to the preferred enjoyment a superiority in quality so far outweighing quantity as to render it, in comparison, of small account.

Now it is an unquestionable fact that those who are equally acquainted with and equally capable of appreciating and enjoying both do give a most marked preference to the manner of existence which employs their higher faculties. Few human creatures would consent to be changed into any of the lower animals for a promise of the fullest allowance of a beast's pleasures; no intelligent human being would consent to be a fool, no instructed person would be an ignoramus, no person of feeling and conscience would be selfish and base, even though they should be persuaded that the fool, the dunce, or the rascal is better satisfied with his lot than they are with theirs. They would not resign what they possess more than he for the most complete satisfaction of all the desires which they have in common with him. If they ever fancy they would, it is only in cases of unhappiness so extreme that to escape from it they would exchange their lot for almost any other, however undesirable in their own eyes. A being of higher faculties requires more to make him happy, is capable probably of more acute suffering, and certainly accessible to it at more points, than one of an inferior type; but in spite of these liabilities, he can never really wish to sink into what he feels to be a lower grade of existence. . . .

It is better to be a human being dissatisfied than a pig satisfied; better to be Socrates dissatisfied than a fool satisfied. And if the fool, or the pig, are of a different opinion, it is because they only know their own side of the question. The other party to the comparison knows both sides. . . .

From this verdict of the only competent judges, I apprehend there can be no appeal. On a question which is the best worth having of two pleasures, or which of two modes of existence is the most grateful to the feelings, apart from its moral attributes and from its consequences, the judgment of those who are qualified by knowledge of both, or, if they differ, that of the majority among them, must be admitted as final. And there needs be the less hesitation to accept this judgment respecting the quality of pleasures, since there is no other tribunal to be referred to even on the question of quantity. What means are there of determining which is the acutest of two pains, or the intensest of two pleasurable sensations, except the general suffrage of those who are familiar with both?. . . .

I have dwelt on this point as being a necessary part of a perfectly just conception of utility or happiness considered as the directive rule of human conduct. But it is by no means an indispensable condition to the acceptance of the utilitarian standard; for that standard is not the agent's own greatest happiness, but the greatest amount of happiness altogether; and if it may possibly be doubted whether a noble character is always the happier for its nobleness, there can be no doubt that it makes other people happier, and that the world in general is immensely a gainer by it. Utilitarianism, therefore, could only attain its end by the general cultivation of nobleness of character, even if each individual were only benefited by the nobleness of others, and his own, so far as happiness is concerned, were a sheer deduction from the benefit. But the bare enunciation of such an absurdity as this last renders refutation superfluous.

According to the greatest happiness principle, as above explained, the ultimate end, with reference to and for the sake of which all other things are desirable—whether we are considering our own good or that of other people—is an existence exempt as far as possible from pain, and as rich as possible in enjoyments, both in point of quantity and quality; the test of quality and the rule for measuring it against quantity being the preference felt by those who, in their opportunities of experience, to which must be added their habits of self-consciousness and self-observation, are best furnished with the means of comparison. This, being according to the utilitarian opinion the end of human action, is necessarily also the standard of morality, which may accordingly be defined "the rules and precepts for human conduct," by the observance of which an existence such as has been described might be, to the greatest extent possible, secured to all mankind; and not to them only, but, so far as the nature of things admits, to the whole sentient creation. . . .

I must again repeat what the assailants of utilitarianism seldom have the justice to acknowledge, that the happiness which forms the utilitarian standard of what is right in conduct is not the agent's own happiness but that of all concerned. As between his own happiness and that of others, utilitarianism requires him to be as strictly impartial as a disinterested and benevolent spectator. In the golden rule of Jesus of Nazareth, we read the complete spirit of the ethics of utility. "To do as you would be done by," and "to love your neighbor as yourself," constitute the ideal perfection of utilitarian morality. As the means of making the nearest approach to this ideal, utility would enjoin, first, that laws and social arrangements should place the happiness or (as, speaking practically, it may be called) the interest of every individual as nearly as possible in harmony with the interest of the whole; and, secondly, that education and opinion, which have so vast a power over human character, should so use that power as to establish in the mind of every individual an indissoluble association between his own happiness and the good of the whole, especially between his own happiness and the practice of such modes of conduct, negative and positive, as regard for the universal happiness prescribes; so that not only he may be unable to conceive the possibility of happiness to himself, consistently with conduct opposed to the general good, but also that a direct impulse to promote the general good may be in every individual one of the habitual motives of action, and the sentiments connected therewith may fill a large and prominent place in every human being's sentient existence. If the impugners of the utilitarian morality represented it to their own minds in this its true character, I know not what recommendation possessed by any other morality they could possibly affirm to be wanting to it; what more beautiful or more exalted developments of human nature any other ethical system can be supposed to foster, or what springs of action, not accessible to the utilitarian, such systems rely on for giving effect to their mandates.

The objectors to utilitarianism cannot always be charged with representing it in a discreditable light. On the contrary, those among them who entertain anything like a just idea of its disinterested character sometimes find fault with its standard as being too high for humanity. They say it is exacting too much to require that people shall always act from the inducement of promoting the general interests of society. But this is to mistake the very meaning of a standard of morals and confound the rule of action with the motive of it. It is the business of ethics to tell us what are our duties, or by what test we may know them; but no system of ethics requires that the sole motive of all we do shall be a feeling of duty; on the contrary, ninety-nine hundredths of all our actions are done from other motives, and rightly so done if the rule of duty does not condemn them. It is the more unjust to utilitarianism that this particular misapprehension should be made a ground of objection to it, inasmuch as utilitarian moralists have gone beyond almost all others in affirming that the motive has nothing to do with the morality of the action, though much with the worth of the agent. He who saves a fellow creature from drowning does what is morally right, whether his motive be duty or the hope of being paid for his trouble; he who betrays the friend that trusts him is guilty of a crime, even if his object be to serve another friend to whom he is under greater obligations. But to speak only of actions done from the motive of duty, and in direct obedience to principle: it is a misapprehension of the utilitarian mode of thought to conceive it as implying that people should fix their minds upon so wide a generality as the world, or society at large. The great majority of good actions are intended not for the benefit of the world, but for that of individuals, of which the good of the world is made up; and the thoughts of the most virtuous man need not on these occasions travel beyond the particular persons concerned, except so far as is necessary to assure himself that in benefiting them he is not violating the rights, that is,

the legitimate and authorized expectations, of anyone else. The multiplica-
tion of happiness is, according to the utilitarian ethics, the object of virtue:
the occasions on which any person (except one in a thousand) has it in his
power to do this on an extended scale—in other words, to be a public benefactor—are but exceptional; and on these occasions alone is he called on to
consider public utility; in every other case, private utility, the interest or happiness of some few persons, is all he has to attend to. Those alone the influence of whose actions extends to society in general need concern themselves
habitually about so large an object. In the case of abstinences indeed—of
things which people forbear to do from moral considerations, though the
consequences in the particular case might be beneficial—it would be unworthy of an intelligent agent not to be consciously aware that the action is of a
class which, if practiced generally, would be generally injurious, and that
this is the ground of the obligation to abstain from it. The amount of regard
for the public interest implied in this recognition is no greater than is demanded by every system of morals, for they all enjoin to abstain from whatever is manifestly pernicious to society. . . .

Again, utility is often summarily stigmatized as an immoral doctrine by
giving it the name of "expediency," and taking advantage of the popular use
of that term to contrast it with principle. But the expedient, in the sense in
which it is opposed to the right, generally means that which is expedient for
the particular interest of the agent himself; as when a minister sacrifices the
interests of his country to keep himself in place. When it means anything better than this, it means that which is expedient for some immediate object,
some temporary purpose, but which violates a rule whose observance is expedient in a much higher degree. The expedient, in this sense, instead of being the same thing with the useful, is a branch of the hurtful. Thus it would
often be expedient, for the purpose of getting over some momentary embarrassment, or attaining some object immediately useful to ourselves or others,
to tell a lie. But inasmuch as the cultivation in ourselves of a sensitive feeling
on the subject of veracity is one of the most useful, and the enfeeblement of
that feeling one of the most hurtful, things to which our conduct can be instrumental; and inasmuch as any, even unintentional, deviation from truth
does that much toward weakening the trustworthiness of human assertion,
which is not only the principal support of all present social well-being, but
the insufficiency of which does more than any one thing that can be named
to keep back civilization, virtue, everything on which human happiness on
the largest scale depends—we feel that the violation, for a present advantage, of a rule of such transcendent expediency is not expedient, and that he
who, for the sake of convenience to himself or to some other individual, does
what depends on him to deprive mankind of the good, and inflict upon them
the evil, involved in the greater or less reliance which they can place in each
other's word, acts the part of one of their worst enemies. Yet that even this
rule, sacred as it is, admits of possible exceptions is acknowledged by all
moralists; the chief of which is when the withholding of some fact (as of in-

formation from a malefactor, or of bad news from a person dangerously ill) would save an individual (especially an individual other than oneself) from great and unmerited evil, and when the withholding can only be effected by denial. But in order that the exception may not extend itself beyond the need, and may have the least possible effect in weakening reliance on veracity, it ought to be recognized and, if possible, its limits defined; and, if the principle of utility is good for anything, it must be good for weighing these conflicting utilities against one another and marking out the region within which one or the other preponderates.

PART 6

SOCIETY

Democracy

✿✿

JOHN DEWEY

Social and political philosophy focuses on ethical issues related to the structure of society and the practices of government. One long-standing area of inquiry within the field is the nature of democracy and its relative advantages or disadvantages compared to alternative systems.

Our next selection is devoted to this subject. Its author is John Dewey (1859–1952), the foremost American philosopher of the first half of the twentieth century. Born and bred in Burlington, Vermont, his life and thought reflected the commitment to social equality he found exemplified in the life of his boyhood New England community.

Dewey made contributions to virtually every area of philosophical inquiry, and his collected works, now available in a standard edition, occupy thirty-seven volumes. He spent most of his academic career as Professor of Philosophy at Columbia University and served as President of both the American Psychological Association and the American Philosophical Association. In celebration of his eightieth birthday, the American Philosophical Association bestowed upon him for the duration of his life the title of Honorary President.

Reprinted here is the text of a talk he delivered in 1937 to a meeting of educational administrators. It offers, in brief, his account of democracy.

[D]emocracy is much broader than a special political form, a method of conducting government, of making laws and carrying on governmental administration by means of popular suffrage and elected officers. It is that of course. But it is something broader and deeper than that.

The political and governmental phase of democracy is a means, the best means so far found, for realizing ends that lie in the wide domain of human relationships and the development of human personality. It is, as we often say, though perhaps without appreciating all that is involved in the saying, a way of life, social and individual. The key-note of democracy as a way of life may be expressed, it seems to me, as the necessity for the participation of every mature human being in formation of the values that regulate the living of men together—which is necessary from the standpoint of both the general social welfare and the full development of human beings as individuals.

Universal suffrage, recurring elections, responsibility of those who are in political power to the voters, and the other factors of democratic government are means that have been found expedient for realizing democracy as the truly human way of living. They are not a final end and a final value. They are to be judged on the basis of their contribution to an end. It is a form of idolatry to erect means into the end which they serve. Democratic political forms are simply the best means that human wit has devised up to a special time in history. But they rest back upon the idea that no man or limited set of men is wise enough or good enough to rule others without their consent; the positive meaning of this statement is that all those who are affected by social institutions must have a share in producing and managing them. The two facts that each one is influenced in what he does and enjoys and in what he becomes by the institutions under which he lives, and that therefore he shall have, in a democracy, a voice in shaping them, are the passive and active sides of the same fact.

The development of political democracy came about through substitution of the method of mutual consultation and voluntary agreement for the method of subordination of the many to the few enforced from above. Social arrangements which involve fixed subordination are maintained by coercion. The coercion need not be physical. There have existed, for short periods, benevolent despotisms. But coercion of some sort there has been; perhaps economic, certainly psychological and moral. The very fact of exclusion from participation is a subtle form of suppression. It gives individuals no opportunity to reflect and decide upon what is good for them. Others who are supposed to be wiser and who in any case have more power decide the question for them and also decide the methods and means by which subjects may arrive at the enjoyment of what in good for them. This form of coercion and suppression is more subtle and more effective than is overt intimidation and restraint. When it is habitual and embodied in social institutions, it seems the normal and natural state of affairs. The mass usually become unaware that they have a claim to a development of their own powers. Their experience is so restricted that they are not conscious of restriction. It is part of the democratic conception that they as individuals are not the only sufferers, but that the whole social body is deprived of the potential resources that should be at its service. The individuals of the submerged mass may not be very wise. But there is one thing they are wiser about than anybody else can be, and that is where the shoe pinches, the troubles they suffer from.

The foundation of democracy is faith in the capacities of human nature; faith in human intelligence, and in the power of pooled and cooperative experience. It is not belief that these things are complete but that if given a show they will grow and be able to generate progressively the knowledge and wisdom needed to guide collective action. Every autocratic and authoritarian scheme of social action rests on a belief that the needed intelligence is confined to a superior few who because of inherent natural gifts are endowed with the ability and the right to control the conduct of others; laying down principles and rules and directing the ways in which they are carried out. It would be foolish to deny that much can be said for this point of view. It is that which controlled human relations in social groups for much the greater part of human history. The democratic faith has emerged very, very recently in the history of mankind. Even where democracies now exist, men's minds and feelings are still permeated with ideas about leadership imposed from above, ideas that developed in the long early history of mankind. After democratic political institutions were nominally established, beliefs and ways of looking at life and of acting that originated when men and women were externally controlled and subjected to arbitrary power, persisted in the family, the church, business and the school, and experience shows that as long as they persist there, political democracy is not secure.

Belief in equality is an element of the democratic credo. It is not, however, belief in equality of natural endowments. Those who proclaimed the idea of equality did not suppose they were enunciating a psychological doctrine, but a legal and political one. All individuals are entitled to equality of treatment by law and in its administration. Each one is affected equally in quality if not in quantity by the institutions under which he lives and has an equal right to express his judgment, although the weight of his judgment may not be equal in amount when it enters into the pooled result to that of others. In short, each one is equally an individual and entitled to equal opportunity of development of his own capacities, be they large or small in range. Moreover, each has needs of his own, as significant to him as those of others are to them. The very fact of natural and psychological inequality is all the more reason for establishment by law of equality of opportunity, since otherwise the former becomes a means of oppression of the less gifted.

While what we call intelligence be distributed in unequal amounts, it is the democratic faith that it is sufficiently general so that each individual has something to contribute whose value can be assessed only as it enters into the final pooled intelligence constituted by the contributions of all. Every authoritarian scheme, on the contrary assumes that its value may be assessed by some *prior* principle, if not of family and birth or race and color or possession of material wealth, then by the position and rank a person occupies in the existing social scheme. The democratic faith in equality is the faith that each individual shall have the chance and opportunity to contribute whatever he is capable of contributing, and that the value of his contribution be decided by its place and function in the organized total of similar contributions—not on the basis of prior status of any kind whatever.

I have emphasized in what precedes the importance of the effective release of intelligence in connection with personal experience in the democratic way of living. I have done so purposely because democracy is so often and so naturally associated in our minds with freedom of *action*, forgetting the importance of freed intelligence which is necessary to direct and to warrant freedom of action. Unless freedom of individual action has intelligence and informed conviction back of it, its manifestation is almost sure to result in confusion and disorder. The democratic idea of freedom is not the right of each individual to *do* as he pleases, even if it be qualified by adding "provided he does not interfere with the same freedom on the part of others." While the idea is not always, not often enough, expressed in words, the basic freedom is that of freedom of *mind* and of whatever degree of freedom of action and experience is necessary to produce freedom of intelligence. The modes of freedom guaranteed in the Bill of Rights are all of this nature: Freedom of belief and conscience, of expression of opinion, of assembly for discussion and conference, of the press as an organ of communication. They are guaranteed because without them individuals are not free to develop and society is deprived of what they might contribute. . . .

There is some kind of government, of control, wherever affairs that concern a number of persons who act together are engaged in. It is a superficial view that holds government is located in Washington and Albany. There is government in the family, in business, in the church, in every social group. There are regulations, due to custom if not to enactment, that settle how individuals in a group act in connection with one another.

It is a disputed question of theory and practice just how far a democratic political government should go in control of the conditions of action within special groups. At the present time, for example, there are those who think the federal and state governments leave too much freedom of independent action to industrial and financial groups and there are others who think the Government is going altogether too far at the present time. I do not need to discuss this phase of the problem much less to try to settle it. But it must be pointed out that if the methods of regulation and administration in vogue in the conduct of secondary social groups are non-democratic, whether directly or indirectly or both, there is bound to be an unfavorable reaction back into the habits of feeling, thought and action of citizenship in the broadest sense of that word. The way in which any organized social interest is controlled necessarily plays an important part in forming the dispositions and tastes, the attitudes, interests, purposes and desires, of those engaged in carrying on the activities of the group. For illustration, I do not need to do more than point to the moral, emotional, and intellectual effect upon both employers and laborers of the existing industrial system. Just what the effects specifically are is a matter about which we know very little. But I suppose that every one who reflects upon the subject admits that it is impossible that the ways in which activities are carried on for the greater part of the waking hours of the day; and the way in which the shares of individuals are involved in the management of affairs in such a matter as gaining a livelihood and attaining material and social security, can only be a highly important factor in shaping personal dispositions; in short, forming character and intelligence.

In the broad and final sense all institutions are educational in the sense that they operate to form the attitudes, dispositions, abilities, and disabilities that constitute a concrete personality. The principle applies with special force to the school. For it is the main business of the family and the school to influence directly the formation and growth of attitudes and dispositions, emotional, intellectual and moral. Whether this educative process is carried on in a predominantly democratic or non-democratic way becomes therefore a question of transcendent importance not only for education itself but for its final effect upon all the interests and activities of a society that is committed to the democratic way of life. . . .

[T]here are certain corollaries which clarify the meaning of the issue. Absence of participation tends to produce lack of interest and concern on the part of those shut out. The result is a corresponding lack of effective responsibility. Automatically and unconsciously, if not consciously, the feeling develops, "this is none of our affair; it is the business of those at the top; let that particular set of Georges do what needs to be done." The countries in which autocratic government prevails are just those in which there is least public spirit and the greatest indifference to matters of general as distinct from personal concern. . . . Where there is little power, there is correspondingly little sense of positive responsibility—It is enough to do what one is told to do sufficiently well to escape flagrant unfavorable notice. About larger matters a spirit of passivity is engendered. . . .

[I]t still is also true that incapacity to assume the responsibilities involved in having a voice in shaping policies is bred and increased by conditions in which that responsibility is denied. I suppose there has never been an autocrat, big or little, who did not justify his conduct on the ground of the unfitness of his subjects to take part in government. . . . But, as was said earlier, habitual exclusion has the effect of reducing a sense of responsibility for what is done and its consequences. What the argument for democracy implies is that the best way to produce initiative and constructive power is to exercise it. Power, as well as interest, comes by use and practice. . . .

The fundamental beliefs and practices of democracy are now challenged as they never have been before. In some nations they are more than challenged. They are ruthlessly and systematically destroyed. Everywhere there are waves of criticism and doubt as to whether democracy can meet pressing problems of order and security. The causes for the destruction of political democracy in countries where it was nominally established are complex. But of one thing I think we may be sure. Wherever it has fallen it was too exclusively political in nature. It had not become part of the bone and blood of the people in daily conduct of its life. Democratic forms were limited to Parliament, elections, and combats between parties. What is happening proves conclusively, I think, that unless democratic habits of thought and action are part of the fiber of a people, political democracy is insecure. It cannot stand in isolation. It must be buttressed by the presence of democratic methods in all social relationships. The relations that exist in educational institutions are second only in importance in this respect to those which exist in industry and business, perhaps not even to them. . . .

I can think of nothing so important in this country at present as a re-thinking of the whole problem of democracy and its implications. Neither the rethinking nor the action it should produce can be brought into being in a day or year. The democratic idea itself demands that the thinking and activity proceed cooperatively.

Political Action:
The Problem of Dirty Hands

❖❖

MICHAEL WALZER

> Michael Walzer is Professor of Political Science at the Institute for Advanced Studies in Princeton, New Jersey. In the next selection he considers a situation likely to be faced by those elected to political office. In order to accomplish their goals, they may be forced to compromise their ideals. Assuming they do so, will they feel guilty? In other words, will they have dirty hands?
>
> Walzer's view is that politicians should compromise and then feel guilty about having done so. As he sees it, a politician who claims falsely to have clean hands reveals moral insensitivity; one who actually has clean hands displays political impracticality. So we should want politicians with dirty hands, that is, those who have moral scruples but can overcome them.
>
> Some readers will accept Walzer's conclusion. Those who find it overly cynical should try to locate any misstep in his argument.

Let me begin . . . with a piece of conventional wisdom to the effect that politicians are a good deal worse, morally worse, than the rest of us (it is the wisdom of the rest of us). Without either endorsing it or pretending to disbelieve it, I am going to expound this convention. . . .

From Walzer, Michael, "Political Action," *Philosophy and Public Affairs*, 2. Copyright © 1973 by Princeton University Press. Reprinted by permission of Princeton University Press.

Why is the politician singled out? Isn't he like the other entrepreneurs in an open society, who hustle, lie, intrigue, wear masks, smile, and are villains? He is not, no doubt for many reasons, three of which I need to consider. First of all, the politician claims to play a different part than other entrepreneurs. He doesn't merely cater to our interests; he acts on our behalf, even in our name. He has purposes in mind, causes and projects that require the support and redound to the benefit, not of each of us individually, but of all of us together. He hustles, lies, and intrigues *for us*—or so he claims. Perhaps he is right, or at least sincere, but we suspect that he acts for himself also. Indeed, he cannot serve us without serving himself, for success brings him power and glory, the greatest rewards that men can win from their fellows. The competition for these two is fierce; the risks are often great, but the temptations are greater. We imagine ourselves succumbing. Why should our representatives act differently? Even if they would like to act differently, they probably cannot: for other men are all too ready to hustle and lie for power and glory, and it is the others who set the terms of the competition. Hustling and lying are necessary because power and glory are so desirable—that is, so widely desired. And so the men who act for us and in our name are necessarily hustlers and liars.

Politicians are also thought to be worse than the rest of us because they rule over us, and the pleasures of ruling are much greater than the pleasures of being ruled. The successful politician becomes the visible architect of our restraint. He taxes us, licenses us, forbids and permits us, directs us to this or that distant goal—all for our greater good. Moreover, he takes chances for our greater good that put us, or some of us, in danger. Sometimes he puts himself in danger too, but politics, after all, is his adventure. It is not always ours. There are undoubtedly times when it is good or necessary to direct the affairs of other people and to put them in danger. But we are a little frightened of the man who seeks, ordinarily and every day, the power to do so. And the fear is reasonable enough. The politician has, or pretends to have, a kind of confidence in his own judgment that the rest of us know to be presumptuous in any man.

The presumption is especially great because the victorious politician uses violence and the threat of violence—not only against foreign nations in our defense but also against us, and again ostensibly for our greater good. This . . . point . . . has not, so far as I can tell, played an overt or obvious part in the development of the convention I am examining. The stock figure is the lying, not the murderous, politician—though the murderer lurks in the background, appearing most often in the form of the revolutionary or terrorist, very rarely as an ordinary magistrate or official. Nevertheless, the sheer weight of official violence in human history does suggest the kind of power to which politicians aspire, the kind of power they want to wield, and it may point to the roots of our half-conscious dislike and unease. The men who act for us and in our name are often killers, or seem to become killers too quickly and too easily.

Knowing all this or most of it, good and decent people still enter political life, aiming at some specific reform or seeking a general reformation. . . .
They can do no good themselves unless . . . they are willing and able to use
the necessary means. So we are suspicious even of the best of winners. It is
not a sign of our perversity if we think them only more clever than the rest.
They have not won, after all, because they were good, or not only because of
that, but also because they were not good. No one succeeds in politics without getting his hands dirty. This is conventional wisdom again, and again I
don't mean to insist that it is true without qualification. I repeat it only to disclose the moral dilemma inherent in the convention. For sometimes it is right
to try to succeed, and then it must also be right to get one's hands dirty. But
one's hands get dirty from doing what it is wrong to do. And how can it be
wrong to do what is right? Or, how can we get our hands dirty by doing
what we ought to do?

It will be best to turn quickly to some examples. I have chosen two, one
relating to the struggle for power and one to its exercise. I should stress that
in both these cases the men who face the dilemma of dirty hands have in an
important sense chosen to do so; the cases tell us nothing about what it
would be like, so to speak, to fall into the dilemma; nor shall I say anything
about that here. Politicians often argue that they have no right to keep their
hands clean, and that may well be true of them, but it is not so clearly true of
the rest of us. Probably we do have a right to avoid, if we possibly can, those
positions in which we might be forced to do terrible things. This might be regarded as the moral equivalent of our legal right not to incriminate ourselves. Good men will be in no hurry to surrender it, though there are reasons for doing so sometimes, and among these are or might be the reasons
good men have for entering politics. But let us imagine a politician who does
not agree to that: he wants to do good only by doing good, or at least he is
certain that he can stop short of the most corrupting and brutal uses of political power. Very quickly that certainty is tested. What do we think of him
then?

He wants to win the election, someone says, but he doesn't want to get
his hands dirty. This is meant as a disparagement, even though it also means
that the man being criticized is the sort of man who will not lie, cheat, bargain behind the backs of his supporters, shout absurdities at public meetings, or manipulate other men and women. Assuming that this particular
election ought to be won, it is clear, I think, that the disparagement is justified. If the candidate didn't want to get his hands dirty, he should have
stayed at home; if he can't stand the heat, he should get out of the kitchen,
and so on. His decision to run was a commitment (to all of us who think the
election important) to try to win, that is, to do within rational limits whatever is necessary to win. But the candidate is a moral man. He has principles
and a history of adherence to those principles. That is why we are supporting him. Perhaps when he refuses to dirty his hands, he is simply insisting
on being the sort of man he is. And isn't that the sort of man we want?

Let us look more closely at this case. In order to win the election the candidate must make a deal with a dishonest ward boss, involving the granting of contracts for school construction over the next four years. Should he make the deal? Well, at least he shouldn't be surprised by the offer, most of us would probably say (a conventional piece of sarcasm). And he should accept it or not, depending on exactly what is at stake in the election. But that is not the candidate's view. He is extremely reluctant even to consider the deal, puts off his aides when they remind him of it, refuses to calculate its possible effects upon the campaign. Now, if he is acting this way because the very thought of bargaining with that particular ward boss makes him feel unclean, his reluctance isn't very interesting. His feelings by themselves are not important. But he may also have reasons for his reluctance. He may know, for example, that some of his supporters support him precisely because they believe he is a good man, and this means to them a man who won't make such deals. Or he may doubt his own motives for considering the deal, wondering whether it is the political campaign or his own candidacy that makes the bargain at all tempting. Or he may believe that if he makes deals of this sort now he may not be able later on to achieve those ends that make the campaign worthwhile, and he may not feel entitled to take such risks with a future that is not only his own future. Or he may simply think that the deal is dishonest and therefore wrong, corrupting not only himself but all those human relations in which he is involved.

Because he has scruples of this sort, we know him to be a good man. But we view the campaign in a certain light, estimate its importance in a certain way, and hope that he will overcome his scruples and make the deal. It is important to stress that we don't want just *anyone* to make the deal; we want *him* to make it, precisely because he has scruples about it. We know he is doing right when he makes the deal because he knows he is doing wrong. I don't mean merely that he will feel badly or even very badly after he makes the deal. If he is the good man I am imagining him to be, he will feel guilty; that is, he will believe himself to be guilty. That is what it means to have dirty hands.

All this may become clearer if we look at a more dramatic example, for we are, perhaps, a little blasé about political deals and disinclined to worry much about the man who makes one. So consider a politician who has seized upon a national crisis—a prolonged colonial war—to reach for power. He and his friends win office pledged to decolonization and peace; they are honestly committed to both, though not without some sense of the advantages of the commitment. In any case, they have no responsibility for the war; they have steadfastly opposed it. Immediately, the politician goes off to the colonial capital to open negotiations with the rebels. But the capital is in the grip of a terrorist campaign, and the first decision the new leader faces is this: he is asked to authorize the torture of a captured rebel leader who knows or probably knows the location of a number of bombs hidden in apartment buildings around the city, set to go off within the next twenty-four hours. He orders the man tortured, convinced that he must do so for the sake of the people who might otherwise die in the explosions—even though he believes that torture is wrong, indeed abominable, not just sometimes, but always.[1] He had expressed this belief often and angrily during his own campaign; the rest of us took it as a sign of his goodness. How should we regard him now? (How should he regard himself?)

Once again, it does not seem enough to say that he should feel very badly. . . . Surely we have a right to expect more than melancholy from him now. When he ordered the prisoner tortured, he committed a moral crime and he accepted a moral burden. Now he is a guilty man. His willingness to acknowledge and bear (and perhaps to repent and do penance for) his guilt is evidence, and it is the only evidence he can offer us, both that he is not too good for politics and that he is good enough. Here is the moral politician: it is by his dirty hands that we know him. If he were a moral man and nothing else, his hands would not be dirty; if he were a politician and nothing else, he would pretend that they were clean.

NOTE

1. I leave aside the question of whether the prisoner is himself responsible for the terrorist campaign. Perhaps he opposed it in meetings of the rebel organization. In any case, whether he deserves to be punished or not, he does not deserve to be tortured.

Privacy

❖❖

CHARLES FRIED

> We all value our privacy. We resent the efforts of those organizations or individuals who pry into our lives and seek to know more than is appropriate about ourselves and our activities. But why is privacy so important to us?
>
> Our next author addresses this question. He is Charles Fried, who served as associate justice of the Massachusetts Supreme Judi-

Reprinted by permission of the publisher from *An Anatomy of Values*, by Charles Fried, Cambridge, Mass.: Harvard University Press. Copyright © 1970 by the President and Fellows of Harvard College.

cial Court, and is professor of law at Harvard University. The subtle answers he gives have influenced many subsequent writers on this increasingly important topic.

It is my thesis that privacy is . . . necessarily related to ends and relations of the most fundamental sort: respect, love, friendship, and trust. Privacy is not merely a good technique for furthering these fundamental relations; rather without privacy they are simply inconceivable. They require a context of privacy or the possibility of privacy for their existence. To make clear the necessity of privacy as a context for respect, love, friendship, and trust is to bring out also why a threat to privacy seems to threaten our very integrity as persons. To respect, love, trust, or feel affection for others and to regard ourselves as the objects of love, trust, and affection is at the heart of our notion of ourselves as persons among persons, and privacy is the necessary atmosphere for these attitudes and actions, as oxygen is for combustion.

Before going further, it is necessary to sharpen the intuitive concept of privacy. As a first approximation, privacy seems to be related to secrecy, to limiting the knowledge of others about oneself. This notion must be refined. It is not true, for instance, that the less that is known about us the more privacy we have. Privacy is not simply an absence of information about us in the minds of others; rather it is the control we have over information about ourselves.

To refer, for instance, to the privacy of a lonely man on a desert island would be to engage in irony. The person who enjoys privacy is able to grant or deny access to others. Even when one considers private situations into which outsiders could not possibly intrude, the context implies some alternative situation where the intrusion is possible. A man's house may be private, for instance, but that is because it is constructed—with doors, windows, window shades—to allow it to be made private, and because the law entitles a man to exclude unauthorized persons. And even the remote vacation hideaway is private just because one resorts to it in order—in part—to preclude access to unauthorized persons.

Privacy, thus, is control over knowledge about oneself. But it is not simply control over the quality of information abroad; there are modulations in the quality of the knowledge as well. We may not mind that a person knows a general fact about us, and yet feel our privacy invaded if he knows the details. For instance, a casual acquaintance may comfortably know that I am sick, but it would violate my privacy if he knew the nature of the illness. Or a good friend may know what particular illness I am suffering from, but it would violate my privacy if he were actually to witness my suffering from some symptom which he must know is associated with the disease.

Privacy in its dimension of control over information is an aspect of personal liberty. Acts derive their meaning partly from their social context—

from how many people know about them and what the knowledge consists of. For instance, a reproof administered out of the hearing of third persons may be an act of kindness, but if administered in public it becomes cruel and degrading. Thus if a man cannot be sure that third persons are not listening—if his privacy is not secure—he is denied the freedom to do what he regards as an act of kindness.

Besides giving us control over the context in which we act, privacy has a more defensive role in protecting our liberty. We may wish to do or say things not forbidden by the restraints of morality but nevertheless unpopular or unconventional. If we thought that our every word and deed were public, fear of disapproval or more tangible retaliation might keep us from doing or saying things which we would do or say if we could be sure of keeping them to ourselves or within a circle of those who we know approve or tolerate our tastes.

These reasons support the familiar arguments for the right of privacy. Yet they leave privacy with less security than we feel it deserves; they leave it vulnerable to arguments that a particular invasion of privacy will secure to us other kinds of liberty which more than compensate for what is lost. To present privacy, then, only as an aspect of or an aid to general liberty is to miss some of its most significant differentiating features. The value of control over information about ourselves is more nearly absolute than that. For privacy is the necessary context for relationships which we would hardly be human if we had to do without—the relationships of love, friendship, and trust.

Love and friendship . . . involve the initial respect for the rights of others which morality requires of everyone. They further involve the voluntary and spontaneous relinquishment of something between friend and friend, lover and lover. The title to information about oneself conferred by privacy provides the necessary something. To be friends or lovers persons must be intimate to some degree with each other. Intimacy is the sharing of information about one's actions, beliefs or emotions which one does not share with all, and which one has the right not to share with anyone. By conferring this right, privacy creates the moral capital which we spend in friendship and love.

The entitlements of privacy are not just one kind of entitlement among many which a lover can surrender to show his love. Love or friendship can be partially expressed by the gift of other rights—gifts of property or of service. But these gifts, without the intimacy of shared private information, cannot alone constitute love or friendship. The man who is generous with his possessions, but not with himself, can hardly be a friend, nor—and this more clearly shows the necessity of privacy for love—can the man who, voluntarily or involuntarily, shares everything about himself with the world indiscriminately.

Privacy is essential to friendship and love in another respect besides providing what I call moral capital. The rights of privacy are among those basic entitlements which men must respect in each other; and mutual respect is the minimal precondition for love and friendship.

Privacy also provides the means for modulating those degrees of friendship which fall short of love. Few persons have the emotional resources to be on the most intimate terms with all their friends. Privacy grants the control over information which enables us to maintain degrees of intimacy. Thus even between friends the restraints of privacy apply; since friendship implies a voluntary relinquishment of private information, one will not wish to know what his friend or lover has not chosen to share with him. The rupture of this balance by a third party—the state perhaps—thrusting information concerning one friend upon another might well destroy the limited degree of intimacy the two have achieved.

Finally, there is a more extreme case where privacy serves not to save something which will be "spent" on a friend, but to keep it from all the world. There are thoughts whose expression to a friend or lover would be a hostile act, though the entertaining of them is completely consistent with friendship or love. That is because these thoughts, prior to being given expression, are mere unratified possibilities for action. Only by expressing them do we adopt them, choose them as part of ourselves, and draw them into our relations with others. Now a sophisticated person knows that a friend or lover must entertain thoughts which if expressed would be wounding, and so—it might be objected—why should he attach any significance to their actual expression? In a sense the objection is well taken. If it were possible to give expression to these thoughts and yet make clear to ourselves and to others that we do not thereby ratify them, adopt them as our own, it might be that in some relations, at least, another could be allowed complete access to us. But this possibility is not a very likely one. Thus the most complete form of privacy is perhaps also the most basic, since it is necessary not only to our freedom to define our relations with others but also to our freedom to define ourselves. To be deprived of this control over what we do and who we are is the ultimate assault on liberty, personality, and self-respect.

Trust is the attitude of expectation that another will behave according to the constraints of morality. Insofar as trust is only instrumental to the more convenient conduct of life, its purposes could be as well served by cheap and efficient surveillance of the person upon whom one depends. One does not trust machines or animals; one takes the fullest economically feasible precautions against their going wrong. Often, however, we choose to trust people where it would be safer to take precautions—to watch them or require a bond from them. This must be because . . . we value the relation of trust for its own sake. It is one of those relations, less inspiring than love or friendship but also less tiring, through which we express our humanity.

There can be no trust where there is no possibility of error. More specifically, man cannot know that he is trusted unless he has a right to act without constant surveillance so that he knows he can betray the trust. Privacy confers that essential right. And since . . . trust in its fullest sense is reciprocal, the man who cannot be trusted cannot himself trust or learn to trust. Without privacy and the possibility of error which it protects that aspect of his humanity is denied to him.

The Death Penalty

❖❖

BURTON LEISER

> Is capital punishment ever justified? Our next selection offers an answer to this question that many find persuasive. The author, Burton Leiser, who is Professor of Philosophy at Pace University, maintains that the death penalty is sometimes fitting, but only in response to the most heinous crimes and after all the elements of a fair legal proceeding have been observed. Whether you agree, contrast his views with those offered in the selection that follows this one.

The death penalty has historically been employed for such diverse offenses as murder, espionage, treason, kidnapping, rape, arson, robbery, burglary, and theft. Except for the most serious crimes, it is now agreed that lesser penalties are sufficient. . . . Only the most heinous offenses against the state and against individual persons seem to deserve the ultimate penalty. . . .

Perpetrators of such crimes as genocide (the deliberate extermination of entire peoples, racial, religious, or ethnic groups) deserve a penalty no less severe than death on purely retributive grounds. Those who perpetrate major war crimes, crimes against peace, or crimes against humanity, deliberately and without justification plunging nations into violent conflicts that entail widespread bloodshed or causing needless suffering on a vast scale, deserve no less.

Because of the reckless manner in which they endanger the lives of innocent citizens and their clear intention to take human lives on a massive scale in order to achieve their ends, terrorists should be subject to the death penalty, on retributive grounds, on the ground that it serves as the ultimate form

Liberty, Justice and Morals, by Leiser, © 1979. Reprinted by permission of Prentice-Hall, Inc., Upper Saddle River, NJ.

of incapacitation—guaranteeing that terrorists who are executed will never again deprive an innocent person of his life, and on the ground that no other penalty can reasonably be expected to serve as a deterrent to persons whose colleagues are likely to engage in further acts of terrorism in order to achieve their release from prison.

Major crimes against the peace, security, and integrity of the state constitute particularly heinous offenses, for they shake the very foundations upon which civilization rests and endanger the lives, the liberties, and the fundamental rights of all the people who depend upon the state for protection. Treason, espionage, and sabotage, particularly during times of great danger (as in time of war), ought to be punishable by death.

Murder for personal gain and murder committed in the course of the commission of a felony that is being committed for personal gain or out of a reckless disregard for the lives or fundamental rights and interests of potential victims ought to be punishable by death.

Murder committed by a person who is serving a life sentence ought to be punishable by death, both because of the enormity of the crime itself and because no other penalty is likely to deter such crimes.

Needless to say, if a person is so deranged as to be legally insane, neither death nor any other punishment is appropriate. The very concept of punishment entails the assumption that the person being punished had the capacity, at the time he committed the act for which he is being punished, to act or refrain from acting, and of behaving at least in a minimally rational way. A person who commits a homicide while insane has not, strictly speaking, committed a murder or, for that matter, any crime at all; for no crime *can* (logically or legally) be committed without *mens rea,* the *intention* or *will* to carry it out.

The mere fact, however, that a person has carried out a homicide in a particularly vile, wanton, or malicious way is not sufficient to establish that that person is insane, for such a fact is consistent with many other explanations (e.g., that the perpetrator, making shrewd and calculated judgments as to what would most likely enable him to succeed without being caught, concluded that it would be in his own best interests if the crime *appeared* to be the act of an insane person who happened to be in the neighborhood).

Bearing these caveats in mind, we may conclude that any murder (as opposed to a mere homicide) committed in a particularly vile, wanton, or malicious way ought to be punishable by death.

One of the principal justifications for the state's existence is the protection it offers those who come under its jurisdiction against violations of their fundamental rights. Those who are entrusted with the responsibility for carrying out the duties of administering the state's functions, enforcing its laws, and seeing that justice is done carry an onerous burden and are particularly likely to become the targets of hostile, malicious, or rebellious individuals or groups. Their special vulnerability entitles them to special protection. Hence, any person guilty of murdering a policeman, a fireman, a judge, a governor, a president, a lawmaker, or any other person holding a comparable position while that person is carrying out his official duties or because of the office he holds has struck at the very heart of government and thus at the foundations upon which the state and civilized society depend. The gravity of such a crime warrants imposition of the death penalty.

From the fact that some persons who bring about the deaths of fellow humans do so under conditions that just and humane men would consider sufficient to justify either complete exculpation or penalties less than death, it does not follow that all of them do. If guilt is clearly established beyond a reasonable doubt under circumstances that guarantee a reasonable opportunity for the defendant to confront his accusers, to cross-examine witnesses, to present his case with the assistance of professional counsel, and in general to enjoy the benefits of due process of law; if in addition he has been given the protection of laws that prevent the use of torture to extract confessions and is provided immunity against self-incrimination; if those who are authorized to pass judgment find there were no excusing or mitigating circumstances; if he is found to have committed a wanton, brutal, callous murder or some other crime that is subversive of the very foundations of an ordered society; and if, finally, the representatives of the people, exercising the people's sovereign authority have prescribed death as the penalty for that crime; then the judge and jury are fully justified in imposing that penalty, and the proper authorities are justified in carrying it out.

Capital Punishment

❖❖❖

Hugo Adam Bedau

Hugo Adam Bedau is Professor of Philosophy at Tufts University. In the next selection he develops the case against capital punishment, which he believes is the stronger side of the controversy. Do you agree? Does he offer considerations that overcome the points made by supporters of the death penalty? You may remain unsure, but what will become clear are the reasons that can be offered on both sides of this vexing issue. Understanding the conflicting argumentation is a necessary step in working out a well-justified position.

The Analogy with Self-Defense

Capital punishment, it is sometimes said, is to the body politic what self-defense is to the individual. If the latter is not morally wrong, how can the former be morally wrong? In order to assess the strength of this analogy, we need to inspect rather closely the morality of self-defense.

Except for the absolute pacifists, who believe it is morally wrong to use violence even to defend themselves or others from unprovoked and undeserved aggression, most of us believe that it is not morally wrong and may even be our moral duty to use violence to prevent aggression. The law has long granted persons the right to defend themselves against the unjust aggressions of others, even to the extent of killing a would-be assailant. It is very difficult to think of any convincing argument that would show it is never rational to risk the death of another in order to prevent death or grave injury to oneself or to others. Certainly self-interest dictates the legitimacy of self-defense. So does concern for the well-being of others. So also does justice. If it is unfair for one person to attempt violence on another, then it is hard to see why morality compels the victim to acquiesce in the attempt by another to hurt him or her, rather than to resist it, even if that resistance may involve injury to the assailant.

The foregoing account assumes that the person acting in self-defense is innocent of any provocation of the assailant. It also assumes that there is no alternative to victimization except resistance. In actual life, both assumptions—especially the second—are often false, because there may be a third alternative: escape, or removing oneself from the scene of danger and imminent aggression. Hence, the law imposes on us the so-called "duty to retreat." Before we use violence to resist aggression, we must try to get out of the way, lest unnecessary violence be used to resist aggression. Now suppose that unjust aggression is imminent, and there is no path open for escape. How much violence may justifiably be used to ward off aggression? The answer is: No more violence than is necessary to prevent the aggressive assault. Violence beyond that is unnecessary and therefore unjustified. We may restate the principle governing the use of violence in self-defense in terms of the use of "deadly force" by the police in the discharge of their duties. The rule is this: Use of deadly force is justified only to prevent loss of life in immediate jeopardy where a lesser use of force cannot reasonably be expected to save the life that is threatened.

In real life, violence in self-defense in excess of the minimum necessary to prevent aggression is often excusable. One cannot always tell what will suffice to deter or prevent becoming a victim, and the law looks with a certain tolerance upon the frightened and innocent would-be victim who turns upon a vicious assailant and inflicts a fatal injury even though a lesser injury would have been sufficient. What is not justified is deliberately using far more violence than is necessary to prevent becoming a victim. It is the deliberate, not the impulsive, use of violence that is relevant to the death-penalty controversy, since the death penalty is enacted into law and carried out in each case only after ample time to weigh alternatives. Notice that we are assuming that the act of self-defense is to protect one's person or that of a third party. The reasoning outlined here does not extend to the defense of one's property. Shooting a thief to prevent one's automobile from being stolen cannot be excused or justified in the way that shooting an assailant charging with a knife pointed at one's face can be. In terms of the concept of "deadly force," our criterion is that deadly force is never justified to prevent crimes against property or other violent crimes not immediately threatening the life of a person.

The rationale for self-defense as set out above illustrates two moral principles of great importance to our discussion. . . . One is that if a life is to be risked, then it is better that it be the life of someone who is guilty (in our context, the initial assailant) rather than the life of someone who is not (the innocent potential victim). It is not fair to expect the innocent prospective victim to run the added risk of severe injury or death in order to avoid using violence in self-defense to the extent of possibly killing his assailant. It is only fair that the guilty aggressor run the risk.

The other principle is that taking life deliberately is not justified so long as there is any feasible alternative. One does not expect miracles, of course, but in theory, if shooting a burglar through the foot will stop the burglary and enable one to call the police for help, then there is no reason to shoot to kill. Likewise, if the burglar is unarmed, there is no reason to shoot at all. In actual life, of course, burglars are likely to be shot at by aroused householders because one does not know whether they are armed, and prudence may dictate the assumption that they are. Even so, although the burglar has no right to commit a felony against a person or a person's property, the attempt to do so does not give the chosen victim the right to respond in whatever way he or she pleases in retaliation, and then to excuse or justify such conduct on the ground that he or she was "only acting in self-defense." In these ways the law shows a tacit regard for the life of even a felon and discourages the use of unnecessary violence even by the innocent; morality can hardly do less.

Preventing Crime *versus* Deterring Crime

The analogy between capital punishment and self-defense requires us to face squarely the empirical questions surrounding the preventive and deterrent effects of the death penalty. Let us distinguish first between preventing and deterring crime. Executing a murderer in the name of punishment can be seen as a crime-*preventive* measure just to the extent it is reasonable to believe that if the murderer had not been executed he or she would have committed other crimes (including, but not necessarily confined to, murder). Executing a murderer can be seen as a crime *deterrent* just to the extent it is reasonable to believe that by the example of the execution other persons are frightened off from committing murder. Any punishment can be a crime preventive without being a crime deterrent, and it can be a deterrent without being a preventive. It can also be both or neither. Prevention and deterrence are theoretically independent because they operate by different methods. Crimes can be prevented by taking guns out of the hands of criminals, by putting criminals behind bars, by alerting the public to be less careless and less prone to victimization, and so forth. Crimes can be deterred only by making would-be criminals frightened of being arrested, convicted, and punished for crimes—that is, making persons overcome their desire to commit crimes by a stronger desire to avoid the risk of being caught and punished.

The Death Penalty as a Crime Preventive

Capital punishment is unusual among penalties because its preventive effects limit its deterrent effects. The death penalty can never deter the executed person from further crimes. At most, it can prevent him or her from committing them. Popular discussions of the death penalty are frequently confused and misleading because they so often involve the assumption that the death penalty is a perfect and infallible deterrent so far as the executed criminal is concerned, whereas nothing of the sort is true. It is even an exaggeration to think that in any given case of execution the death penalty has proved to be an infallible crime preventive. What is obviously true is that once a person has been executed, it is physically impossible for him or her to commit any further crimes. But this does not prove that by executing a murderer society has in fact prevented any crimes. To prove this, one would need to know what crimes the executed criminal would have committed if he or she had not been executed and had been punished only in some less severe way (e.g., by imprisonment).

What is the evidence that the death penalty is an effective crime preventive? From the study of imprisonment, and parole and release records, it is clear that in general, if the murderers and other criminals who have been executed are like the murderers who were convicted but not executed, then (a) executing all convicted murderers would have prevented few crimes, but not many murders (less than one convicted murderer in a hundred commits another murder); and (b) convicted murderers, whether inside prison or outside after release, have at least as good a record of no further criminal activity as does any other class of convicted felon.

These facts show that the general public tends to overrate the danger and threat to public safety constituted by the failure to execute every murderer who is caught and convicted. While one would be in error to say that there is no risk such criminals will repeat their crimes—or similar ones—if they are not executed, one would be equally in error to say that by executing every convicted murderer we know that many horrible crimes will never be committed. All we know is that a few such crimes will never be committed; we do not know how many or by whom they would have been committed. (Obviously, if we did we could have prevented them.) This is the nub of the problem. There is no way to know in advance which if any of the incarcerated or released murderers will kill again. It is useful in this connection to remember that the only way to guarantee that no horrible crimes ever occur is to execute *everyone* who might conceivably commit such a crime. Similarly, the only way to guarantee that no convicted murderer ever commits another murder is to execute them all. No society has ever done this, and for 200 years our society has been moving steadily in the opposite direction.

These considerations show that our society has implicitly adopted an attitude toward the risk of murder rather like the attitude it has adopted toward the risk of fatality from other sources, such as automobile accidents, lung cancer, or drowning. Since no one knows when or where or upon whom any of these lethal events will befall, it would be too great an invasion of freedom to undertake the severe restrictions that alone would suffice to prevent any of them from occurring. It is better to take the risks and keep our freedom than to try to eliminate the risks altogether and lose our freedom in the process. Hence, we have lifeguards at the beach, but swimming is not totally prohibited; smokers are warned, but cigarettes are still legally sold; pedestrians may be given the right of way in a crosswalk, but marginally competent drivers are still allowed to operate motor vehicles. Some risk is therefore imposed on the innocent; in the name of our right to freedom, our other rights are not protected by society at all costs.

The Death Penalty as a Crime Deterrent

Determining whether the death penalty is an effective deterrent is even more difficult than determining its effectiveness as a crime preventive. In general, our knowledge about how penalties deter crimes and whether in fact they do—whom they deter, from which crimes, and under what conditions—is distressingly inexact. Most people nevertheless are convinced that punishments do deter, and that the more severe a punishment is the better it will deter. For more than a generation, social scientists have studied the question of whether the death penalty is a deterrent and of whether it is a better deterrent than the alternative of imprisonment. Their verdict, while not unanimous, is fairly clear. Whatever may be true about the deterrence of lesser crimes by other penalties, the deterrence achieved by the death penalty for murder is not measurably greater than the deterrence achieved by long-term imprisonment. In the nature of the case, the evidence is quite indirect. No one can identify for certain any crimes that did not occur because the would-be offender was deterred by the threat of the death penalty and that would not have been deterred by a lesser threat. Likewise, no one can identify any crimes that did occur because the offender was not deterred by the threat of prison even though he would have been deterred by the threat of death. Nevertheless, such evidence as we have fails to show that the more severe penalty (death) is really a better deterrent than the less severe penalty (imprisonment) for such crimes as murder.

If the conclusion stated above is correct, and the death penalty and long-term imprisonment are equally effective (or ineffective) as deterrents to murder, then the argument for the death penalty on grounds of deterrence is seriously weakened. One of the moral principles identified earlier comes into play and requires us to reject the death penalty on moral grounds. This is the principle that unless there is a good reason for choosing a more rather than a less severe punishment for a crime, the less severe penalty is to be preferred. This principle obviously commends itself to anyone who values human life and who concedes that, all other things being equal, less pain and suffering is always better than more. Human life is valued in part to the degree that it is free of pain, suffering, misery, and frustration, and in particular that it is free of such experiences when they serve no purpose. If the death penalty is not a more effective deterrent than imprisonment, then its greater severity than imprisonment is gratuitous, purposeless suffering and deprivation.

A Cost/Benefit Analysis of the Death Penalty

A full study of the costs and benefits involved in the practice of capital punishment would not be confined solely to the question of whether it is a better deterrent or preventive of murder than imprisonment. Any thoroughgoing utilitarian approach to the death-penalty controversy would need to examine carefully other costs and benefits as well, because maximizing the balance of social benefits over social costs is the sole criterion of right and wrong according to utilitarianism. Let us consider, therefore, some of the other costs and benefits to be calculated. Clinical psychologists have presented evidence to suggest that the death penalty actually incites some persons of unstable mind to murder others, either because they are afraid to take their own lives and hope that society will punish them for murder by putting them to death, or because they fancy that they, too, are killing with justification analogously to the justified killing involved in capital punishment. If such evidence is sound, capital punishment can serve as a counter-preventive or an incitement to murder, and these incited murders become part of its social cost. Imprisonment, however, has not been known to incite any murders or other crimes of violence in a comparable fashion. (A possible exception might be found in the imprisonment of terrorists, which has inspired other terrorists to take hostages as part of a scheme to force the authorities to release their imprisoned comrades.) The risks of executing the innocent are also part of the social cost. The historical record is replete with innocent persons indicted, convicted, sentenced, and occasionally legally executed for crimes they did not commit, not to mention the guilty persons unfairly convicted, sentenced to death, and executed on the strength of perjured testimony, fraudulent evidence, subornation of jurors, and other violations of the civil rights and liberties of the accused. Nor is this all. The high costs of a capital trial, of the inevitable appeals, the costly methods of custody most prisons adopt for convicts on "death row," are among the straightforward economic costs that the death penalty incurs. No scientifically valid cost/benefit analysis of capital punishment has ever been conducted, and it is impossible to predict exactly what such a study would show. Nevertheless, based on such evidence as we do have, it is quite possible that a study of this sort would favor abolition of all death penalties rather than their retention.

What If Executions Did Deter?

From the moral point of view, it is quite important to determine what one should think about capital punishment if the evidence clearly showed that the death penalty is a distinctly superior method of social defense by comparison with less severe alternatives. . . . To oppose the death penalty in the face of incontestable evidence that it is an effective method of social defense seems to violate the moral principle that where grave risks are to be run, it is better that they be run by the guilty than by the innocent. Consider in this connection an imaginary world in which by executing a murderer the victim is invariably restored to life, whole and intact, as though the murder had never occurred. In such a miraculous world, it is hard to see how anyone could oppose the death penalty on moral grounds. Why shouldn't a murderer die if that will infallibly bring the victim back to life? What could possibly be morally wrong with taking the murderer's life under such conditions? It would turn the death penalty into an instrument of perfect restitution, and it would give a new and better meaning to *lex talionis,* "a life for a life." The whole idea is fanciful, of course, but it shows better than anything else how opposition to the death penalty cannot be both moral and wholly unconditional. If opposition to the death penalty is to be morally responsible, then it must be conceded that there are conditions (however unlikely) under which that opposition should cease.

But even if the death penalty were known to be a uniquely effective social defense, we could still imagine conditions under which it would be reasonable to oppose it. Suppose that in addition to being a slightly better preventive and deterrent than imprisonment, executions also have a slight incitive effect (so that for every ten murders an execution prevents or deters, it also incites another murder). Suppose also that the administration of criminal justice in capital cases is inefficient, unequal, and tends to secure convictions of murderers who least "deserve" to be sentenced to death (including some death sentences and a few executions of the innocent). Under such conditions, it would still be reasonable to oppose the death penalty, because on the facts supposed more (or not fewer) innocent lives are being threatened and lost by using the death penalty than would be risked by abolishing it. It is important to remember throughout our evaluation of the deterrence controversy that we cannot ever apply the principle . . . that advises us to risk the lives of the guilty in order to save the lives of the innocent. Instead, the most we can do is weigh the risk for the general public against the execution of those who are *found* guilty by an imperfect system of criminal justice. These hypothetical factual assumptions illustrate the contingencies upon which the morality of opposition to the death penalty rests. And not only the morality of opposition; the morality of any defense of the death penalty rests on the same contingencies. This should help us understand why, in resolving the morality of capital punishment one way or the other, it is so important to know, as well as we can, whether the death penalty really does deter, prevent, or incite crime, whether the innocent really are ever executed, and whether any of these things are likely to occur in the future.

How Many Guilty Lives Is One Innocent Life Worth?

The great unanswered question that utilitarians must face concerns the level of social defense that executions should be expected to achieve before it is justifiable to carry them out. Consider three possible situations: (1) At the level of a hundred executions per year, each additional execution of a convicted murderer reduces the number of murder victims by ten. (2) Executing every convicted murderer reduces the number of murders to 5,000 victims annually, whereas executing only one out of ten reduces the number to 5,001. (3) Executing every convicted murderer reduces the murder rate no more than does executing one in a hundred and no more than a random pattern of executions does.

Many people contemplating situation (1) would regard this as a reasonable trade-off: The execution of each further guilty person saves the lives of ten innocent ones. (In fact, situation (1) or something like it may be taken as a description of what most of those who defend the death penalty on grounds of social defense believe is true.) But suppose that, instead of saving 10 lives, the number dropped to 0.5, i.e., one victim avoided for each two additional executions. Would that be a reasonable price to pay? We are on the road toward the situation described in situation (2), where a drastic 90 percent reduction in the number of persons executed causes the level of social defense to drop by only 0.0002 percent. Would it be worth it to execute so many more murderers at the cost of such a slight decrease in social defense? How many guilty lives is one innocent life worth? In situation (3), of course, there is no basis for executing all convicted murderers, since there is no gain in social defense to show for each additional murderer executed after the first out of each hundred murderers has been executed. How, then, should we determine which out of each hundred convicted murderers is the unlucky one to be put to death?

It may be possible, under a complete and thoroughgoing cost/benefit analysis of the death penalty, to answer such questions. But an appeal merely to the moral principle that if lives are to be risked then let it be the lives of the guilty rather than the lives of the innocent will not suffice. (We have already noticed . . . that this abstract principle is of little use in the actual administration of criminal justice, because the police and the courts do not deal with the guilty as such but only with those *judged* guilty.) Nor will it suffice to agree that society deserves all the crime prevention and deterrence it can get by inflicting severe punishments. These principles are consistent with too many different policies. They are too vague by themselves to resolve the choice on grounds of social defense when confronted with hypothetical situations like those proposed above.

Since no adequate cost/benefit analysis of the death penalty exists, there is no way to resolve these questions from this standpoint at the present time. Moreover, it can be argued that we cannot have such an analysis without already establishing in some way or other the relative value of innocent lives versus guilty lives. Far from being a product of a cost/benefit analysis, this comparative evaluation of lives would have to be brought into any such analysis. Without it, no cost/benefit analysis can get off the ground. Finally, it must be noted that we have no knowledge at present that begins to approximate anything like the situation described above in (1), whereas it appears from the evidence we do have that we achieve about the same deterrent and preventive effects whether we punish murder by death or by imprisonment. Therefore, something like the situation in (2) or in (3) may be correct. If so, this shows that the choice between the two policies of capital punishment and life imprisonment for murder will probably have to be made on some basis other than social defense; on that basis the two policies are equivalent and therefore equally acceptable.

Crime Must Be Punished

[T]here cannot be any dispute over this principle. In embracing it, of course, we are not automatically making a fetish of "law and order," in the sense that we would be if we thought that the most important single thing society can do with its resources is to punish crimes. In addition, this principle is not likely to be in dispute between proponents and opponents of the death penalty. Only those who completely oppose punishment for murder and other erstwhile capital crimes would appear to disregard this principle. Even defenders of the death penalty must admit that putting a convicted murderer in prison for years is a punishment of that criminal. The principle that crime must be punished is neutral to our controversy, because both sides acknowledge it and comply with it.

It is the other principle of retributive justice that seems to be a decisive one. Under the principle of retaliation, *lex talionis,* it must always have seemed that murderers ought to be put to death. Proponents of the death penalty, with rare exceptions, have insisted on this point, and it seems that even opponents of the death penalty must give it grudging assent. The strategy for opponents of the death penalty is to show either (a) that this principle is not really a principle of justice after all, or (b) that although it is, other principles outweigh or cancel its dictates. As we shall see, both these objections have merit.

Is Murder Alone to Be Punished by Death?

Let us recall, first, that not even the Biblical world limited the death penalty to the punishment of murder. Many other nonhomicidal crimes also carried this penalty (e.g., kidnapping, witchcraft, cursing one's parents). In our own recent history, persons have been executed for aggravated assault, rape, kidnapping, armed robbery, sabotage, and espionage. It is not possible to defend any of these executions (not to mention some of the more bizarre capital statutes, like the one in Georgia that used to provide an optional death penalty for desecration of a grave) on grounds of just retribution. This entails that either such executions are not justified or that they are justified on some ground other than retribution. In actual practice, few if any defenders of the death penalty have ever been willing to rest their case entirely on the moral principle of just retribution as formulated in terms of "a life for a life." Kant seems to have been a conspicuous exception. Most defenders of the death penalty have implied by their willingness to use executions to defend limb and property, as well as life, that they did not place much value on the lives of criminals when compared to the value of both lives and things belonging to innocent citizens.

Are All Murders to Be Punished by Death?

Our society for several centuries has endeavored to confine the death penalty to some criminal homicides. Even Kant took a casual attitude toward a mother's killing of her illegitimate child. ("A child born into the world outside marriage is outside the law . . . , and consequently it is also outside the protection of the law.")[1] In our society, the development nearly 200 years ago of the distinction between first- and second-degree murder was an attempt to narrow the class of criminal homicides deserving of the death penalty. Yet those dead owing to manslaughter, or to any kind of unintentional, accidental, unpremeditated, unavoidable, unmalicious killing are just as dead as the victims of the most ghastly murder. Both the law in practice and moral reflection show how difficult it is to identify all and only the criminal homicides that are appropriately punished by death (assuming that any are). Individual judges and juries differ in the conclusions they reach. The history of capital punishment for homicides reveals continual efforts, uniformly unsuccessful, to identify before the fact those homicides for which the slayer should die. Benjamin Cardozo, a justice of the United States Supreme Court fifty years ago, said of the distinction between degrees of murder that it was

> . . . so obscure that no jury hearing it for the first time can fairly be expected to assimilate and understand it. I am not at all sure that I understand it myself after trying to apply it for many years and after diligent study of what has been written in the books. Upon the basis of this fine distinction with its obscure and mystifying psychology, scores of men have gone to their death.[2]

Similar skepticism has been registered on the reliability and rationality of death-penalty statutes that give the trial court the discretion to sentence to prison or to death. As Justice John Marshall Harlan of the Supreme Court observed a decade ago,

> Those who have come to grips with the hard task of actually attempting to draft means of channeling capital sentencing discretion have confirmed the lesson taught by history. . . . To identify before the fact those characteristics of criminal homicide and their perpetrators which call for the death penalty, and to express these characteristics in language which can be fairly understood and applied by the sentencing authority, appear to be tasks which are beyond present human ability.[3]

The abstract principle that the punishment of death best fits the crime of murder turns out to be extremely difficult to interpret and apply.

If we look at the matter from the standpoint of the actual practice of criminal justice, we can only conclude that "a life for a life" plays little or no role whatever. Plea bargaining (by means of which one of the persons involved in a crime agrees to accept a lesser sentence in exchange for testifying against the others to enable the prosecutor to get them all convicted), even where murder is concerned, is widespread. Studies of criminal justice reveal that what the courts (trial or appellate) decide on a given day is first-degree murder suitably punished by death in a given jurisdiction could just as well be decided in a neighboring jurisdiction on another day either as second-degree murder or as first-degree murder but without the death penalty. The factors that influence prosecutors in determining the charge under which they will prosecute go far beyond the simple principle of "a life for a life." Nor can it be objected that these facts show that our society does not care about justice. To put it succinctly, either justice in punishment does not consist of retribution, because there are other principles of justice; or there are other moral considerations besides justice that must be honored; or retributive justice is not adequately expressed in the idea of "a life for a life."

Is Death Sufficiently Retributive?

Given the reality of horrible and vicious crimes, one must consider whether there is not a quality of unthinking arbitrariness in advocating capital punishment for murder as the retributively just punishment. Why does death in the electric chair or the gas chamber or before a firing squad or on a gallows meet the requirements of retributive justice? When one thinks of the savage, brutal, wanton character of so many murders, how can retributive justice be served by anything less than equally savage methods of execution for the murderer? From a retributive point of view, the oft-heard exclamation, "Death is too good for him!" has a certain truth. Yet few defenders of the death penalty are willing to embrace this consequence of their own doctrine.

The reason they do not and should not is that, if they did, they would be stooping to the methods and thus to the squalor of the murderer. Where criminals set the limits of just methods of punishment, as they will do if we attempt to give exact and literal implementation to *lex talionis,* society will find itself descending to the cruelties and savagery that criminals employ. But society would be deliberately authorizing such acts, in the cool light of reason, and not (as is often true of vicious criminals) impulsively or in hatred and anger or with an insane or unbalanced mind. Moral restraints, in short, prohibit us from trying to make executions perfectly retributive. Once we grant the role of these restraints, the principle of "a life for a life" itself has been qualified and no longer suffices to justify the execution of murderers.

Other considerations take us in a different direction. Few murders, outside television and movie scripts, involve anything like an execution. An execution, after all, begins with a solemn pronouncement of the death sentence from a judge, is followed by long detention in maximum security awaiting the date of execution, various appeals, perhaps a final sanity hearing, and then "the last mile" to the execution chamber itself. As the French writer Albert Camus remarked,

> For there to be an equivalence, the death penalty would have to punish a criminal who had warned his victim of the date at which he would inflict a horrible death on him and who, from that moment onward, had confined him at his mercy for months. Such a monster is not encountered in private life.[4]

Differential Severity Does Not Require Executions

What, then, emerges from our examination of retributive justice and the death penalty? If retributive justice is thought to consist in *lex talionis,* all one can say is that this principle has never exercised more than a crude and indirect effect on the actual punishments meted out. Other principles interfere with a literal and single-minded application of this one. Some murders seem improperly punished by death at all; other murders would require methods of execution too horrible to inflict; in still other cases any possible execution is too deliberate and monstrous given the nature of the motivation culminating in the murder. Proponents of the death penalty rarely confine themselves to reliance on this principle of just retribution and nothing else, since they rarely confine themselves to supporting the death penalty only for all murders.

But retributive justice need not be thought to consist of *lex talionis.* One may reject that principle as too crude and still embrace the retributive principle that the severity of punishments should be graded according to the gravity of the offense. Even though one need not claim that life imprisonment (or any kind of punishment other than death) "fits" the crime of murder, one can claim that this punishment is the proper one for murder. To do this, the schedule of punishments accepted by society must be arranged so that this mode of imprisonment is the most severe penalty used. Opponents of the death penalty need not reject this principle of retributive justice, even though they must reject a literal *lex talionis.*

Equal Justice and Capital Punishment

During the past generation, the strongest practical objection to the death penalty has been the inequities with which it has been applied. As Supreme Court Justice William O. Douglas once observed, "One searches our chronicles in vain for the execution of any member of the affluent strata of this society."[5] One does not search our chronicles in vain for the crime of murder committed by the affluent. Every study of the death penalty for rape has confirmed that black male rapists (especially where the victim is a white female) are far more likely to be sentenced to death (and executed) than white male rapists. Half of all those under death sentence during 1976 and 1977 were black, and nearly half of all those executed since 1930 were black. All the sociological evidence points to the conclusion that the death penalty is the poor man's justice; as the current street saying has it, "Those without the capital get the punishment."

Let us suppose that the factual basis for such a criticism is sound. What follows for the morality of capital punishment? Many defenders of the death penalty have been quick to point out that since there is nothing intrinsic about the crime of murder or rape that dictates that only the poor or racial-minority males will commit it, and since there is nothing overtly racist about the statutes that authorize the death penalty for murder or rape, it is hardly a fault in the idea of capital punishment if in practice it falls with unfair impact on the poor and the black. There is, in short, nothing in the death penalty that requires it to be applied unfairly and with arbitrary or discriminatory results. It is at worst a fault in the system of administering criminal justice (and some, who dispute the facts cited above, would deny even this).

Presumably, both proponents and opponents of capital punishment would concede that it is a fundamental dictate of justice that a punishment should not be unfairly—inequitably or unevenly—enforced and applied. They should also be able to agree that when the punishment in question is the extremely severe one of death, then the requirement to be fair in using such a punishment becomes even more stringent. Thus, there should be no dispute in the death penalty controversy over these principles of justice. The dispute begins as soon as one attempts to connect these principles with the actual use of this punishment.

In this country, many critics of the death penalty have argued, we would long ago have got rid of it entirely if it had been a condition of its use that it be applied equally and fairly. In the words of the attorneys who argued against the death penalty in the Supreme Court during 1972, "It is a freakish aberration, a random extreme act of violence, visibly arbitrary and discriminatory—a penalty reserved for unusual application because, if it were usually used, it would affront universally shared standards of public decency."[6] It is difficult to dispute this judgment, when one considers that there have been in the United States during the past fifty years about half a million criminal homicides but only about 4,000 executions (all but 50 of which were of men).

We can look at these statistics in another way to illustrate the same point. If we could be assured that the 4,000 persons executed were the worst of the worst, repeated offenders without exception, the most dangerous murderers in captivity—the ones who had killed more than once and were likely to kill again, and the least likely to be confined in prison without imminent danger to other inmates and the staff—then one might accept half a million murders and a few thousand executions with a sense that rough justice had been done. But the truth is otherwise. Persons are sentenced to death and executed not because they have been found to be uncontrollably violent, hopelessly poor parole and release risks, or for other reasons. Instead, they are executed for entirely different reasons. They have a poor defense at trial; they have no funds to bring sympathetic witnesses to court; they are immigrants or strangers in the community where they were tried; the prosecuting attorney wants the publicity that goes with "sending a killer to the chair"; they have inexperienced or overworked counsel at trial; there are no funds for an appeal or for a transcript of the trial record; they are members of a despised racial minority. In short, the actual study of why particular persons have been sentenced to death and executed does not show any careful winnowing of the worst from the bad. It shows that the executed were usually the unlucky victims of prejudice and discrimination, the losers in an arbitrary lottery that could just as well have spared them as killed them, the victims of the disadvantages that almost always go with poverty. A system like this does not enhance respect for human life; it cheapens and degrades it. However heinous murder and other crimes are, the system of capital punishment does not compensate for or erase those crimes. It only tends to add new injuries of its own to the catalogue of our inhumanity to each other.

Conclusion

Our discussion of the death penalty from the moral point of view shows that there is no one moral principle the validity of which is paramount and that decisively favors one side to the controversy. Rather, we have seen how it is possible to argue either for or against the death penalty, and in each case to be appealing to moral principles that derive from the worth, value, or dignity of human life. We have also seen how it is impossible to connect any of these abstract principles with the actual practice of capital punishment without a close study of sociological, psychological, and economic factors. By themselves, the moral principles that are relevant are too abstract and uncertain in application to be of much help. Without the guidance of such principles, of course, the facts (who gets executed, and why) are of little use, either.

My own view of the controversy is that on balance, given the moral principles we have identified in the course of our discussion (including the overriding value of human life), and given the facts about capital punishment and crimes against the person, the side favoring abolition of the death penalty has the better of the argument. And there *is* an alternative to capital punishment: long-term imprisonment. Such a punishment is retributive and can be made appropriately severe to reflect the gravity of the crime for which it is the punishment. It gives adequate (though hardly perfect) protection to the public. It is free of the worst defect to which the death penalty is liable: execution of the innocent. It tacitly acknowledges that there is no way for a criminal, alive or dead, to make amends for murder or other grave crimes against the person. Finally, it has symbolic significance. The death penalty, more than any other kind of killing, is done in the name of society and on its behalf. Each of us has a hand in such a killing, and unless such killings are absolutely necessary they cannot really be justified.

NOTES

1. Immanuel Kant, *The Metaphysical Elements of Justice* (1797), tr. John Ladd, p. 106.
2. Benjamin Cardozo, "What Medicine Can Do for Law" (1928), reprinted in Margaret E. Hall, ed., *Selected Writings of Benjamin Nathan Cardozo* (1947), p. 204.
3. *McGautha v. California*, 402 U.S. 183 (1971), at p. 204.

4. Albert Camus, *Resistance, Rebellion, and Death* (1961), p. 199.
5. *Furman v. Georgia*, 408 U.S. 238 (1972), at pp. 251–252.
6. NAACP Legal Defense and Educational Fund, Brief for Petitioner in *Aikens v. California*, O.T. 1971, No. 68-5027, reprinted in Philip English Mackey, ed., *Voices Against Death: American Opposition to Capital Punishment, 1787–1975* (1975), p. 288.

Two Concepts of Affirmative Action

STEVEN M. CAHN

> Affirmative action is a divisive issue in the United States. With recent attempts by referendum, legislation, and judicial action to change current policies, emotions have intensified.
>
> What is most needed now is not increased passion but greater attention to recognizing and analyzing the subject's complexities. That is one aim of the essay of mine that follows. After providing historical perspective, I try to clarify some major lines of argument and assess their strength. Your conclusion may differ from mine, but I hope you find that the article contributes towards an increased understanding of this difficult matter.

In March 1961, less than two months after assuming office, President John F. Kennedy issued Executive Order 10925, establishing the President's Committee on Equal Employment Opportunity. Its mission was to end discrimination in employment by the government and its contractors. The order required every federal contract to include the pledge that "The contractor will not discriminate against any employe[e] or applicant for employment because of race, creed, color, or national origin. The contractor will take affirmative action to ensure that applicants are employed, and that employe[e]s are treated during employment, without regard to their race, creed, color, or national origin."

Here, for the first time in the context of civil rights, the government called for "affirmative action." The term meant taking appropriate steps to eradicate the then widespread practices of racial, religious, and ethnic discrimination.[1] The goal, as the president stated, was "equal opportunity in employment."

In other words, *procedural* affirmative action, as I shall call it, was instituted to ensure that applicants for positions would be judged without any consideration of their race, religion, or national origin. These criteria were declared irrelevant. Taking them into account was forbidden.

The Civil Rights Act of 1964 restated and broadened the application of this principle. Title VI declared that "No person in the United States shall, on the ground of race, color or national origin, be excluded from participation in, be denied the benefits of, or be subjected to discrimination under any program or activity receiving Federal financial assistance."

But before one year had passed, President Lyndon B. Johnson argued that fairness required more than a commitment to such procedural affirmative action. In his 1965 commencement address at Howard University, he said, "You do not take a person who for years has been hobbled by chains and liberate him, bring him up to the starting line of a race and then say, 'you're free to compete with all the others,' and still justly believe that you have been completely fair."

And so several months later Johnson issued Executive Order 11246, stating that "It is the policy of the Government of the United States to provide equal opportunity in Federal employment for all qualified persons, to prohibit discrimination in employment because of race, creed, color or national origin, and to promote the full realization of equal employment opportunity through a positive, continuing program in each department and agency." Two years later the order was amended to prohibit discrimination on the basis of sex.

While the aim of Johnson's order is stated in language similar to that of Kennedy's, Johnson's abolished the Committee on Equal Employment Opportunity, transferred its responsibilities to the Secretary of Labor, and authorized the secretary to "adopt such rules and regulations and issue such orders as he deems necessary and appropriate to achieve the purposes thereof."

Acting on this mandate, the Department of Labor in December 1971, during the Nixon administration, issued Revised Order No. 4, requiring all federal contractors to develop "an acceptable affirmative action program," including "an analysis of areas within which the contractor is deficient in the utilization of minority groups and women, and further, goals and timetables to which the contractor's good faith efforts must be directed to correct the deficiencies." Contractors were instructed to take the term "minority groups" to refer to "Negroes, American Indians, Orientals, and Spanish Surnamed Americans." (No guidance was given as to whether having only one parent, grandparent, or great-grandparent from a group would suffice to establish group membership.) The concept of "underutilization," according to the Revised Order, meant "having fewer minorities or women in a particular job classification than would reasonably be expected by their availability." "Goals" were not to be "rigid and inflexible quotas," but "targets reasonably attainable by means of applying every good faith effort to make all aspects of the entire affirmative action program work."[2]

Such *preferential* affirmative action, as I shall call it, requires that attention be paid to the same criteria of race, sex, and ethnicity that procedural affirmative action deems irrelevant. Is such use of these criteria justifiable in employment decisions?[3]

Return to President Johnson's claim that a person hobbled by discrimination cannot in fairness be expected to be competitive. How is it to be determined which specific individuals are entitled to a compensatory advantage? To decide each case on its own merits would be possible, but this approach would undermine the argument for instituting preferential affirmative action on a group basis. For if some members of a group are able to compete, why not others? Thus, defenders of preferential affirmative action maintain that the group, not the individual, is to be judged. If the group has suffered discrimination, then all its members are to be treated as hobbled runners.

But note that while a hobbled runner, provided with a sufficient lead in a race, may cross the finish line first, giving that person an edge prevents the individual from being considered as fast a runner as others. An equally fast runner does not need an advantage to be competitive.

This entire racing analogy thus encourages stereotypical thinking. For example, recall those men who played in baseball's Negro Leagues. That these athletes were barred from competing in the Major Leagues is the greatest stain on the history of the sport. But while they suffered discrimination, they were as proficient as their counterparts in the Major Leagues. They needed only to be judged by the same criteria as all others, and ensuring such equality of consideration is the essence of procedural affirmative action.

Granted, if individuals are unprepared or ill-equipped to compete, then they ought to be helped to try to achieve their goals. But such aid is appropriate for all who need it, not merely for members of particular racial, sexual, or ethnic groups.

Victims of discrimination deserve compensation. Former players in the Negro Leagues ought to receive special consideration in the arrangement of pension plans and any other benefits formerly denied them due to unfair treatment. The case for such compensation, however, does not imply that present black players vying for jobs in the Major Leagues should be evaluated in any other way than their performance on the field. To assume their inability to compete is derogatory and erroneous.

Such considerations have led recent defenders of preferential affirmative action to rely less heavily on any argument that implies the attribution of noncompetitiveness to an entire population.[4] Instead the emphasis has been placed on recognizing the benefits society is said to derive from encouraging expression of the varied experiences, outlooks, and values of members of different groups.

This approach makes a virtue of what has come to be called "diversity."[5] As a defense of preferential affirmative action, it has at least two advantages.

First, those previously excluded are now included not as a favor to them but as a means of enriching all. Second, no one is viewed as hobbled; each competes on a par, although with varied strengths.

Note that diversity requires preferential hiring. Those who enhance diversity are to be preferred to those who do not. But those preferred are not being chosen because of their deficiency; the larger group is deficient lacking diversity. By including those who embody it, the group is enhanced.

But what does it mean to say that a group lacks diversity? Or to put the question another way, would it be possible to decide which member of a ten-person group to eliminate in order to decrease most markedly its diversity?

So stated, the question is reminiscent of a provocative puzzle in *The Tyranny of Testing*, a 1962 book by the scientist Banesh Hoffman. In this attack on the importance placed on multiple-choice tests, he quotes the following letter to the editor of the *Times* of London:

> Sir.—Among the "odd one out" type of questions which my son had to answer for a school entrance examination was: "Which is the odd one out among cricket, football, billiards, and hockey?" [In England "football" refers to the game Americans call "soccer," and "hockey" here refers to "field hockey."]

The letter continued:

> I said billiards because it is the only one played indoors. A colleague says football because it is the only one in which the ball is not struck by an implement. A neighbour says cricket because in all the other games the object is to put the ball into a net . . . Could any of your readers put me out of my misery by stating what is the correct answer . . . ?

A day later the *Times* printed the following two letters:

> Sir.—"Billiards" is the obvious answer . . . because it is the only one of the games listed which is not a team game.

> Sir.— . . . football is the odd one out because . . . it is played with an inflated ball as compared with the solid ball used in each of the other three.

Hoffman then continued his own discussion:

> When I had read these three letters it seemed to me that good cases had been made for football and billiards, and that the case for cricket was particularly clever. . . . At first I thought this made hockey easily the worst of the four choices and, in effect, ruled it out. But then I realized that the very fact that hockey was the only one that could be thus ruled out gave it so striking a quality of separateness as to make it an excellent answer after all—perhaps the best.

Fortunately for my piece of mind, it soon occurred to me that hockey is the only one of the four games that is played with a curved implement.

The following day the *Times* published yet another letter, this from a philosophically sophisticated thinker:

Sir.—[The author of the original letter] . . . has put his finger on what has long been a matter of great amusement to me. Of the four—cricket, football, billiards, hockey—each is unique in a multitude of respects. For example, billiards is the only one in which the colour of the balls matters, the only one played with more than one ball at once, the only one played on a green cloth and not on a field. . . .

It seems to me that those who have been responsible for inventing this kind of brain teaser have been ignorant of the elementary philosophical fact that every thing is at once unique and a member of a wider class.

With this sound principle in mind, return to the problem of deciding which member of a ten-person group to eliminate in order to decrease most markedly its diversity. Unless the sort of diversity is specified, the question has no rational answer.

In searches for college and university faculty members, we know what sorts of diversity are typically of present concern: race, sex, and certain ethnicities. Why should these characteristics be given special consideration?

Consider, for example, other nonacademic respects in which prospective faculty appointees can differ: age, religion, nationality, regional background, economic class, social stratum, military experience, bodily appearance, physical soundness, sexual orientation, marital status, ethical standards, political commitments, and cultural values. Why should we not seek diversity of these sorts?

To some extent schools do. Many colleges and universities indicate in advertisements for faculty positions that they seek persons with disabilities or Vietnam War veterans. The City University of New York requires all searches to give preference to individuals of Italian–American descent.

The crucial point is that the appeal to diversity never favors any particular candidate. Each one adds to some sort of diversity but not another. In a department of ten, one individual might be the only black, another the only woman, another the only bachelor, another the only veteran, another the only one over 50, another the only Catholic, another the only Republican, another the only Scandinavian, another the only socialist, and the tenth the only Southerner.

Suppose the suggestion is made that the sorts of diversity to be sought are those of groups that have suffered discrimination. This approach leads to another problem, clearly put by the philosopher John Kekes:

It is true that American blacks, Native Americans, Hispanics, and women have suffered injustice as a group. But so have homosexuals, epileptics, the urban and the rural poor, the physically ugly, those whose careers were ruined by McCarthyism, prostitutes, the obese, and so forth. . . .

There have been some attempts to deny that there is an analogy between these two classes of victims. It has been said that the first were unjustly discriminated against due to racial or sexual prejudice and that this is not true of the second. This is indeed so. But why should we accept the suggestion . . . that the only form of injustice relevant to preferential treatment is that which is due to racial or sexual prejudice? Injustice occurs in many forms, and those who value justice will surely object to all of them.[6]

Kekes's reasoning is cogent. But another difficulty looms for the proposal to seek diversity only of groups that have suffered discrimination. For diversity is supposed to be valued not as compensation to the disadvantaged, but as a means of enriching all.

Consider, for example, a department in which most of the faculty members are women. In certain fields such as nursing and elementary education, such departments are common. If diversity by sex is of value, then such a department, when making its next appointment, should prefer a man. But men as a group have not been victims of discrimination. So, to achieve valued sorts of diversity, the question is not which groups have been discriminated against, but which valued groups are not represented. The question thus reappears as to which sorts of diversity are to be most highly valued. I know of no compelling answer.

Seeking to justify preferential affirmative action in terms of its contribution to diversity raises yet another difficulty. For preferential affirmative action is commonly defended as a temporary rather than a permanent measure.[7] Yet preferential affirmative action to achieve diversity is not temporary.

Suppose it were. Then once an institution had appointed an appropriate number of members of a particular group, preferential affirmative action would no longer be in effect. Yet the institution may later find that it has too few members of that group. Since lack of valuable diversity is presumably no more acceptable at one time than another, preferential affirmative action would have to be reinstituted. Thereby it would in effect become a permanent policy.

Why do so many of its defenders wish it to be only transitional? They believe the policy was instituted in response to irrelevant criteria for appointment having been mistakenly treated as relevant. To adopt any policy that continues to treat essentially irrelevant criteria as relevant is to share the guilt of those who discriminated originally. Irrelevant criteria should be recognized as such and abandoned as soon as feasible.

Some defenders of preferential affirmative action argue, however, that an individual's race, sex, or ethnicity is germane to fulfilling the responsibilities of a faculty member. They believe, therefore, that preferential affirmative action should be a permanent feature of search processes, since it takes account of criteria that should be considered in every appointment.

At least three reasons have been offered to justify the claim that those of a particular race, sex, or ethnicity are particularly well-suited to be faculty members. First, it has been argued that they would be especially effective teachers of any student who shares their race, sex, or ethnicity.[8] Second, they have been supposed to be particularly insightful researchers due to their experiencing the world from distinctive standpoints.[9] Third, they have been taken to be role models, demonstrating that those of a particular race, sex, or ethnicity can perform effectively as faculty members.[10]

Consider each of these claims in turn. As to the presumed teaching effectiveness of the individuals in question, no empirical study supports the claim.[11] But assume compelling evidence were presented. It would have no implications for individual cases. A particular person who does not share race, sex, or ethnicity with students might teach them superbly. An individual of the students' own race, sex, or ethnicity might be ineffective. Regardless of statistical correlations, what is crucial is that individuals be able to teach effectively all sorts of students, and it is entirely consistent with procedural affirmative action to seek individuals who give evidence of satisfying this criterion. But knowing an individual's race, sex, or ethnicity does not reveal whether that person will be effective in the classroom.

Do members of a particular race, sex, or ethnicity share a distinctive intellectual perspective that enhances their scholarship? The philosopher Celia Wolf-Devine has aptly described this claim as a form of "stereotyping" that is "demeaning." As she puts it, "A Hispanic who is a Republican is no less a Hispanic, and a woman who is not a feminist is no less a woman."[12] Furthermore, are Hispanic men and women supposed to have the same point of view in virtue of their common ethnicity, or are they supposed to have different points of view in virtue of their different sexes?

If our standpoints are thought to be determined by our race, sex, and ethnicity, why not also by the numerous other significant respects in which people differ, such as age, religion, sexual orientation, and so on? Since each of us is unique, can anyone else share my point of view?

That my own experience is my own is a tautology that does not imply the keenness of my insight into my experience. The victim of a crime may as a result embrace an outlandish theory of racism. But neither who you are nor what you experience guarantees the truth of your theories.

To be an effective researcher calls for discernment, imagination, and perseverance. These attributes are not tied to one's race, sex, ethnicity, age, or religion. Black scholars, for example, may be more inclined to study black literature than are non-black scholars. But some non-black literary critics are more interested in and more knowledgeable about black literature than are some black literary critics. Why make decisions based on fallible racial generalizations when judgments of individual merit are obtainable and more reliable?

Perhaps the answer lies in the claim that only those of a particular race,

sex, or ethnicity can serve as role models, exemplifying to members of a particular group the possibility of their success. Again, no empirical study supports the claim, but in this case it has often been taken as self-evident that,
for instance, only a woman can be a role model for a woman, only a black for
a black, only a Catholic for a Catholic. In other words, the crucial feature of a
person is supposed to be not what the person does but who the person *is*.

The logic of the situation, however, is not so clear. Consider, for example,
a black man who is a Catholic. Presumably he serves as a role model for
blacks, men, and Catholics. Does he serve as a role model for black women,
or can only a black woman serve that purpose? Does he serve as a role model for all Catholics or only for those who are black? Can I serve as a role model for anyone else, since no one else shares all my characteristics? Or perhaps
I can serve as a role model for everyone else, since everyone else belongs to
at least one group to which I belong.

Putting aside these conundrums, the critical point is supposed to be that
in a field in which discrimination has been rife, a successful individual who
belongs to the discriminated group demonstrates that members of the group
can succeed in that field. Obviously success is possible without a role model,
for the first successful individual had none. But suppose persuasive evidence were offered that a role model, while not necessary, sometimes is helpful, not only to those who belong to the group in question, but also to those
prone to believe that no members of the group can perform effectively within the field. Role models would then both encourage members of a group
that had suffered discrimination and discourage further discrimination
against the group.

To serve these purposes, however, the person chosen would need to be
viewed as having been selected by the same criteria as all others. If not,
members of the group that has suffered discrimination as well as those prone
to discriminate would be confirmed in their common view that members of
the group never would have been chosen unless membership in the group
had been taken into account. Those who suffered discrimination would conclude that it still exists, while those prone to discriminate would conclude
that members of the group lack the necessary attributes to compete equally.

How can we ensure that a person chosen for a position has been selected
by the same criteria as all others? Preferential affirmative action fails to serve
the purpose, since by definition it differentiates among people on the basis of
criteria other than performance. The approach that ensures merit selection is
procedural affirmative action. By its demand for vigilance against every
form of discrimination, it maximizes equal opportunity for all.

The policy of appointing others than the best qualified has not produced
a harmonious society in which prejudice is transcended and all enjoy the
benefits of self-esteem. Rather, the practice has bred doubts about the abilities of those chosen while generating resentment in those passed over.

Procedural affirmative action had barely begun before it was replaced by
preferential affirmative action. The difficulties with the latter are now clear.
Before deeming them necessary evils in the struggle to overcome pervasive

prejudice, why not try scrupulous enforcement of procedural affirmative action? We might thereby most directly achieve that equitable society so ardently desired by every person of good will.

NOTES

1. A comprehensive history of one well-documented case of such discrimination is Dan A. Oren, *Joining the Club: A History of Jews and Yale* (New Haven and London: Yale University Press, 1985). Prior to the end of World War II, no Jew had ever been appointed to the rank of full professor in Yale College.

2. 41 C.F.R. 60-2.12. The Order provides no suggestion as to whether a "good faith effort" implies only showing preference among equally qualified candidates (the "tie-breaking" model), preferring a strong candidate to an even stronger one (the "plus factor" model), preferring a merely qualified candidate to a strongly qualified candidate (the "trumping" model), or cancelling a search unless a qualified candidate of the preferred sort is available (the "quota" model).

   A significant source of misunderstanding about affirmative action results from both the government's failure to clarify which type of preference is called for by a "good faith effort" and the failure on the part of those conducting searches to inform applicants which type of preference is in use. Regarding the latter issue, see my "Colleges Should Be Explicit About Who Will Be Considered for Jobs," *The Chronicle of Higher Education, XXXV* (30), 1989, reprinted in *Affirmative Action and the University: A Philosophical Inquiry*, Steven M. Cahn (ed.), (Philadelphia: Temple University Press, 1993), pp. 3–4.

3. Whether their use is appropriate in a school's admission and scholarship decisions is a different issue, involving other considerations, and I shall not explore that subject in this article.

4. See, for example, Leslie Pickering Francis, "In Defense of Affirmative Action," in Cahn, *op. cit.,* especially pp. 24–26. She raises concerns about unfairness to those individuals forced by circumstances not of their own making to bear all the costs of compensation, as well as injustices to those who have been equally victimized but are not members of specified groups.

5. The term gained currency when Justice Lewis Powell, in his pivotal opinion in the Supreme Court's 1978 *Bakke* decision, found "the attainment of a diverse student body" to be a goal that might justify the use of race in student admissions. An incisive analysis of that decision is Carl Cohen, *Naked Racial Preference* (Lanham, Md.: Madison Books, 1995), pp. 55–80.

6. Cahn, *op. cit.*, p. 151.

7. Consider Michael Rosenfeld, *Affirmative Action and Justice: A Philosophical and Constitutional Inquiry* (New Haven and London: Yale University Press, 1991), p. 336: "Ironically, the sooner affirmative action is allowed to complete its mission, the sooner the need for it will altogether disappear."

8. See, for example, Francis, *op. cit.,* p. 31.

9. See, for example, Richard Wasserstrom, "The University and the Case for Preferential Treatment," *American Philosophical Quarterly, 13* (4), 1976, pp. 165–170.

10. See, for example, Joel J. Kupperman, "Affirmative Action: Relevant Knowledge and Relevant Ignorance," in Cahn, *op. cit.,* pp. 181–188.

11. Consider Judith Jarvis Thomson, "Preferential Hiring," *Philosophy and Public Af-*

fairs, 2 (4), 1973, p. 368: "I do not think that as a student I learned any better, or any more, from the women who taught me than from the men, and I do not think that my own women students now learn any better or any more from me than they do from my male colleagues."
12. Cahn, *op. cit.*, p. 230.

Are Quotas Sometimes Justified?

❖❖

JAMES RACHELS

> You have already read some work of James Rachels (pp. 245–255; 288–294). Here he addresses the question of whether circumstances could ever justify the imposition of a racial or sexual quota in the process of appointing a faculty member. His answer may surprise you, but the challenge, as usual, is to assess his argument and decide whether it is sound.

Of the many kinds of policies that have been devised to combat discrimination, quotas are the most despised. Almost no one has a good word to say about them. Even those who defend other varieties of preferential treatment are eager, more often than not, to make it known that they do not approve of quotas. In an area in which there is little agreement about anything else, there is a remarkable consensus about this.

Why are quotas thought to be so objectionable? The key idea seems to be that justice is blind, or at least that it should be blind where race and gender are concerned. Jobs should go to the best qualified applicants, regardless of race or sex; anything else is unacceptably discriminatory. A race- or gender-based quota contradicts this fundamental principle. A hiring quota seems to involve—necessarily—the idea that a less qualified black or woman may be hired ahead of a better qualified white male. But if it is wrong to discriminate against blacks and women, how can it be right to discriminate against white men? This point seems to many people to be so obviously correct that quotas are ruled out peremptorily. It is no wonder that the very word has acquired a bad smell.

With so many other issues still unresolved, it may seem perverse to question the one thing about which there is agreement. Nevertheless, I believe that the prevailing consensus concerning quotas is misguided. There is nothing wrong with a quota used in the right circumstances and for the right reason. It needs to be emphasized, however, that there are significant differences in the ways that quotas may be used. They may be imposed in various sorts of circumstances and for various purposes. In what follows I describe a set of circumstances in which I believe the imposition of a quota is justified. I do not conclude from this that the imposition of quotas is in general a good thing or that they should be widely used. If only because they cause such resentment, they should be used sparingly. But I do conclude that the near-universal condemnation of quotas is misguided. It is wrong to think they should never be used.

Suppose you are the dean of a college—let us say that it is a good college, but not one of the most prestigious in the country—and you are concerned that only the best qualified scholars are hired for your faculty. Your college uses the standard procedure for selecting new faculty: The relevant department solicits applications, reviews them, and then recommends the best qualified to you. You then authorize the formal offer of employment. Your role is mainly that of an overseer; so long as everything seems to be in order, you go along with the departments' recommendations.

In your philosophy department, there are vacancies almost every year. You notice, however, that women are almost never hired to fill them. (One woman was hired years ago, so there is a token female. But that's as far as it has gone.) So you investigate. You discover that there are, indeed, lots of female philosophers looking for jobs each year. And you have no reason to think that these women are, on average, any less capable than their male counterparts. On the contrary, all available evidence suggests that they are equally as good. So you talk to the (male) chairperson of the philosophy department and you urge him to be careful to give full and fair consideration to the female applicants. Being a good liberal fellow, he finds this agreeable enough—although he may be a little offended by the suggestion that he is not already giving women due consideration. But your admonition has little apparent effect. Each time there is a vacancy in the philosophy faculty, and candidates are being considered, he continues to report, with evident sincerity, that in the particular group under review a male has turned out to be the best qualified. And so, he says each year, if we want to hire the best qualified applicant we have to hire the man, at least this time.

This is repeated annually, with minor variations. One of the variations is that the best female philosopher in the pool may be listed as the department's top choice. But when, predictably enough, she turns out to be unavailable (having been snapped up by a more prestigious university), no women in the second tier are considered to be good alternatives. Here you notice a peculiar asymmetry: namely, that although the very best males are also going to other universities, the males in the second tier are considered good alternatives. Momentarily, then, you consider whether the problem could be that philosophical talent is distributed in a funny way: While the very best women are equal to the very best men, at the next level down the men suddenly dominate. But that seems unlikely.

After further efforts have been made along these lines, without result, you might eventually conclude that there is an unconscious prejudice at work. Your department, despite its good intentions and its one female member, is biased. It isn't hard to understand why this could be so. In addition to the usual sources of prejudice against women—the stereotypes, the picture of women as less rational than men, and so forth—an all-male or mostly male group enjoys a kind of camaraderie that might seem impossible if females were significantly included. In choosing a new colleague the matter of how someone would "fit in" with the existing group will always have some influence. This will work against females, no matter what their talents as teachers and scholars.

Finally, then, you reach two conclusions. First, you are not getting the best qualified scholars for your faculty. Better qualified women are being passed over in favor of less qualified men. Second, this problem is unlikely to be corrected if the "standard" procedure of permitting the philosophy department to choose its own new members is continued.

Therefore, you issue a new instruction: You tell the philosophy department that it *must* hire some additional women, in numbers at least in proportion to the number of women in the applicant pool. (Why that number? Because, if talent is equally distributed among men and women, that is the number most likely to result in the best qualified individuals being hired.) The department's reaction is easily predictable. It will be objected that this policy could result in hiring a less qualified woman over a better qualified man. That would be unfair. Faculty should be hired, it will be said, according to their qualifications and not according to their gender.

But you agree that the best qualified should be hired. That is precisely what you are trying to achieve. You are not out to give women a special break. You are not trying to redress the injustices they have suffered in the past; nor are you trying to provide "role models" for female students. You may be pleased if your policy has these effects, but the purpose of your new instruction is not to achieve them. Your only purpose is to get the best qualified scholars for your faculty, regardless of gender. The question is simply what selection procedure will best serve that purpose. The fact of unconscious prejudice makes the usual system of simply allowing your experts—the philosophy department—to exercise their judgment an ineffective method. Allowing them to exercise their judgment within the limits of a quota, on the other hand, might be more effective because it reduces the influence of unconscious prejudice. The department's objection, along with all the other usual objections to quotas, misses the point.

That's the argument. It is worth emphasizing that this argument takes into account a feature of the selection process that is often ignored when "preferential treatment" is discussed. Often, the question is put like this: Assuming that X (a white man) is better qualified than Y (a black or a woman), is it justifiable to adopt a policy that would permit hiring or promoting Y rather than X? Then the debate begins, and various reasons are produced that might justify such a policy, such as that it redresses wrongs or that it helps to combat racism or sexism. The debate focuses on whether such reasons are sufficient, and the critical issue appears to be justice versus social utility: Justice argues for hiring X, while reasons of social utility weigh in on behalf of hiring Y.

When the issue is approached in this way, a crucial point is overlooked. People do not come prelabeled as better or worse qualified. Before we can say that X is better qualified than Y, someone has to have made that judgment. And this is where prejudice is most likely to enter the picture. A male philosopher, judging other philosophers, might very well rate women lower, without even realizing he is doing so. The argument we are considering is intended to address this problem, which arises before the terms of the conventional discussion are even set.

Of course, this argument does not purport to show that any system of quotas, applied in any circumstances, is fair. It implies nothing at all about whether schools should establish quotas for the admission of minority students, for example; nor does it imply anything about whether a certain number of government contracts should be set aside for minority businesses. Those remain separate issues. Moreover, the argument does not even say that hiring quotas should be used for all academic appointments. The argument is only a defense of quotas used in a certain way in certain particular circumstances.

But the type of circumstances I have described is not uncommon. Actual quota systems, of the sort that have been established and tested in the courts in recent years, often have just this character. They are instituted to counter the prejudice, conscious or otherwise, that corrupts judgments of merit. When Federal District Court Judge Frank Johnson ordered the Alabama State Police to hire black officers—an order that was widely condemned as just another objectionable "quota"—he was not attempting to redress past injustices or anything of the sort. He was, instead, attempting to curb present injustices against blacks whose qualifications were being systematically underrated by white officials. University people are likely to feel superior to the Alabama police officers: *They* may be guilty of bias, it will be said, but *we* are not. But of course it is almost always a mistake to think oneself an exception to tendencies that are well-nigh universal among human beings. Few of us are saints.

To summarize: Our argument envisions the imposition of a quota as a corrective to a "normal" decision-making process that has gone wrong. We may define a "normal" process as follows: (1) The goal of the process is to identify the best qualified individuals for the purpose at hand. (2) The nature of the qualifications is specified. (3) A pool of candidates is assembled. (4) The qualifications of the individuals in the pool are assessed, using the specified criteria, and the candidates are ranked from best to worst. (5) The jobs, promotions, or whatever are awarded to the best qualified individuals.

This process may go wrong in any number of ways, of course, some of them not involving prejudice. We are not concerned here with all the ways in which things can go wrong. We are concerned only with this possibility: First, we notice that, as the selection process is carried out, individuals from a certain group are regularly rated higher than members of another group. Second, we can find no reason to think that the members of the former group are in fact superior to the members of the latter group—on the contrary, there is reason to think the members of the two groups are, on average, equally well qualified. Moreover, the distribution of qualifications within the two groups seems normal, from top to bottom. And third, there is reason to think that the people performing the assessments are prejudiced against members of the latter group. These are the circumstances in which our argument says the imposition of a quota may be justified, if other corrective steps cannot do the job. The quota is justified as an effective method for making sure that the best qualified win out, despite the prejudices that inescapably operate against them. The quota does not introduce a new element of prejudice. It merely cancels out an old one.

In deciding what should be done, the policies that have the best reasons on their side should come out on top. In this area, however, emotions run so high that reason often takes second place, and arguments are adduced only to support views to which people are already viscerally committed. I cannot say for certain that the argument I have presented does not contain some flaw that has escaped my notice. But even if it is unassailable, I am pessimistic about whether it will make much difference in the public debate. The emotions that surround this whole subject are too powerful, and the lines that have been drawn are too firmly in place, to allow much optimism on behalf of reason. Nevertheless, if this argument is sound, it does show that the prevailing consensus against quotas does not have reason on its side, no matter how powerful are the emotions that sustain it.

What Is a Liberal Education?

SIDNEY HOOK

> In a previous selection (pp. 321–326) John Dewey stressed that the welfare of a democratic community depends on the understanding and capability of its citizenry. But what knowledge, skills, and val-

ues do we all require to enable us to make a success of our experiment in self-government? That is the question addressed in our next
essay, which is written by Dewey's student Sidney Hook, whose
work we read before (pp. 300–302).

What, concretely, should the modern man know in order to live intelligently
in the world today? What should we require that he learn of subject matters
and skills in his educational career in order that he may acquire maturity in
feeling, in judgment, in action? Can we indicate the minimum indispens-
ables of a liberal education in the modern world? This approach recognizes
that no subject per se is inherently liberal at all times and places. But it also
recognizes that within a given age in a given culture, the enlightenment and
maturity, the freedom and power, which liberal education aims to impart, is
more likely to be achieved by mastery of some subject matters and skills than
by others. In short, principles must bear fruit in specific programs in specific
times. In what follows I shall speak of studies rather than of conventional
courses.

  1. The liberally educated person should be intellectually at home in the
world of physical nature. He should know something about the earth he in-
habits and its place in the solar system, about the solar system and its relation to the cosmos. He should know something about mechanics, heat, light,
electricity, and magnetism as the universal forces that condition anything he
is or may become. He should be just as intimately acquainted with the nature of man as a biological species, his evolution, and the discoveries of experimental genetics. He should know something about the structure of his
own body and mind, and the cycle of birth, growth, learning, and decline. To
have even a glimmer of understanding of these things, he must go beyond
the level of primary description and acquire some grasp of the principles
that explain what he observes. Where an intelligent grasp of principles requires a knowledge of mathematics, its fundamental ideas should be presented in such a way that students carry away the sense of mathematics not
only as a tool for the solution of problems but as a study of types of order,
system, and language.

  Such knowledge is important to the individual *not* merely because of its
intrinsic fascination. Every subject from numismatics to Sanskrit possesses
an intrinsic interest to those who are curious about it. It is important because
it helps make everyday experience more intelligible; because it furnishes a
continuous exemplification of scientific method in action; because our world
is literally being remade by the consequences and applications of science; because the fate of nations and the vocations of men depend upon the use of
this knowledge; and because it provides the instruments to reduce our vast
helplessness and dependence in an uncertain world.

  Such knowledge is no less important because it bears upon the formation of *rational belief* about the place of man in the universe. Whatever views a man professes today about God, human freedom, Cosmic Purpose, and personal survival, he cannot reasonably hold them in ignorance of the scientific account of the world and man.

These are some of the reasons why the study of the natural sciences, and the elementary mathematical notions they involve, should be *required* of everyone. Making such study required imposes a heavy obligation and a difficult task of pedagogical discovery upon those who teach it. It is commonly recognized that the sciences today are taught as if all students enrolled in science courses were preparing to be professional scientists. Most of them are not. Naturally they seek to escape a study whose wider and larger uses they do not see because many of their teachers do not see it. Here is not the place to canvass and evaluate the attempts being made to organize instruction in the sciences. The best experience seems to show that one science should not be taken as the exemplar of all, but that the basic subject matter of astronomy, physics, chemistry, geology, in one group, and biology and psychology in another, should be covered. For when only one science is taught it tends to be treated professionally. Similarly, the best experience indicates that instruction should be interdepartmental—any competent teacher from one of these fields in either group should be able to teach all of them in the group, instead of having a succession of different teachers each representing his own field. This usually destroys both the continuity and the cumulative effect of the teaching as a whole.

2. Every student should be required to become intelligently aware of how the society in which he lives functions, of the great forces molding contemporary civilization, and of the crucial problems of our age which await decision. The studies most appropriate to this awareness have been conventionally separated into history, economics, government, sociology, social psychology, and anthropology. This separation is an intellectual scandal. For it is impossible to have an adequate grasp of the problems of government without a knowledge of economics, and vice versa. Except for some special domains of professional interest, the same is true for the other subjects as well.

The place of the social studies, properly integrated around problems and issues, is fundamental in the curriculum of modern education. It is one of the dividing points between the major conflicting schools of educational thought. The question of its justification must be sharply distinguished from discussion of the relative merits of this or that mode of approach to the social studies.

The knowledge and insight that the social studies can give are necessary for every student because no matter what his specialized pursuits may later be, the extent to which he can follow them, and the "contextual" developments within these fields, depend upon the total social situation of which they are in some sense a part. An engineer today whose knowledge is restricted only to technical matters of engineering, or a physician whose competence extends only to the subject matter of traditional medical training, is ill-prepared to plan intelligently for a life-career or to understand the basic problems that face his profession. He is often unable to cope adequately with those specific problems in his own domain that involve, as so many problems of social and personal health do, economic and psychological difficulties. No matter what an individual's vocation, the conditions of his effective functioning depend upon pervasive social tendencies which set the occasions for the application of knowledge, provide the opportunities of employment, and not seldom determine even the direction of research.

More important, the whole presupposition of the theory of democracy is that the electorate will be able to make intelligent decisions on the issues before it. These issues are basically political, social, and economic. Their specific character changes from year to year. But their generic form, and the character of the basic problems, do not. Nor, most essential of all, do the proper intellectual habits of meeting them change. It is undeniably true that the world we live in is one marked by greater changes, because of the impact of technology, than ever before. This does not necessitate changing the curriculum daily to catch up with today's newspapers, nor does it justify a concentration on presumably eternal problems as if these problems had significance independent of cultural place–time. The fact that we are living in a world where the rate of cultural change is greater than at any time in the past, together with its ramifications, may itself become a central consideration for analysis. . . .

3. Everyone recognizes a distinction between knowledge and wisdom. This distinction is not clarified by making a mystery of wisdom and speaking of it as if it were begotten by divine inspiration while knowledge had a more lowly source. Wisdom is a kind of knowledge. It is knowledge of the nature, career, and consequences of *human values*. Since these cannot be separated from the human organism and the social scene, the moral ways of man cannot be understood without knowledge of the ways of things and institutions.

To study social affairs without an analysis of policies is to lose oneself in factual minutiae that lack interest and relevance. But knowledge of values is a prerequisite of the intelligent determination of policy. Philosophy, most broadly viewed, is the critical survey of existence from the standpoint of value. This points to the twofold role of philosophy in the curriculum of the college.

The world of physical nature may be studied without reference to human values. But history, art, literature, and particularly the social studies involve problems of value at every turn. A social philosophy whose implications are worked out is a series of proposals that something be *done* in the world. It includes a set of *plans* to conserve or change aspects of social life. Today the community is arrayed under different banners without a clear understanding of the basic issues involved. In the press of controversy, the ideals and values at the heart of every social philosophy are widely affirmed as articles of blind faith. They are partisan commitments justified only by the emotional security they give to believers. They spread by contagion, unchecked by critical safeguards; yet the future of civilization largely depends upon them and how they are held. It is therefore requisite that their study be made an integral part of the liberal arts curriculum. Systematic and critical instruction should be given in the great maps of life—the ways to heaven, hell, and earth—which are being unrolled in the world today.

Ideals and philosophies of life are not parts of the world of nature; but it is a pernicious illusion to imagine that they cannot be studied "scientifically." Their historical origins, their concatenation of doctrine, their controlling assumptions, their means, methods, and consequences in practice, can and should be investigated in a scientific spirit. There are certain social philosophies that would forbid such an investigation for fear of not being able to survive it; but it is one of the great merits of the democratic way of life and one of its strongest claims for acceptance that it can withstand analysis of this sort. It is incumbent upon the liberal arts college to provide for close study of the dominant social and political philosophies, ranging from one end of the color spectrum to the other. Proper study will disclose that these philosophies cannot be narrowly considered in their own terms. They involve an examination of the great ways of life—of the great visions of philosophy which come into play whenever we try to arrange our values in a preference scale in order to choose the better between conflicting goods. Philosophy is best taught when the issues of moral choice arise naturally out of the problems of social life. The effective integration of concrete materials from history, literature, and social studies can easily be achieved within a philosophical perspective.

4. Instruction in the natural, social, and technological forces shaping the world, and in the dominant conflicting ideals in behalf of which these forces are to be controlled, goes a long way. But not far enough. Far more important than knowledge is the method by which it is reached, and the ability to recognize when it constitutes *evidence* and when not; and more important than any particular ideal is the way in which it is held, and the capacity to evaluate it in relation to other ideals. From first to last, in season and out, our educational institutions, especially on the college level, must emphasize *methods* of analysis. They must build up in students a critical sense of evidence, relevance, and validity against which the multitudinous seas of propaganda will wash in vain. They must strengthen the powers of independent reflection, which will enable students to confront the claims of ideals and values by their alternatives and the relative costs of achieving them. . . .

The field of language, of inference and argument, is a broad field but a definite one in which specific training can be given to all students. How to read intelligently, how to recognize good from bad reasoning, how to evaluate evidence, how to distinguish between a definition and a hypothesis and between a hypothesis and a resolution, can be taught in such a way as to build up permanent habits of logic in action. The result of thorough training in "semantic" analysis—using that term in its broadest sense without invidious distinctions between different schools—is an intellectual sophistication without which a man may be learned but not intelligent.

Judging by past and present curricular achievements in developing students with intellectual sophistication and maturity, our colleges must be pronounced, in the main, dismal failures. The main reason for the failure is the absence of serious effort, except in a few institutions, to realize this goal. The necessity of the task is not even recognized. This failure is not only intellectually reprehensible; it is socially dangerous. For the natural susceptibility of youth to enthusiasms, its tendency to glorify action, and its limited experience make it easy recruiting material for all sorts of demagogic movements which flatter its strength and impatience. Recent history furnishes many illustrations of how, in the absence of strong critical sense, youthful strength can lead to cruelty, and youthful impatience to folly. It is true that people who are incapable of thinking cannot be taught how to think, and that the incapacity for thought is not restricted to those who learn. But the first cannot be judged without being exposed to the processes of critical instruction, and the second should be eliminated from the ranks of the teachers. There is considerable evidence to show that students who are capable of completing high school can be so taught that they are aware of *whether* they are thinking or not. There is hope that, with better pedagogic skill and inspiration, they may become capable of grasping the main thought of *what* they are reading or hearing in non-technical fields—of developing a sense of *what validly follows from what*, an accompanying sensitiveness to the dominant types of fallacies, and a habit of weighing evidence for conclusions advanced.

My own experience has led me to the conclusion that this is *not* accomplished by courses in formal logic which, when given in a rigorous and elegant way, accomplish little more than courses in pure mathematics. There is an approach to the study of logic that on an elementary level is much more successful in achieving the ends described above than the traditional course in formal logic. This plunges the student into an analysis of language material around him. By constant use of concrete illustrations drawn from all fields, but especially the fields of politics and social study, insight is developed into the logical principles of definition, the structure of analogies, dilemmas, types of fallacies and the reasons *why* they are fallacies, the criteria of good hypotheses, and related topics. Such training may legitimately be required of all students. Although philosophers are usually best able to give it, any teacher who combines logical capacity with pedagogic skill can make this study a stimulating experience.

5. There is less controversy about the desirability of the study of composition and literature than about any other subject in the traditional or modern curriculum. It is appreciated that among the essentials of clear thought are good language habits and that, except in the higher strata of philosophic discourse, tortuous obscurities of expression are more likely to be an indication of plain confusion than of stuttering profundity. It is also widely recog-

nized that nothing can take the place of literature in developing the imagination, and in imparting a sense of the inexhaustible richness of human personality. The questions that arise at this point are not of justification, but of method, technique, and scope of comprehensiveness.

If good language habits are to be acquired *only* in order to acquire facility in thinking, little can be said for the conventional courses in English composition. Students cannot acquire facility in clear expression in the space of a year, by developing sundry themes from varied sources, under the tutelage of instructors whose training and interest may not qualify them for sustained critical thought. Clear thinking is best controlled by those who are at home in the field in which thinking is done. If language instruction is to be motivated only by the desire to strengthen the power of organizing ideas in written discourse, it should be left to properly trained instructors in other disciplines.

But there are other justifications for teaching students English composition. The first is that there are certain rules of intelligent reading that are essential to—if they do not constitute—understanding. These rules are very elementary. By themselves they do not tell us how to understand a poem, a mathematical demonstration, a scientific text, or a religious prayer—all of which require special skills. But they make it easier for the student to uncover the nature of the "argument"—what is being said, what is being assumed, what is being presented as evidence—in any piece of prose that is not a narrative or simply informational in content. In a sense these rules are integral to the study of logic in action, but in such an introductory way that they are usually not considered part of logical study which begins its work after basic meanings have been established, or in independence of the meaning of logical symbols.

Another reason for teaching English composition independently is its uses in learning how to write. "Effective writing" is not necessarily the same thing as logical writing. The purpose for which we write determines whether our writing is effective. And there are many situations in which we write not to convince or to prove but to explain, arouse, confess, challenge, or assuage. To write *interestingly* may sometimes be just as important as to write soundly because getting a hearing and keeping attention may depend upon it. How much of the skills of writing can be taught is difficult to say. That it is worth making the effort to teach these skills is indisputable.

The place of language in the curriculum involves not merely our native language but *foreign* languages. Vocational considerations aside, should knowledge of a foreign language be required, and why? . . .

The main reason why students should be requested to learn another language is that it is the most effective medium by which, when properly taught, they can acquire a sensitivity to language, to the subtle tones, undertones, and overtones of words, and to the licit ambiguities of imaginative discourse. No one who has not translated prose or poetry from one language to another can appreciate both the unique richness and the unique limitations of his own language. This is particularly true where the life of the emotions is concerned; and it is particularly important that it should be realized. For the appreciation of emotions, perhaps even their recognition in certain cases, depends upon their linguistic identification. The spectrum of human emotions is much more dense than the words by which we render them. Knowledge of different languages, and the attempts made to communicate back and forth between them in our own minds, broaden and diversify our own feelings. They multiply points of view, and liberate us from the prejudice that words—*our* words—are the natural signs of things and events. The genius of a culture is exemplified in a preeminent way in the characteristic idioms of its language. In learning another language we enable ourselves to appreciate both the cultural similarities and differences of the Western world. . . .

The place of literature in the curriculum is justified by so many considerations that it is secure against all criticism. Here, too, what is at issue is not whether literature—Greek, Latin, English, European, American—should be read and studied in the schools but what should be read, when, and by what methods. These are details, important details—but outside the scope of our inquiry.

Something should be said about the unique opportunity which the teaching of literature provides, not only in giving delight by heightening perception of the formal values of literary craftsmanship, but in giving insight into people. The opposite of a liberal education, William James somewhere suggests, is a literal education. A literal education is one which equips a person to read formulas and equations, straightforward prose, doggerel verse, and advertising signs. It does not equip one to read the language of metaphor, of paradox, of indirect analogy, of serious fancy in which the emotions and passions and half-believed ideas of human beings express themselves. To read great literature is to read men—their fears and motives, their needs and hopes. Every great novelist is a *Menschenkenner* who opens the hearts of others to us and helps us to read our own hearts as well. The intelligent study of literature should never directly aim to strengthen morals and improve manners. For its natural consequences are a delicacy of perception and an emotional tact that are defeated by preaching and didactic teaching.

A liberal education will impart an awareness of the amazing and precious complexity of human relationships. Since those relationships are violated more often out of insensitiveness than out of deliberate intent, whatever increases sensitiveness of perception and understanding humanizes life. Literature in all its forms is the great humanizing medium of life. It must therefore be representative of life; not only of past life but of our own; not only of our own culture but of different cultures.

6. An unfailing mark of philistinism in education is reference to the study of art and music as "the frills and fads" of schooling. Insofar as those who speak this way are not tone-deaf or color-blind, they are themselves products of a narrow education, unaware of the profound experiences which

are uniquely bound up with the trained perception of color and form. There is no reason to believe that the capacity for the appreciation of art and music shows a markedly different curve of distribution from what is observable in the measurement of capacity of drawing inferences or recalling relevant information. A sufficient justification for making some study of art and music required in modern education is that it provides an unfailing source of delight in personal experience, a certain grace in living, and a variety of dimensions of meaning by which to interpret the world around us. This is a sufficient justification: there are others, quite subsidiary, related to the themes, the occasions, the history and backgrounds of the works studied. Perhaps one should add—although this expresses only a reasonable hope—that a community whose citizens have developed tastes would not tolerate the stridency, the ugliness and squalor which assault us in our factories, our cities, and our countryside.

One of the reasons why the study of art and music has not received as much attention as it should by educators, particularly on the college level, is that instruction in these subjects often suffers from two opposite defects. Sometimes courses in art and music are given as if all students enrolled in them were planning a career as practicing artists or as professional *teachers* of the arts. Sometimes they are given as hours for passive enjoyment or relaxation in which the teacher does the performing or talking and in which there is no call upon the students to make an intelligent response.

The key-stress in courses in art and music should be *discrimination* and *interpretation*, rather than appreciation and cultivation. The latter can take care of themselves, when the student has learned to discriminate and interpret intelligently.

Briefly summarized: the answer to the question *What should we teach?* is selected materials from the fields of mathematics and the natural sciences; social studies, including history; language and literature; philosophy and logic; art and music. The knowledge imparted by such study should be acquired in such a way as to strengthen the skills of reading and writing, of thinking and imaginative interpretation, of criticism and evaluation.

Crito

❖❖

PLATO

The *Crito*, probably written about the time of the *Defence of Socrates*, relates a conversation Socrates has in prison, while awaiting death. His lifelong friend Crito urges Socrates to run away, assuring him that his rescue can be arranged. Socrates refuses to try to escape, arguing that he is morally obligated to submit to the sentence of the Court, for he accepts its authority and does not wish to bring the system of laws into disrepute.

A much-discussed issue is whether the view Socrates adopts in the *Crito* coheres with the opinions he espouses in his *Defence*. As our translator, David Gallop, explains the apparent inconsistency:

> To some readers the positions adopted by Socrates in the two works have seemed utterly opposed. In the *Defence* he comes across as a champion of intellectual liberty, an individualist bravely defying the conservative Athenian establishment; whereas in the *Crito* he appears to be advocating the most abject submission of the citizen to state authority.

Gallop believes the supposed conflict is illusory, and many commentators agree. Yet they have not reached consensus as to how the reconciliation is to be achieved. I have a suggestion to offer but urge that you proceed now to the *Crito* and return here after finishing it.

The notes are the translator's. The *Index of Names* he prepared can be found at the end of the *Defence of Socrates* in Part I (pp. 38–40).

In my view the key to recognizing the consistency of Socrates' position is found near the end of the dialogue (p. 385), where a distinction is drawn, in essence, between unjust laws and unjust application of just laws. Socrates believes his fellow citizens decided his case wrongly, but he accepts the fairness of the laws under which he was tried and convicted. If he believed the laws themselves were unfair, he would break them. As he says in his *Defence* (p. 25), were a law to be passed banning the study of philosophy, he would disobey it. But he will not evade his death sentence, for "he has been treated unjustly not by . . . Laws but by human beings."

Whether you accept this analysis, you can see why the life of Socrates has so fascinated subsequent generations. He embodies the spirit of philosophical inquiry and the ideal of intellectual integrity.

SOCRATES: Why have you come at this hour, Crito? It's still very early, isn't it?

CRITO: Yes, very.

SOCRATES: About what time?

CRITO: Just before daybreak.

SOCRATES: I'm surprised the prison-warder was willing to answer the door.

CRITO: He knows me by now, Socrates, because I come and go here so often; and besides, I've done him a small favour.

SOCRATES: Have you just arrived, or have you been here for a while?

CRITO: For quite a while.

SOCRATES: Then why didn't you wake me up right away instead of sitting by me in silence?

CRITO: Well *of course* I didn't wake you, Socrates! I only wish I weren't so sleepless and wretched myself. I've been marvelling all this time as I saw how peacefully you were sleeping, and I deliberately kept from waking you, so that you could pass the time as peacefully as possible. I've often admired your disposition in the past, in fact all your life; but more than ever in your present plight, you bear it so easily and patiently.

SOCRATES: Well, Crito, it really would be tiresome for a man of my age to get upset if the time has come when he must end his life.

CRITO: And yet others of your age, Socrates, are overtaken by similar troubles, but their age brings them no relief from being upset at the fate which faces them.

SOCRATES: That's true. But tell me, why *have* you come so early?

CRITO: I bring painful news, Socrates—not painful for you, I suppose, but painful and hard for me and all your friends—and hardest of all for me to bear, I think.

SOCRATES: What news is that? Is it that the ship has come back from Delos,[1] the one on whose return I must die?

CRITO: Well no, it hasn't arrived yet, but I think it will get here today, judging from reports of people who've come from Sunium,[2] where they disembarked. That makes it obvious that it will get here today; and so tomorrow, Socrates, you will have to end your life.

SOCRATES: Well, may that be for the best, Crito. If it so please the gods, so be it. All the same, I don't think it will get here today.

CRITO: What makes you think that?

SOCRATES: I'll tell you. You see, I am to die on the day after the ship arrives, am I not?

CRITO: At least that's what the authorities say.

SOCRATES: Then I don't think it will get here on the day that is just dawning, but on the next one. I infer that from a certain dream I had in the night—a short time ago, so it may be just as well that you didn't wake me.

CRITO: And what was your dream?

SOCRATES: I dreamt that a lovely, handsome woman approached me, robed in white. She called me and said: "Socrates,

Thou shalt reach fertile Phthia upon the third day."[3]

CRITO: What a curious dream, Socrates.

SOCRATES: Yet its meaning is clear, I think, Crito.

CRITO: All too clear, it would seem. But please, Socrates, my dear friend, there is still time to take my advice, and make your escape—because if you die, I shall suffer more than one misfortune: not only shall I lose such a friend as I'll never find again, but it will look to many people, who hardly know you or me, as if I'd abandoned you—since I could have rescued you if I'd been willing to put up the money. And yet what could be more shameful than a reputation for valuing money more highly than friends? Most people won't believe that it was you who refused to leave this place yourself, despite our urging you to do so.

SOCRATES: But why should we care so much, my good Crito, about what most people believe? All the most capable people, whom we should take more seriously, will think the matter has been handled exactly as it has been.

CRITO: Yet surely, Socrates, you can see that one must heed popular opinion too. Your present plight shows by itself that the populace can inflict not the least of evils, but just about the worst, if someone has been slandered in their presence.

SOCRATES: Ah Crito, if only the populace could inflict the worst of evils! Then they would also be capable of providing the greatest of goods, and a fine thing that would be. But the fact is that they can do neither: they are unable to give anyone understanding or lack of it, no matter what they do.

CRITO: Well, if you say so. But tell me this, Socrates: can it be that you are worried for me and your other friends, in case the blackmailers[4] give us trouble, if you escape, for having smuggled you out of here? Are you worried that we might be forced to forfeit all our property as well, or pay heavy fines, or even incur some further penalty? If you're afraid of anything like that, put it out of your mind. In rescuing you we are surely justified in taking that risk, or even worse if need be. Come on, listen to me and do as I say.

SOCRATES: Yes, those risks do worry me, Crito—amongst many others.

CRITO: Then put those fears aside—because no great sum is needed to pay people who are willing to rescue you and get you out of here. Besides, you can surely see that those blackmailers are cheap, and it wouldn't take much to buy them off. My own means are available to you and would be ample, I'm sure. Then again, even if—out of concern on my behalf—you think you shouldn't be spending my money, there are visitors here who are ready to spend theirs. One of them, Simmias from Thebes, has actually brought enough money for this very purpose, while Cebes and quite a number of others are also prepared to contribute. So, as I say, you shouldn't hesitate to save yourself on account of those fears.

And don't let it trouble you, as you were saying in court, that you wouldn't know what to do with yourself if you went into exile. There will be people to welcome you anywhere else you may go: if you want to go to Thessaly,[5] I have friends there who will make much of you and give you safe refuge, so that no one from anywhere in Thessaly will trouble you.

Next, Socrates, I don't think that what you propose—giving yourself up, when you could be rescued—is even just. You are actually hastening to bring upon yourself just the sorts of thing which your enemies would hasten to bring upon you—indeed, they have done so—in their wish to destroy you.

What's more, I think you're betraying those sons of yours. You will be deserting them, if you go off when you could be raising and educating them: as far as you're concerned, they will fare as best they may. In all likelihood, they'll meet the sort of fate which usually befalls orphans once they've lost their parents. Surely, one should either not have children at all, or else see the toil and trouble of their upbringing and education through to the end; yet you seem to me to prefer the easiest path. One should rather choose the path that a good and resolute man would choose, particularly if one professes to cultivate goodness all one's life. Frankly, I'm ashamed for you and for us, your friends: it may appear that this whole predicament of yours has been handled with a certain feebleness on our part. What with the bringing of your case to court when that could have been avoided, the actual conduct of the trial, and now, to crown it all, this absurd outcome of the business, it may seem that the problem has eluded us through some fault or feebleness on our part—in that we failed to save you, and you failed to save yourself, when that was quite possible and feasible, if we had been any use at all.

Make sure, Socrates, that all this doesn't turn out badly, and a disgrace to you as well as us. Come now, form a plan—or rather, don't even plan, because the time for that is past, and only a single plan remains. Everything needs to be carried out during the coming night; and if we go on waiting around, it won't be possible or feasible any longer. Come on, Socrates, do all you can to take my advice, and do exactly what I say.

SOCRATES: My dear Crito, your zeal will be invaluable if it should have right on its side; but otherwise, the greater it is, the harder it makes matters. We must therefore consider whether or not the course you urge should be followed—because it is in my nature, not just now for the first time but always, to follow nothing within me but the principle which appears to me, upon reflection, to be best.

I cannot now reject the very principles that I previously adopted, just because this fate has overtaken me; rather, they appear to me much the same as ever, and I respect and honour the same ones that I did before. If we cannot find better ones to maintain in the present situation, you can be sure that I won't agree with you—not even if the power of the populace threatens us, like children, with more bogeymen than it does now, by visiting us with imprisonment, execution, or confiscation of property.

What, then, is the most reasonable way to consider the matter? Suppose we first take up the point you make about what people will think. Was it always an acceptable principle that one should pay heed to some opinions but not to others, or was it not? Or was it acceptable before I had to die, while now it is exposed as an idle assertion made for the sake of talk, when it is really childish nonsense? For my part, Crito, I'm eager to look into this together with you, to see whether the principle is to be viewed any differently, or in the same way, now that I'm in this position, and whether we should disregard or follow it.

As I recall, the following principle always used to be affirmed by people who thought they were talking sense: the principle, as I was just saying, that one should have a high regard for some opinions held by human beings, but not for others. Come now, Crito: don't you think that was a good principle? I ask because you are not, in all foreseeable likelihood, going to die tomorrow, and my present trouble shouldn't impair your judgement. Consider, then: don't you think it a good principle, that one shouldn't respect all human opinions, but only some and not others; or, again, that one shouldn't respect everyone's opinions, but those of some people, and not those of others? What do you say? Isn't that a good principle?

CRITO: It is.

SOCRATES: And one should respect the good ones, but not the bad ones?

CRITO: Yes.

SOCRATES: And good ones are those of people with understanding, whereas bad ones are those of people without it?

CRITO: Of course.

SOCRATES: Now then, once again, how were such points established? When a man is in training, and concentrating upon that, does he pay heed to the praise or censure or opinion of each and every man, or only to those of the individual who happens to be his doctor or trainer?

CRITO: Only to that individual's.

SOCRATES: Then he should fear the censures, and welcome the praises of that individual, but not those of most people.

CRITO: Obviously.

SOCRATES: So he must base his actions and exercises, his eating and drinking, upon the opinion of the individual, the expert supervisor, rather than upon everyone else's.

CRITO: True.

SOCRATES: Very well. If he disobeys that individual and disregards his opinion and his praises, but respects those of most people, who are ignorant, he'll suffer harm, won't he?

CRITO: Of course.

SOCRATES: And what is that harm? What does it affect? What element within the disobedient man?

CRITO: Obviously, it affects his body, because that's what it spoils.

SOCRATES: A good answer. And in other fields too, Crito—we needn't go through them all, but they surely include matters of just and unjust, honourable and dishonourable, good and bad, the subjects of our present deliberation—is it the opinion of most people that we should follow and fear, or is it that of the individual authority—assuming that some expert exists who should be respected and feared above all others? If we don't follow that person, won't we corrupt and impair the element which (as we agreed) is made better by what is just, but is spoilt by what is unjust? Or is there nothing in all that?

CRITO: I accept it myself, Socrates.

SOCRATES: Well now, if we spoil the part of us that is improved by what is healthy but corrupted by what is unhealthy, because it is not expert opinion that we are following, are our lives worth living once it has been corrupted? The part in question is, of course, the body, isn't it?

CRITO: Yes.

SOCRATES: And are our lives worth living with a poor or corrupted body?

CRITO: Definitely not.

SOCRATES: Well then, are they worth living if the element which is impaired by what is unjust and benefited by what is just has been corrupted? Or do we consider the element to which justice or injustice belongs, whichever part of us it is, to be of less value than the body?

CRITO: By no means.

SOCRATES: On the contrary, it is more precious?

CRITO: Far more.

SOCRATES: Then, my good friend, we shouldn't care all that much about what the populace will say of us, but about what the expert on matters of justice and injustice will say, the individual authority, or Truth. In the first place, then, your proposal that we should care about popular opinion regarding just, honourable, or good actions, and their opposites, is mistaken.

"Even so," someone might say, "the populace has the power to put us to death."

CRITO: *That*'s certainly clear enough; one might say that, Socrates.

SOCRATES: You're right. But the principle we've rehearsed, my dear friend, still remains as true as it was before—for me at any rate. And now consider this further one, to see whether or not it still holds good for us. We should attach the highest value, shouldn't we, not to living, but to living well?

CRITO: Why yes, that still holds.

SOCRATES: And living well is the same as living honourably or justly? Does that still hold or not?

CRITO: Yes, it does.

SOCRATES: Then in the light of those admissions, we must ask the following question: is it just, or is it not, for me to try to get out of here, when Athenian authorities are unwilling to release me? Then, if it does seem just, let us attempt it; but if it doesn't, let us abandon the idea.

As for the questions you raise about expenses and reputation and bringing up children, I suspect they are the concerns of those who cheerfully put people to death, and would bring them back to life if they could, without any intelligence, namely, the populace. For us, however, because our principle so demands, there is no other question to ask except the one we just raised: shall we be acting justly—we who are rescued as well as the rescuers themselves—if we pay money and do favours to those who would get me out of here? Or shall we in truth be acting unjustly if we do all those things? And if it is clear that we shall be acting unjustly in taking that course, then the question whether we shall have to die through standing firm and holding our peace, or suffer in any other way, ought not to weigh with us in comparison with acting unjustly.

CRITO: I think that's finely *said*, Socrates; but do please consider what we should *do*.

SOCRATES: Let's examine that question together, dear friend; and if you have objections to anything I say, please raise them, and I'll listen to you—otherwise, good fellow, it's time to stop telling me, again and again, that I should leave here against the will of Athens. You see, I set great store upon persuading you as to my course of action, and not acting against your will. Come now, just consider whether you find the starting-point of our inquiry acceptable, and try to answer my questions according to your real beliefs.

CRITO: All right, I'll try.

SOCRATES: Do we maintain that people should on no account whatever do injustice willingly? Or may it be done in some circumstances but not in others? Is acting unjustly in no way good or honourable, as we frequently agreed in the past? Or have all those former agreements been jettisoned during these last few days? Can it be, Crito, that men of our age have long failed to notice, as we earnestly conversed with each other, that we ourselves were no better than children? Or is what we then used to say true above all else? Whether most people say so or not, and whether we must be treated more harshly or more leniently than at present, isn't it a fact, all the same, that acting unjustly is utterly bad and shameful for the agent? Yes or no?

CRITO: Yes.

SOCRATES: So one must not act unjustly at all.

CRITO: Absolutely not.

SOCRATES: Then, even if one is unjustly treated, one should not return injustice, as most people believe—given that one should act not unjustly at all.

CRITO: Apparently not.

SOCRATES: Well now, Crito, should one ever ill-treat anybody or not?

CRITO: Surely not, Socrates.

SOCRATES: And again, when one suffers ill-treatment, is it just to return it, as most people maintain, or isn't it?

CRITO: It is not just at all.

SOCRATES: Because there's no difference, I take it, between ill-treating people and treating them unjustly.

CRITO: Correct.

SOCRATES: Then one shouldn't return injustice or ill-treatment to any human being, no matter how one may be treated by that person. And in making those admissions, Crito, watch out that you're not agreeing to anything contrary to your real beliefs. I say that, because I realize that the belief is held by few people, and always will be. Those who hold it share no common counsel with those who don't; but each group is bound to regard the other with contempt when they observe one another's decisions. You too, therefore, should consider very carefully whether you share that belief with me, and whether we may begin our deliberations from the following premise: neither doing nor returning injustice is ever right, nor should one who is ill-treated defend himself by retaliation. Do you agree? Or do you dissent and not share my belief in that premise? I've long been of that opinion myself, and I still am now; but if you've formed any different view, say so, and explain it. If you stand by our former view, however, then listen to my next point.

CRITO: Well, I do stand by it and share that view, so go ahead.

SOCRATES: All right, I'll make my next point—or rather, ask a question. Should the things one agrees with someone else be done, provided they are just, or should one cheat?

CRITO: They should be done.

SOCRATES: Then consider what follows. If we leave this place without having persuaded our city, are we or are we not ill-treating certain people, indeed people whom we ought least of all to be ill-treating? And would we be abiding by the things we agreed, those things being just, or not?

CRITO: I can't answer your question, Socrates, because I don't understand it.

SOCRATES: Well, look at it this way. Suppose we were on the point of running away from here, or whatever else one should call it. Then the Laws, or the State of Athens, might come and confront us, and they might speak as follows:

"Please tell us, Socrates, what do you have in mind? With this action you are attempting, do you intend anything short of destroying us, the Laws and the city as a whole, to the best of your ability? Do you think that a city can still exist without being overturned, if the legal judgments rendered within it possess no force, but are nullified or invalidated by individuals?"

What shall we say, Crito, in answer to that and other such questions? Because somebody, particularly a legal advocate,[6] might say a great deal on behalf of the law that is being invalidated here, the one requiring that judgments, once rendered, shall have authority. Shall we tell them: "Yes, that is our intention, because the city was treating us unjustly, by not judging our case correctly"? Is that to be our answer, or what?

CRITO: Indeed it is, Socrates.

SOCRATES: And what if the Laws say: "And was that also part of the agreement between you and us, Socrates? Or did you agree to abide by whatever judgments the city rendered?"

Then, if we were surprised by their words, perhaps they might say: "Don't be surprised at what we are saying, Socrates, but answer us, seeing that you like to use question-and-answer. What complaint, pray, do you have against the city and ourselves, that you should now attempt to destroy us? In the first place, was it not we who gave you birth? Did your father not marry your mother and beget you under our auspices? So will you inform those of us here who regulate marriages whether you have any criticism of them as poorly framed?"

"No, I have none," I should say.

"Well then, what of the laws dealing with children's upbringing and education, under which you were educated yourself? Did those of us Laws who are in charge of that area not give proper direction, when they required your father to educate you in the arts and physical training?"[7]

"They did," I should say.

"Very good. In view of your birth, upbringing, and education, can you deny, first, that you belong to us as our offspring and slave, as your forebears also did? And if so, do you imagine that you are on equal terms with us in regard to what is just, and that whatever treatment we may accord to you, it is just for you to do the same thing back to us? You weren't on equal terms with your father, or your master (assuming you had one), making it just for you to return the treatment you received— answering back when you were scolded, or striking back when you were struck, or doing many other things of the same sort. Will you then have licence against your fatherland and its Laws, if we try to destroy you, in the belief that that is just? Will you try to destroy us in return, to the best of your ability? And will you claim that in doing so you are acting justly, you who are genuinely exercised about goodness? Or are you, in your wisdom, unaware that, in comparison with your mother and father and all your other forebears, your fatherland is more precious and venerable, more sacred and held in higher esteem among gods, as well as among human beings who have any sense; and that you should revere your fatherland, deferring to it and appeasing it when it is angry, more than your own father? You must either persuade it, or else do whatever it commands; and if it ordains that you must submit to certain treatment, then you must hold your peace and submit to it: whether that means being beaten or put in bonds, or whether it leads you into war to be wounded or killed, you must act accordingly, and that is what is just; you must neither give way nor retreat, nor leave your position; rather, in warfare, in court, and everywhere else, you must do whatever your city or fatherland commands, or else persuade it as to what is truly just; and if it is sinful to use violence against your mother or father, it is far more so to use it against your fatherland."

What shall we say to that, Crito? That the Laws are right or not?

CRITO: I think they are.

SOCRATES: "Consider then, Socrates," the Laws might go on, "whether the following is also true: in your present undertaking you are not proposing to treat us justly. We gave you birth, upbringing, and education, and a share in all the benefits we could provide for you along with all your fellow citizens. Nevertheless, we proclaim, by the formal granting of permission, that any Athenian who wishes, once he has been admitted to adult status,[8] and has observed the conduct of city business and ourselves, the Laws, may—if he is dissatisfied with us—go wherever he pleases and take his property. Not one of us Laws hinders or forbids that: whether any of you wishes to emigrate to a colony, or to go and live as an alien elsewhere, he may go wherever he pleases and keep his property, if we and the city fail to satisfy him.

"We do say, however, that if any of you remains here after he has observed the system by which we dispense justice and otherwise manage our city, then he has agreed with us by his conduct to obey whatever orders we give him. And thus we claim that anyone who fails to obey is guilty on three counts: he disobeys us as his parents; he disobeys those who nurtured him; and after agreeing to obey us he neither obeys nor persuades us if we are doing anything amiss, even though we offer him a choice, and do not harshly insist that he must do whatever we command. Instead, we give him two options: he must either persuade us or else do as we say; yet he does neither. Those are the charges, Socrates, to which we say you too will be liable if you carry out your intention; and among Athenians, you will be not the least liable, but one of the most."

And if I were to say, "How so?" perhaps they could fairly reproach me, observing that I am actually among those Athenians who have made that agreement with them most emphatically.

"Socrates," they would say, "we have every indication that you were content with us, as well as with our city, because you would never have stayed home here, more than is normal for all other Athenians, unless you were abnormally content. You never left our city for a festival—except once to go to the Isthmus[9]—nor did you go elsewhere for other purposes, apart from military service. You never travelled abroad, as other people do; nor were you eager for acquaintance with a different city or different laws: we and our city sufficed for you. Thus, you emphatically opted for us, and agreed to be a citizen on our terms. In particular, you fathered children in our city, which would suggest that you were content with it.

"Moreover, during your actual trial it was open to you, had you wished, to propose exile as your penalty; thus, what you are now attempting to do without the city's consent, you could then have done with it. On that occasion, you kept priding yourself that it would not trouble you if you had to die: you would choose death ahead of exile, so you said. Yet now you dishonour those words, and show no regard for us, the Laws, in your effort to destroy us. You are acting as the meanest slave would act, by trying to run away in spite of those compacts and agreements you made with us, whereby you agreed to be a citizen on our terms.

"First, then, answer us this question: are we right in claiming that you agreed, by your conduct if not verbally, that you would be a citizen on our terms? Or is that untrue?"

What shall we say in reply to that, Crito? Mustn't we agree?

CRITO: We must, Socrates.

SOCRATES: "Then what does your action amount to," they would say, "except breaking the compacts and agreements you made with us? By your own admission, you were not coerced or tricked into making them, or forced to reach a decision in a short time: you had seventy years in which it was open to you to leave if you were not happy with us, or if you thought those agreements unfair. Yet you preferred neither Lacedaemon nor Crete[10]—places you often say are well governed—nor any other Greek or foreign city: in fact, you went abroad less often than the lame and the blind or other cripples. Obviously, then, amongst Athenians you were exceptionally content with our city and with us, its Laws—because who would care for a city apart from its laws? Won't you, then, abide by your agreements now? Yes you will, if you listen to us, Socrates; and then at least you won't make yourself an object of derision by leaving the city.

"Just consider: if you break those agreements, and commit any of those offences, what good will you do yourself or those friends of yours? Your friends, pretty obviously, will risk being exiled themselves, as well as being disenfranchised or losing their property. As for you, first of all, if you go to one of the nearest cities, Thebes or Megara[11]—they are both well governed—you will arrive as an enemy of their political systems, Socrates: all who are concerned for their own cities will look askance at you, regarding you as a subverter of laws. You will also confirm your jurors in their judgment, making them think they decided your case correctly: any subverter of laws, presumably, might well be thought to be a corrupter of young, unthinking people.

"Will you, then, avoid the best-governed cities and the most respectable of men? And if so, will your life be worth living? Or will you associate with those people, and be shameless enough to converse with them? And what will you say to them, Socrates? The things you used to say here, that goodness and justice are most precious to mankind, along with institutions and laws? Don't you think that the predicament of Socrates will cut an ugly figure? Surely you must.

"Or will you take leave of those spots, and go to stay with those friends of Crito's up in Thessaly? That, of course, is a region of the utmost disorder and licence; so perhaps they would enjoy hearing from you about your comical escape from gaol, when you dressed up in some outfit, wore a leather jerkin or some other runaway's garb, and altered your appearance. Will no one observe that you, an old man with probably only a short time left to live, had the nerve to cling so greedily to life by violating the most important laws? Perhaps not, so long as you don't trouble anyone. Otherwise, Socrates, you will hear a great deal to your own discredit. You will live as every person's toady and lackey; and what will you be doing—apart from living it up in Thessaly, as if you had travelled all the way to Thessaly to have dinner? As for those principles of yours about justice and goodness in general—tell us, where will they be then?

"Well then, is it for your children's sake that you wish to live, in order to bring them up and give them an education? How so? Will you bring them up and educate them by taking them off to Thessaly and making foreigners of them, so that they may gain that advantage too? Or if, instead of that, they are brought up here, will they be better brought up and educated just because you are alive, if you are not with them? Yes, you may say, because those friends of yours will take care of them. Then will they take care of them if you travel to Thessaly, but not take care of them if you travel to Hades? Surely if those professing to be your friends are of any use at all, you must believe that they will.

"No, Socrates, listen to us, your own nurturers: do not place a higher value upon children, upon life, or upon anything else, than upon what is just, so that when you leave for Hades, this may be your whole defence before the authorities there: to take that course seems neither better nor more just or holy, for you or for any of your friends here in this world. Nor will it be better for you when you reach the next. As things stand, you will leave this world (if you do) as one who has been treated unjustly not by us Laws, but by human beings; whereas if you go into exile, thereby shamefully returning injustice for injustice and ill-treatment for ill-treatment, breaking the agreements and compacts you made with us, and inflicting harm upon the people you should least harm— yourself, your friends, your fatherland, and ourselves—then we shall be angry with you in your lifetime; and our brother Laws in Hades will not receive you kindly there, knowing that you tried, to the best of your ability, to destroy us too. Come then, do not let Crito persuade you to take his advice rather than ours."

That, Crito, my dear comrade, is what I seem to hear them saying, I do assure you. I am like the Corybantic revellers[12] who think they are still hearing the music of pipes: the sound of those arguments is ringing loudly in my head, and makes me unable to hear the others. As far as these present thoughts of mine go, then, you may be sure that if you object to them, you will plead in vain. None the less, if you think you will do any good, speak up.

CRITO: No, Socrates, I've nothing to say.

SOCRATES: Then let it be, Crito, and let us act accordingly, because that is the direction in which God is guiding us.

NOTES

1. The small island of Delos was sacred to the god Apollo. A mission sailed there annually from Athens to commemorate her deliverance by Theseus from servitude to King Minos of Crete. No executions could be carried out in Athens until the sacred ship returned.
2. The headland at the south-eastern extremity of Attica, about 50 kilometres from Athens. The winds were unfavourable at the time; so the ship may have been taking shelter at Sunium when the travellers left it there.
3. In Homer's *Iliad* (ix. 363) Achilles says, "on the third day I may return to fertile Phthia," meaning that he can get home in three days.
4. Athens had no public prosecutors. Prosecutions were undertaken by private citizens, who sometimes threatened legal action for personal, political, or financial gain.
5. The region of northern Greece, lying 200–300 kilometres north-west of Attica.
6. It was customary in Athens to appoint a public advocate to defend laws which it was proposed to abrogate.
7. The standard components of traditional Athenian education.
8. Admission to Athenian citizenship was not automatic, but required formal registration by males at the age of 17 or 18, with proof of age and parental citizenship.
9. The Isthmus was the strip of land linking the Peloponnese with the rest of Greece. Socrates may have attended the Isthmian Games, which were held every two years at Corinth.
10. Lacedaemon was the official name for the territory of Sparta. Sparta and Crete were both authoritarian and "closed" societies, which forbade their citizens to live abroad.
11. Thebes was the chief city in Boeotia, the region lying to the north-west of Attica; Megara was on the Isthmus. Both lay within easy reach of Athens.
12. The Corybantes performed orgiastic rites and dances to the sound of pipe and drum music. Their music sometimes induced a state of frenzy in emotionally disordered people, which was followed by a deep sleep from which the patients awoke cured.

On Liberty

✿✿

JOHN STUART MILL

Bring to your mind an opinion so outrageous that it would be repudiated by any sensible person. Now suppose that stating this opin-

From *On Liberty* (1859).

ion openly would be an affront to the vast majority of listeners. Under such circumstances, why shouldn't the representatives of the people be empowered to pass a law banning the public expression of this foolishness, thus ensuring that no one is offended by it or tempted to repeat it?

One answer might be that the First Amendment to the Constitution of the United States prohibits any law abridging the freedom of speech. But if an opinion is wrongheaded and repugnant, why does it merit protection?

The most celebrated and eloquent reply is provided in John Stuart Mill's classic work, *On Liberty.* It is dedicated to Harriet Taylor, "the inspirer, and in part the author, of all that is best in my writings."

What is most surprising about Mill's presentation is that he defends an individual's free speech by appealing not to the majority's kindheartedness but to its own welfare. Yet how can it be in anyone's self-interest to allow blatantly false views to be expressed? Let us consider Mill's argument.

Chapter I

Introductory

The object of this essay is to assert one very simple principle, as entitled to govern absolutely the dealings of society with the individual in the way of compulsion and control, whether the means used be physical force in the form of legal penalties or the moral coercion of public opinion. That principle is that the sole end for which mankind are warranted, individually or collectively, in interfering with the liberty of action of any of their number is self-protection. That the only purpose for which power can be rightfully exercised over any member of a civilized community, against his will, is to prevent harm to others. His own good, either physical or moral, is not a sufficient warrant. He cannot rightfully be compelled to do or forbear because it will be better for him to do so, because it will make him happier, because, in the opinions of others, to do so would be wise or even right. These are good reasons for remonstrating with him, or reasoning with him, or persuading him, or entreating him, but not for compelling him or visiting him with any evil in case he do otherwise. To justify that, the conduct from which it is desired to deter him must be calculated to produce evil to someone else. The only part of the conduct of anyone for which he is amenable to society is that which concerns others. In the part which merely concerns himself, his independence is, of right, absolute. Over himself, over his own body and mind, the individual is sovereign. . . .

This, then, is the appropriate region of human liberty. It comprises, first, the inward domain of consciousness, demanding liberty of conscience in the most comprehensive sense, liberty of thought and feeling, absolute freedom of opinion and sentiment on all subjects, practical or speculative, scientific, moral, or theological. The liberty of expressing and publishing opinions may seem to fall under a different principle, since it belongs to that part of the conduct of an individual which concerns other people, but, being almost of as much importance as the liberty of thought itself and resting in great part on the same reasons, is practically inseparable from it. Secondly, the principle requires liberty of tastes and pursuits, of framing the plan of our life to suit our own character, of doing as we like, subject to such consequences as may follow, without impediment from our fellow creatures, so long as what we do does not harm them, even though they should think our conduct foolish, perverse, or wrong. Thirdly, from this liberty of each individual follows the liberty, within the same limits, of combination among individuals; freedom to unite for any purpose not involving harm to others: the persons combining being supposed to be of full age and not forced or deceived.

No society in which these liberties are not, on the whole, respected is free, whatever may be its form of government; and none is completely free in which they do not exist absolute and unqualified. The only freedom which deserves the name is that of pursuing our own good in our own way, so long as we do not attempt to deprive others of theirs or impede their efforts to obtain it. Each is the proper guardian of his own health, whether bodily *or* mental and spiritual. Mankind are greater gainers by suffering each other to live as seems good to themselves than by compelling each to live as seems good to the rest. . . .

It will be convenient for the argument if, instead of at once entering upon the general thesis, we confine ourselves in the first instance to a single branch of it on which the principle here stated is, if not fully, yet to a certain point, recognized by the current opinions. This one branch is the Liberty of Thought, from which it is impossible to separate the cognate liberty of speaking and of writing. Although these liberties, to some considerable amount, form part of the political morality of all countries which profess religious toleration and free institutions, the grounds, both philosophical and practical, on which they rest are perhaps not so familiar to the general mind, nor so thoroughly appreciated by many, even of the leaders of opinion, as might have been expected. . . .

Chapter II

Of the Liberty of Thought and Discussion

The time, it is to be hoped, is gone by when any defense would be necessary of the "liberty of the press" as one of the securities against corrupt or tyrannical government. No argument, we may suppose, can now be needed against permitting a legislature or an executive, not identified in interest with the people, to prescribe opinions to them and determine what doctrines or what arguments they shall be allowed to hear. . . . Let us suppose, therefore, that the government is entirely at one with the people, and never thinks of exerting any power of coercion unless in agreement with what it conceives to be their voice. But I deny the right of the people to exercise such coercion, either by themselves or by their government. The power itself is illegitimate. The best government has no more title to it than the worst. It is as noxious, or more noxious, when exerted in accordance with public opinion than when in opposition to it. If all mankind minus one were of one opinion, mankind would be no more justified in silencing that one person than he, if he had the power, would be justified in silencing mankind. Were an opinion a personal possession of no value except to the owner, if to be obstructed in the enjoyment of it were simply a private injury, it would make some difference whether the injury was inflicted only on a few persons or on many. But the peculiar evil of silencing the expression of an opinion is that it is robbing the human race, posterity as well as the existing generation—those who dissent from the opinion, still more than those who hold it. If the opinion is right, they are deprived of the opportunity of exchanging error for truth; if wrong, they lose, what is almost as great a benefit, the clearer perception and livelier impression of truth produced by its collision with error.

It is necessary to consider separately these two hypotheses, each of which has a distinct branch of the argument corresponding to it. We can never be sure that the opinion we are endeavoring to stifle is a false opinion; and if we were sure, stifling it would be an evil still.

First, the opinion which it is attempted to suppress by authority may possibly be true. Those who desire to suppress it, of course, deny its truth; but they are not infallible. They have no authority to decide the question for all mankind and exclude every other person from the means of judging. To refuse a hearing to an opinion because they are sure that it is false is to assume that *their* certainty is the same thing as *absolute* certainty. All silencing of discussion is an assumption of infallibility. Its condemnation may be allowed to rest on this common argument, not the worse for being common.

Unfortunately for the good sense of mankind, the fact of their fallibility is far from carrying the weight in their practical judgment which is always allowed to it in theory; for while everyone well knows himself to be fallible, few think it necessary to take any precautions against their own fallibility, or admit the supposition that any opinion of which they feel very certain may be one of the examples of the error to which they acknowledge themselves to be liable. Absolute princes, or others who are accustomed to unlimited deference, usually feel this complete confidence in their own opinions on nearly all subjects. People more happily situated, who sometimes hear their opinions disputed and are not wholly unused to be set right when they are wrong, place the same unbounded reliance only on such of their opinions as are shared by all who surround them, or to whom they habitually defer; for in proportion to a man's want of confidence in his own solitary judgment does he usually repose, with implicit trust, on the infallibility of "the world" in general. And the world, to each individual, means the part of it with which he comes in contact: his party, his sect, his church, his class of society; the man may be called, by comparison, almost liberal and large-minded to whom it means anything so comprehensive as his own country or his own age. Nor is his faith in this collective authority at all shaken by his being aware that other ages, countries, sects, churches, classes, and parties have thought, and even now think, the exact reverse. He devolves upon his own world the responsibility of being in the right against the dissentient worlds of other people; and it never troubles him that mere accident has decided which of these numerous worlds is the object of his reliance, and that the same causes which make him a churchman in London would have made him a Buddhist or a Confucian in Peking. Yet it is as evident in itself, as any amount of argument can make it, that ages are no more infallible than individuals—every age having held many opinions which subsequent ages have deemed not only false but absurd; and it is as certain that many opinions, now general, will be rejected by future ages, as it is that many, once general, are rejected by the present.

The objection likely to be made to this argument would probably take some such form as the following. There is no greater assumption of infallibility in forbidding the propagation of error than in any other thing which is done by public authority on its own judgment and responsibility. Judgment is given to men that they may use it. Because it may be used erroneously, are men to be told that they ought not to use it at all? To prohibit what they think pernicious is not claiming exemption from error, but fulfilling the duty incumbent on them, although fallible, of acting on their conscientious conviction. If we were never to act on our opinions, because those opinions may be wrong, we should leave all our interests uncared for, and all our duties unperformed. An objection which applies to all conduct can be no valid objection to any conduct in particular. It is the duty of governments, and of individuals, to form the truest opinions they can; to form them carefully, and never impose them upon others unless they are quite sure of being right. But when they are sure (such reasoners may say), it is not conscientiousness but cowardice to shrink from acting on their opinions and allow doctrines which they honestly think dangerous to the welfare of mankind, either in this life or in another, to be scattered abroad without restraint, because other people, in less enlightened times, have persecuted opinions now believed to be true. Let us take care, it may be said, not to make the same mistake; but governments and nations have made mistakes in other things which are not denied to be fit subjects for the exercise of authority: they have laid on bad taxes, made unjust wars. Ought we therefore to lay on no taxes and, under whatever provocation, make no wars? Men and governments must act to the best of their ability. There is no such thing as absolute certainty, but there is as-

surance sufficient for the purposes of human life. We may, and must, assume
our opinion to be true for the guidance of our own conduct; and it is assuming no more when we forbid bad men to pervert society by the propagation
of opinions which we regard as false and pernicious.

I answer, that it is assuming very much more. There is the greatest difference between presuming an opinion to be true because, with every opportunity for contesting it, it has not been refuted, and assuming its truth for the
purpose of not permitting its refutation. Complete liberty of contradicting
and disproving our opinion is the very condition which justifies us in assuming its truth for purposes of action; and on no other terms can a being
with human faculties have any rational assurance of being right.

When we consider either the history of opinion or the ordinary conduct
of human life, to what is it to be ascribed that the one and the other are no
worse than they are? Not certainly to the inherent force of the human understanding, for on any matter not self-evident there are ninety-nine persons totally incapable of judging of it for one who is capable; and the capacity of the
hundredth person is only comparative, for the majority of the eminent men
of every past generation held many opinions now known to be erroneous,
and did or approved numerous things which no one will now justify. Why is
it, then, that there is on the whole a preponderance among mankind of rational opinions and rational conduct? If there really is this preponderance—
which there must be unless human affairs are, and have always been, in an
almost desperate state—it is owing to a quality of the human mind, the
source of everything respectable in man either as an intellectual or as a moral
being, namely, that his errors are corrigible. He is capable of rectifying his
mistakes by discussion and experience. Not by experience alone. There must
be discussion to show how experience is to be interpreted. Wrong opinions
and practices gradually yield to fact and argument; but facts and arguments,
to produce any effect on the mind, must be brought before it. Very few facts
are able to tell their own story, without comments to bring out their meaning. The whole strength and value, then, of human judgment depending on
the one property, that it can be set right when it is wrong, reliance can be
placed on it only when the means of setting it right are kept constantly at
hand. In the case of any person whose judgment is really deserving of confidence, how has it become so? Because he has kept his mind open to criticism
of his opinions and conduct. Because it has been his practice to listen to all
that could be said against him; to profit by as much of it as was just, and to
expound to himself, and upon occasion to others, the fallacy of what was fallacious. Because he has felt that the only way in which a human being can
make some approach to knowing the whole of a subject is by hearing what
can be said about it by persons of every variety of opinion, and studying all
modes in which it can be looked at by every character of mind. No wise man
ever acquired his wisdom in any mode but this; nor is it in the nature of human intellect to become wise in any other manner. The steady habit of correcting and completing his own opinion by collating it with those of others,

so far from causing doubt and hesitation in carrying it into practice, is the only stable foundation for a just reliance on it; for, being cognizant of all that can, at least obviously, be said against him, and having taken up his position against all gainsayers—knowing that he has sought for objections and difficulties instead of avoiding them, and has shut out no light which can be thrown upon the subject from any quarter—he has a right to think his judgment better than that of any person, or any multitude, who have not gone through a similar process.

It is not too much to require that what the wisest of mankind, those who are best entitled to trust their own judgment, find necessary to warrant their relying on it, should be submitted to by that miscellaneous collection of a few wise and many foolish individuals called the public. The . . . Roman Catholic Church, even at the canonization of a saint, admits, and listens patiently to, a "devil's advocate." The holiest of men, it appears, cannot be admitted to posthumous honors until all that the devil could say against him is known and weighed. If even the Newtonian philosophy were not permitted to be questioned, mankind could not feel as complete assurance of its truth as they now do. The beliefs which we have most warrant for have no safeguard to rest on but a standing invitation to the whole world to prove them unfounded. If the challenge is not accepted, or is accepted and the attempt fails, we are far enough from certainty still, but we have done the best that the existing state of human reason admits of: we have neglected nothing that could give the truth a chance of reaching us; if the lists are kept open, we may hope that, if there be a better truth, it will be found when the human mind is capable of receiving it; and in the meantime we may rely on having attained such approach to truth as is possible in our own day. This is the amount of certainty attainable by a fallible being, and this the sole way of attaining it.

Strange it is that men should admit the validity of the arguments for free discussion, but object to their being "pushed to an extreme," not seeing that unless the reasons are good for an extreme case, they are not good for any case. Strange that they should imagine that they are not assuming infallibility when they acknowledge that there should be free discussion on all subjects which can possibly be *doubtful*, but think that some particular principle or doctrine should be forbidden to be questioned because it is so *certain*, that is, because *they are certain* that it is certain. To call any proposition certain, while there is anyone who would deny its certainty if permitted, but who is not permitted, is to assume that we ourselves, and those who agree with us, are the judges of certainty, and judges without hearing the other side. . . .

In order more fully to illustrate the mischief of denying a hearing to opinions because we, in our own judgment, have condemned them, it will be desirable to fix down the discussion to a concrete case; and I choose, by preference, the cases which are least favorable to me—in which the argument against freedom of opinion, both on the score of truth and on that of utility, is considered the strongest. Let the opinions impugned be the belief in a God and in a future state, or any of the commonly received doctrines of morality. To fight the battle on such ground gives a great advantage to an unfair antagonist, since he will be sure to say (and many who have no desire to be unfair will say it internally), Are these the doctrines which you do not deem sufficiently certain to be taken under the protection of law? Is the belief in a God one of the opinions to feel sure of which you hold to be assuming infallibility? But I must be permitted to observe that it is not the feeling sure of a doctrine (be it what it may) which I call an assumption of infallibility. It is the undertaking to decide that question *for others*, without allowing them to hear what can be said on the contrary side. And I denounce and reprobate this pretension not the less if put forth on the side of my most solemn convictions. However positive anyone's persuasion may be, not only of the falsity but of the pernicious consequences—not only of the pernicious consequences, but (to adopt expressions which I altogether condemn) the immorality and impiety of an opinion—yet if, in pursuance of that private judgment, though backed by the public judgment of his country or his contemporaries, he prevents the opinion from being heard in its defense, he assumes infallibility. And so far from the assumption being less objectionable or less dangerous because the opinion is called immoral or impious, this is the case of all others in which it is most fatal. These are exactly the occasions on which the men of one generation commit those dreadful mistakes which excite the astonishment and horror of posterity. It is among such that we find the instances memorable in history, when the arm of the law has been employed to root out the best men and the noblest doctrines; with deplorable success as to the men, though some of the doctrines have survived to be (as if in mockery) invoked in defense of similar conduct toward those who dissent from *them*, or from their received interpretation.

Mankind can hardly be too often reminded that there was once a man called Socrates, between whom and the legal authorities and public opinion of his time there took place a memorable collision. Born in an age and country abounding in individual greatness, this man has been handed down to us by those who best knew both him and the age as the most virtuous man in it. . . . This acknowledged master of all the eminent thinkers who have since lived—whose fame, still growing after more than two thousand years, all but outweighs the whole remainder of the names which make his native city illustrious—was put to death by his countrymen, after a judicial conviction, for impiety and immorality. Impiety, in denying the gods recognized by the State; indeed, his accuser asserted (see the *Apologia*) that he believed in no gods at all. Immorality, in being, by his doctrines and instructions, a "corruptor of youth." Of these charges the tribunal, there is every ground for believing, honestly found him guilty, and condemned the man who probably of all then born had deserved best of mankind to be put to death as a criminal.

To pass from this to the only other instance of judicial iniquity, the mention of which, after the condemnation of Socrates, would not be an anticlimax: the event which took place on Calvary rather more than eighteen hundred years ago. The man who left on the memory of those who witnessed his life and conversation such an impression of his moral grandeur that eighteen subsequent centuries have done homage to him as the Almighty in person, was ignominiously put to death, as what? As a blasphemer. Men did not merely mistake their benefactor, they mistook him for the exact contrary of what he was and treated him as that prodigy of impiety which they themselves are now held to be for their treatment of him. The feelings with which mankind now regard these lamentable transactions, especially the later of the two, render them extremely unjust in their judgment of the unhappy actors. These were, to all appearance, not bad men—not worse than men commonly are, but rather the contrary; men who possessed in a full, or somewhat more than a full measure, the religious, moral, and patriotic feelings of their time and people: the very kind of men who, in all times, our own included, have every chance of passing through life blameless and respected. The high priest who rent his garments when the words were pronounced, which, according to all the ideas of his country, constituted the blackest guilt, was in all probability quite as sincere in his horror and indignation as the generality of respectable and pious men now are in the religious and moral sentiments they profess; and most of those who now shudder at his conduct, if they had lived in his time . . . would have acted precisely as he did. Orthodox Christians who are tempted to think that those who stoned to death the first martyrs must have been worse men than they themselves are ought to remember that one of those persecutors was Saint Paul. . . .

Let us now pass to the second division of the argument, and dismissing the supposition that any of the received opinions may be false, let us assume them to be true and examine into the worth of the manner in which they are likely to be held when their truth is not freely and openly canvassed. However unwillingly a person who has a strong opinion may admit the possibility that his opinion may be false, he ought to be moved by the consideration that, however true it may be, if it is not fully, frequently, and fearlessly discussed, it will be held as a dead dogma, not a living truth.

There is a class of persons (happily not quite so numerous as formerly) who think it enough if a person assents undoubtingly to what they think true, though he has no knowledge whatever of the grounds of the opinion and could not make a tenable defense of it against the most superficial objections. Such persons, if they can once get their creed taught from authority, naturally think that no good, and some harm, comes of its being allowed to be questioned. Where their influence prevails, they make it nearly impossible for the received opinion to be rejected wisely and considerately, though it may still be rejected rashly and ignorantly; for to shut out discussion entirely is seldom possible, and when it once gets in, beliefs not grounded on conviction are apt to give way before the slightest semblance of an argument. Waiving, however, this possibility—assuming that the true opinion abides in the mind, but abides as a prejudice, a belief independent of, and proof against, argument—this is not the way in which truth ought to be held by a rational being. This is not knowing the truth. Truth, thus held, is but one superstition the more, accidentally clinging to the words which enunciate a truth.

If the intellect and judgment of mankind ought to be cultivated, a thing which Protestants at least do not deny, on what can these faculties be more appropriately exercised by anyone than on the things which concern him so much that it is considered necessary for him to hold opinions on them? If the cultivation of the understanding consists in one thing more than in another, it is surely in learning the grounds of one's own opinions. Whatever people believe, on subjects on which it is of the first importance to believe rightly, they ought to be able to defend against at least the common objections. But, someone may say, "Let them be *taught* the grounds of their opinions. It does not follow that opinions must be merely parroted because they are never heard controverted. Persons who learn geometry do not simply commit the theorems to memory, but understand and learn likewise the demonstrations; and it would be absurd to say that they remain ignorant of the grounds of geometrical truths because they never hear anyone deny and attempt to disprove them." Undoubtedly: and such teaching suffices on a subject like mathematics, where there is nothing at all to be said on the wrong side of the question. The peculiarity of the evidence of mathematical truths is that all the argument is on one side. There are no objections, and no answers to objections. But on every subject on which difference of opinion is possible, the truth depends on a balance to be struck between two sets of conflicting reasons. Even in natural philosophy, there is always some other explanation possible of the same facts; some geocentric theory instead of heliocentric, some phlogiston instead of oxygen; and it has to be shown why that other theory cannot be the true one; and until this is shown, and until we know how it is shown, we do not understand the grounds of our opinion. But when we turn to subjects infinitely more complicated, to morals, religion, politics, social relations, and the business of life, three-fourths of the arguments for every disputed opinion consist in dispelling the appearances which favor some opinion different from it. The greatest orator, save one, of antiquity, has left it on record that he always studied his adversary's case with as great, if not still greater, intensity than even his own. What Cicero practiced as the means of forensic success requires to be imitated by all who study any subject in order to arrive at the truth. He who knows only his own side of the case knows little of that. His reasons may be good, and no one may have been able to refute them. But if he is equally unable to refute the reasons on the opposite side, if he does not so much as know what they are, he has no ground for preferring either opinion. The rational position for him would be suspension of judgment, and unless he contents himself with that, he is either led by authority or adopts, like the generality of the world, the side to which he feels most inclination. Nor is it enough that he should hear the arguments of adversaries from his own teachers, presented as they state them, and accompanied by what they offer as refutations. That is not the way to do justice to the arguments or bring them into real contact with his own mind. He must be able to hear them from persons who actually believe them, who defend them in earnest and do their very utmost for them. He must know them in their most plausible and persuasive form; he must feel the whole force of the difficulty which the true view of the subject has to encounter and dispose of, else he will never really possess himself of the portion of truth which meets and removes that difficulty. Ninety-nine in a hundred of what are called educated men are in this condition, even of those who can argue fluently for their opinions. Their conclusion may be true, but it might be false for anything they know; they have never thrown themselves into the mental position of those who think differently from them, and considered what such persons may have to say; and, consequently, they do not, in any proper sense of the word, know the doctrine which they themselves profess. They do not know those parts of it which explain and justify the remainder—the considerations which show that a fact which seemingly conflicts with another is reconcilable with it, or that, of two apparently strong reasons, one and not the other ought to be preferred. All that part of the truth which turns the scale and decides the judgment of a completely informed mind, they are strangers to; nor is it ever really known but to those who have attended equally and impartially to both sides and endeavored to see the reasons of both in the strongest light. So essential is this discipline to a real understanding of moral and human subjects that, if opponents of all-important truths do not exist, it is indispensable to imagine them and supply them with the strongest arguments which the most skillful devil's advocate can conjure up.

To abate the force of these considerations, an enemy of free discussion may be supposed to say that there is no necessity for mankind in general to know and understand all that can be said against or for their opinions by philosophers and theologians. That it is not needful for common men to be able to expose all the misstatements or fallacies of an ingenious opponent. That it is enough if there is always somebody capable of answering them, so that nothing likely to mislead uninstructed persons remains unrefuted. That simple minds, having been taught the obvious grounds of the truths inculcated in them, may trust to authority for the rest and, being aware that they have neither knowledge nor talent to resolve every difficulty which can be raised, may repose in the assurance that all those which have been raised have been or can be answered by those who are specially trained to the task.

Conceding to this view of the subject the utmost that can be claimed for it by those most easily satisfied with the amount of understanding of truth which ought to accompany the belief of it, even so, the argument for free discussion is noway weakened. For even this doctrine acknowledges that mankind ought to have a rational assurance that all objections have been satisfactorily answered; and how are they to be answered if that which requires to be answered is not spoken? Or how can the answer be known to be satisfactory if the objectors have no opportunity of showing that it is unsatisfactory? If not the public, at least the philosophers and theologians who are to resolve the difficulties must make themselves familiar with those difficulties in their most puzzling form; and this cannot be accomplished unless they are freely stated and placed in the most advantageous light which they admit of. . . . If the teachers of mankind are to be cognizant of all that they ought to know, everything must be free to be written and published without restraint.

If, however, the mischievous operation of the absence of free discussion, when the received opinions are true, were confined to leaving men ignorant of the grounds of those opinions, it might be thought that this, if an intellectual, is no moral evil and does not affect the worth of the opinions, regarded in their influence on the character. The fact, however, is that not only the grounds of the opinion are forgotten in the absence of discussion, but too often the meaning of the opinion itself. The words which convey it cease to suggest ideas, or suggest only a small portion of those they were originally employed to communicate. Instead of a vivid conception and a living belief, there remain only a few phrases retained by rote; or, if any part, the shell and husk only of the meaning is retained, the finer essence being lost. The great chapter in human history which this fact occupies and fills cannot be too earnestly studied and meditated on.

It is illustrated in the experience of almost all ethical doctrines and religious creeds. They are all full of meaning and vitality to those who originate them, and to the direct disciples of the originators. Their meaning continues to be felt in undiminished strength, and is perhaps brought out into even fuller consciousness, so long as the struggle lasts to give the doctrine or creed an ascendancy over other creeds. At last it either prevails and becomes the general opinion, or its progress stops; it keeps possession of the ground it has gained, but ceases to spread further. When either of these results has become apparent, controversy on the subject flags, and gradually dies away. The doctrine has taken its place, if not as a received opinion, as one of the admitted sects or divisions of opinion; those who hold it have generally inherited, not adopted it; and conversion from one of these doctrines to another, being now an exceptional fact, occupies little place in the thoughts of their professors. Instead of being, as at first, constantly on the alert either to defend themselves against the world or to bring the world over to them, they have subsided into acquiescence and neither listen, when they can help it, to arguments against their creed, nor trouble dissentients (if there be such) with arguments in its favor. From this time may usually be dated the decline in the living power of the doctrine. We often hear the teachers of all creeds lamenting the difficulty of keeping up in the minds of believers a lively apprehension of the truth which they nominally recognize, so that it may penetrate the feelings and acquire a real mastery over the conduct. No such difficulty is complained of while the creed is still fighting for its existence; even the weaker combatants then know and feel what they are fighting for, and the difference between it and other doctrines; and in that period of every creed's existence not a few persons may be found who have realized its fundamental principles in all the forms of thought, have weighed and considered them in all their important bearings, and have experienced the full effect on the character which belief in that creed ought to produce in a mind thoroughly imbued with it. But when it has come to be an hereditary creed, and to be received passively, not actively—when the mind is no longer compelled, in the same degree as at first, to exercise its vital powers on the questions which its belief presents to it, there is a progressive tendency to forget all of the belief except the formularies, or to give it a dull and torpid assent, as if accepting it on trust dispensed with the necessity of realizing it in consciousness, or testing it by personal experience, until it almost ceases to connect itself at all with the inner life of the human being. Then are seen the cases, so frequent in this age of the world as almost to form the majority, in which the creed remains as it were outside the mind, incrusting and petrifying it against all other influences addressed to the higher parts of our nature; manifesting its power by not suffering any fresh and living conviction to get in, but itself doing nothing for the mind or heart except standing sentinel over them to keep them vacant. . . .

We have hitherto considered only two possibilities: that the received opinion may be false, and some other opinion, consequently, true; or that, the received opinion being true, a conflict with the opposite error is essential to a clear apprehension and deep feeling of its truth. But there is a commoner case than either of these: when the conflicting doctrines, instead of being one true and the other false, share the truth between them, and the nonconforming opinion is needed to supply the remainder of the truth of which the received doctrine embodies only a part. Popular opinions, on subjects not palpable to sense, are often true, but seldom or never the whole truth. They are a part of the truth, sometimes a greater, sometimes a smaller part, but exaggerated, distorted, and disjointed from the truths by which they ought to be accompanied and limited. Heretical opinions, on the other hand, are generally some of these suppressed and neglected truths, bursting the bonds which kept them down, and either seeking reconciliation with the truth contained in the common opinion, or fronting it as enemies, and setting themselves up, with similar exclusiveness, as the whole truth. The latter case is hitherto the most frequent, as, in the human mind, one-sidedness has always been the rule, and many-sidedness the exception. Hence, even in revolutions of opinion, one part of the truth usually sets while another rises. Even progress, which ought to superadd, for the most part only substitutes one partial and incomplete truth for another; improvement consisting chiefly in this, that the new fragment of truth is more wanted, more adapted to the needs of the time than that which it displaces. Such being the partial character of prevailing opinions, even when resting on a true foundation, every opinion which embodies somewhat of the portion of truth which the common opinion omits ought to be considered precious, with whatever amount of error and confusion that truth may be blended. No sober judge of human affairs will feel bound to be indignant because those who force on our notice truths which we should otherwise have overlooked, overlook some of those which we see. Rather, he will think that so long as popular truth is one-sided, it is more desirable than otherwise that unpopular truth should have one-sided assertors, too, such being usually the most energetic and the most likely to compel reluctant attention to the fragment of wisdom which they proclaim as if it were the whole . . .

I do not pretend that the most unlimited use of the freedom of enunciating all possible opinions would put an end to the evils of religious or philosophical sectarianism. Every truth which men of narrow capacity are in earnest about is sure to be asserted, inculcated, and in many ways even acted on, as if no other truth existed in the world, or at all events none that could limit or qualify the first. I acknowledge that the tendency of all opinions to become sectarian is not cured by the freest discussion, but is often heightened and exacerbated thereby; the truth which ought to have been, but was not, seen, being rejected all the more violently because proclaimed by persons regarded as opponents. But it is not on the impassioned partisan, it is on the calmer and more disinterested bystander, that this collision of opinions works its salutary effect. Not the violent conflict between parts of the truth, but the quiet suppression of half of it, is the formidable evil; there is always hope when people are forced to listen to both sides; it is when they attend only to one that errors harden into prejudices, and truth itself ceases to have the effect of truth by being exaggerated into falsehood. And since there are few mental attributes more rare than that judicial faculty which can sit in intelligent judgment between two sides of a question, of which only one is represented by an advocate before it, truth has no chance but in proportion as every side of it, every opinion which embodies any fraction of the truth, not only finds advocates, but is so advocated as to be listened to.

We have now recognized the necessity to the mental well-being of mankind (on which all their other well-being depends) of freedom of opinion, and freedom of the expression of opinion, on four distinct grounds, which we will now briefly recapitulate:

First, if any opinion is compelled to silence, that opinion may, for aught we can certainly know, be true. To deny this is to assume our own infallibility.

Secondly, though the silenced opinion be an error, it may, and very commonly does, contain a portion of truth; and since the general or prevailing opinion on any subject is rarely or never the whole truth, it is only by the collision of adverse opinions that the remainder of the truth has any chance of being supplied.

Thirdly, even if the received opinion be not only true, but the whole truth; unless it is suffered to be, and actually is, vigorously and earnestly contested, it will, by most of those who receive it, be held in the manner of a prejudice, with little comprehension or feeling of its rational grounds. And not only this, but, fourthly, the meaning of the doctrine itself will be in danger of being lost or enfeebled, and deprived of its vital effect on the character and conduct: the dogma becoming a mere formal profession, inefficacious for good, but cumbering the ground and preventing the growth of any real and heartfelt conviction from reason or personal experience.

Before quitting the subject of freedom of opinion, it is fit to take some notice of those who say that the free expression of all opinions should be permitted on condition that the manner be temperate, and do not pass the bounds of fair discussion. Much might be said on the impossibility of fixing where these supposed bounds are to be placed; for if the test be offense to those whose opinions are attacked, I think experience testifies that this offense is given whenever the attack is telling and powerful, and that every opponent who pushes them hard, and whom they find it difficult to answer, appears to them, if he shows any strong feeling on the subject, an intemperate opponent. But this, though an important consideration in a practical point of view, merges in a more fundamental objection. Undoubtedly, the manner of asserting an opinion, even though it be a true one, may be very objectionable and may justly incur severe censure. But the principal offenses of the kind are such as it is mostly impossible, unless by accidental self-betrayal, to bring home to conviction. The gravest of them is, to argue sophistically, to suppress facts or arguments, to misstate the elements of the case, or misrepresent the opposite opinion. But all this, even to the most aggravated degree, is so continually done in perfect good faith by persons who are not considered, and in many other respects may not deserve to be considered, ignorant or incompetent, that it is rarely possible, on adequate grounds, conscientiously to stamp the misrepresentation as morally culpable, and still less could law presume to interfere with this kind of controversial misconduct. With regard to what is commonly meant by intemperate discussion, namely invective, sarcasm, personality, and the like, the denunciation of these weapons would deserve more sympathy if it were ever proposed to interdict them equally to both sides; but it is only desired to restrain the employment of them against the prevailing opinion; against the unprevailing they may not only be used without general disapproval, but will be likely to obtain for him who uses them the praise of honest zeal and righteous indignation. Yet whatever mischief arises from their use is greatest when they are employed against the comparatively defenceless; and whatever unfair advantage can be derived by any opinion from this mode of asserting it accrues almost exclusively to received opinions. The worst offense of this kind which can be committed by a polemic is to stigmatize those who hold the contrary opinion as bad and immoral men. To calumny of this sort, those who hold any unpopular opinion are peculiarly exposed, because they are in general few and uninfluential, and nobody but themselves feels much interested in seeing justice done them; but this weapon is, from the nature of the case, denied to those who attack a prevailing opinion: they can neither use it with safety to themselves, nor, if they could, would it do anything but recoil on their own cause. In general, opinions contrary to those commonly received can only obtain a hearing by studied moderation of language and the most cautious avoidance of unnecessary offense, from which they hardly ever deviate even in a slight degree without losing ground, while unmeasured vituperation employed on the side of the prevailing opinion really does deter people from professing contrary opinions and from listening to those who profess them. For the interest, therefore, of truth and justice it is far more important to restrain this employment of vituperative language than the other; and, for example, if it were necessary to choose, there would be much more need to discourage offensive attacks on infidelity than on religion. It is, however, obvious that law and authority have no business with restraining either, while opinion ought, in every instance, to determine its verdict by the circumstances of the individual case—condemning everyone, on whichever side of the argument he places himself, in whose mode of advocacy either want of candor, or malignity, bigotry, or intolerance of feeling manifest themselves; but not inferring these vices from the side which a person takes, though it be the contrary side of the question to our own; and giving merited honor to everyone, whatever opinion he may hold, who has calmness to see and honesty to state what his opponents and their opinions really are, exaggerating nothing to their discredit, keeping nothing back which tells, or can be supposed to tell, in their favor. This is the real morality of public discussion; and if often violated, I am happy to think that there are many controversialists who to a great extent observe it, and a still greater number who conscientiously strive toward it.

PART 7

CONCLUSION

The Meaning of Life

✧✧

RICHARD TAYLOR

> As I mentioned earlier (p. 113), those who begin the study of phi-
> losophy often assume the subject will focus on the meaning of life.
> However, this supposedly crucial topic is rarely mentioned. Yet
> philosophers do occasionally consider the issue, as witness our
> next selection. Its author is Richard Taylor, whose work we read pre-
> viously (pp. 101–112; 202–205).

The question whether life has any meaning is difficult to interpret, and the more one concentrates his critical faculty on it the more it seems to elude him, or to evaporate as any intelligible question. One wants to turn it aside, as a source of embarrassment, as something that, if it cannot be abolished, should at least be decently covered. And yet I think any reflective person recognizes that the question it raises is important, and that it ought to have a significant answer.

If the idea of meaningfulness is difficult to grasp in this context, so that we are unsure what sort of thing would amount to answering the question, the idea of meaninglessness is perhaps less so. If, then, we can bring before our minds a clear image of meaningless existence, then perhaps we can take a step toward coping with our original question by seeing to what extent our lives, as we actually find them, resemble that image, and draw such lessons as we are able to from the comparison.

Meaningless Existence

A perfect image of meaninglessness, of the kind we are seeking, is found in the ancient myth of Sisyphus. Sisyphus, it will be remembered, betrayed divine secrets to mortals, and for this he was condemned by the gods to roll a stone to the top of a hill, the stone then immediately to roll back down, again to be pushed to the top by Sisyphus, to roll down once more, and so on again and again, *forever*. Now in this we have the picture of meaningless, pointless toil, of a meaningless existence that is absolutely *never* redeemed. It is not even redeemed by a death that, if it were to accomplish nothing more, would at least bring this idiotic cycle to a close. If we were invited to imagine Sisyphus struggling for awhile and accomplishing nothing, perhaps eventually

From Richard Taylor, *Good and Evil*, pp. 256–268 (Amherst, NY: Prometheus Books). Copyright © 1984. Reprinted by permission of the publisher.

falling from exhaustion, so that we might suppose him then eventually turning to something having some sort of promise, then the meaninglessness of that chapter of his life would not be so stark. It would be a dark and dreadful dream, from which he eventually awakens to sunlight and reality. But he does not awaken, for there is nothing for him to awaken to. His repetitive toil is his life and reality, and it goes on forever, and it is without any meaning whatever. Nothing ever comes of what he is doing, except simply, more of the same. Not by one step, nor by a thousand, nor by ten thousand does he even expiate by the smallest token the sin against the gods that led him into this fate. Nothing comes of it, nothing at all.

This ancient myth has always enchanted men, for countless meanings can be read into it. Some of the ancients apparently thought it symbolized the perpetual rising and setting of the sun, and others the repetitious crashing of the waves upon the shore. Probably the commonest interpretation is that it symbolizes man's eternal struggle and unquenchable spirit, his determination always to try once more in the face of overwhelming discouragement. This interpretation is further supported by that version of the myth according to which Sisyphus was commanded to roll the stone *over* the hill, so that it would finally roll down the other side, but was never quite able to make it.

I am not concerned with rendering or defending any interpretation of this myth, however. I have cited it only for the one element it does unmistakably contain, namely, that of a repetitious, cyclic activity that never comes to anything. We could contrive other images of this that would serve just as well, and no myth-makers are needed to supply the materials of it. Thus, we can imagine two persons transporting a stone—or even a precious gem, it does not matter—back and forth, relay style. One carries it to a near or distant point where it is received by the other; it is returned to its starting point, there to be recovered by the first, and the process is repeated over and over. Except in this relay nothing counts as winning, and nothing brings the contest to any close, each step only leads to a repetition of itself. Or we can imagine two groups of prisoners, one of them engaged in digging a prodigious hole in the ground that is no sooner finished than it is filled in again by the other group, the latter then digging a new hole that is at once filled in by the first group, and so on and on endlessly.

Now what stands out in all such pictures as oppressive and dejecting is not that the beings who enact these roles suffer any torture or pain, for it need not be assumed that they do. Nor is it that their labors are great, for they are no greater than the labors commonly undertaken by most men most of the time. According to the original myth, the stone is so large that Sisyphus never quite gets it to the top and must groan under every step, so that his enormous labor is all for nought. But this is not what appalls. It is not that his great struggle comes to nothing, but that his existence itself is without meaning. Even if we suppose, for example, that the stone is but a pebble that can be carried effortlessly, or that the holes dug by the prisoners are but small ones, not the slightest meaning is introduced into their lives. The stone that Sisyphus moves to the top of the hill, whether we think of it as large or small, still rolls back every time, and the process is repeated forever. Nothing comes of it, and the work is simply pointless. That is the element of the myth that I wish to capture.

Again, it is not the fact that the labors of Sisyphus continue forever that deprives them of meaning. It is, rather, the implication of this: that they come to nothing. The image would not be changed by our supposing him to push a different stone up every time, each to roll down again. But if we supposed that these stones, instead of rolling back to their places as if they had never been moved, were assembled at the top of the hill and there incorporated, say, in a beautiful and enduring temple, then the aspect of meaninglessness would disappear. His labors would then have a point, something would come of them all, and although one could perhaps still say it was not worth it, one could not say that the life of Sisyphus was devoid of meaning altogether. Meaningfulness would at least have made an appearance, and we could see what it was.

That point will need remembering. But in the meantime, let us note another way in which the image of meaninglessness can be altered by making only a very slight change. Let us suppose that the gods, while condemning Sisyphus to the fate just described, at the same time, as an afterthought, waxed perversely merciful by implanting in him a strange and irrational impulse; namely, a compulsive impulse to roll stones. We may if we like, to make this more graphic, suppose they accomplish this by implanting in him some substance that has this effect on his character and drives. I call this perverse, because from our point of view there is clearly no reason why anyone should have a persistent and insatiable desire to do something so pointless as that. Nevertheless, suppose that is Sisyphus' condition. He has but one obsession, which is to roll stones, and it is an obsession that is only for the moment appeased by his rolling them—he no sooner gets a stone rolled to the top of the hill than he is restless to roll up another.

Now it can be seen why this little afterthought of the gods, which I called perverse, was also in fact merciful. For they have by this device managed to give Sisyphus precisely what he wants—by making him want precisely what they inflict on him. However it may appear to us, Sisyphus' fate now does not appear to him as a condemnation, but the very reverse. His one desire in life is to roll stones, and he is absolutely guaranteed its endless fulfillment. Where otherwise he might profoundly have wished surcease, and even welcomed the quiet of death to release him from endless boredom and meaninglessness, his life is now filled with mission and meaning, and he seems to himself to have been given an entry to heaven. Nor need he even fear death, for the gods have promised him an endless opportunity to indulge his single purpose, without concern or frustration. He will be able to roll stones *forever*.

What we need to mark most carefully at this point is that the picture with which we began has not really been changed in the least by adding this supposition. Exactly the same things happen as before. The only change is in

Sisyphus' view of them. The picture before was the image of meaningless activity and existence. It was created precisely to be an image of that. It has not lost that meaninglessness, it has now gained not the least shred of meaningfulness. The stones still roll back as before, each phase of Sisyphus' life still exactly resembles all the others, the task is never completed, nothing comes of it, no temple ever begins to rise, and all this cycle of the same pointless thing over and over goes on forever in this picture as in the other. The *only* thing that has happened is this: Sisyphus has been reconciled to it, and indeed more, he has been led to embrace it. Not, however, by reason or persuasion, but by nothing more rational than the potency of a new substance in his veins.

The Meaninglessness of Life

I believe the foregoing provides a fairly clear content to the idea of meaninglessness and, through it, some hint of what meaningfulness, in this sense, might be. Meaninglessness is essentially endless pointlessness, and meaningfulness is therefore the opposite. Activity, and even long drawn out and repetitive activity, has a meaning if it has some significant culmination, some more or less lasting end that can be considered to have been the direction and purpose of the activity. But the descriptions so far also provide something else; namely, the suggestion of how an existence that is objectively meaningless, in this sense, can nevertheless acquire a meaning for him whose existence it is.

Now let us ask: Which of these pictures does life in fact resemble? And let us not begin with our own lives, for here both our prejudices and wishes are great, but with the life in general that we share with the rest of creation. We shall find, I think, that it all has a certain pattern, and that this pattern is by now easily recognized.

We can begin anywhere, only saving human existence for our last consideration. We can, for example, begin with any animal. It does not matter where we begin, because the result is going to be exactly the same.

Thus, for example, there are caves in New Zealand, deep and dark, whose floors are quiet pools and whose walls and ceilings are covered with soft light. As one gazes in wonder in the stillness of these caves it seems that the Creator has reproduced there in microcosm the heavens themselves, until one scarcely remembers the enclosing presence of the walls. As one looks more closely, however, the scene is explained. Each dot of light identifies an ugly worm, whose luminous tail is meant to attract insects from the surrounding darkness. As from time to time one of these insects draws near it becomes entangled in a sticky thread lowered by the worm, and is eaten. This goes on month after month, the blind worm lying there in the barren stillness waiting to entrap an occasional bit of nourishment that will only sustain it to another bit of nourishment until. . . . Until what? What great thing awaits all this long and repetitious effort and makes it worthwhile? Really nothing. The larva just transforms itself finally to a tiny winged adult that lacks even mouth parts to feed and lives only a day or two. These adults, as soon as they have mated and laid eggs, are themselves caught in the threads and are devoured by the cannibalist worms, often without having ventured into the day, the only point to their existence having now been fulfilled. This has been going on for millions of years, and to no end other than that the same meaningless cycle may continue for another millions of years.

All living things present essentially the same spectacle. The larva of a certain cicada burrows in the darkness of the earth for seventeen years, through season after season, to emerge finally into the daylight for a brief flight, lay its eggs, and die—this all to repeat itself during the next seventeen years, and so on to eternity. . . . Some birds span an entire side of the globe each year and then return, only to insure that others may follow the same incredibly long path again and again. One is led to wonder what the point of it all is, with what great triumph this ceaseless effort, repeating itself through millions of years, might finally culminate, and why it should go on and on for so long, accomplishing nothing, getting nowhere. But then one realizes that there is no point to it at all, that it really culminates in nothing, that each of these cycles, so filled with toil, is to be followed only by more of the same. The point of any living thing's life is, evidently, nothing but life itself.

This life of the world thus presents itself to our eyes as a vast machine, feeding on itself, running on and on forever to nothing. And we are part of that life. To be sure, we are not just the same, but the differences are not so great as we like to think; many are merely invented, and none really cancels the kind of meaninglessness that we found in Sisyphus and that we find all around, wherever anything lives. We are conscious of our activity. Our goals, whether in any significant sense we choose them or not, are things of which we are at least partly aware and can therefore in some sense appraise. More significantly, perhaps, men have a history, as other animals do not, such that each generation does not precisely resemble all those before. Still, if we can in imagination disengage our wills from our lives and disregard the deep interest each man has in his own existence, we shall find that they do not so little resemble the existence of Sisyphus. We toil after goals, most of them—indeed every single one of them—of transitory significance and, having gained one of them, we immediately set forth for the next, as if that one had never been, with this next one being essentially more of the same. Look at a busy street any day, and observe the throng going hither and thither. To what? Some office or shop, where the same things will be done today as were done yesterday, and are done now so they may be repeated tomorrow. And if we think that, unlike Sisyphus, these labors do have a point, that they culminate in something lasting and, independently of our own deep interests in them, very worthwhile, then we simply have not considered the thing closely enough. Most such effort is directed only to the establishment and perpetuation of home and family; that is, to the begetting of others who will follow in our steps to do more of the same. Each man's life thus resembles one of Sisyphus' climbs to the summit of his hill, and each day of it one of his steps; the difference is that whereas Sisyphus himself returns to push the stone up again, we leave this to our children. We at one point imagined that the labors of Sisyphus finally culminated in the creation of a temple, but for this to make any difference it had to be a temple that would at least endure, adding beauty to the world for the remainder of time. Our achievements, even though they are often beautiful, are mostly bubbles; and those that do last, like the sand-swept pyramids, soon become mere curiosities while around them the rest of mankind continues its perpetual toting of rocks, only to see them roll down. Nations are built upon the bones of their founders and pioneers, but only to decay and crumble before long, their rubble then becoming the foundation for others directed to exactly the same fate. The picture of Sisyphus is the picture of existence of the individual man, great or unknown, of nations, of the race of men, and of the very life of the world.

On a country road one sometimes comes upon the ruined hulks of a house and once extensive buildings, all in collapse and spread over with weeds. A curious eye can in imagination reconstruct from what is left a once warm and thriving life, filled with purpose. There was the hearth, where a family once talked, sang, and made plans; there were the rooms, where people loved, and babes were born to a rejoicing mother; there are the musty remains of a sofa, infested with bugs, once bought at a dear price to enhance an ever-growing comfort, beauty, and warmth. Every small piece of junk fills the mind with what once, not long ago, was utterly real, with children's voices, plans made, and enterprises embarked upon. That is how these stones of Sisyphus were rolled up, and that is how they became incorporated into a beautiful temple, and that temple is what now lies before you. Meanwhile other buildings, institutions, nations, and civilizations spring up all around, only to share the same fate before long. And if the question "What for?" is now asked, the answer is clear: so that just this may go on forever.

The two pictures—of Sisyphus and of our own lives, if we look at them from a distance—are in outline the same and convey to the mind the same image. It is not surprising, then, that men invent ways of denying it, their religious proclaiming a heaven that does not crumble, their hymnals and prayer books declaring a significance to life of which our eyes provide no hint whatever.[1] Even our philosophies portray some permanent and lasting good at which all may aim, from the changeless forms invented by Plato to the beatific vision of St. Thomas and the ideals of permanence contrived by the moderns. When these fail to convince, then earthly ideals such as universal justice and brotherhood are conjured up to take their places and give meaning to man's seemingly endless pilgrimage, some final state that will be ushered in when the last obstacle is removed and the last stone pushed to the hilltop. No one believes, of course, that any such state will be final, or even wants it to be in case it means that human existence would then cease to be a struggle; but in the meantime such ideas serve a very real need.

The Meaning of Life

We noted that Sisyphus' existence would have meaning if there were some point to his labors, if his efforts ever culminated in something that was not just an occasion for fresh labors of the same kind. But that is precisely the meaning it lacks. And human existence resembles his in that respect. Men do achieve things—they scale their towers and raise their stones to their hilltops—but every such accomplishment fades, providing only an occasion for renewed labors of the same kind.

But here we need to note something else that has been mentioned, but its significance not explored, and that is the state of mind and feeling with which such labors are undertaken. We noted that if Sisyphus had a keen and unappeasable desire to be doing just what he found himself doing, then, although his life would in no way be changed, it would nevertheless have a meaning for him. It would be an irrational one, no doubt, because the desire itself would be only the product of the substance in his veins, and not any that reason could discover, but a meaning nevertheless.

And would it not, in fact, be a meaning incomparably better than the other? For let us examine again the first kind of meaning it could have. Let us suppose that, without having any interest in rolling stones, as such, and finding this, in fact, a galling toil, Sisyphus did nevertheless have a deep interest in raising a temple, one that would be beautiful and lasting. And let us suppose he succeeded in this, that after ages of dreadful toil, all directed at this final result, he did at last complete his temple, such that now he could say his work was done, and he could rest and forever enjoy the result. Now what? What picture now presents itself to our minds? It is precisely the picture of infinite boredom! Of Sisyphus doing nothing ever again, but contemplating what he has already wrought and can no longer add anything to, and contemplating it for an eternity! Now in this picture we have a meaning for Sisyphus' existence, a point for his prodigious labor, because we have put it there; yet, at the same time, that which is really worthwhile seems to have slipped away entirely. Where before we were presented with the nightmare of eternal and pointless activity, we are now confronted with the hell of its eternal absence.

Our second picture, then, wherein we imagined Sisyphus to have had inflicted on him the irrational desire to be doing just what he found himself doing, should not have been dismissed so abruptly. The meaning that picture lacked was no meaning that he or anyone could crave, and the strange meaning it had was perhaps just what we were seeking.

At this point, then, we can reintroduce what has been until now, it is hoped, resolutely pushed aside in an effort to view our lives and human existence with objectivity; namely, our own wills, our deep interest in what we find ourselves doing. If we do this we find that our lives do indeed still resemble that of Sisyphus, but that the meaningfulness they thus lack is precisely the meaningfulness of infinite boredom. At the same time, the strange meaningfulness they possess is that of the inner compulsion to be doing just what we were put here to do, and to go on doing it forever. This is the nearest we may hope to get to heaven, but the redeeming side of that fact is that we do thereby avoid a genuine hell.

If the builders of a great and flourishing ancient civilization could somehow return now to see archaeologists unearthing the trivial remnants of what they had once accomplished with such effort—see the fragments of pots and vases, a few broken statues, and such tokens of another age and greatness—they could indeed ask themselves what the point of it all was, if this is all it finally came to. Yet, it did not seem so to them then, for it was just the building, and not what was finally built, that gave their life meaning. Similarly, if the builders of the ruined home and farm that I described a short while ago could be brought back to see what is left, they would have the same feelings. What we construct in our imaginations as we look over these decayed and rusting pieces would reconstruct itself in their very memories, and certainly with unspeakable sadness. The piece of a sled at our feet would revive in them a warm Christmas. And what rich memories would there be in the broken crib? And the weed-covered remains of a fence would reproduce the scene of a great herd of livestock, so laboriously built up over so many years. What was it all worth, if this is the final result? Yet, again, it did not seem so to them through those many years of struggle and toil, and they did not imagine they were building a Gibraltar. The things to which they bent their backs day after day, realizing one by one their ephemeral plans, were precisely the things in which their wills were deeply involved, precisely the things in which their interests lay, and there was no need then to ask questions. There is no more need of them now—the day was sufficient to itself, and so was the life.

This is surely the way to look at all of life—at one's own life, and each day and moment it contains; of the life of a nation; of the species; of the life of the world; and of everything that breathes. Even the glow worms I described, whose cycles of existence over the millions of years seem so pointless when looked at by us, will seem entirely different to us if we can somehow try to view their existence from within. Their endless activity, which gets nowhere, is just what it is their will to pursue. This is its whole justification and meaning. Nor would it be any salvation to the birds who span the globe every year, back and forth, to have a home made for them in a cage with plenty of food and protection, so that they would not have to migrate any more. It would be their condemnation, for it is the doing that counts for them, and not what they hope to win by it. Flying these prodigious distances, never ending, is what it is in their veins to do, exactly as it was in Sisyphus' veins to roll stones, without end, after the gods had waxed merciful and implanted this in him.

A human being no sooner draws his first breath than he responds to the will that is in him to live. He no more asks whether it will be worthwhile, or whether anything of significance will come of it, than the worms and the birds. The point of his living is simply to be living, in the manner that it is his nature to be living. He goes through his life building his castles, each of these beginning to fade into time as the next is begun; yet, it would be no salvation to rest from all this. It would be a condemnation, and one that would in no way be redeemed were he able to gaze upon the things he has done, even if these were beautiful and absolutely permanent, as they never are. What counts is that one should be able to begin a new task, a new castle, a new bubble. It counts only because it is there to be done and he has the will to do it. The same will be the life of his children, and of theirs; and if the philosopher is apt to see in this a pattern similar to the unending cycles of the existence of Sisyphus, and to despair, then it is indeed because the meaning and point he is seeking is not there—but mercifully so. The meaning of life is from within us, it is not bestowed from without, and it far exceeds in both its beauty and permanence any heaven of which men have ever dreamed or yearned for.

NOTE

1. A popular Christian hymn, sung often at funerals and typical of many hymns, expresses this thought:
    Swift to its close ebbs out life's little day;
    Earth's joys grow dim, its glories pass away;
    Change and decay in all around I see:
    O thou who changest not, abide with me.

The Value of Philosophy

✿✿

BERTRAND RUSSELL

We approach the end of this introduction to philosophy. I hope you now have a clearer sense of what the subject is and why it has captivated so many generations of thinkers.

But since the questions of philosophy receive uncertain answers, what is the point of the inquiry? For a reply we turn to
Bertrand Russell, whose work we read earlier (pp. 71–74; 80–83),
and whose thoughts on the value of philosophy many have found
insightful or even inspirational.

Having now come to the end of our brief and very incomplete review of the
problems of philosophy, it will be well to consider, in conclusion, what is the
value of philosophy and why it ought to be studied. It is the more necessary
to consider this question, in view of the fact that many men, under the influence of science or of practical affairs, are inclined to doubt whether philosophy is anything better than innocent but useless trifling, hair-splitting distinctions, and controversies on matters concerning which knowledge is
impossible.

This view of philosophy appears to result, partly from a wrong conception of the ends of life, partly from a wrong conception of the kind of goods
which philosophy strives to achieve. Physical science, through the medium
of inventions, is useful to innumerable people who are wholly ignorant of it;
thus the study of physical science is to be recommended, not only, or primarily, because of the effect on the student, but rather because of the effect on
mankind in general. Thus utility does not belong to philosophy. If the study
of philosophy has any value at all for others than students of philosophy, it
must be only indirectly, through its effects upon the lives of those who study
it. It is in these effects, therefore, if anywhere, that the value of philosophy
must be primarily sought.

But further, if we are not to fail in our endeavour to determine the value
of philosophy, we must first free our minds from the prejudices of what are
wrongly called "practical" men. The "practical" man, as this word is often
used, is one who recognizes only material needs, who realizes that men must
have food for the body, but is oblivious of the necessity of providing food for
the mind. If all men were well off, if poverty and disease had been reduced
to their lowest possible point, there would still remain much to be done to
produce a valuable society; and even in the existing world the goods of the
mind are at least as important as the goods of the body. It is exclusively
among the goods of the mind that the value of philosophy is to be found;
and only those who are not indifferent to these goods can be persuaded that
the study of philosophy is not a waste of time.

Philosophy, like all other studies, aims primarily at knowledge. The
knowledge it aims at is the kind of knowledge which gives unity and system
to the body of the sciences, and the kind which results from a critical examination of the grounds of our convictions, prejudices, and beliefs. But it cannot be maintained that philosophy has had any very great measure of success in its attempts to provide definite answers to its questions. If you ask a

mathematician, a mineralogist, a historian, or any other man of learning, what definite body of truths has been ascertained by his science, his answer will last as long as you are willing to listen. But if you put the same question to a philosopher, he will, if he is candid, have to confess that his study has not achieved positive results such as have been achieved by other sciences. It is true that this is partly accounted for by the fact that, as soon as definite knowledge concerning any subject becomes possible, this subject ceases to be called philosophy, and becomes a separate science. The whole study of the heavens, which now belongs to astronomy, was once included in philosophy; Newton's great work was called "the mathematical principles of natural philosophy." Similarly, the study of the human mind, which was a part of philosophy, has now been separated from philosophy and has become the science of psychology. Thus, to a great extent, the uncertainty of philosophy is more apparent than real: those questions which are already capable of definite answers are placed in the sciences, while those only to which, at present, no definite answer can be given, remain to form the residue which is called philosophy.

This is, however, only a part of the truth concerning the uncertainty of philosophy. There are many questions—and among them those that are of the profoundest interest to our spiritual life—which, so far as we can see, must remain insoluble to the human intellect unless its powers become of quite a different order from what they are now. Has the universe any unity of plan or purpose, or is it a fortuitous concourse of atoms? Is consciousness a permanent part of the universe, giving hope of indefinite growth in wisdom, or is it a transitory accident on a small planet on which life must ultimately become impossible? Are good and evil of importance to the universe or only to man? Such questions are asked by philosophy, and variously answered by various philosophers. But it would seem that, whether answers be otherwise discoverable or not, the answers suggested by philosophy are none of them demonstrably true. Yet, however slight may be the hope of discovering an answer, it is part of the business of philosophy to continue the consideration of such questions, to make us aware of their importance, to examine all the approaches to them, and to keep alive that speculative interest in the universe which is apt to be killed by confining ourselves to definitely ascertainable knowledge. . . .

The value of philosophy is, in fact, to be sought largely in its very uncertainty. The man who has no tincture of philosophy goes through life imprisoned in the prejudices derived from common sense, from the habitual beliefs of his age or his nation, and from convictions which have grown up in his mind without the co-operation or consent of his deliberate reason. To such a man the world tends to become definite, finite, obvious; common objects rouse no questions, and unfamiliar possibilities are contemptuously rejected. As soon as we begin to philosophize, on the contrary, we find . . . that even the most everyday things lead to problems to which only very incomplete answers can be given. Philosophy, though unable to tell us with certainty what is the true answer to the doubts which it raises, is able to suggest many possibilities which enlarge our thoughts and free them from the tyranny of custom. Thus, while diminishing our feeling of certainty as to what things are, it greatly increases our knowledge as to what they may be; it removes the somewhat arrogant dogmatism of those who have never travelled into the region of liberating doubt, and it keeps alive our sense of wonder by showing familiar things in an unfamiliar aspect.

Apart from its utility in showing unsuspected possibilities, philosophy has a value—perhaps its chief value—through the greatness of the objects which it contemplates, and the freedom from narrow and personal aims resulting from this contemplation. The life of the instinctive man is shut up within the circle of his private interests: family and friends may be included, but the outer world is not regarded except as it may help or hinder what comes within the circle of instinctive wishes. In such a life there is something feverish and confined, in comparison with which the philosophic life is calm and free. The private world of instinctive interests is a small one, set in the midst of a great and powerful world which must, sooner or later, lay our private world in ruins. Unless we can so enlarge our interests as to include the whole outer world, we remain like a garrison in a beleagured fortress, knowing that the enemy prevents escape and that ultimate surrender is inevitable. In such a life there is no peace, but a constant strife between the insistence of desire and the powerlessness of will. In one way or another, if our life is to be great and free, we must escape this prison and this strife. . . .

Thus, to sum up our discussion of the value of philosophy: Philosophy is to be studied, not for the sake of any definite answers to its questions, since no definite answers can, as a rule, be known to be true, but rather for the sake of the questions themselves; because these questions enlarge our conception of what is possible, enrich our intellectual imagination and diminish the dogmatic assurance which closes the mind against speculation; but above all because, through the greatness of the universe which philosophy contemplates, the mind also is rendered great, and becomes capable of that union with the universe which constitutes its highest good.

Phaedo

❖❖❖

PLATO

> The *Phaedo,* one of Plato's greatest and most complex works, is set
> in the Athenian prison on the day of Socrates' death. The discussion
> focuses on Plato's attempts to prove the immortality of the soul.
> Near the end of the dialogue, from which our selection is taken,
> Socrates utters his final thoughts, drinks poison, and dies. What
> then begins is his enormous influence on the history of Western
> thought.

When he'd spoken, Crito said: "Very well, Socrates: what instructions have
you for these others or for me, about your children or about anything else?
What could we do, that would be of most service to you?"

"What I'm always telling you, Crito," said he, "and nothing very new: if
you take care for yourselves, your actions will be of service to me and mine,
and to yourselves too, whatever they may be, even if you make no promises
now; but if you take no care for yourselves, and are unwilling to pursue your
lives along the tracks, as it were, marked by our present and earlier discussions, then even if you make many firm promises at this time, you'll do no
good at all."

"Then we'll strive to do as you say," he said; "but in what fashion are we
to bury you?"

"However you wish," said he; "provided you catch me, that is, and I
don't get away from you." And with this he laughed quietly, looked towards
us and said: "Friends, I can't persuade Crito that I am Socrates here, the one
who is now conversing and arranging each of the things being discussed;
but he imagines I'm that dead body he'll see in a little while, so he goes and
asks how he's to bury me! But as for the great case I've been arguing all this
time, that when I drink the poison,[1] I shall no longer remain with you, but
shall go off and depart for some happy state of the blessed, this, I think, I'm
putting to him in vain, while comforting you and myself alike. So please
stand surety for me with Crito, the opposite surety to that which he stood for
me with the judges: his guarantee was that I *would* stay behind, whereas you
must guarantee that, when I die, I shall *not* stay behind, but shall go off and

depart; then Crito will bear it more easily, and when he sees the burning or interment of my body, he won't be distressed for me, as if I were suffering dreadful things, and won't say at the funeral that it is Socrates they are laying out or bearing to the grave or interring. Because you can be sure, my dear Crito, that misuse of words is not only troublesome in itself, but actually has a bad effect on the soul. Rather, you should have confidence, and say you are burying my body; and bury it however you please, and think most proper."

After saying this, he rose and went into a room to take a bath, and Crito followed him but told us to wait. So we waited, talking among ourselves about what had been said and reviewing it, and then again dwelling on how great a misfortune had befallen us, literally thinking of it as if we were deprived of a father and would lead the rest of our life as orphans. After he'd bathed and his children had been brought to him—he had two little sons and one big one—and those women of his household had come, he talked with them in Crito's presence, and gave certain directions as to his wishes; he then told the women and children to leave, and himself returned to us.

By now it was close to sunset, as he'd spent a long time inside. So he came and sat down, fresh from his bath, and there wasn't much talk after that. Then the prison official came in, stepped up to him and said: "Socrates, I shan't reproach you as I reproach others for being angry with me and cursing, whenever by order of the rulers I direct them to drink the poison. In your time here I've known you for the most generous and gentlest and best of men who have ever come to this place; and now especially, I feel sure it isn't with me that you're angry, but with others, because you know who are responsible. Well now, you know the message I've come to bring: good-bye, then, and try to bear the inevitable as easily as you can." And with this he turned away in tears, and went off.

Socrates looked up at him and said: "Good-bye to you too, and we'll do as you say." And to us he added: "What a civil man he is! Throughout my time here he's been to see me, and sometimes talked with me, and been the best of fellows; and now how generous of him to weep for me! But come on, Crito, let's obey him: let someone bring in the poison, if it has been prepared; if not, let the man prepare it."

Crito said: "But Socrates, I think the sun is still on the mountains and hasn't yet gone down. And besides, I know of others who've taken the draught long after the order had been given them, and after dining well and drinking plenty, and even in some cases enjoying themselves with those they fancied. Be in no hurry, then: there's still time left."

Socrates said: "It's reasonable for those you speak of to do those things— because they think they gain by doing them; for myself, it's reasonable not to do them; because I think I'll gain nothing by taking the draught a little later: I'll only earn my own ridicule by clinging to life, and being sparing when there's nothing more left. Go on now; do as I ask, and nothing else."

Hearing this, Crito nodded to the boy who was standing nearby. The boy went out, and after spending a long time away he returned, bringing the man who was going to administer the poison, and was carrying it ready-pounded in a cup. When he saw the man, Socrates said: "Well, my friend, you're an expert in these things: what must one do?"

"Simply drink it," he said, "and walk about till a heaviness comes over your legs; then lie down, and it will act of itself." And with this he held out the cup to Socrates.

He took it perfectly calmly, Echecrates, without a tremor, or any change of colour or countenance; but looking up at the man, and fixing him with his customary stare, he said: "What do you say to pouring someone a libation from this drink? Is it allowed or not?"

"We only prepare as much as we judge the proper dose, Socrates," he said.

"I understand," he said; "but at least one may pray to the gods, and so one should, that the removal from this world to the next will be a happy one; that is my own prayer: so may it be." With these words he pressed the cup to his lips, and drank it off with good humour and without the least distaste.

Till then most of us had been fairly well able to restrain our tears; but when we saw he was drinking, that he'd actually drunk it, we could do so no longer. In my own case, the tears came pouring out in spite of myself, so that I covered my face and wept for myself—not for him, no, but for my own misfortune in being deprived of such a man for a companion. Even before me, Crito had moved away, when he was unable to restrain his tears. And Apollodorus, who even earlier had been continuously in tears, now burst forth into such a storm of weeping and grieving, that he made everyone present break down except Socrates himself.

But Socrates said: "What a way to behave, my strange friends! Why, it was mainly for this reason that I sent the women away, so that they shouldn't make this sort of trouble; in fact, I've heard one should die in silence. Come now, calm yourselves and have strength."

When we heard this, we were ashamed and checked our tears. He walked about, and when he said that his legs felt heavy he lay down on his back—as the man told him—and then the man, this one who'd given him the poison, felt him, and after an interval examined his feet and legs; he then pinched his foot hard and asked if he could feel it, and Socrates said not. After that he felt his shins once more; and moving upwards in this way, he showed us that he was becoming cold and numb. He went on feeling him, and said that when the coldness reached his heart, he would be gone.

By this time the coldness was somewhere in the region of his abdomen, when he uncovered his face—it had been covered over—and spoke; and this was in fact his last utterance: "Crito," he said, "we owe a cock to Asclepius: please pay the debt, and don't neglect it."[2]

"It shall be done," said Crito; "have you anything else to say?"

To this question he made no answer, but after a short interval he stirred, and when the man uncovered him his eyes were fixed; when he saw this, Crito closed his mouth and his eyes.

And that, Echecrates, was the end of our companion, a man who, among those of his time we knew, was—so we should say—the best, the wisest too, and the most just.

NOTES

(prepared by Andrea Tschemplik)

1. The poison was hemlock, frequently used in ancient executions.
2. Asclepius was the hero or god of healing. A provocative, but disputed, interpretation of Socrates' final instruction is that he considers death the cure for life and, therefore, wishes to make an offering in gratitude to the god of health.

Suggestions for Further Reading

To learn more about any aspect of philosophy, an excellent source to consult is the ten-volume *Routledge Encyclopedia of Philosophy* (London and New York: Routledge, 1998), edited by Edward Craig, which contains detailed entries with bibliographies on every significant topic in the field. Reliable, single-volume guides to the entire subject are Ted Honderich, ed., *The Oxford Companion to Philosophy* (Oxford and New York: Oxford University Press, 1995), Robert Audi, ed., *The Cambridge Dictionary of Philosophy* (Cambridge and New York: Cambridge University Press, 1995), and a shorter single-authored work, Simon Blackburn, *The Oxford Dictionary of Philosophy* (Oxford and New York: Oxford University Press, 1994).

An accessible one-volume history of philosophy is Anthony Kenny, *A Brief History of Western Philosophy* (Oxford and Malden, MA: Blackwell Publishers, 1998). A convenient collection of major writings in the history of philosophy is Steven M. Cahn, ed., *Classics of Western Philosophy*, Fifth Edition (Indianapolis and Cambridge, MA: Hackett Publishing Company, 1999).

A classic text in informal logic newly reprinted and edited is Morris R. Cohen and Ernest Nagel, *An Introduction to Logic* (Indianapolis and Cambridge, MA: Hackett Publishing Company, 1993). A recommended introduction to formal logic is Stephen F. Barker, *Elements of Logic*, Fifth Edition (New York: McGraw-Hill, 1988).

A superb introduction to the philosophy of science is Carl G. Hempel, *Philosophy of Natural Science* (Englewood Cliffs, NJ: Prentice-Hall, 1966). A comprehensive anthology in the area is Martin Curd and J. A. Cover, *Philosophy of Science: The Central Issues* (New York and London: W. W. Norton & Company, 1998).

A basic work in the theory of knowledge is Charles Landesman, *An Introduction to Epistemology* (Cambridge, MA and Oxford: Blackwell Publishers, 1997). A useful reader is Louis J. Pojman, *Theory of Knowledge: Classical and Contemporary Readings, Second Edition* (Belmont, CA: Wadsworth Publishing Company, 1999).

An incisive study of the problem of free will is Robert Kane, *The Significance of Free Will* (New York and Oxford: Oxford University Press, 1996). A convenient collection of articles on the issue is Gary Watson, ed., *Free Will* (New York and Oxford: Oxford University Press, 1982).

A helpful text surveying issues in the philosophy of mind is Jaegwon Kim, *Philosophy of Mind* (Boulder, CO: Westview Press, 1996). A comprehensive anthology of the subject is David M. Rosenthal, ed., *The Nature of Mind* (New York and Oxford: Oxford University Press, 1991).

An accessible text in the philosophy of religion is John H. Hick, *Philosophy of Religion*, Fourth Edition (Englewood Cliffs, NJ: Prentice-Hall, 1989). A comprehensive anthology of the area is Louis J. Pojman, ed., *Philosophy of Religion: An Anthology*, Third Edition (Belmont, CA: Wadsworth Publishing Company, 1998).

An engaging introduction to ethics is James Rachels, *The Elements of Moral Philosophy*, Third Edition (New York: McGraw-Hill, 1998). A thorough survey of the field is Steven M. Cahn and Peter Markie, eds., *Ethics: History, Theory, and Contemporary Issues* (New York and Oxford: Oxford University Press, 1998).

A balanced collection concerning abortion is Louis P. Pojman, ed., *The Abortion Controversy: A Reader*, Second Edition (Belmont, CA: Wadsworth Publishing Company, 1998). Regarding euthanasia and the distinction between killing and letting die, see Bonnie Steinbock and Alastair Norcross, eds., *Killing and Letting Die*, Second Edition (New York: Fordham University Press, 1994).

A useful introduction to political philosophy is Jonathan Wolff, *An Introduction to Political Philosophy* (Oxford and New York: Oxford University Press, 1996). A collection of major works in the modern history of the subject is Steven M. Cahn, ed., *Classics of Modern Political Theory: Machiavelli to Mill* (New York and Oxford: Oxford University Press, 1997). Recent essays are collected in George Sher and Baruch A. Brody, eds., *Social and Political Philosophy: Contemporary Readings* (Fort Worth, TX: Harcourt Brace College Publishers, 1999).

Regarding affirmative action, see Steven M. Cahn, ed., *The Affirmative Action Debate* (New York and London: Routledge, 1995). Regarding democracy, see John Arthur, ed., *Democracy: Theory and Practice* (Belmont, CA: Wadsworth Publishing Company, 1992). Regarding privacy, see Ferdinand Schoeman, ed., *Philosophical Dimensions of Privacy: An Anthology* (Cambridge: Cambridge University Press, 1984). Regarding capital punishment, see Hugo Adam Bedau, ed., *The Death Penalty in America*, Third Edition (New York: Oxford University Press, 1982).

An introduction to the philosophy of education is Nel Noddings, *Philosophy of Education* (Boulder, CO: Westview Press, 1995). A comprehensive anthology of the field is Steven M. Cahn, ed., *Classic and Contemporary Readings in the Philosophy of Education* (New York: McGraw-Hill, 1997).

A variety of essays concerning the meaning of life are collected in E. D. Klemke, ed., *The Meaning of Life* (New York and Oxford: Oxford University Press, 1981).

Each of the historical works included whole or in part in this volume has been the subject of voluminous commentary. Regarding the *Defence of Socrates*, see Thomas C. Brickhouse and Nicholas D. Smith, *Socrates on Trial* (Princeton: Princeton University Press, 1989). Regarding the *Meno* and *Euthyphro*, see R. E. Allen, *The Dialogues of Plato*, vol. I (New Haven and London: Yale University Press, 1984). Regarding the *Crito*, see Richard Kraut,

Socrates and the State (Princeton: Princeton University Press, 1984). An overall guide to the study of Plato is Richard Kraut, ed., *The Cambridge Companion to Plato* (Cambridge: Cambridge University Press, 1992).

Regarding Aristotle's *Nicomachean Ethics,* see Nancy Sherman, ed., *Aristotle's Nichomachean Ethics: Critical Essays* (Lanham, MD: Rowman & Littlefield Publishers, 1999). Aquinas' proofs for the existence of God are analyzed in Anthony Kenny, *The Five Ways: St. Thomas Aquinas' Proofs of God's Existence* (New York: Schocken Books, 1969). Regarding Descartes' *Meditations,* see Vere Chappell, ed., *Descartes's Meditations: Critical Essays* (Lanham, MD: Rowman & Littlefield Publishers, 1997).

Regarding Hume's *Enquiry,* see Antony Flew, *Hume's Philosophy of Belief: A Study of His First "Inquiry"* (London: Routledge & Kegan Paul, 1961). Regarding Kant's *Groundwork,* see Paul Guyer, ed., *Kant's Groundwork of the Metaphysics of Morals: Critical Essays* (Lanham, MD: Rowman & Littlefield Publishers, 1998). Regarding Mill's *Utilitarianism,* see David Lyons, ed., *Mill's Utilitarianism: Critical Essays* (Lanham, MD: Rowman & Littlefield Publishers, 1997). Regarding Mill's *On Liberty,* see Gerald Dworkin, ed., *Mill's On Liberty: Critical Essays* (Lanham, MD: Rowman & Littlefield Publishers, 1997).

Index

About the Author

Steven M. Cahn is Professor of Philosophy at The Graduate School of The City University of New York, where he served as Provost and Vice-President for Academic Affairs and then as Acting President. He received his A.B. from Columbia College and his Ph.D. from Columbia University. He previously taught at Dartmouth College, Vassar College, the University of Rochester, New York University, and the University of Vermont, where he headed the Department of Philosophy.

He served as a program officer at the Exxon Education Foundation, as acting director for humanities at The Rockefeller Foundation, and as director of the Division of General Programs at the National Endowment for the Humanities. He chaired the American Philosophical Association's Committee on the Teaching of Philosophy and is President of The John Dewey Foundation.

Dr. Cahn is the author of *Fate, Logic, and Time, A New Introduction to Philosophy, The Eclipse of Excellence, Education and the Democratic Ideal, Philosophical Explorations: Freedom, God and Goodness,* and *Saints and Scamps: Ethics in Academia.* He has edited numerous other volumes, including *Classics of Western Philosophy, Morality, Responsibility and the University: Studies in Academic Ethics, The Affirmative Action Debate, Classics of Modern Political Theory: Machiavelli to Mill,* and *Classic and Contemporary Readings in the Philosophy of Education.*